CHILDI NCE

D0863340

CHILDREN
EXPOSED TO VIOLENCE

edited by

Margaret M. Feerick, Ph.D.
Feerick Consulting
Laytonsville, Maryland

and

Gerald B. Silverman, M.Ed., M.S.W.
Office of the Assistant Secretary for Planning and Evaluation
U.S. Department of Health and Human Services
Washington, D.C.

Baltimore • London • Sydney

Paul H. Brookes Publishing Co.
Post Office Box 10624
Baltimore, Maryland 21285-0624

www.brookespublishing.com

Typeset by Barton Matheson Willse & Worthington, Baltimore, Maryland.
Manufactured in the United States of America by
Versa Press, Inc., East Peoria, Illinois.

Library of Congress Cataloging-in-Publication Data

Children exposed to violence / edited by Margaret M. Feerick & Gerald B. Silverman.
   p.   cm.
 Includes bibliographical references and index.
 ISBN-13: 978-1-55766-804-2
 ISBN-10: 1-55766-804-3
 1. Abused children. 2. Family violence. 3. Children and violence. 4. Children
and terrorism. I. Feerick, Margaret Mary, 1967– II. Silverman, Gerald B.

HV6626.5.C558 2006
362.76—dc22   2006000232

British Library Cataloguing in Publication data are available from the British Library.

CONTENTS

About the Editors

Margaret M. Feerick, Ph.D., Psychologist and Independent Consultant, Feerick Consulting, 21021 Brooke Knolls Road, Laytonsville, Maryland 20882. Dr. Feerick holds a bachelor's degree in English and a master's degree in developmental psychology from Columbia University and a doctorate in developmental psychology from Cornell University. Early in her career, Dr. Feerick worked as a language arts teacher and director of development/contributions at an independent junior high school in New York City while also working as a freelance editor/reader for Penguin Books, U.S.A. She has also served in research and statistical consultant positions on several federally funded research projects at St. Luke's-Roosevelt Hospital in New York City and at the New York State Research Institute on Alcoholism and Addictions and the National Data Archive on Child Abuse and Neglect. She has published articles and book chapters addressing various aspects of child maltreatment and family violence. Dr. Feerick has been the recipient of numerous fellowships and awards, including an individual National Research Service Award from the National Institutes of Health (NIH) and a Society for Research in Child Development (SRCD) Executive Branch Policy Fellowship. From 1998 to 2004, Dr. Feerick served as a Health Scientist Administrator/Program Director at the National Institute of Child Health and Human Development, where she directed a large research and training program on child development, family processes, and child maltreatment and violence, in addition to serving on numerous inter-agency work groups and committees, including the Federal Inter-agency Work Group on Child Abuse and Neglect, the NIH Child Abuse and Neglect Working Group (which she co-chaired) and the Inter-Agency Work Group on Children Exposed to Violence (which she developed and chaired). She is currently working as an independent consultant, a freelance science writer, a Liaison for the Section on Child Maltreatment of the Division on Children, Youth, and Families of the American Psychological Association, and a reviewer for several peer-reviewed journals, while completing several writing projects and raising her two children.

Gerald (Jerry) B. Silverman, M.Ed., M.S.W., Social Science Analyst, Office of the Assistant Secretary for Planning and Evaluation (ASPE), U.S. Department of Health and Human Services (HHS), 450G, 200 Independence Avenue, SW, Washington, D.C. 20201. Mr. Silverman has been a senior policy analyst in ASPE for more than 30 years, where he has played a leading role in addressing domestic violence, the overlap of domestic violence and child maltreatment, child welfare reform legislation, and the social aspects of pediatric AIDS, as well as coordinating community-based responses to family problems. This work has included staffing the department's Steering Committee on Violence Against Women, participating in the department's Interagency Work Group on Child Abuse and Neglect, helping to define the domestic violence regulatory provisions of the welfare reform legislation of 1996, and playing a major role in the child welfare reform efforts of 1980. In the past few years, he has been leading the federal multi-agency program referred to as the "Greenbook" initiative, community demonstrations addressing domestic violence and child maltreatment. This initiative focuses on system change to better serve battered women and children in child welfare agencies, domestic violence programs, and juvenile and family courts. Mr. Silverman also served on the original technical work group for the National Conference of Juvenile and Family Court Judges that developed the Greenbook. Prior to coming to HHS, he was a school teacher and public welfare case worker in New York City and poverty program director for the Washington State Office of Economic Opportunity. He holds both bachelor's and master's degrees in education from New York University and a master's degree in social work from the University of California at Los Angeles.

About the Contributors

Steven J. Berkowitz, M.D., Assistant Professor of Psychiatry, Yale University School of Medicine, Child Study Center, 230 South Frontage Road, New Haven, Connecticut 06520-7900. Dr. Berkowitz is Medical Director of the National Center for Children Exposed to Violence (NCCE) at Yale University. Dr. Berkowitz has been one of the primary developers and proponents of the Child Development–Community Policing Program, a nationally replicated program between law enforcement and child mental health professionals. This program is the core intervention project of the NCCE and provides immediate and follow-up collaborative mental health and law enforcement intervention for children who witness and are victimized by violence in their homes, schools, and communities. Dr. Berkowitz has helped develop several other community-based initiatives for children and families that are at high risk for poor developmental and psychiatric outcomes. He is a founder and Medical Director of the Intensive In-home Child and Adolescent Psychiatry Service (IICAPS), a model of intensive home- and community-based treatment that has become a core service for disadvantaged children and their families in Connecticut. The majority of children served by the IICAPS have histories of violence exposure.

Theresa Stichick Betancourt, Sc.D., M.A., Assistant Professor, Department of Child and Adolescent Psychiatry/Center for Medical and Refugee Trauma, Boston University School of Medicine and Department of International Health, Boston University School of Public Health, Dowling 1 North, One Boston Medical Center Place, Boston, Massachusetts 02118. Dr. Betancourt completed her doctorate of science in maternal and child health with concentrations in population and international health and psychiatric epidemiology at the Harvard School of Public Health in 2003. She also holds a master of arts in expressive arts therapy from the University of Louisville. She has worked as a mental health clinician in both school and community settings and has consulted for international non-governmental organizations and the United Nations' agencies on international children's mental health issues. She has particular expertise in research, policy, and programming for children affected by armed conflict and has worked for the Special Representative of the United Nations Secretary-General for Children and Armed Conflict. Her field experience includes the design and implementation of emergency education programs for Kosovar refugee children in Albania (1998) and youth displaced by the war in Chechnya (1999). Her research focuses on the mental health and psychosocial development of children and adolescents affected by complex humanitarian emergencies. In collaboration with the International Rescue Committee (IRC), she has developed several research projects on resilience in war-affected children in numerous settings including the Russian Federation, Ethiopia, and Sierra Leone. She is currently working with colleagues at the Boston University School of Public Health on the development of locally meaningful and valid mental health measures for war-affected children in northern Uganda. She is currently Principal Investigator for a study of psychosocial adjustment and community reintegration of child ex-combatants in Sierra Leone.

Jacquelyn Campbell, Ph.D., RN, Anna D. Wolf Endowed Professor, The Johns Hopkins University School of Nursing, 525 North Wolfe Street, Baltimore, Maryland 21205-2110. Dr. Campbell is the Associate Dean for Faculty Affairs in The Johns Hopkins University School of Nursing with a joint appointment in the Bloomberg School of Public Health. Her bachelor of science, master of science, and doctorate are from Duke University, Wright State University, and the University of Rochester, respectively. She has been conducting advocacy, policy work, and research in the area of domestic violence since 1980. Dr. Campbell has been Principal Investigator of nine major National Institutes of Health, National Institute of Justice, or Centers for Disease Control and Prevention research grants and has published more than 125 articles and 6 books on domestic violence. She is an elected member of the Institute of Medicine and the American Academy of Nursing, is on the Boards of Directors of the Family Violence Prevention Fund and the House of Ruth Battered Women's Shelter, and was a member of the congressionally appointed U.S. Department of Defense Task Force on Domestic Violence.

Lisa M. Cullins, M.D., Assistant Professor of Psychiatry and Behavioral Sciences, Children's National Medical Center, 111 Michigan Avenue, NW, Washington, D.C. 20010. Dr. Cullins received her medical degree from the University of Illinois College of Medicine in Chicago. She obtained her training in general psychiatry at the UCLA Neuropsychiatric Institute and Hospital in Los Angeles and her training in child and adolescent psychiatry at Columbia Presbyterian Hospital in New York City. Dr. Cullins is the Director of Mental Health Services for DCKIDS at the Children's National Medical Center, which provides comprehensive mental health services to children in foster care in the District of Columbia. Dr. Cullins is a strong advocate for underserved children and adolescents and their families. She has led family groups on urban community violence and participated on a collaborative community board for a family-oriented psycho-educational HIV program. Dr. Cullins has been an invited speaker at the International Traumatic Stress Studies Conference and has given lectures on cross-cultural psychiatry. Her research interests lie in community psychiatry and systems of psychiatric care for high risk and minority populations.

Jeffrey L. Edleson, Ph.D., Professor, University of Minnesota School of Social Work, 105 Peters Hall, 1404 Gortner Avenue, St. Paul, Minnesota 55108-6142. Dr. Edleson is Director of the Minnesota Center Against Violence and Abuse (www.mincava.umn.edu). He has published more than 90 articles and 7 books on domestic violence, group work, and program evaluation. Dr. Edleson has conducted intervention research at the Domestic Abuse Project in Minneapolis over the past two decades. He is a consultant to the Centers for Disease Control and Prevention and to the National Council of Juvenile and Family Court Judges. Dr. Edleson is an Associate Editor of the journal *Violence Against Women* and has served on the editorial boards of several other journals. His most recent books are entitled *Domestic Violence in the Lives of Children: The Future of Research, Intervention, and Social Policy* (co-edited with Sandra Graham-Bermann, 2001, American Psychological Association Books), *Sourcebook on Violence Against Women* (co-edited with Claire Renzetti and Raquel Kennedy Bergen, 2001, Sage Publications), and *Domestic Violence: Classic Papers* (co-edited with Claire Renzetti and Raquel Kennedy Bergen, 2005, Allyn & Bacon).

B. Heidi Ellis, Ph.D., Assistant Professor of Psychiatry and Psychology, Department of Child Psychiatry, Boston University Medical Center, Center for Medical and Refugee Trauma, Dowling 1 North, One Boston Medical Center Place, Boston, Massachusetts 02118. Dr. Ellis is the Associate Director of the Center for Medical and Refugee Trauma, a partner of the National Child Traumatic Stress Network. Dr. Ellis' work focuses on the development and dissemination of interventions for refugee children and their families. As Co-chair of the Refugee Trauma Task Force, a part of the National Child Traumatic Stress Network (NCTSN), Dr. Ellis is actively working with leaders in the child refugee mental health field nationally to promote models of best practice for providing mental health services for refugee children. Dr. Ellis also provides direct clinical service to traumatized children and their families, specializing in work with refugee families and survivors of war and torture. She is co-author of *Comprehensive Care for Traumatized Children: The Trauma Systems Therapy Approach*, a manualized treatment for children in complex social environments. In addition, she is Principal

Investigator of a National Institute of Mental Health–funded research project examining the role of stigma and discrimination in the mental health of resettled Somali adolescents.

Faye A. Gary, Ed.D., RN, FAAN, Professor, Case Western Reserve University, Francis Payne Bolden School of Nursing, 10900 Euclid Avenue, Cleveland, Ohio 44106-4904. Dr. Gary is the Medical Mutual of Ohio Professor of Nursing for Vulnerable and At-Risk Persons at the Frances Payne Bolton School of Nursing at Case Western Reserve University. Her research and practice focus on children and families with mental illnesses or those who are at risk for mental illness. Within this context, her work addresses violence and abuse in the family and community, attention-deficit/hyperactivity disorder, help-seeking behaviors among parents whose children have mental health problems, and community-based initiatives to reduce health disparities. Dr. Gary is also active in exploring the overlap between violence and HIV/AIDS prevention among youth.

Abigail Gewirtz, Ph.D., LP, Clinical Assistant Professor, College of Education and Human Development, University of Minnesota, N-218 Elliott Hall, 75 East River Road, Minneapolis, Minnesota 55455. Dr. Gewirtz is a child psychologist and clinical assistant professor at the University of Minnesota where she teaches and conducts research at the Institute of Child Development and the Department of Psychology. She is engaged in several prevention research and longitudinal projects that investigate the nature of recovery and functioning among high-risk children exposed to violence. Dr. Gewirtz is also Director of Research at the Twin Cities–based Tubman Family Alliance, one of the largest family violence resource agencies in the country, and Project Director for the Minnesota Child Response Initiative, a multi-agency, multi-disciplinary initiative to meet the needs of children exposed to violence. Formerly Director of Operations for the National Center for Children Exposed to Violence at Yale University's Child Study Center, Dr. Gewirtz has extensive experience in clinical and policy work with children and families exposed to violence and in the provision of training and technical assistance to communities across the United States of America implementing multi-system efforts to intervene with children exposed to violence. She has presented widely at both the local and national level on working with high-risk children affected by violence.

Betsy McAlister Groves, LICSW, Director, Child Witness to Violence Project, Boston University School of Medicine, Boston Medical Center, MAT 5, Boston, Massachusetts 02118. Ms. Groves is Associate Professor in the Department of Pediatrics at the Boston University School of Medicine and the founding Director of the Child Witness to Violence Project at Boston Medical Center. She is the past recipient of a fellowship from the Open Society Institute and has been a fellow at the Malcolm Weiner Center of Social Policy at Harvard University. She has lectured widely, providing training to police, social workers, health providers, judges and court personnel, and teachers on a range of topics associated with children and violence. Her publications include a book, *Children Who See Too Much: Lessons from the Child Witness to Violence Project* (2002), and articles in the *Journal of the American Medical Association, Pediatrics, Harvard Mental Health Letter*, and *Topics in Early Childhood Special Education*. Ms. Groves received her master's degree from Boston University School of Social Work and her undergraduate degree from the College of William and Mary.

Janice Humphreys, Ph.D., RN, CS, PNP, Associate Professor and Vice-Chair for Faculty Practice, Department of Family Health Care Nursing, 2 Koret Way, Box 0606, University of California at San Francisco, San Francisco, California 94143-0606. Dr. Humphreys has been conducting research and providing nursing care to abused women and their children for more than 20 years. She is the author of numerous publications and the co-editor with Jacquelyn Campbell of *Family Violence and Nursing Practice*.

Paramjit T. Joshi, M.D., Professor, George Washington University School of Medicine, Room 700/2.5W, 111 Michigan Avenue, NW, Washington, D.C. 20010. Dr. Joshi is Chair of the Department of Psychiatry and Behavioral Sciences at the Children's National Medical Center (CNMC) and Professor of Psychiatry, Behavioral Sciences & Pediatrics at the George Washington University School of Medicine in Washington, D.C. Over the past 20 years, Dr. Joshi has developed expertise in the study of psychological effects of violence, crisis, and trauma in children. She has received numerous grants to direct research and provide outreach services, including programs in Croatia, Bosnia-Hercegovina, and Macedonia. Since the mid-1990s Dr. Joshi has charted local and international efforts to identify and treat children traumatized by violence—in wars abroad and closer to home on the United States' streets and schools and through its media. Dr. Joshi joined CNMC in 1999, after serving as Director of Clinical Services at Johns Hopkins Hospital in the Division of Child and Adolescent Psychiatry. She obtained her medical degree from the Christian Medical College and Brown Memorial Hospital, Punjab University in India, where she first trained as a pediatrician. She completed her training in general and child and adolescent psychiatry at Johns Hopkins Hospital, where she remained for 22 years before coming to CNMC. Dr. Joshi is a fellow of the American Psychiatric Association (APA) and a recipient of the APA's Bruno Lima award for outstanding contributions in the care and understanding of disaster psychiatry. In addition, the National Alliance on Mental Illness (NAMI) honored her with the Annual Exemplary Psychiatrist Award for her contributions to a greater understanding of brain disorders.

Shulamit M. Lewin, M.H.S., Program Manager, International Center to Heal Our Children (ICHOC), Department of Psychiatry and Behavioral Sciences, Children's National Medical Center, 111 Michigan Avenue, NW, Washington, D.C. 20010. Ms. Lewin received a master's of health sciences in social and behavioral sciences, health education, and health communications from the Department of Health Policy and Management at The Johns Hopkins School of Hygiene and Public Health. Ms. Lewin has experience working with national organizations and federal agencies on child-related issues. Prior to managing the ICHOC, Ms. Lewin served as the Child Care and School Health Specialist at the Emergency Medical Services for Children's National Resource Center, where she provided technical support to state, national, and federal programs. She has expertise in emergency preparedness, violence and intentional injury prevention, school health, mental health, family-centered care, and health communications and has presented widely on these issues. Currently, Ms. Lewin oversees all ICHOC national and international training and outreach programs and development of health education resources. Ms. Lewin serves on several national task forces addressing pediatric emergency and disaster mental health issues including the Hospital Bioterrorism Preparedness, Pediatric, and Mental Health Advisory Committees of the U.S. Department of Health and Human Services.

Annie Lewis-O'Connor, RNCS, M.P.H., SANE, Doctoral Candidate, Boston University, 715 Albany St, Boston, Massachusetts 02118-2526. Ms. Lewis-O'Connor is a Pediatric and Ob-Gyn Nurse Practitioner and a certified Sexual Assault Nurse Examiner. She is recognized as an expert on child sexual abuse, physical abuse, and domestic violence. In 1994, Governor Weld of Massachusetts appointed Ms. O'Connor to the Governor's Commission on Domestic Violence. In 2004, Governor Romney commissioned Ms. Lewis-O'Connor to the Governor's Commission on Sexual Assault and Domestic Abuse. She lectures to a broad spectrum of providers, specifically on medical and nursing approaches to caring for victims of violence. Her work emphasizes the need to educate and cross-train medical, nursing, and social services professionals. She holds faculty appointments at Boston University, Boston College, and Simmons College. Ms. O'Connor has testified as an expert witness in more than 30 cases of child abuse, sexual assault, and domestic violence. Ms. O' Connor is a nurse practitioner in the Emergency Department of Boston Medical Center and has worked in women's health at Neponset Health Center since the early 1990s. Ms. O'Connor received her master's in primary care nursing from Simmons College in Boston and her master's in public health from Boston University. Her doctoral dissertation, which has been funded by the National Institutes of Health/National Institute of Nursing Research, will address screening mothers for domestic abuse during their child's pediatric visits.

Alicia F. Lieberman, Ph.D., Professor of Psychology, Department of Psychiatry, University of California, San Francisco, 401 Parnassus Avenue, San Francisco, California 94143-0984. Dr. Lieberman is Director of the Child Trauma Research Project at the University of California, San Francisco, and Project Director for the Early Trauma Treatment Network, a program of the Substance Abuse and Mental Health Services Administration–funded National Child Traumatic Stress Network. Born in Paraguay, she received her bachelor's degree at the Hebrew University of Jerusalem and her doctorate from The Johns Hopkins University. She is Vice-President of ZERO TO THREE: National Center for Infants, Toddlers and Families and a member of the Professional Advisory Board of the Johnson & Johnson Pediatric Institute. She is the author of *The Emotional Life of the Toddler*, which has been translated into seven languages, senior editor of *DC:0-3 Casebook: a Guide to the Use of ZERO TO THREE'S Diagnostic Classification of Mental Health and Developmental Disorders of Infancy and Early Childhood*, and senior author of the books *Losing a Parent to Death in the Early Years: Guidelines for the Treatment of Traumatic Bereavement in Infancy and Early Childhood* and *"Don't Hit My Mommy!": A Manual for Child-Parent Psychotherapy with Young Witnesses of Family Violence*.

Michael Lynch, Ph.D., Assistant Professor, Department of Psychology, SUNY Geneseo, 1 College Circle, Geneseo, New York 14454. Dr. Lynch received his doctoral degree from the University of Rochester, working with advisor Dante Cicchetti. Prior to joining the faculty at Geneseo, Dr. Lynch worked for nearly 15 years at the Mt. Hope Family Center in Rochester, where he supervised intervention programs for multi-risk urban children and coordinated a major longitudinal investigation of child abuse and neglect. Throughout his career, Dr. Lynch has been interested in the development of psychopathology. His research has focused on the effects of child maltreatment and exposure to community violence. Dr. Lynch is a former Research Fellow for the National Center on Child Abuse and Neglect. He is a current member of the Federal Child Neglect Research Consortium, where he is a co-principal investigator on a 5-year study of child neglect entitled "Processes Linking Child Neglect and Adaptation to School." He also is a founding board member for the Charter School of Science and Technology in Rochester where he is working to integrate knowledge about the effects of ecological adversity into school-based approaches for supporting children and families.

Steven Marans, Ph.D., Harris Associate Professor of Child Psychoanalysis, Yale Child Study Center, Yale University, School of Medicine, 230 South Frontage Road, Post Office Box 207900, New Haven, Connecticut 05420-7900. Dr. Marans is Director of the National Center for Children Exposed to Violence (NCCEV) and the Center for Childhood Violent Trauma. Dr. Marans is also the founder of the Child Development-Community Policing Program (upon which the NCCEV is founded). The primary goals of the NCCEV are to raise public awareness of the effects of violence on children and families; to serve as a national resource center for information about the effects of violence on children and families; and to provide training and technical assistance to communities throughout the country that respond to children and families exposed to violence. The Center for Childhood Violent Trauma is part of the National Childhood Traumatic Stress Network and is involved in program evaluation and research regarding acute response to violent trauma. The Child Study Center programs provide direct services for children, families, and communities in the aftermath of violent events and traumatic reactions. In addition, Dr. Marans has consulted and worked closely with ranking members of the U.S. Department of Justice, Congress, and the White House on issues related to trauma, youth violence, and law enforcement. Dr. Marans has led the NCCEV in responding to September 11th with the 3rd Congressional District, the State of Connecticut, nationally, and within New York City.

Deborah A. O'Donnell, Ph.D., Assistant Professor of Psychology, St. Mary's College of Maryland, 18952 E. Fisher Road, St. Mary's City, Maryland 20686. Dr. O'Donnell received a doctorate in clinical psychology from Yale University in 2002. She serves as Research Consultant to the International Center to Heal Our Children at Children's National Medical Center and Clinical Consultant to Child Nurture and Relief, a non-profit organization working for the psychosocial rehabilitation of orphaned children in conflict areas. Her research interests include cross-cultural processes of risk and resilience among violence-exposed youth, the role of self-regulation in overcoming adversity, and prevention and intervention design with a focus on the use of meditative and movement treatment approaches for children with traumatic stress reactions. Dr. O'Donnell coordinates the St. Mary's College undergraduate psychological research program in The Gambia, West Africa. She is a licensed clinical psychologist in Maryland and has written chapters and peer-reviewed manuscripts on a variety of topics related to her clinical research interests.

Audrey Rubin, M.D., M.P.H., Clinical Assistant Professor, Department of Psychiatry, Boston University School of Medicine; Instructor in Psychiatry, Harvard Medical School, Cambridge Health Alliance, 1493 Cambridge Street, Cambridge

Massachusetts 02139. Dr. Rubin is a child and adolescent psychiatrist and was a consultant to the Center for Medical and Refugee Trauma, Boston Medical Center. She has more than 15 years of experience providing clinical care to refugee children and adults, primarily from Southeast Asia and East Africa, both in the United States of America and in first asylum camps overseas. For 4 years she co-directed Help Each Other Reach the Sky (HERS), a community-based multi-modal after-school and summer program for at-risk Cambodian girls in Seattle, funded by the U.S. Department of Justice. She was a consultant and trainer for a program to train lay mental health counselors in Cambodia, developed by the Harvard Program in Refugee Trauma. Her research has focused on the intergenerational transmission of trauma in Cambodian families.

Glenn Saxe, Ph.D., Chair, Department of Child and Adolescent Psychiatry, Boston University School of Medicine, Dowling 1 North, Boston Medical Center, One Boston Medical Center Place, Boston, Massachusetts 02118. Responsible for the overall clinical, research, and educational programs in the Department of Child and Adolescent Psychiatry, Dr. Saxe studied medicine at McMaster University Medical School in Hamilton, Ontario. He completed a residency in adult psychiatry at Harvard Medical School/ Massachusetts Mental Health Center and two post-residency fellowships: a PTSD Fellowship at Harvard Medical School/ Massachusetts General Hospital and a Child and Adolescent Psychiatry Fellowship at Harvard Medical School/The Cambridge Hospital. Dr. Saxe's primary research and clinical interests are the psychological consequences of traumatic events in children. He was a research psychiatrist at the National Center for PTSD, where his work with traumatized women prompted the book *Violence Against Women: A Physician's Guide to Identification and Management* (co-authored with Liebschutz and Frayne; American College of Physician's Press). Dr. Saxe is Director of the Center for Medical and Refugee Trauma, a SAMHSA-funded center within the National Child Traumatic Stress Network. He is Principal Investigator on a 5-year, NIMH-funded longitudinal study of Acute Stress Disorder (ASD) and PTSD in injured children and has completed another 5-year NIMH-funded study of risk factors for PTSD in burned children. Dr. Saxe and his team have developed Trauma Systems Therapy, an intervention for children with traumatic stress who live in environments with ongoing stressors, and manualized it in *Comprehensive Care of Traumatized Children: The Trauma Systems Therapy Approach* (co-authored with Ellis and Kaplow, in press, Guilford Press).

Phyllis W. Sharps, Ph.D., RN, FAAN, Associate Professor, The Johns Hopkins University, School of Nursing, 525 North Wolfe Street, Room 464, Baltimore, Maryland 21205-2110. Dr. Sharps is the Director of the Master's Program at The Johns Hopkins University School of Nursing. Her practice and research focus on the consequences of intimate partner abuse against girls and women. Her work has emphasized the physical and mental health outcomes of family violence, including its effects on pregnancy and children, and the use of health care by victims of partner violence. Other investigations have examined the role of alcohol and substance use in partner violence and domestic abuse and mental health and perinatal outcomes in military pregnant women.

Patricia M. Sullivan, Ph.D., Director, Center for the Study of Children's Issues, Creighton University, 11111 Mill Valley Road, Omaha, Nebraska 68154. Dr. Sullivan is Professor of Neurology in the School of Medicine and Professor of Psychology in the College of Arts and Sciences at Creighton University. She is also the Director of the Center for the Study of Children's Issues, a university-wide center dedicated to conducting research on issues affecting children and their families. Dr. Sullivan previously directed the Center for Abused Children with Disabilities at the Boys Town National Research Hospital, a division of Father Flanagan's Boys Town. Dr. Sullivan's research has focused on children and youth with disabilities as victims and perpetrators of physical and sexual violence, including child maltreatment and domestic violence. Her research has addressed institutional abuse, the prevalence of maltreatment among children and youth with disabilities, and co-occurring factors of that maltreatment, including domestic violence and runaway behavior as they relate to disability status. She is investigating violence linkages among children and youth with and without disabilities, including both perpetrator and victim outcomes in adulthood.

Patricia Van Horn, J.D., Ph.D., Child Trauma Research Project, University of California, San Francisco (UCSF), San Francisco General Hospital, Building 20, Suite 2100, Room 2122, 1001 Potrero Avenue, San Francisco, California 94110. Dr. Van Horn is Assistant Clinical Professor in the Department of Psychiatry at UCSF and Director of Training of the UCSF Child Trauma Research Project. She received her juris doctor in 1970 from the University of Colorado School of Law and her doctorate in 1996 from the Pacific Graduate School of Psychology. Dr. Van Horn was the lead planner for the San Francisco Safe Start Initiative and is a consultant to San Francisco Safe Start in its implementation period. She is a member of the steering committee of the Youth Family Violence Court in the San Francisco Unified Family Court. She is co-author of the books *Losing a Parent to Death in the Early Years: Guidelines for the Treatment of Traumatic Bereavement in Infancy and Early Childhood* and *"Don't Hit My Mommy!": A Manual for Child-Parent Psychotherapy with Young Witnesses of Family Violence.*

FOREWORD

In the early 1990s, the American Psychological Association's Committee on Children, Youth, and Families developed an initiative on violence against children in the family and the community. This resulted first in a conference and then a book of the same name. This initiative focused on integrating what was known about the impact of different forms of violence experienced by children on their development and fostering communication, and maybe even collaboration, among researchers and scholars from different perspectives and disciplines who had been examining the causes of different forms of violence, treatment, or prevention of the adverse consequences of the violence or pertinent policy issues. It was concluded at that time that although there were still serious gaps in knowledge, considerably more was known about the impact of child abuse, particularly physical abuse, on children, how to ameliorate its negative effects, and how to approach prevention efforts than was known about children's exposure to domestic or community violence.

Children Exposed to Violence illustrates wonderfully how far the field has come since the American Psychological Association conference. The chapters in the first section provide much recent knowledge about the prevalence and consequences of children's violence exposure in the family or the community as well as about children exposed to war. It is especially exciting that this book brings together so much research-based knowledge about treatment services and other interventions designed to ameliorate the negative mental health consequences of violence exposure for children and integrates this knowledge into public policy recommendations. It is very encouraging to see that the field has produced such a large cadre of energetic and integrative researchers and scholars dedicated to remediating these horrible social problems.

Penelope K. Trickett, Ph.D.
David Lawrence Stein/Violet Goldberg Sachs
Professor of Mental Health
University of Southern California

ACKNOWLEDGMENTS

We extend our deep appreciation to a number of individuals who contributed significantly to the preparation and completion of this book. First, our sincere thanks to all those who participated in and contributed to the Workshop on Children Exposed to Violence and to this book. The 3-day workshop was truly a learning experience for all involved. The work presented during the workshop and the ideas and suggestions generated as a result of several discussion groups during the workshop have led to a number of significant products, including two special journal issues of *Clinical Child and Family Psychology Review*, a 3-year NIH-sponsored program announcement on children exposed to violence, and this book. We cannot thank enough all of those who contributed to each of these activities.

Thanks also to the staff of Brookes Publishing for their support and insights throughout the publication process. Clearly, this book would not be a reality without their dedication to this important area of science.

Finally, we thank our families, friends, and colleagues for their ongoing support during the process of completing this book. In particular, we thank Kyle Snow, Joan Meier, Emalie and John Feerick, Kate and Patty Ethridge, Priscilla Meza, Martha Morehouse, Reid Lyon, and Peggy McCardle, without whose support this book would not have been completed in a timely manner.

To our children,

Dylan and Caitlyn Snow,

and Douglas, Michael, and Emily Silverman,

and Penina Meier-Silverman,

who have taught us the meaning of parenthood and

who continue to give us hope for the future.

May they live in a world that is safe and free

from the pain and suffering wrought by violence.

INTRODUCTION

In July 2002, 10 different federal institutes or agencies—the National Institute of Child Health and Human Development, the National Institute on Drug Abuse, the National Institute of Mental Health, the Fogarty International Center, and the Office of Behavioral and Social Sciences at the National Institutes of Health; the Office of the Assistant Secretary for Planning and Evaluation, the Centers for Disease Control and Prevention, and the Substance Abuse and Mental Health Services Administration in the U.S. Department of Health and Human Services; the National Institute of Justice in the U.S. Department of Justice; and the Office of Special Education Programs in the U.S. Department of Education—cosponsored a 3-day workshop in Washington, D.C., on children exposed to violence. The workshop was stimulated by the interest in and attention to the problems of domestic violence, school and community violence, and war/terrorism in the United States of America and around the world. During the past two decades, much has been learned about children exposed to violence, in terms of prevalence, consequences, and mediators and moderators of violence exposure and promising interventions and approaches. However, significant gaps remain in our knowledge and understanding.

The tremendous public interest in this topic and the potential policy and intervention implications for a new understanding of the nature and extent of children's violence exposure and the consequences of such exposure on child development provided the impetus for the workshop, which brought together researchers, practitioners, and policy makers to provide perspectives on the current state of knowledge regarding children exposed to violence and to identify research gaps and promising avenues for future research. In addition, the workshop discussions were intended to assist in the development of a clearly focused comprehensive research agenda that would reflect the current needs of the field as well as those of the larger public. We hope not only that this book will stimulate additional research on children exposed to violence but also that it will serve as a resource for practitioners and professionals who work with these children and who seek to conduct or develop evidence-based services and interventions.

The book is divided into three main sections. Section I is about the prevalence and consequences of different types of violence exposure (domestic violence, community/school violence, and war/terrorism). In these chapters, the authors—Annie Lewis-O'Connor and her colleagues, Michael Lynch, and Paramjit T. Joshi and her colleagues—detail what is known about how often and in what settings children are exposed to violence, the consequences of exposure to violence on a number of child developmental processes, and risk and protective factors related to violence exposure and successful coping and adaptation among children.

Section II reviews what is known about evidence-based services and interventions for children exposed to different types of violence. Patricia Van Horn and Alicia F. Lieberman discuss a collaborative effort, the Early Trauma Treatment Network, that aims to improve the way that mental health services are delivered to traumatized young children and their families. Betsy McAlister Groves and Abigail Gewirtz review interventions and promising approaches for children exposed to domestic violence, considering the goals for intervention and proposing core principles for good practice with children. Steven J. Berkowitz and Steven Marans provide an overview of current approaches to secondary prevention and what is known about effective crisis and early intervention strategies. Finally, B. Heidi Ellis and her colleagues review interventions for children exposed to war or terrorism, using a social-ecological model as their framework. They conclude that there is a tremendous need for theoretically driven, culturally sensitive, and empirically supported treatments, especially given the fact the need for interventions for children affected by war and terrorism is unlikely to diminish in coming years.

Section III discusses legal and policy issues related to children exposed to violence. Jeffrey L. Edleson discusses specific public policies and the practices they support related to children exposed to domestic violence, focusing on the intended and unintended impacts of these policies. He outlines a set of basic values that desirable public policy would promote for children exposed to domestic violence and suggests a public policy and research agenda that maximizes safety for children exposed to violence and their families. Patricia M. Sullivan analyzes legal and policy issues affecting children with special needs (e.g., children with developmental disabilities), noting the tremendous lack of research focus on this vulnerable population.

Finally, Margaret M. Feerick and Jerry B. Silverman conclude by summarizing a number of common themes across the different types of violence exposure discussed and current and future research needs, making several recommendations for work in this area. Our goal is to stimulate additional thought, collaboration, and research on children exposed to violence so that we can move closer to finding effective ways of preventing the problem, with the ultimate goal of eliminating it.

I

CHILDREN EXPOSED TO VIOLENCE

Prevalence and Consequences

1

Children Exposed to Intimate Partner Violence

Annie Lewis-O'Connor, Phyllis W. Sharps,
Janice Humphreys, Faye A. Gary, and Jacquelyn Campbell

In most homes where intimate partner violence (IPV) occurs, there are children. In order to appreciate the enormity of the problem of children exposed to IPV[1] one needs to understand the context of family and culture in which IPV occurs. The following definition of IPV has been condensed from that developed by a consensus panel for the Centers for Disease Control and Prevention (CDC): physical and/or sexual assault or threats of assault against a married, cohabitating, or dating current or estranged intimate partner by the other partner, including emotional abuse and controlling behaviors in a relationship where there has been physical and/or sexual assault (Saltzman, Fanslow, McMahon, & Shelley, 1999). This chapter begins with a summary of what is known about the incidence and prevalence of IPV, followed by a discussion of IPV during pregnancy, and then a review of the literature on behavioral and mental health consequences of IPV and health responses to IPV for children. An integrative model for research on children's exposure to IPV is proposed, and future directions for research and practice given.

INCIDENCE AND PREVALENCE
OF INTIMATE PARTNER VIOLENCE

The extent of IPV is difficult to measure accurately due to imprecise definitions of the phenomenon and underreporting. Population-based studies over the past several years suggest that 8%–12% of women experience some form of IPV in any

---

[1]Although the term "domestic violence" is often used to denote what we refer to as "intimate partner violence," we use the latter term since it is broader in covering all partner relationships in which abuse/violence is occurring (whereas domestic violence may be misconstrued as only couples living together) and since many state statutes refer to "intimate partner violence."

given year (Humphreys, Parker, & Campbell, 2001; Wilt & Olson, 1996). Nearly one third of American women (31%) report being physically abused by their husbands or boyfriends at some point in their lives (Collins et al., 1999). In 2001, more than half a million women and slightly more than 100,000 men experienced some form of IPV. About 85% of these victimizations were against women (Rennison & Welchans, 2003). Profound morbidity and mortality have been reported in relation to IPV (Coker et al., 2002).

According to a 1994 report, 37% of all women who sought care in an emergency department for a violence-related injury were injured by a current or former spouse, boyfriend, or girlfriend (Rand, 1997). In 2000, 1,247 women—more than three women per day—were murdered by an intimate partner (Rennison & Welchans, 2003).

Based on these statistics, it is rather daunting to envision just how many children may be exposed to IPV. Estimates are between 3.3 million and 10 million children per year (Edleson, 1999a). The variation is due to differences in definitions, the source of the interviews, and the age of the children exposed. Because very young children are not always able to get out of harm's way, and adolescents often try to intervene to protect the parent from being abused, these two groups are believed to be the most vulnerable to witnessing IPV (Christian, Scribano, Seidi, & Pinto-Martin, 1997). A study of 120 homicides of female intimate partners found that in approximately two thirds of cases there were children in the home and that each of the households had an average of two children (Lewandowski, McFarlane, Campbell, Gary, & Barenski, 2004). Tragically, more than a third of the children actually witnessed the femicide, and in another 37% of the cases, a child was the first to find his or her mother's body.

Studies suggest that mothers in certain ethnic minority groups are exposed to IPV at greater rates than other groups (Greenfeld et al., 1998; Parker, McFarlane, Silva, Soeken, & Reel, 1999). Specifically, African American and Latino mothers are often reported as experiencing higher rates of IPV than their European American counterparts; and they, as a rule, have more children than Caucasians (Gjelsvik, Verhoek-Oftedahl, & Pearlman, 2003). However, other researchers have reported that when socioeconomic status is controlled, racial and ethnic differences lessen or disappear (Beadnell, Baker, Morrison, & Knox, 2000; Schollenberger et al., 2002; Vogeltanz et al., 1999).

INTIMATE PARTNER VIOLENCE
IN THE CONTEXT OF PREGNANCY

Homicide has been documented as the leading cause of mortality among pregnant women and those within a year of childbirth in several urban areas in the United States (Frye, Wilt, & Schomburg, 2000; Horon & Cheng, 2001; Nannini, Weiss, Goldstein, & Fogerty, 2002). Because these studies use medical examiner data that currently are not combined with criminal justice data, the perpetrator of these homicides is unknown. However, the largest single perpetrator category of homicide of women nationally is a current or ex-intimate partner, suggesting this important but generally unrecognized cause of maternal mortality is IPV. These studies as well as a study of intimate partner femicide and the increased risk among women who have been abused during pregnancy call urgent attention to the associated risks of IPV and pregnancy (McFarlane, Campbell, Sharps, & Watson, 2002).

To truly understand just how many pregnant women are abused requires clear definition of the population and the instruments used. Horon and Cheng (2001) expanded the definition of maternal deaths to include deaths caused by accident, homicides, and suicides. Their study compared the homicide rate of pregnant or recently pregnant women with that for women "aged 14–44 years who had not had a pregnancy in the year preceding death" (p. 1455). The study found that the homicide rate was significantly higher for the first group (20.2%) than the non-pregnant group (11.2%) when adjusted for race and maternal age. In addition, this study found that homicide was the leading cause of death during pregnancy (43.4%) and during the first year year after a delivery or termination (23.3%). In Massachusetts, similar findings were found in reviewing pregnancy-associated deaths. In this report, homicide was also found to be the leading cause of death, with two of three homicides caused by domestic abuse (Nannini et al., 2002).

The prevalence of abuse during pregnancy ranges from 3.9% to 8.3% in most North American samples (Gazmararian, Lazorick, Spitz, Ballard, Saltzman, et al., 1996), with a prevalence rate of 10.4% to 24.4% of women during the year before pregnancy (Amaro, Fried, Cabral, & Zuckerman, 1990; Parker, McFarlane, & Soeken, 1994). Torres and colleagues (2000) examined the prevalence of abuse during pregnancy and the influence of cultural norms and acculturation on abuse in approximately 1,000 Mexican American, Puerto Rican, Cuban American, Central American, African American, and Anglo American women. The results of this study indicated that cultural norm indicators, such as beliefs in the supremacy of the wife/mother role, were significantly related to abuse. A partner's belief in wife/mother role supremacy and cultural group acceptability of men hitting women were significantly positively related to both physical and emotional abuse.

Pregnancy-associated hospitalizations related to assaults signify severe risks to women and children (Weiss, Lawrence, & Miller, 2002). A number of studies have demonstrated a positive association between severe violence and preterm labor and delivery, low birthweight infants, low Apgar scores of infants, and smoking and illicit drug use among pregnant women (Bullock & McFarlane, 1989; Campbell et al., 1999; Campbell, Soeken, McFarlane, & Parker, 1998;

Kearney, Haggerty, Munro, & Hawkins, 2002; McFarlane, Parker, & Soeken, 1996; Murphy, Schei, Myhr, & Du Mont, 2001), and maternal depression and suicide attempts (Amaro et al., 1990; McFarlane et al., 1996).

Not only do infants born to abused women start out with lower birth-weights, but when exposure to violence continues their weight disparity contin-ues (Murphy et al., 2001). Low birthweight and premature babies can require major medical and social supports during the first year of life, and it is likely that these stressors cause added strain to a relationship in which abuse is occuring. Mc-Farlane and Soeken (1999) examined the rate of weight changes among infants ages birth to 12 months who were born to women subjected to abuse. An ethni-cally stratified cohort of 121 infants and their mothers were followed, and the in-fants were weighed at birth, 6 months, and 12 months of age. During this same time, the mothers were asked about the abuse and if it had ended. The rate of change in infant weight from 6 to 12 months was significantly greater for those infants whose mothers reported that the abuse had ended by 12 months and even greater if the mother reported that the abuse had ended by 6 months.

Ethnic differences in rates of domestic abuse during pregnancy presents chal-lenges to all medical providers in how to best identify victim of IPV. Although some have reported higher or lower rates among different ethnic groups, one prospective survey of pregnant women in public prenatal facilities, including substantial pro-portions of African American, Caucasian, and first-generation Mexican American women, found that abuse occurred often during pregnancy in all groups, and for most women (55%) the abuse also occurred prior to pregnancy (McFarlane, Parker, Soeken, Silva, & Reel, 1999). In several studies, however, abuse during pregnancy occurred at significantly lower rates among Mexican American and Central Amer-ican women than among African American and Caucasian women (Gaffney, Choi, Yi, Jones, & Bowman, 1997; McFarlane et al., 1999; Torres et al., 2000).

Screening

The well-being of an infant is best assessed when health care providers concur-rently explore the safety and well-being of the mother during a child's pediatric visit. In 2004, however, the United States Preventive Services Task Force (USP-STF) released a controversial document on their findings related to IPV screening. This document has been subjected to much criticism. The USPSTF recommenda-tions stated that there was "insufficient evidence to recommend for or against rou-tine screening of parents or guardians for the physical abuse or neglect of children, of women for IPV, or of older adults or their caregivers for elder abuse" (p. 387)—their rationale being "we found no direct evidence that screening for family and IPV leads to decreased disability or premature death. We found no existing stud-ies that determine the accuracy of screening tools for identifying family and IPV among children, women, or older adults in the general population" (p. 387). The members of the task force were primarily physicians.

A discussion of a few keys points is warranted as the task force's conclusions may be potentially harmful. The task force members used an overly narrow approach in examining screening for domestic violence; they proposed that detecting IPV requires a medical screener rather than a behavioral assessment tool, such as assessments for substance abuse, unintended pregnancy, and safety practices require; this is a mistake. Hundreds of studies on this topic were not reviewed simply because researchers did not use control groups. Morse (1991) suggested, "researchers who purport to subscribe to the philosophical underpinnings of only one research approach have lost sight of the fact that research methodologies are merely tools, instruments to be used to facilitate understanding" (p. 122). The most scholarly researchers from all over the world have expressed concern about using control groups, because they raise moral and ethical questions about withholding help from patients in danger.

In an editorial accompanying the USPSTF report, Mark S. Lachs, M.D., M.P.H., wrote,

> Sometimes humanity trumps evidence, for some conditions that clinicians regularly encounter, robotic devotion to evidence-based medicine risks dehumanizing certain aspects of doctoring. Any clinician who has extricated a family violence victim from an abusive situation understands this . . . We should also act because it's difficult to read about the dizzying prevalence of family violence and simply conclude that there's nothing to do because of a lack of proof. What proof is required? . . . Our patients and families are suffering, and the relief of suffering is among our mandates.

President-elect John Nelson of the American Medical Association was quoted as stating,

> We stand by our existing policy of routine inquiry about abuse. Our experience confirms what common sense tells us: When doctors and other health care providers talk to patients about domestic violence and offer referrals and help to those who are victims, battered patients are more likely to take steps to protect themselves and their children. It would be a tragedy if any provider stopped inquiring about family violence as a result of this new recommendation.

The USPSTF seems to have consciously omitted the rich body of rigorous qualitative and quantitative research, particularly the studies focused on pregnant women. Screening for IPV is every bit as vital as screening for breast cancer, cardiac disease, or smoking. Screening mothers during their children's pediatric visits makes sense, yet the feasibility and safety issues involved with this population have yet to be explored.

CONSEQUENCES OF EXPOSURE TO IPV FOR CHILDREN

Recognizing that abuse occurs in pregnancy, one must assume that once a child is born, the potential for ongoing abuse is substantial, with resulting impacts on the mother–child dyad and any siblings. Children of abused women are at increased risk for either direct abuse and or witnessing violence (Edleson, 1999a; Groves, 2002). Developmental theory has been used to understand and classify children's responses to IPV. According to this perspective, how IPV affects children depends on the child's developmental stage and history, as well as a number of endogenous and exogenous factors. Since the 1990s, there has been a dramatic growth in research on brain development and the role of early experiences in child development. This research sugggests that IPV has a variety of negative consequences on children, many of which may last into adulthood (Dong et al., 2004; Felitti et al., 1998).

Effects on Infants and Young Children

Social, Emotional, and Cognitive Deficits Several developmental theorists believe that infants and toddlers are attempting to establish trust and autonomy during the first few years of life (e.g., Bowlby, 1969/1982; Erikson, 1950). Failure to achieve these milestones is thought to be associated with insecure attachment and difficulties in establishing a sense of autonomy (Bell & Jenkins, 1991; McCloskey, Figuerdo, & Koss, 1995; Osofsky & Fenichel, 1993). This research has emphasized the first 3 years of life as the critical window of opportunity.

Concurrent with this research are studies of the effects of traumatic events on very young children (e.g., Cicchetti, 2002). Cummings (1987) was among the first to report on young children's sensitivity to inter-adult conflict. Cummings and his colleagues have argued that children become sensitized to inter-adult conflicts and that rather than habituate to such conflicts, children of conflictual relationships become increasingly reactive to inter-adult anger (Cummings, 1987; Cummings & Davies, 1994; Davies & Cummings, 1998). Moreover, children's sensitivity to interparental anger is posed as an important link between IPV and very young children's adjustment problems (Martin & Clements, 2002). In support of this perspective, a number of studies have demonstrated that children exposed to IPV experience a variety of intellectual, emotional, and behavioral problems (Campbell & Lewandowski, 1997; Onyskiw, 2003). Symptoms such as excessive irritability, immature behavior, sleep disturbances, emotional distress, fear of being alone, and regression in toileting and language have all been noted (Jaffe, Wolfe, & Wilson, 1990; Zeanah & Scheering, 1996).

Huth-Bocks, Levendosky, and Semel (2001) studied 3- to 5-year-old children, half of whom had mothers who experienced IPV and half of whom did not.

The children who witnessed violence against their mothers had significantly poorer verbal abilities than nonwitnesses.

Brain Chemistry and Functioning   Early exposure to IPV may alter brain development. Perry (1994) and others (e.g., Bremner & Vermetten, 2001; De Bellis et al., 1999) have demonstrated that violence exposure in early life may indelibly affect both the chemistry and structures of the developing brain. Koenen, Moffitt, Caspi, Taylor, and Purcell (2003) studied 1,116 identical and fraternal 5-year-old twins. Even in children this young, those exposed to high levels of IPV had IQs that were on average 8 points lower than those of nonexposed children. They hypothesized that the extreme stress of living in a home with IPV affected brain development. The findings are provocative and provide an important foundation for future studies.

Health Outcomes   Higher levels of IPV appear to result in more severe child dysfunction (Campbell & Lewandowski, 1997; Lemmey et al., 2001). In one of the few longitudinal studies of the effects of IPV, McNeal and Amato (1998) found that the consequences lasted far into adulthood and that parents' reports of IPV predicted child outcomes. These findings and the work of others (e.g., Cummings & Davies, 1994) suggest that even very young children are sensitive to interparental verbal and physical aggression. Exposure to IPV also has other health consequences. Huth-Bocks, Levendosky, and Bogat (2002) reported that even during the first 2 months of life, infants born to mothers who experienced IPV were more likely to be hospitalized, seen in the emergency department, and taken to physicians for visits other than well-baby check-ups than were infants of women who were not abused. Important to note, Huth-Bocks and colleagues (2002) reported that maternal social support moderated both maternal and infant health outcomes.

Children exposed to IPV may have a variety of somatic complaints, such as headaches, stomachaches, nausea and diarrhea, eating disorders, sleep difficulties, and lapses in bowel control (Berman, 1999; Campbell & Lewandowski, 1997; Lemmey et al., 2001). Problems with speech, hearing, vision, and immunization adherence have also been reported (Attala & McSweeney, 1997).

Posttraumatic Stress   Some researchers have suggested that young children exposed to IPV manifest behaviors similar to posttraumatic stress disorder in adults (i.e., re-experiencing of traumatic events, avoidance, numbing of responses, and increased arousal) (Drell, Siegel, & Gaensbauer, 1993; Levendosky, Huth-Bocks, Semel, & Shapiro, 2002). However, these findings are often confounded by other factors such as other disruptive events in children's lives, including non-IPV trauma, poverty, and mothers' and siblings' responses to IPV. In addition, the absence of reliable and valid instruments to measure these symptoms in very young children contributes to diversity of opinion on outcomes (Berman, Hardesty, & Humphreys, 2004).

Effects on School-Age and Older Children

Specific problems of exposure to IPV vary according to developmental stage (Augustyn, Frank, Posner, & Zuckerman, 2002; Groves, 2002; McKibben, De Vos, & Newberger, 1989; Zuckerman, Augustyn, Groves, & Parker, 1995). Infants and preschoolers may have sleep problems or separation anxiety, school-age children may have somatic complaints, and teenagers may become depressed or suicidal (Socolar, 2000). Adolescents are more likely to attempt suicide, abuse drugs and alcohol, smoke, run away from home, engage in concerning weight control measures, and engage in high-risk activity (Silverman, Raj, Mucci, & Hathaway, 2001). The repercussions on performance at school and in their communities are of paramount concern.

Mental Health and Substance Problems Children of abused women are at higher risk for mental health problems and subsequent problems with alcohol and drug abuse (Parker et al., 1999; Rossman, 2001). In a study of abused mothers and their children recruited from a special family violence unit of a large urban police department, all mothers reported that their children were affected by their abuse, as evidenced by symptoms of child distress, including sleep disturbances, aggressive behaviors, school problems, and issues with the abuser and/or the mother (Goodwin, Gazmararian, Johnson, Gilbert, & Saltzman, 2000).

According to Edleson's (1999a) review of 31 studies, children who witnessed IPV exhibited more behavioral and emotional problems than non-exposed children. Such behavioral problems have been labeled as "externalizing" behaviors (e.g., aggression, delinquency, antisocial behaviors, hyperactivity, conduct problems, anger/temperament problems) and "internalizing" behaviors (e.g., anxiety, depression, low self-esteem, social withdrawal, somatic complaints). These children have also been found to lack the ability to empathize with others, and they demonstrate low social competence (Campbell & Lewandowski, 1997).

O'Keefe (1994) found that witnessing violence was associated with externalizing problems even after controlling for parent–child aggression, and it was more predictive of behavior problems for boys than for girls. The severity of violence experienced by the mother is also associated with more behavior problems in child witnesses, especially depression and anxiety (Holden & Ritchie, 1995). In another study, children who witnessed violence were more likely to report depressive symptoms such as feeling sad, unwanted, and less healthy than their peers (Sternberg et al., 1993).

Ware and colleagues (2001) conducted a longitudinal study of 401 children residing in a shelter for battered women. Using multiple measures, they found that 30% of the children between the ages of 4 and 10 were reported to have clinical levels of externalizing behaviors, and 37% met the DSM-IV criteria for behavior disorders. This is consistent with earlier reported prevalence rates of behavior problems ranging between 29% and 45% (Christopoulos et al., 1987; Hughes & Luke, 1998; O'Keefe, 1994).

Attitudes About Violence   Witnessing violence may also influence children's attitudes about violent behavior. Children, especially boys, may adopt the attitude that violence is acceptable and may learn to use it in their own relationships. Girls may learn not to question violence used against them (Campbell & Parker, 1999; Socolar, 2000). In support of this view, Wolak and Finkelhor (1998) cited several studies that noted gender differences in relation to the behavioral responses of children exposed to family violence. In these studies, boys who witnessed severe violence tended to demonstrate more aggressive behaviors, while girls tended to withdraw or become more introverted. However, at least two studies have found no differences in gender related to behavioral problems (Kerig, Fedorowicz, Brown, Patenaude, & Warren, 1998; Spaccarelli, Sandler, & Roosa, 1994).

Factors Influencing the Effects of IPV

Possible influences affecting those that witness violence include the frequency and severity of abuse, time since witnessing violence, quality of parent–child relationships, the presence of child abuse in addition to IPV, and the presence of protective factors (e.g., community supports, positive adult role models) (Socolar, 2000). Although race and ethnicity may be associated with specific outcomes, Edleson (1999a) found no differences in outcomes according to ethnicity for children who witnessed domestic violence.

The degree to which children experience negative effects from witnessing IPV is influenced by contextual as well as individual factors. For example, families with violence may have other contextual stressors (e.g., poverty, job and family instability, residential instability, parental stress, and social isolation) that affect their children's health. Multiple risk factors may increase the negative effects for children (Mohr, Noone Lutz, Fantuzzo, & Perry, 2000).

HEALTH CARE RESPONSES TO IPV

For too long, adult and child victims of family violence have been treated for injuries in health care settings with less than optimal inquiries into the causes of those injuries and then discharged to the same homes where the injuries were afflicted (Cohn, Salmon, & Stobo, 2002; Glass, Dearwater, & Campbell, 2001). From research with adult abused women, we know that untreated injuries can result in long-term health problems (Campbell, 2002). Moreover, research suggests that children are more frequently traumatized by witnessing violence in their own homes than by witnessing community violence (Plichta & Falik, 2001; Tjaden & Thoennes, 2000). Little is known about the long-term consequences of unmet health needs of these children, however.

Victims of violence, including children, present to health care providers in every type of clinical setting, and health care providers have opportunities to deliver primary (routine screening and education), secondary (intervention for suspicious clinical findings), and tertiary (treating injuries, whether physical and/or behavioral) interventions. However, to date, little has been done to address the health care needs of battered women and their children, although health care providers and organizations were first challenged formally to provide such services by the Joint Commission on Accreditation of Healthcare Organizations (JCAHO) in 1995.

Screening for Intimate Partner Violence

Recognizing the potential for profound effects of IPV on children, the American Academy of Pediatrics, Committee on Child Abuse and Neglect (1998) recommended that all pediatric providers incorporate IPV screening as a routine assessment. However, screening mothers in a pediatric setting presents many challenges. First, using tools to assess maternal abuse that have been found valid and reliable in adult settings can be problematic if the tools have not been tested in pediatric settings. Second, it is difficult to imagine how a provider could ask sensitive questions about abuse in front of a child, especially when those questions are usually related to the father or father figure of the child. While pediatric providers agreed on screening practices in mothers of children younger than the age of 2 (where it was considered acceptable for the child to be present during screening), they disagreed when the child was older than 2. Third, there is a risk that the child may tell the abusive parent about the medical provider's queries. Fourth, documenting abuse in the child's medical chart is problematic because both parents have legal access to the child's medical records. Fifth, there are profound intervention and legal implications because of the lack of clarity about when a child's witnessing domestic abuse is considered child maltreatment (see Chapter 8).

Because screening for IPV in pediatric settings raises many issues, it is recommended that screening be a routine part of assessment in adult health care settings. Over the past decade, nurse-researchers have developed and/or tested several instruments to assess for IPV:

- The Abuse Assessment Screen (AAS) (Parker & McFarlane, 1991)

- The Index of Spouse Abuse (ISA) (Hudson & McIntosh, 1981), now the Partner Abuse Scale (PAS) (Hudson, 1990)

- The Partner Violence Screen (PVS) (Feldhaus, Koziol-McLain, & Ambury, 1997)

- The Danger Assessment (Campbell, 1995)

In many adult settings, a brief screen identifies a subset of women at high risk for verbal, physical, and sexual partner abuse (Koziol-McLain, Coates, & Lowenstein, 2001). Some studies in adult settings have suggested that direct verbal screening is superior to written questionnaires (Feldhaus et al., 1997; Glass et al., 2001). In several studies, both abused and nonabused women stated that they favored routine assessment for abuse (Gielen et al., 2000). The findings have been similar in pediatric settings. Across several studies, screening was found to be supported by mothers and pediatric health care providers in pediatric health care settings (Dowd, Kennedy, Knapp, & Stallbaumer-Rouyer, 2002; Hathaway, Willis, & Zimmer, 2002; Wright, Wright, & Isaac, 1997; Zink, 2000).

Mandated Reporting and Treatment Issues

Some states have stringent laws that require mandated child abuse reporters to notify child protective services of IPV when children are first identified; in other states child exposure to IPV does not automatically require such a report. There is significant overlap between IPV and child abuse (Edleson, 1999b); thus, recognizing one form of family violence may lead to discovering the other, which may help mothers and children get needed services. Although little research has explored this issue, some research suggests that abused mothers will seek treatment on behalf of their children. For example, Martin, Mackie, Kupper, Buescher, and Moracco (2001) found that although more than three quarters of women who were abused after pregnancy were injured, less than one quarter of these women received medical treatment for their injuries. However, this study also found that both abused and nonabused women utilized well-baby care and that the numbers did not differ significantly by maternal patterns of abuse.

CULTURAL CONSIDERATIONS FOR CHILDREN EXPOSED TO INTIMATE PARTNER VIOLENCE: USE OF AN INTEGRATIVE MODEL

The effect of IPV on children from ethnic minority groups as well as the influence of their cultural backgrounds and experiences requires a knowledge and understanding of complex factors such as those described in the integrative model for the study of developmental competencies in minority children developed by Garcia-Coll et al. (1996). This model's components include 1) social position (race, social class, ethnicity, gender); 2) racism, prejudice, discrimination; 3) residential and economic contexts; 4) promoting/inhibiting environments; 5) adaptive cultures; 6) child characteristics; 7) family characteristics; and 8) developmental competencies. This model is useful for understanding developmental challenges that children are likely to confront, including potential psychosocial and mental health outcomes. The use of this integrative model may guide providers and researchers who focus on unraveling questions that will help to illuminate the complexities associated with IPV. This model is a beginning point for conceptualizing how ethnic minority group membership and diverse cultural backgrounds can serve as protective or harmful factors among children who are exposed to IPV.

Culture and Social Class

Using the integrative model for children exposed to IPV suggests that the stratification or a society's hierarchy has a significant impact on children's physical and mental health outcomes. In the United States, members from ethnic/minority groups are often relegated to the lower social classes, typically because of their lower income, educational status, and occupations. Lower income household members often experience IPV at higher rates than higher income household members, thereby increasing the exposure risk for children living in these homes (Rennison & Planty, 2003). Racism experienced by members of minority groups is often associated with inequitable distribution of resources, education, and employment, making it more difficult for these families to provide adequate care for their children—often leading to less than optimal outcomes for their children (National Research Council, 1993). However, helping professionals must be careful not to assume that membership in an ethnic minority group automatically increases a child's exposure to IPV. There is a complex relationship between poverty and IPV, and it should be carefully researched from the perspective of cultural diversity by culturally competent teams of researchers.

Lower social class is also associated with living in segregated residential areas, often characterized by high crime rates and economic isolation, as well as families being alienated from each other due to fear of victimization and other barriers. Such neighborhoods usually have less cohesion and access to fewer resources that promote optimal physical and mental health outcomes for children (Rennison & Planty, 2003). By any standard, these conditions do not create a nurturing environment for children.

Culture and Social Experience

The integrative model also helps to identify characteristics in the environment that promote or inhibit the health and welfare of ethnic minority children exposed to IPV. For example, often members of ethnic minority groups do not trust helping agencies and agents because of several factors, including years of abuse and violence perpetrated against ethnic minority individuals, personal negative experiences with authority figures, and a general perceived sense of powerlessness.

Victims of IPV may not always trust health providers. Some studies have shown social mistrust to be highly correlated with being African American and having little income and low educational attainment (Carlson & Chamberlain, 2003). This may be due to perceived negative attitudes toward them, which may be based on stereotypes, a lack of understanding about IPV, or a particular community's culture and values. These dynamics could also account for the reluctance of many minorities to call for help from law enforcement officers (perceived by some as helping professionals) because of the potential for harsher legal sentences and overrepresentation of men of color in the criminal justice system. In a similar manner, women with children are often reluctant to use shelters as a place of refuge and help because of the perceived lack of cultural competence among shelter staff.

In addition, ethnic minority mothers may be reluctant to disclose that they and their children are living in an abusive situation as they may fear losing their children to child protective services or being reported to immigration authorities. The reluctance to use helping agencies may prolong ethnic/racial minority children's exposure to IPV and increase their risks (Bent-Goodley, 2001).

Culture and Beliefs and Values

To further understand the effects of exposure to IPV for ethnic/minority children, it is important to understand the influence of culture, which may define the individual's values and beliefs about IPV. For example, loud arguing and psychological abuse may be acceptable in some cultural groups (Chalk & King, 1998). When such behaviors become manifest, they may cause negative stereotypes toward the families. Such responses could increase the family members' reluctance to label themselves as victims of IPV. If they do not perceive themselves as victims of IPV, then resources for marital counseling, child rearing classes, parenting support groups, respite care, and other community-based programs will not be seen as appropriate by the family members. Thus, needed services may not be attained. Hence, the child's prolonged exposure to IPV may also initiate his or her use of verbal abuse as acceptable behavior.

The historical context of African immigrants' experiences in this country, the slavery experience, and the oppression and discrimination that African Americans have experienced for more than 200 years have led some scholars to theorize that IPV is a maladaptive behavior that evolved over time to cope with these negative experiences (Oliver, 1999; Williams, 1993). These experiences may further contribute to women believing that the IPV they experience is no different from the other types of abuse that they experience (e.g., mistrust, disrespect, rudeness, physical threats) from helping agencies and law enforcement agents. These perpetual thoughts might help to conceal IPV.

Ethnic minority populations have significant strengths that may protect them from abuse or mitigate the harmful effects of exposure to IPV. For instance, abuse during pregnancy is apparently lower among Mexican American and Central American women, perhaps because of the prevalence of familism, or the primacy of the family over the individual, among this cultural group. This lower level of abuse may continue through the postpartum period and thereby lessen the exposure of young Hispanic children to violence; this has not been studied specifically.

Culture and Child Characteristics

Characteristics of ethnic minority children may also influence the impact of exposure to IPV on their health and well-being. Although, in general, racial background does not appear to be associated with different outcomes for children (e.g., Edleson, 1999a), one study found that children from lower income groups, primarily ethnic minorities, showed poorer performance on the Child Behavior Checklist (Achenbach, 1991) than other children (Kernic et al., 2003). However, parental low socioeconomic status, maternal depression, and use of alcohol may confound these findings; more research is needed to understand the relationships among the various variables and how they impact minority children (Kernic et al., 2003).

Several studies suggest that mothers' perceptions of their children vary by ethnic background. A study of 206 low-income, predominantly African American children of mothers experiencing IPV revealed that their mothers reported that the children had more internalizing (depression) and externalizing (disruptive) behaviors compared to children whose mothers had not been victimized (Morrel, Dubowitz, Kerr, & Black, 2003). However, other studies of abused women have found that while Caucasian, Latino, and African American mothers report that their children have serious behavioral and emotional problems, African American mothers rate their children as more competent when compared to other mothers (O'Keefe, 1994).

PARENTING CONSIDERATIONS

Researchers have long stressed the intimate tie between mothers and their very young children. The relationship between one essential adult, usually the mother, and a child is thought to be necessary for human life and development (Bowlby, 1969/1982, 1980). Research findings suggest that mothers experiencing IPV often make major life decisions based upon the perceived effects of IPV on their children rather than themselves (DeVoe & Smith, 2002; Ulrich, 1991; Zink, Elder, & Jacobson, 2003). Although some research has noted that mothers tend to underestimate children's knowledge of violence, DeVoe and Smith found that the mothers in their focus groups "were acutely aware of the myriad ways in which their children had been exposed to domestic violence" (2002, p. 1096).

Parental Influences

Another body of research suggests that children's responses to IPV may only be in part due to observing the violence between adults. The more important influence, it is posed, is a mother's responses to IPV and its effect upon the mother's abilities to parent her children (McIntosh, 2002). It is suggested that when mothers are too numbed, frightened, and/or depressed to deal with their own responses to IPV, they are equally limited in their abilities to parent their children (Radford & Hester, 2001). English, Marshall, and Stewart (2003) suggested an even more complex relationship. In their study of homes in which women experienced domestic violence, they concluded that IPV indirectly affected children via a household "of emotional harshness and occasional physical violence" (p. 55). Jaffee, Muffitt, Caspe, Taylor, and Arseneault (2002), in a study of 5-year-old twins, reported that domestic violence affected children directly and through shared environmental factors rather than through some genetic risk. These findings are consistent with Humphreys' (2001a, 2001b) qualitative study of resilient adult daughters of abused women. In Humphreys' study and that of Bennett (1991), children viewed fathers who abused their mothers as creating homes full of fear, tension, and periodic violent outbursts.

Family Context

The family context of a minority child exposed to IPV may be either protective or further contribute to the negative consequences of the exposure to IPV. Some studies have suggested that minority mothers who are victimized as children later manifest maternal depression and stress, which are associated with negative and abusive parenting styles (Lutenbacher, 2002). Exposure to these negative parenting styles is likely to further contribute to the negative consequences of children exposed to parental IPV. Other studies have reported that depression is more prevalent among minority women, and maternal depression has been associated with less than optimal outcomes for infants and children (Beck & Beck, 1989; Hall, Gurley, Sachs, & Kryscio, 1991; Kessler et al., 2003; Lutenbacher & Hall, 1998).

Parenting Style

Parenting styles may also influence outcomes for minority children exposed to IPV. Often the parenting styles of Latino families are perceived as coercive (Garcia-Coll & Pachter, 2002; Jambunathanm, Burts, & Pierce, 2000) and those of African American families as controlling (Deater-Deckard & Dodge, 1997; Deater-Deckard, Dodge, Bates, & Petit, 1996). However, these parenting styles, when combined with love and warmth, have been associated with positive developmental and cognitive outcomes for their children.

Resilience

Studies have shown that the development of resilience may also be influenced by ethnic background. For example, Hughes and Luke (1998) found that among African American children less parental hostility and more competent parenting was associated with better adjustment, but for Caucasian children maternal mental health status predicted children's resilience. For both groups of children, not being exposed to child abuse was also associated with increased resiliency. Other studies have reported that a child's nurturing relationship with even one person can be protective when children are exposed to parental IPV (Grych, Jouriles, Swank, McDonald, & Norwood, 2000; Jouriles, Norwood, McDonald, Vincent, & Mahoney, 1996; Nader, Pynoos, Fairbanks, & Frederick, 1990). Many ethnic minority families are characterized by extended family members living in close proximity, which provides these children with some opportunity to develop relationships with other family members. These relationships may serve as buffers of the effects of exposure to IPV.

LESSONS LEARNED FROM
EXPOSURE TO IPV: LOOKING TO THE FUTURE

The knowledge gained about the effects of IPV on children serves to inform clinical practice and policy and provides direction for future research.

Research Implications

Prinz and Feerick (2003) outlined an extensive research agenda on the effects of IPV on children that focuses on best models, methods, and instruments. Researchers must use tools that are valid and reliable in each study group and in each ethnic population; researchers cannot assume that one tool will work for all. We must be clear about defining and measuring IPV; having better definitions is critical to having the best impact on the interventions we develop. Further, the research efforts need to apply innovative research designs and analyses. In addition, Prinz and Feerick (2003) suggested that research needs to focus on examining the theoretical basis of the impact of IPV on parenting, family functioning, and the family as a system; such studies would provide an empirical basis for prevention and intervention programs. Finally, intervention studies that measure successful outcomes may be instrumental in stemming the harmful consequences of exposure to IPV.

To truly understand the experiences of children exposed to IPV, consideration of contextual factors that affect their responses, such as poverty, family structure, and source of violence need close consideration. As health disparities among ethnic minority groups continue to widen, with ethnic minorities carrying the greatest disease burdens, more studies will be needed that clearly define ethnicity and minority group or race as major components to be studied. For example, if race is the concept that is used to measure culture, then clearer definitions of culture and race are needed. Conversely, if exposure to racism and its impact on IPV as well as its consequences are what need to be explored, then a more rigorous definition of racism is needed (LaVeist, 1996).

Understanding the consequences of minority children's exposure to parental IPV also requires consideration of the complex relationships, interactions, and influences of social stratification, poverty, and racism that occur daily in the lives of ethnic minority persons. We need to understand how IPV exposure impacts children's physical and mental health over their short- and long- term growth and development (Olin, 1999; Pescosolido, Wright, Alegria, & Vera, 1998; Reyes, Routh, Jean-Gilles, Sanfilippo, & Fawcett, 1991; Reynolds, Wallace, Hill, Waits, & LA, 2001; Schreiber, Stern, & Wilson, 2000; U.S. Department of Health and Human Services, 2001). We also need to better understand mothers' perceptions of these child characteristics and determine what they mean within specific cultural contexts. Thoughtful approaches to these complex relationships and interactions are necessary in our efforts to plan specific programs based on ethnic minority group membership and background experiences of children exposed to IPV. Jaffe, Crooks, and Wolfe (2003) suggest that legislative efforts consider the full range of empirical evidence on the effects of IPV on children prior to initiating programs and legislation. Failure to undertake thoughtful analysis and consideration of the potential consequences can result in flawed programs and inadvertently damaging legislation.

Appreciation of the unique relationship that exists between mothers and very young children suggests that interventions directed toward one member of the dyad must also consider the other. Hester (2000) noted that there is a growing consensus in the IPV literature that indicates that providing support for, and ensuring the safety of, mothers is an effective way to improve the welfare of their children. Likewise, other researchers have noted that failure to involve mothers in interventions with children leads to less than ideal results (Radford & Hester, 2001). However, only limited research has addressed the practical steps that women take to compensate their children for living with IPV, and even less research has focused on what mothers themselves want or have found most influential in the process of surviving IPV and in caring for their children.

Practice Implications

It seems that if children grow up in violent homes, from a very early age they learn lessons that are profoundly flawed, and thus adjustment to social norms is even more difficult than for children who grow up in non-violent homes. Children exposed to IPV find it acceptable to use violence to assert their viewpoints and to relieve stress, and they feel justified using violence in their own relationships (Osofsky, 1999; Pfefferbaum & Allen, 1998).

It is very important that helping professionals truly understand the cultural values of the communities that they serve and the historical, social, immigration, acculturation, assimilation, and current contextual conditions that influence cultural beliefs and values. Their clinical practice, including interventions and long-term plans of care, must be compatible with the cultural beliefs and values of the ethnic minority communities that are being served.

Ethnic diversification of the helping professions is needed in order to include professionals from ethnic minority groups who may help to advance our understanding of the cultural contexts, values, and beliefs that exist among ethnic minority families. Continued professional training that provides more than awareness about ethnic minority people and their similarities and differences is critical to increasing health professionals' capacities to provide supportive and effective interventions that promote optimal physical and mental development among ethnic minority children exposed to IPV.

Health care systems have made significant progress in meeting the health care needs of abused women. However, there is a need to develop protocols and test interventions that address the health needs of children who witness domestic violence (Campbell & Parker, 1999). Brief clinical interventions have proven effective in increasing abused women's safety-seeking behaviors (McFarlane, Parker, & Cross, 2001; McFarlane, Parker, Soeken, Silva, & Reel, 1998). A window of opportunity to screen for domestic violence exists during child heath visits. Home visitation is another ideal time to systematically assess for IPV and intervene. Ideally, health care providers should assess for the presence of IPV in the home just as they assess for all health problems. Unfortunately, such screening is not routinely performed.

Health care providers can support mothers in helping their children cope with the effects of IPV. In one study, Ericksen and Henderson (1998) found that abused mothers reported that their children had enormous unmet needs, and the mothers felt inadequate in helping their children. However, another study demonstrated that most abused women are nonetheless competent mothers (Sullivan, Nguyen, Allen, Bybee, & Juras, 2000). Some mothers may need encouragement and facilitation of basic parenting skills, while those who are having problems in their parenting may need assistance for these skills as well as interventions to help end the violence. Health care providers can help mothers understand their children's responses, behaviors, and needs. They also can provide appropriate referrals for needed services, such as mental health counseling. Health care providers should be knowledgeable about the community resources available to abused women and their children and connect women to those services that would be most appropriate for them.

In sum, evidence indicates that witnessing IPV results in negative physical and mental health effects for children. Thus, early identification and intervention in the lives of children is necessary to reduce the potential detrimental effects of witnessing IPV.

REFERENCES

Achenbach, T.M. (1991). *Manual for the Child Behavior Checklist 4–18 and 1991 Profile.* Burlington: University of Vermont.

Amaro, H., Fried, L., Cabral, H., & Zuckerman, B. (1990). Violence during pregnancy and substance use. *American Journal of Public Health, 80,* 575–579.

American Academy of Pediatrics, Committee on Child Abuse and Neglect. (1998). The role of the pediatrician in recognizing and intervening on behalf of abused women. *Pediatrics, 101,* 1091–1092.

Attala, J., & McSweeney, M. (1997). Preschool children of battered women identified in a community setting. *Issues in Comprehensive Pediatric Nursing, 20,* 217–225.

Augustyn, M., Frank, D., Posner, M., & Zuckerman, B. (2002). Children who witness violence, and parent report of children's behavior. *Archives of Pediatric and Adolescent Medicine, 156,* 800–803.

Beadnell, B., Baker, S.A., Morrison, D.M., & Knox, K. (2000). HIV/STD risk factors for women with violent male partners. *Sex Roles, 42,* 661–689.

Beck, A., & Beck, S. (1989). The incidence of depression in extended households among middle-aged black and white women: Estimates from a 15-year panel study. *Journal of Family Issues, 10,* 147–168.

Bell, C.C., & Jenkins, E.J. (1991). Traumatic stress and children. *Journal of Health Care for the Poor and Underserved, 21,* 175–185.

Bennett, L. (1991). Adolescent girls' experience of witnessing marital violence: A phenomenological study. *Journal of Advanced Nursing, 16,* 431–438.

Bent-Goodley, T.B. (2001). Eradicating domestic violence in the African American community: A literature review and action agenda. *Trauma, Violence & Abuse, 2,* 316–330.

Berman, H. (1999). Health in the aftermath of violence: A critical narrative study of children of war and children of battered women. *Canadian Journal of Family Therapy, 31,* 89–109.

Berman, H., Hardesty, J., & Humphreys, J. (2004). Children of abused women. In J. Humphreys & J. Campbell (Eds.), *Family violence and nursing practice* (pp. 150–185). Philadelphia: Lippincott Williams & Wilkins.

Bowlby, J. (1969/1982). *Attachment and loss: Vol. I: Attachment.* New York: Basic Books.

Bowlby, J. (1980). *Attachment and loss: Vol. III: Loss: Sadness and depression.* New York: Basic Books.

Bremner, J.D., & Vermetten, E. (2001). Stress and development: Behavioral and biological consequences. *Development and Psychopathology, 13,* 473–489.

Bullock, L., & McFarlane, J. (1989). The birthweight-battering connection. *American Journal of Nursing, 89,* 1153–1155.

Campbell, J. (1995). *Assessing dangerousness.* Thousand Oaks, CA: Sage.

Campbell, J.C. (2002). Health consequences of IPV. *Lancet, 359,* 1331–1336.

Campbell, J.C., & Lewandowski, L.A. (1997). Mental and physical effects of intimate partner violence on women and children. *Psychiatric Clinics of North America, 20,* 353–374.

Campbell, J.C., & Parker, B. (1999). Clinical nursing research on battered women and their children. In A.S. Hinshaw, S.L. Feetham, & J.L. Shaver (Eds.), *Handbook of clinical nursing research* (pp. 535–559). Thousand Oaks, CA: Sage.

Campbell, J.C., Ryan, J., Campbell, D.W., Torres, S., King, C., Stallings, R., et al. (1999). Physical and nonphysical abuse and other risk factors for low birthweight among term and preterm babies: A multiethnic case control study. *American Journal of Epidemiology, 150,* 714–726.

Campbell, J., Soeken, K., McFarlane, J., & Parker, B. (1998). Risk factors for femicide among pregnant and non-pregnant battered women. In J.C. Campbell (Ed.), *Empowering survivors of abuse: Health care for battered women and their children* (pp. 195–204). Thousand Oaks, CA: Sage.

Carlson, E.D., & Chamberlain, R.M. (2003). Social capital, health and health disparities. *Journal of Nursing Scholarship, 35*(4), 325–331.

Chalk, R., & King. P.A. (Eds.). (1998). *Violence in families: Assessing prevention and treatment programs.* Washington, DC: National Academy Press.

Christian, C., Scribano, P., Seidi, T., & Pinto-Martin, J. (1997). Pediatric injury resulting from family violence. *Pediatrics, 99,* 208–212.

Christopoulos, C., Shaw, D.S., Joyce, S., Sullivan-Hanson, H.J., Kraft, S.P., & Emery, R.E. (1987). Children of abused women: Adjustment at time of shelter residence. *Journal of Marriage and the Family, 49,* 611–619.

Cicchetti, D. (2002). The impact of social experience on neurobiological systems: Illustration from a constructivist view of child maltreatment. *Cognitive Development, 171,* 1407–1428.

Cohn, F., Salmon, M., & Stobo, J. (2002). *Confronting chronic neglect: The education and training of health professionals on family violence.* Washington, DC: Institute of Medicine, National Academy Press.

Coker, A., Davis, K., Arias, H., Desai, S., Sanderson, M., Brandt, H., et al. (2002). Physical and mental health effects of IPV for men and women. *American Journal of Preventive Medicine, 23,* 260–268.

Cummings, E.M. (1987). Coping with background anger in early childhood. *Child Development, 58,* 976–984.

Cummings, E.M., & Davies, P.T. (1994). *Children and marital conflict: The impact of family dispute and resolution.* London: Guilford Press.

Davies, P.T., & Cummings, E.M. (1998). Exploring children's emotional security as a mediator of the link between marital relations and child adjustment. *Child Development, 69,* 124–139.

Deater-Deckard, K., & Dodge, K.A. (1997). Externalizing behavior problems and discipline revisited: Nonlinear effects and variation by culture, context, and gender. *Psychological Inquiry, 32,* 1065–1072.

Deater-Deckard, K., Dodge, K.A., Bates, J.E., & Petit, G.S. (1996). Physical discipline among African American and European mothers: Links to children's externalizing behaviors. *Developmental Psychology, 32*, 1065–1072.

DeBellis, M.D., Keshavan, M.S., Clark, D.B., Casey, B.J., Giedd, J.N., Boring, A.M. et al. (1999). Developmental traumatology: Part II. Brain development. *Biological Psychiatry, 45*, 1271–1284.

DeVoe, E.R., & Smith, E.L. (2002). The impact of domestic violence on urban preschool children. *Journal of Interpersonal Violence, 17*, 1075–1101.

Dong, M., Anda, R., Felitti, V., Dube, S., Williamson, D., Thompson, T., Loo, C, M, & Giles, W. (2004). The interrelatedness of multiple forms of childhood abuse, Neglect., and household dysfunction. *Child Abuse and Neglect, 28*, 771–784.

Dowd, D., Kennedy, C., Knapp, J., & Stallbaumer-Rouyer, J. (2002). Mother's and health care providers' perspectives on screening for IPV in a pediatric emergency department. *Archives of Pediatric and Adolescent Medicine, 156*, 794–799.

Drell, M., Siegel, C., & Gaensbauer, T. (1993). Posttraumatic stress disorders. In C. Zeanah (Ed.), *Handbook of infant mental health* (pp. 291–304). New York: Guilford Press.

Edleson, J. (1999a). Children's witnessing of adult domestic violence. *Journal of Interpersonal Violence, 14*, 839–870.

Edleson, J. (1999b). The overlap between child maltreatment and women battering. *Violence Against Women, 5*, 134–154.

English, D.J., Marshall, D.B., & Stewart, A.J. (2003). Effects of family violence on child behavior and health during early childhood. *Journal of Family Violence, 19*, 43–57.

Ericksen, J.R., & Henderson, A.D. (1998). Diverging realities: Abused women and their children. In J.C. Campbell (Ed.), *Advocacy health care for battered women and their children* (pp. 138–155). Thousand Oaks, CA: Sage.

Erikson, E. (1950). *Childhood and society.* New York: Norton.

Feldhaus, K., Koziol-McLain, J., & Ambury, H. (1997). Accuracy of 3 brief screening questions for detecting IPV in the ED. *Journal of the American Medical Association, 277*, 1357–1361.

Felitti, V., Anda, R., Nordenberg D., Williamson, D., Spitz, A., et al. (1998). The relationship of adult health status to childhood abuse and household dysfunction. *American Journal of Preventive Medicine, 14*, 245–258.

Frye, V., Wilt, S., & Schomburg, D. (2000). *Female homicide in New York City: 1990–1997.* New York: New York City Department of Health.

Gaffney, K., Choi, E., Yi, K., Jones, G.B., Bowman, C., & Tavangar, N.N. (1997). Stressful events among pregnant Salvadoran women: A cross-cultural comparison. *Journal of Obstetric, Gynecologic, and Neonatal Nursing, 26*, 303–310.

Garcia-Coll, C., Lamberty, G., Jenkins, R., McAdoo, H., Crnic, K., Wasik, B., et al. (1996). An integrative model for the study of developmental competencies in minority children. *Child Development, 67*(5), 1891–1914.

Garcia-Coll, C., & Pachter, L. M. (2002). Ethnic and minority parenting. In M.H. Bornstein (Ed.), *Handbook of parenting* (2nd ed., Vol. 4, pp. 1–20). Mahwah, NJ: Erlbaum.

Gazmararian, J., Lazorick, S., Spitz, A., Ballard, T., Saltzman, L., & Marks, J. (1996). Prevalence of violence against pregnant women: A review of the literature. *Journal of the American Medical Association, 275*, 1915–1920.

Gielen, A.C., O'Campo, P., Campbell, J.C., Schollenberger, J., Woods, A.B., Jones, A.S., et al. (2000). Women's opinions about domestic violence screening and mandatory reporting. *American Journal of Preventive Medicine, 19*(4), 279–285.

Gjelsvik, A., Verhoek-Oftedahl, W., & Pearlman, D.N. (2003). Domestic violence incidents with children witnesses: Findings from Rhode Island surveillance data. *Women's Health Issues, 13*, 68–73.

Glass, N., Dearwater, S., & Campbell, J. (2001). IPV screening and intervention: Data from eleven Pennsylvania and California community hospital emergency departments. *Journal of Emergency Nursing, 27*, 141–149.

Goodwin, M.M., Gazmararian, J.A., Johnson, C.H., Gilbert, B.C., & Saltzman, L.E. (2000). Pregnancy intendedness and physical abuse around the time of pregnancy: Findings from the pregnancy risk assessment monitoring system, 1996–1997. PRAMS Working Group. Pregnancy Risk Assessment Monitoring System. *Maternal Child Health Journal, 4*, 85–92.

Greenfeld, L.A., Rand, M.R., Craven, D., Laus, P.A., Ringel, C., Warchol, G., et al. (1998). *Violence by intimates: Analysis of data on crimes by current or former spouses, boyfriends, and girlfriends.* Washington, DC: Department of Justice.

Groves, B.M. (2002). *Children who see too much: Lessons from the child witness to violence project.* Boston: Beacon Press.

Grych, J., Jouriles, E., Swank, P., McDonald, R., & Norwood, W. (2000). Patterns of adjustment among children of battered women. *Journal of Consulting & Clinical Psychology, 68*, 84–94.

Hall, L.A., Gurley, D.N., Sachs, B., & Kryscio, R.J. (1991). Psychosocial predictors of maternal depressive symptoms, parenting attitudes and child behavior in single-parent families. *Nursing Research, 40*, 214–220.

Hathaway, J., Willis, G., & Zimmer, B. (2002). Listening to survivor's voices. *Violence Against Women, 8*, 687–719.

Hester, M. (2000). Child protection and domestic violence: Findings from a Rowntree/NSPCC study. In J. Hanmer & C. Itzin (Eds.), *Home truths about domestic violence: Feminist influences on policy and practice: A reader* (pp. 96–112). New York: Routledge.

Holden, G., & Ritchie, K. L. (1995). Linking extreme marital discord, child rearing, and child behavior problems: Evidence from battered women. *Child Development, 62*, 311–327.

Horon, I., & Cheng, D. (2001). Enhanced surveillance for pregnancy-associated mortality: Maryland, 1993–1998. *Journal of the American Medical Association, 285*, 1455–1459.

Hudson, W. (1990). *Partner Abuse Scale: Physical.* Tempe, AZ: Walmyr.

Hudson, W., & McIntosh, S. (1981). The assessment of spouse abuse: Two quantifiable dimensions. *Journal of Marriage and the Family, 43*, 873–888.

Hughes, H.M., & Luke, D.A. (1998). Heterogeneity in adjustment among children of battered women. In G.W. Holden, R. Geffner, & E.N. Jouriles (Eds.), *Children exposed to marital violence: Theory, research, and applied issues.* Washington, DC: American Psychological Association.

Humphreys, J. (2001a). Growing up in a violent home: The lived experience of daughters of battered women. *Journal of Family Nursing, 7*, 244–260.

Humphreys, J. (2001b). Turning points and adaptations in resilient adult daughters of battered women. *Journal of Nursing Scholarship, 33*, 245–251.

Humphreys, J.C., Parker, B., & Campbell, J.C. (2001). IPV against women. In D. Taylor & N. Fugate-Woods (Eds.), *Annual review of nursing research* (pp. 275–306). New York: Springer.

Huth-Bocks, A.C., Levendosky, A.A., & Bogat, G.A. (2002). The effects of domestic violence during pregnancy on maternal and infant health. *Violence and Victims, 17*, 169–184.

Huth-Bocks, A., Levendosky, A., & Semel, M. (2001). The direct and indirect effects of domestic violence on young children's intellectual functioning. *Journal of Family Violence, 16*, 269–290.

Jaffe, P., Crooks, C., & Wolfe, D. (2003). Legal and policy responses to children exposed to domestic violence: The need to evaluate intended and unintended consequences. *Clinical Child and Family Psychology Review, 6*, 205–213.

Jaffe, P.G., Wolfe, D.A., & Wilson, S.K. (1990). *Children of battered women.* Thousand Oaks, CA: Sage.

Jaffee, S.R., Moffitt, T.E., Caspi, A., Taylor, A., & Arseneault, L. (2002). Influence of adult domestic violence on children's internalizing and externalizing problems: An environmentally informative twin study. *Journal of the American Academy of Child & Adolescent Psychiatry, 41*, 1095–1103.

Jambunathanm, S., Burts, D.C., & Pierce, S. (2000). Comparisons of parenting attitudes among five ethnic groups in the United States. *Journal of Comparative Family Studies, 31*, 395–406.

Joint Commission on Accreditation of Healthcare Organizations (JCAHO). (1995). *Accreditation manual for hospitals.* Oakbrook Terrace, IL: Author.

Jouriles, E., Norwood, W., McDonald, R., Vincent, J., & Mahoney, A. (1996). Physical violence and other forms of marital aggression: Links with children's behavior problems. *Journal of Family Psychology, 10*, 223–234.

Kearney, M., Haggerty, L., Munro, B., Hawkins, J. (2002). Birth outcomes and maternal morbidity in abused women—public versus private health insurance. *Nursing Scholarship, 35*, 345–349.

Kerig, P.K., Fedorowicz, A.E., Brown, C.A., Patenaude, R.L., & Warren, M. (1998). When warriors are worriers: Gender and children's coping with interparental violence. *Journal of Emotional Abuse, 1*, 89–115.

Kernic, M.A., Wolf, M.E., Holt, V.L., McKnight, B., Huebner, C.E., & Rivara, F.P. (2003). Behavioral problems among children whose mothers are abused by an intimate partner. *Child Abuse & Neglect, 27*, 1231–1246.

Kessler, R., Berglund, P., Demler, O., Jin, P., Koretz, D., Merikangas, K., et al. (2003). The epidemiology of major depressive disorder: Results from the National Comorbidity Survey replication (NCS-R). *Journal of the American Medical Association, 289*, 3095–3105.

Koenen, K.C., Moffitt, T.E., Caspi, A., Taylor, A., & Purcell, S. (2003). Domestic violence is associated with environmental suppression of IQ in young children. *Development and Psychopathology, 15*, 297–311.

Koziol-McLain, J., Coates, C., & Lowenstein, S. (2001). Predictive validity of a screen for partner violence against women. *American Journal of Preventive Medicine, 21*, 93–100.

LaVeist, T.A. (1996). Why we should continue to study race . . . but do a better job: An essay on race, racism and health. *Ethnicity and Disease, 6*, 21–29.

Lemmey, D., Malecha, A., McFarlane, J., Wilson, P., Watson, K., Gist, J. H., et al. (2001). Severity of violence against women correlates with behavioral problems in their children. *Pediatric Nursing, 27*, 265–270.

Levendosky, A., Huth-Bocks, A.D., Semel, M.A., & Shapiro, D.L. (2002). Trauma symptoms in preschool-age children exposed to domestic violence. *Journal of Interpersonal Violence, 17*, 150–164.

Lewandowski, L., McFarlane, J., Campbell, J.C., Gary, F., & Barenski, C. (2004). He killed my mommy: Children of murdered mothers. *Journal of Family Violence, 19*, 211–220.

Lutenbacher, M. (2002). Relationships between psychosocial factors and abusive parenting attitudes in low-income single mothers. *Nursing Research, 51*, 158–167.

Lutenbacher, M., & Hall, L. A. (1998). The effects of maternal psychosocial factors on parenting attitudes of low-income, single mothers with young children. *Nursing Research, 47*, 25–34.

Martin, S.E., & Clements, M.L. (2002). Young children's responding to interparental conflict: Associations with marital aggression and child adjustment. *Journal of Child and Family Studies, 11*, 231–244.

Martin, S., Mackie, L., Kupper, L., Buescher, P., & Moracco, K. (2001). Physical abuse of women before, during, and after pregnancy. *Journal of the American Medical Association, 285*, 1581–1584.

McCloskey, L.A., Figuerdo, A., & Koss, M. (1995). The effects of systemic family violence on children's mental health. *Child Development, 66*, 1239–1261.

McFarlane, J., Campbell, J.C., Sharps, P.W., & Watson, K. (2002). Abuse during pregnancy and femicide: Urgent implications for women's health. *Obstetrics and Gynecology, 100*, 27–36.

McFarlane, J., Parker, B., & Cross, B. (2001). *Abuse during pregnancy: A protocol for prevention and intervention* (2nd ed.). New York: National March of Dimes Birth Defects Foundation.

McFarlane, J., Parker, B., & Soeken, K. (1996). Physical abuse, smoking, and substance use during pregnancy: Prevalence, interrelationships and effects on birthweight. *Journal of Obstetric, Gynecologic, and Neonatal Nursing, 25*, 313–320.

McFarlane, J., Parker, B., Soeken, K., Silva, C., & Reel, S. (1998). Safety behaviors of abused women after an intervention during pregnancy. *Journal of Obstetric, Gynecologic, and Neonatal Nursing, 27*, 64–69.

McFarlane, J., Parker, B., Soeken, K., Silva, C., & Reel, S. (1999). Severity of abuse before and during pregnancy for African American, Hispanic, and Anglo women. *Journal of Nurse-Midwifery, 44*, 139–144.

McFarlane, J., & Soeken, K. (1999). Weight changes of infants, age birth to 12 months, born to abused women. *Pediatric Nursing, 25*, 19–23.

McIntosh, J.E. (2002). Commentary: Thought in the face of violence: A child's need. *Child Abuse and Neglect, 26*, 229–241.

McKibben, L., De Vos, E., & Newberger, E. (1989). Victimization of mothers of abused children: A controlled study. *Pediatrics, 84*, 531–535.

McNeal, C., & Amato, P. (1998). Parents' marital violence: Long-term consequences for children. *Journal of Family Issues, 19*, 123–139.

Mohr, W.R., Noone Lutz , M.J., Fantuzzo, J.W., & Perry, M.A. (2000). Children exposed to family violence: A review of empirical research from a developmental-ecological perspective. *Trauma, Violence & Abuse, 1*, 264–283.

Morrel, T.M., Dubowitz, H., Kerr, M.A., & Black, M.M. (2003). The effect of maternal victimization on children: A cross-informant study. *Journal of Family Violence, 18*, 29–41.

Murphy, C.C., Schei, B., Myhr, T.L., & Du Mont, J. (2001). Abuse: A risk factor for low birth weight? A systematic review and meta-analysis. *Canadian Medical Association Journal, 164*, 1567–1572.

Nader, K., Pynoos, R., Fairbanks, L., & Frederick, C. (1990). Children's PTSD reactions one year after a sniper attack at school. *American Journal of Psychiatry, 147*, 1526–1530.

Nannini, A., Weiss, J., Goldstein, R., & Fogerty, S. (2002). Pregnancy-associated mortality at the end of the twentieth century: Massachusetts, 1990–1999. *Journal of the American Women's Association, 57*, 140–143.

National Research Council. (1993). *Understanding child abuse and neglect.* Washington, DC: National Academy Press.

O'Keefe, M. (1994). Racial/ethnic differences among battered women and their children. *Journal of Child and Family Studies, 3*, 285–305.

Olin, S. (1999). *Report of the Surgeon General's Conference on Children's Mental Health: A National Action Agenda.* Washington, DC: Department of Health and Human Services.

Oliver, W. (1999). Sexual conquests and patterns of Black-on-Black violence: A sociocultural perspective. *Violence and Victims, 4*, 257–274.

Onyskiw, J.E. (2003). Domestic violence and children's adjustment: A review of research. *Journal of Emotional Abuse, 3*, 11–45.

Osofsky, J. (1999). The impact of violence on children. *Future of Children, 9*, 33–49.

Osofsky, J.D., & Fenichel, E. (Eds.). (1993). Caring for infants and toddlers in violent environments: Hurt, healing, and hope. *Zero to Three, 14*, 1–48.

Parker, B., & McFarlane, J. (1991). Nursing assessment of the battered pregnant woman. *American Journal of Maternal and Child Health Nursing, 16*, 162–164.

Parker, B., McFarlane, J., Silva, C., Soeken, K., & Reel, S. (1999). Testing an intervention to prevent further abuse to pregnant women. *Research in Nursing and Health, 22,* 59–66.

Parker, B., McFarlane, J., & Soeken, K. (1994). Abuse during pregnancy: Effects on maternal complications and birthweight in adult and teenage women. *Obstetrics & Gynecology, 84,* 323–328.

Perry, B. D. (1994). Neurobiological sequelae of childhood trauma: PTSD in children. In M. Murburg (Ed.), *Catecholamine function in posttraumatic stress disorder: Emerging concepts* (pp. 233–255). Washington, DC: American Psychiatric Press.

Pescosolido, B., Wright, E., Alegria, M., & Vera, M. (1998). Social networks and patterns of use among the poor with mental health problems in Puerto Rico. *Medical Care 36,* 1057–1072.

Pfefferbaum, B., & Allen, J. (1998). Stress in children exposed to violence. *Child and Adolescent Psychiatric Clinics of North America, 7,* 121–135.

Plichta, S.B., & Falik, M.K. (2001). Prevalence of violence and its implications for women's health. *Women's Health Issues, 11,* 244–258.

Prinz, R., & Feerick, M.M. (2003). Next steps in research on children exposed to domestic violence. *Clinical Child and Family Psychology Review, 6,* 215–219.

Radford, L., & Hester, M. (2001). Overcoming mother blaming? In S.A. Graham-Bermann & J.L. Edleson (Eds.), *Domestic violence in the lives of children* (pp. 135–155). Washington, DC: American Psychological Association.

Rand, M.R. (1997, August). Violence-related injuries treated in hospital emergency departments. *Bureau of Justice Statistics Special Report* (pp. 1–11). Washington, DC: U.S. Department of Justice.

Rennison, C., & Planty, M. (2003). Nonlethal IPV: Examining race, gender, and income patterns. *Violence and Victims, 18*(4), 433–443.

Rennison, C.M., & Welchans, S. (2003). *IPV 1993–2001.* U.S. Department of Justice Bureau of Justice Statistics. Washington, DC. Retrieved March 10, 2004. http://www.ojp.usdoj.gov.bjs/abstract/ipv01.htm.

Reyes, M.B., Routh, D.K., Jean-Gilles, M.M., Sanfilippo, M.D., & Fawcett, N. (1991). Ethnic differences in parenting children in fearful situations. *Journal of Pediatric Psychology, 16*(6), 717–726.

Reynolds, M.W., Wallace, J., Hill, T.F., Waits, M.D., & LA, N. (2001). The relationship between gender, depression, and self-esteem in children who have witnessed domestic violence. *Child Abuse & Neglect, 25,* 1201–1206.

Rossman, B.B.R. (2001). Time heals all: How much and for whom? *Journal of Emotional Abuse, 2,* 31–50.

Saltzman, L.E., Fanslow, J.L., McMahon, P.M., & Shelley, G.A. (1999). *IPV surveillance: Uniform definitions and recommended data elements, Version 1.0.* Atlanta, GA: National Center for Injury Prevention and Control, Centers for Disease Control and Prevention.

Schollenberger, J., Campbell, J.C., Sharps, P., O'Campo, P., Gielen, A.C., Dienemann, J., et al. (2002). African American HMO enrollees: Their experiences with partner abuse and its effect on their health and utilization of medical services. *Violence and Victims, 9,* 599–618.

Schreiber, R., Stern, P., & Wilson, C. (2000). Being strong: How black West-Indian Canadian women manage depression and its stigma. *Journal of Nursing Scholarship, 32,* 39–45.

Silverman, J.G., Raj, A., Mucci, L.A., & Hathaway, J.E. (2001). Dating violence against adolescent girls and associated substance use, unhealthy weight control, sexual risk behavior, pregnancy, and suicidality. *Journal of the American Medical Association, 286,* 572–579.

Socolar, R.R.S. (2000). Domestic violence and children: A review. *North Carolina Medical Journal, 61,* 279–283.

Spaccarelli, S., Sandler, I.N., & Roosa, M.W. (1994). History of spouse violence against mother: Correlated risks and unique effects in child mental health. *Journal of Family Violence, 9,* 79–98.

Sternberg, K.J., Lamb, M.E., Greenbaum, C., Cicchetti, D., Dawud, S., Krispin, O., et al. (1993). Effects of violence on children's behavior problems and depression. *Developmental Psychology, 29,* 44–52.

Sullivan, C.M., Nguyen, H., Allen, N.E., Bybee, D.I., & Juras, J. (2000). Beyond searching for deficits: Evidence that physically and emotional abused women are nurturing parents. *Journal of Emotional Abuse* 2, 51–70.

Tjaden, P., & Thoennes, N. (2000). *Extent, nature and consequences of intimate partner violence: Findings from the National Violence Against Women Survey* (Report publication No. NCJ-181867). Washington, DC: US Department of Justice, Office of Justice Programs.

Torres, S., Campbell, J., Campbell, D., Ryan, J., King, C., Price, P., et al. (2000). Abuse during and before pregnancy: Prevalence and cultural correlates. *Violence and Victims, 15,* 303–321.

Ulrich, Y.C. (1991). Women's reasons for leaving abusive spouses. *Health Care for Women International, 12,* 465–473.

U.S. Department of Health and Human Services. (2001). *Mental health: Culture, race, and ethnicity—A supplement to Mental health: A report of the Surgeon General.* Rockville, MD: Center for Mental Health Services, Substance Abuse and Mental Health Services Administration, U.S. Department of Health and Human Services.

U.S. Preventive Services Task Force. (2004). Screening for Family and Intimate Partner Violence: Recommendations Statement. *Annals of Internal Medicine, 140,* 382–386.

Vogeltanz, N.D., Wilsnack, S.C., Harris, T.R., Wilsnack, R.W., Wonderlich, S.A. & Kristjanson, A.F. (1999). Prevalence and risk factors for childhood sexual abuse in women: National survey findings. *Child Abuse & Neglect, 23,* 579–592.

Ware, H.S., Jouriles, E.N., Spiller, L.C., McDonald, R., Swank, P., & Norwood, W.D. (2001). Conduct problems among children at battered women's shelters: Prevalence and stability of maternal reports. *Journal of Family Violence, 16,* 291–307.

Weiss, H., Lawrence, B., & Miller, T. (2002). Pregnancy-associated assault hospitalizations. *Obstetrics & Gynecology, 100,* 773–780.

Williams, O.J. (1993). Developing an African American perspective to reduce spouse abuse: Considerations for community action. *The Black Caucus: Journal of the National Association of Black Social Workers, 2,* 1–8.

Wilt, S., & Olson, S. (1996). Prevalence of domestic violence in the United States. *Journal of the American Medical Women's Association, 51,* 77–82.

Wolak, J. & Finkelhor, D. (1998). Children exposed to partner violence. In J. L. Jasinski, & L.M. Williams (Eds.), *Partner violence: A comprehensive review of 20 years of research* (pp. 73–112). Thousand Oaks, CA: Sage.

Wright, R.J., Wright, R.O., & Isaac, N. (1997). Response to battered mothers in the pediatric emergency department: A call for an interdisciplinary approach to family violence. *Pediatrics, 99,* 186–192.

Zeanah, C.Z., & Scheering, M. (1996). Evaluation of posttraumatic symptomatology in infants and young children exposed to violence. *Zero to Three, 16,* 9–14.

Zink, T. (2000). Should children be present when a mother is screened for IPV? *Journal of Family Practice, 49,* 130–136.

Zink, T., Elder, N., & Jacobson, J. (2003). How children affect the mother/victim's process in IPV. *Archives of Pediatric and Adolescent Medicine, 157,* 587–592.

Zuckerman, B., Augustyn, M., Groves, B.M., & Parker, S. (1995). Silent victims revisited: The special case of domestic violence. *Pediatrics, 96,* 511–513.

2

Children Exposed to Community Violence

Michael Lynch

I n the early 1990s, several landmark studies began alerting scientists and practitioners to the serious issues surrounding children's exposure to violence in
their communities (Fitzpatrick & Boldizar, 1993; Freeman, Mokros, & Poznanski, 1993; Gladstein, Rusonis, & Heald, 1992; Richters & Martinez, 1993).
Since that time, much has been learned about the rates at which children are exposed to community violence and the ways in which they respond to such violence (Lynch, 2003; Margolin & Gordis, 2000; Salzinger, Feldman, Stockhammer, & Hood, 2002). Investigators have identified factors associated with
increased risk for exposure to community violence and have specified a variety of
main effects. In recent years, more has been learned about variables that mediate
the relationship between exposure to community violence and children's adaptation and about factors that moderate children's response to community violence.
A greater understanding of these mediators and moderators is critical for explaining how exposure to community violence affects the course of development. As
the consequences of children's exposure to community violence are further uncov-
ered, it is important to examine whether there are factors that may protect children from the harmful effects of such exposure.

PREVALENCE OF EXPOSURE

After peaking in the early 1990s, rates of violent crime have shown a relative decline (U.S. Department of Justice, 2002). However, despite these declines, youth

From Lynch, M. (2003). Consequences of children's exposure to community violence. *Clinical
Child and Family Psychology Review, 6,* 265–274. With kind permission of Springer Science and Business Media; adapted with permission.

between the ages of 12 and 19 are victimized by violence at a higher rate than any other age group (Klaus & Rennison, 2002). In examining child exposure to community violence, Stein and his colleagues distinguished between rates of direct exposure resulting from victimization and rates of indirect exposure resulting from witnessing violence (Stein, Jaycox, Kataoka, Rhodes, & Vestal, 2003). Government statistics indicate that large numbers of children are exposed to violent events in their communities and neighborhoods (Federal Interagency Forum on Child and Family Statistics, 2002; Kilpatrick, Saunders, & Smith, 2003). In fact, rates of witnessing acts of violence are higher than rates of actual victimization (Stein et al., 2003). Prevalence rates vary widely from community to community, with rates generally being higher in urban communities than in rural and suburban communities (Stein et al., 2003). Although estimates of the proportion of inner-city children who are exposed to community violence are alarmingly high (Fitzpatrick & Boldizar, 1993; Kliewer, Lepore, Oskin, & Johnson, 1998), research indicates that rural children are not immune to community violence exposure and its consequences (Slovak & Singer, 2002). Specific estimates of witnessing physical violence (e.g., beating, hitting, punching) approach 80% in some cases (Bell & Jenkins, 1993; Muller, Goebel-Fabbri, Diamond, & Dinklage, 2000; Richters & Martinez, 1993; Singer, Anglin, Song, & Lunghofer, 1995). Moreover, in a study of a nationally representative sample of 4,590 high school students, almost 20% reported that they had been victimized by at least one form of violence in the past year (Guterman, Hahm, & Cameron, 2002).

RISK FOR EXPOSURE

A number of factors increase risk for exposure to community violence, including children's gender, ethnicity, and age (Salzinger et al., 2002; Stein et al., 2003). Boys are more likely than girls to be victimized by violence (Fitzpatrick & Boldizar, 1993; Schwab-Stone et al., 1995; Singer et al., 1995; Weist, Acosta, & Youngstom, 2001) and to witness violence (Schwab-Stone et al., 1995). Ethnic minority youth, especially African Americans, are exposed to more community violence on average than Caucasian youth (Berton & Stabb, 1996; Schwab-Stone et al., 1995; Selner-O'Hagan, Kindlon, Buka, Raudenbusch, & Earls, 1998). And older children generally are exposed to more community violence than younger children, although some studies have found little correlation between exposure and age (see Stein et al., 2003).

In addition, economic disadvantage—both at the neighborhood and individual household levels—increases risk for exposure to community violence (Crouch, Hanson, Saunders, Kilpatrick, & Resnick, 2000; Esbensen & Huizinga, 1991; Schwab-Stone et al., 1995). Economic resources may provide protection against exposure to violence as a result of the increased opportunities they provide to individuals and families with respect to education, employment, and living conditions, as well as through the community services and programs they make available (Salzinger et al., 2002). The absence of economic resources may contribute to social disorder and decline in communities as they decrease the opportunities available to individuals.

A number of family characteristics have been associated with an increased likelihood of exposure to community violence, including father absence (Bell & Jenkins, 1993), family conflict (Osofsky, Wewers, Hann, & Fick, 1993), and poor parenting practices (Esbensen, Huizinga, & Menard, 1999). However, the nature of the relationship between family characteristics and community violence is not yet clear. It may be that poor functioning families have difficulty protecting their children from exposure to community violence. However, violent communities may undermine family functioning as the result of the stress they create for families.

CUMULATIVE RISK AND UNIQUE EFFECTS

In trying to understand the likely impact of exposure to community violence on children's development, researchers must address a number of challenges. First and foremost is the nature of the cumulative risk that children growing up in violent communities face. Not only are many children exposed to violence in their communities, but these children are disproportionately likely to live in the inner city, be economically disadvantaged, be of ethnic minority status, and come from troubled families. Each of these factors is associated with documented risks for children. However, the accumulation of multiple psychosocial and environmental risks—as is frequently the case among children exposed to community violence— may be especially toxic (Evans, 2004).

In trying to identify the specific consequences of children's exposure to community violence, researchers must be able to disentangle co-occurring risk factors. Much of the research on community violence has been conducted with economically disadvantaged ethnic minority urban youth. Clearly, there is logic in the rationale for using such samples, based largely on the fact that these children tend to experience violence at higher rates than other children. But when investigators target samples where the rates of community violence are high, they indirectly target other risk factors as well. Not only is exposure to community violence associated with factors such as poverty, overcrowding, inadequate medical care, scarcity of community resources, and parental unemployment—all of which contribute their own risks to child development (Cicchetti & Lynch, 1993)—but it also may contribute to general family instability and disorganization. Several studies have shown links between exposure to community violence and increased risks for parental distress and both domestic violence and child maltreatment (Linares et al., 2001; Lynch & Cicchetti, 1998a; Osofsky et al., 1993). The stress of living in violent neighborhoods may impair parents' ability to cope (Linares et al., 2001). As a result, they may be more likely to maltreat their children or abuse their partners (Lynch & Cicchetti, 1998a; Osofsky et al., 1993).

The presence of co-existing risk conditions has limited researchers' ability to specify the unique effects of exposure to community violence on children's development. The challenge for researchers is to identify and account for these co-morbid risk factors. Only then will it be possible to indicate the specific effects of exposure to community violence and whether these effects are direct or perhaps mediated or moderated by other co-occurring conditions. In the absence of this type of specificity, the best that we can say is that environments characterized by cumulative risk—including community violence and its correlates—may compromise adaptive development. To date, researchers have addressed the issue of co-morbid risk factors in a limited way. Some investigators have attempted to control for demographics and concurrent life stressors (Kliewer et al., 1998); others have included non-urban participants in their studies (Singer et al., 1995; Slovak & Singer, 2002). More work is needed to determine the specific effects of exposure to community violence.

ECOLOGICAL-TRANSACTIONAL PROCESSES

An ecological-transactional model provides a framework for understanding the unique effects of community violence and how it shapes developmental outcomes (Bronfenbrenner, 1977; Cicchetti & Lynch, 1993). According to this framework, four distinct ecological systems operate in synchrony, representing different levels of the child's environment:

1. The *macrosystem* (representing societal values)

2. The *exosystem* (representing community characteristics)

3. The *microsystem* (representing immediate experiences and settings)

4. The level of *ontogenic (individual) development*

Each of these factors interacts with the others over time, and these transactions influence the unfolding of particular developmental pathways. As a result, exposure to community violence is not viewed as a singular and sufficient cause of dysfunction. Rather, it is considered within a broader context of risk and protective factors operating across all levels of the social ecology (Cicchetti & Lynch, 1993). The balance of these reciprocal risk and protective factors determines the evolving adaptation of the child (Cicchetti & Rizley, 1981). The presence of some risk factors associated with different levels of the ecology may *moderate* the effects of exposure to community violence by exacerbating poor outcomes for violence-exposed children through the added stress they create for individuals and families. In contrast, compensatory or protective influences may ameliorate children's responses to violence and facilitate improved adaptation. As a result, it is important to identify factors in the child's environment that may moderate the child's responses to exposure to community violence.

The individual's own ontogenic development also is viewed as an important part of the child's ecology. According to an organizational perspective, development is seen as consisting of a number of important age- and stage-appropriate tasks that, once they emerge, remain critical to the child's continual adaptation (Cicchetti, 1987; Sroufe, 1979). Development builds upon itself throughout the lifespan. Conversely, failure in resolving stage-salient developmental issues increases the likelihood of continued difficulty with future developmental tasks. However, change remains possible throughout the lifespan. If a given factor (e.g., exposure to community violence) affects early development, then it is possible that early development may *mediate* the effects of that factor on subsequent development.

METHODOLOGICAL ISSUES

The way in which community violence has been conceptualized and measured undoubtedly has an effect on the understanding of its consequences. As operationalized in most studies, measures of community violence are based on parent or child reports of violent events that have been experienced personally, either through witnessing violence or having been victimized directly. However, beyond the common reliance on participant reports, the operationalization of the community violence construct has not been very clear or uniform. As Trickett, Duran, and Horn (2003) argued, there is great variability across studies and across measures of community violence regarding what constitutes the "community" and what counts as "violence." There has been little explicit discussion among researchers regarding their conceptualization of these core elements. As a result, researchers' implicit definition of community has included the neighborhood, the school, the family, or the media, or some combination of these things. With little agreement on what the community setting includes, it is difficult to compare rates of violence reported across studies and to generalize findings on the effects of violence reported in those studies.

There also is no clear consensus on what types of events should be assessed (Trickett et al., 2003). Currently, a wide range of events is included on most community violence surveys. However, it is not clear what the criteria are that establish these events as being violent. Some events may be clearly violent (e.g., seeing someone get beaten); other events are less clear (e.g., seeing a drug deal). Very few investigators have explicitly stated what counts as a violent event in their studies. As a result, there is little agreement across studies on the sets of items that are assessed. In addition, there is little discussion of the relative significance of individual events. Many studies simply add up the number of violent events to which participants have been exposed and create a summary score that reflects the degree of exposure to community violence. By taking this approach, researchers are acting on the untested assumption that all events are weighted equally (Trickett et al., 2003). Perhaps creating weighted composites, where different weights are afforded to events based on their severity, would be more appropriate. In any event, researchers need to examine their assumptions more directly so that the measurement of community violence accurately reflects the nature of people's experiences (Trickett et al., 2003).

In general, there is a need for greater clarity in what researchers refer to as community violence. In the most common operationalization based on participant reports, the measure of community violence is tied directly to the subject's personal experiences. One may assume that individuals' personal experiences provide an approximation of the true rates of violence occurring in their communities, but for various reasons these reports may be over- or under-estimates. In examining the effects of community violence, it is probably relevant to assess both the individual's direct personal experiences of violence as well as the actual amount of violence that is occurring in the surrounding environment (which the person may or may not be experiencing directly). This distinction is akin to Bronfenbrenner's (1977) distinction between the microsystem and the exosystem. Direct experiences of violence are part of the child's immediate environment (or microsystem). These direct experiences occur within a broader context—the exosystem—that provides a backdrop for the child's immediate experiences. Rates of violent crime in a neighborhood, for example, provide a measure of how much violence is occurring in a community, even though the child may not be directly experiencing it him- or herself. But these more remote, ambient occurrences of violence still can exert influences on children's development, both through how they affect the availability and adequacy of resources and supports, and how they affect the family's emotional well-being and approach to daily life.

Both direct (microsystemic) and indirect (exosystemic) experiences of community violence are important and relevant to investigate, and each may affect children's adaptation. An important advancement in this regard was made by Gershoff and her colleagues who assessed participants' direct microsystemic experiences of violence through traditional self-reports, as well as the ambient exosystemic violence that participants were exposed to through neighborhood level crime data (Gershoff, Pedersen, Ware, & Aber, 2004). More work is needed in examining the effects of direct and indirect experiences of violence in the community, and researchers need to be clear in specifying what they are measuring so that predictions and conclusions can be more precise.

CONSEQUENCES OF EXPOSURE TO COMMUNITY VIOLENCE

Despite these measurement challenges, much has been learned. Exposure to community violence has been linked both to the presence of clinical symptomatology and impairments in typical development (Garbarino, Dubrow, Kostelny, & Pardo, 1992; Lynch, 2003; Margolin & Gordis, 2000; Osofsky, 1995; Richters & Martinez, 1993). For example, children exposed to traumatic forms of community violence display difficulties in exploring and mastering their environments, forming trusting and secure relationships, developing autonomy, and regulating their emotions (Osofsky, 1995; Pynoos, 1993; Schwartz & Proctor, 2000). More specific clinical syndromes and symptomatology also have been associated with experiences of community violence, including anxiety, depression, aggression, and posttraumatic stress (Fitzpatrick & Boldizar, 1993; Gorman-Smith & Tolan, 1998; Kliewer et al., 1998; Lynch & Cicchetti, 1998a; Overstreet & Braun, 2000). What follows is an overview of the identified main effects of exposure to community violence. For the purpose of this review and for conceptual clarity, community includes neighborhoods and schools, and the effects of violence occurring in these settings (as opposed to home and the media) are discussed.

Psychobiological Effects

The clinical research literature contains many studies documenting the neurological and physiological effects of trauma on individual arousal and stress reactions (see Perry, 2001). In response to normal stress, the central nervous system activates brain structures that influence the individual's overall arousal and ability to regulate stress. For example, the hypothalamic-pituitary-adrenal (HPA) axis plays a central role in regulating the stress response; an initial increase in the production of cortisol contributes to autonomic arousal, including increased heart rate, blood pressure, and an exaggerated startle response. Exposure to chronic or traumatic stress appears to result in dysregulation of the HPA axis that can lead to either chronic hyperarousal—which may contribute to hypervigilance and symptoms of posttraumatic stress disorder—or a dissociative pattern of decreased responsiveness that may contribute to feelings of helplessness and depression (Margolin & Gordis, 2000; Perry, 2001). Very few studies, however, have examined the link between exposure to community violence *per se* and psychobiological sequelae.

High exposure to community violence was associated with a lower resting heart rate in a sample of urban school-age children (Krenichyn, Saegert, & Evans, 2001). In a separate sample of urban high school students, adolescents who had been exposed to high levels of community violence had lower baseline heart rates than less exposed subjects in response to watching media violence (Cooley-Quille, Boyd, Frantz, & Walsh, 2001). These findings may indicate that children exposed to high levels of community violence are beginning to desensitize to witnessing acts of violence. Parenting appears to moderate some of these physiological reactions. For example, Krenichyn et al. (2001) reported that the high exposure children in their sample who also had experienced harsh parenting showed significantly lower systolic and diastolic blood pressure than children whose parenting had not been as harsh.

In contrast, other researchers have reported evidence of *hyperarousal* in response to exposure to community violence. For example, African American children who either witnessed or were victimized by violence were less likely to show a normal drop in blood pressure at night (Wilson, Kliewer, Teasley, Plybon, & Sica, 2002). In addition, having heard about violence in the community was associated with daytime secretion of epinephrine in these children. Both of these effects were seen particularly in *males*.

Differences in physiologic response have also been observed in college-age individuals with differing histories of exposure to community violence. Individuals from an urban subsidized housing community showed significantly higher levels of arousal—as measured by galvanic skin conductance and blood pressure volume—in response to viewing movie clips depicting varying types of violence than did individuals from an affluent undergraduate university (Frost & Stauffer, 1987).

No studies in the literature demonstrate a direct relationship between exposure to community violence and cortisol production. However, work by Scarpa and Ollendick (2003) suggested that the relationship between cortisol production and aggressive behavior may differ between those who have been victimized by community violence and those who have not. In their study, increases in cortisol following a stressful task predicted increases in self-reported aggression among victims of community violence but not among nonvictims (Scarpa & Ollendick, 2003). This type of physiologic reactivity might increase the risk for aggressive behavior among those who have been chronically stressed (e.g., victims of community violence).

More research is needed to clarify how violence exposure impacts specific physiological systems and their response (e.g., hyper- versus hypo-arousal). The timing and chronicity of violence exposure are important to consider (Perry, 2001). In addition, future studies should investigate whether individual physiological responses mediate or moderate the relation between violence exposure and subsequent symptomatology and behavior.

Posttraumatic Stress Disorder

Not surprising, many studies have demonstrated that exposure to community violence can be traumatic for children. Exposure to community violence has been positively correlated with symptoms of posttraumatic stress disorder (PTSD) in children ranging in age from the early elementary years through adolescence (Berton & Stabb, 1996; Fitzpatrick & Boldizar, 1993; Horowitz, Weine, & Jekel, 1995; Lynch & Cicchetti, 1998a; Overstreet, Dempsey, Graham, & Moely, 1999). Although all forms of exposure appear to have some effect, *chronic* exposure to community violence and personal *victimization* by violence are especially relevant in the development of symptomatology (Lynch & Cicchetti 1998a; Terr, 1991). Victimization by community violence has been shown to predict levels of traumatic stress even when demographic variables and prior symptomatology have been controlled (Lynch & Cicchetti, 1998a). In addition, victimization by community violence was found to predict symptoms of traumatic stress in a sample of urban children who had been maltreated by a caregiver even after the effects of maltreatment severity were taken into account (Lynch & Cicchetti, 1998a).

There is some evidence that females may be more vulnerable than males to the effects of victimization, based on PTSD symptomatology (Fitzpatrick & Boldizar, 1993). Moreover, higher levels of symptomatology have been reported in association with victimization by violence among children raised in homes where there are few or no stable male figures present (e.g., Fitzpatrick & Boldizar, 1993).

Substance Abuse

Some investigators have suggested that substance use may represent one strategy to cope with the stress produced by violence exposure (Kilpatrick, Acierno, Resnick, Saunders, & Best, 1997). Along these lines, a growing body of research is demonstrating links between exposure to community violence and substance abuse. Kilpatrick and his colleagues have found that adolescents who have been assaulted or who have witnessed violence are at increased risk for substance abuse, even after controlling for the effects of pre-assault substance use (Kilpatrick et al., 1997, 2000). Although the Kilpatrick data do not allow for a clear distinction between violence that occurs in the community and abuse that happens at home, other researchers have demonstrated a correlation between community violence and substance use. More specifically, exposure to community violence has been linked to increased alcohol use among urban sixth through tenth graders (Schwab-Stone et al., 1995) and with increased drug use among 12- to 18-year-old psychiatric in-patients (Fehon, Grilo, & Lipschitz, 2001). Gershoff and her colleagues reported a link between victimization by violence in the community and increased use of alcohol and marijuana among urban adolescents (Gershoff et al., 2004). However, the strength of this relationship appeared to depend on the demographic characteristics of the neighborhood in which victims lived.

Externalizing Behavior Problems

Many studies have documented a relationship between exposure to community violence and increased risk for various types of externalizing behavior problems. Violence exposure has been shown to correlate positively with both parent- and self-reported antisocial behavior in children ranging from 6 to 15 years old (Miller, Wasserman, Neugebauer, Gorman-Smith, & Kamboukos, 1999; Schwab-Stone et al., 1995), even when controlling for prior antisocial behavior. Likewise, positive correlations between violence exposure and both self- and multi-informant indices of aggression have been reported among inner city first- through tenth-grade children (Gorman-Smith & Tolan, 1998; Guerra, Huesmann, & Spindler, 2003; Schwab-Stone et al., 1995). Again, this relationship seems to persist even when levels of prior aggression are controlled. Self-reported violent behavior also has been linked to exposure to community violence in samples of urban adolescents (DuRant, Cadenhead, Pendergrast, Slavens, & Linder, 1994; Farrell & Bruce, 1997). However, Farrell and Bruce (1997) reported some sex differences. They followed their sample over three points in time during the course of an 8-month period and reported that once previous violent behavior was controlled, exposure was associated with increased violent behavior only among adolescent girls.

Plybon and Kliewer (2001) examined the effects of background violence within the exosystem. They used a cluster analysis of objective census and crime data to identify different types of neighborhoods and found that 8- to 12-year-old urban children living in high-crime, high-poverty neighborhoods demonstrated more broad-band externalizing behavior problems than children living in relatively low-crime, low-poverty neighborhoods. Other research shows evidence of a negative feedback loop that may exist between exposure to community violence and externalizing behavior problems. Lynch and Cicchetti (1998a) reported that externalizing behavior among urban 7- to 12-year-olds predicted increased exposure to community violence a year later, even when prior exposure was controlled. Putting these findings together, it appears that a self-perpetuating cycle between exposure to community violence and externalizing behavior may exist.

Some have suggested that early childhood may represent an especially important developmental period for the influence of neighborhood-based effects on the risk for antisocial behavior problems (Ingoldsby & Shaw, 2002). However, this conclusion is limited by the fact that so little research has been done on preschool-age children. In any event, evidence suggests that these externalizing problems may persist into young adulthood, even among samples of relatively low-risk college students (Scarpa, 2001).

Internalizing Problems

The picture is somewhat more complex with respect to internalizing behavior problems. Although a number of researchers have reported links between exposure to community violence and internalizing behavior problems, not all have. For example, Farrell and Bruce (1997) reported that community violence exposure was unrelated to measures of emotional distress in their study of urban adolescents. This finding appears to be the exception, however. Exposure to community violence has been shown to correlate positively with symptoms of anxiety and depression in samples of urban children between the ages of 7 and 15 years (Gorman-Smith & Tolan, 1998; Kliewer et al., 1998; Lynch & Cicchetti, 1998a; Schwab-Stone et al., 1995). It appears that internalizing problems may be linked more strongly to certain types of violence exposure. Fitzpatrick (1993) reported that depression was linked to experiences of victimization by violence in the community, but it was not related to witnessing violence. In a multi-risk sample of urban children, Lynch and Cicchetti (1998a) reported that victimization (but not witnessing violence) significantly predicted depressed symptomatology even after various demographic variables and the severity of child maltreatment were controlled. Another study found that the risk of suicidal ideation and acts of deliberate self-harm were significantly increased among those who had been victims (but not witnesses) of community violence (Vermeiren, Ruchkin, Leckman, Deboutte, & Schwab-Stone, 2002).

It also may make a difference whether the child is familiar with those involved in violent events in the community. Depressed symptomatology was positively correlated with exposure to violence in a sample of urban fifth and sixth graders when the violent events involved individuals known to the child but not when they involved strangers (Martinez & Richters, 1993).

Other factors appear to play a role in the relationship between violence exposure and internalizing problems as well. For example, levels of depression may be reduced significantly when children exposed to violence are raised in mother-present (versus mother-absent) homes (Fitzpatrick, 1993). There also is converging evidence for specific developmental differences in the relationship between violence exposure and internalizing behavior problems. Community violence seems to have the strongest effect on depression among early-adolescent (as opposed to preadolescent or older adolescent) children (Fitzpatrick, 1993; Schwab-Stone et al., 1999).

In addition to symptoms of depression and anxiety, victimization by community violence has been related to lower self-esteem among urban children between the ages of 6 and 12 years (Freeman et al., 1993; Lynch & Cicchetti, 1998a). Moreover, urban children exposed to high levels of violence—whether through victimization or witnessing—have reported significantly higher levels of separation anxiety and significantly less secure feelings of relatedness with maternal caregivers (Lynch & Cicchetti, 2002). With regard to feelings of security, *females* appear to be affected in a more adverse way than males. Preadolescent urban girls who have been victimized by high levels of violence report feeling significantly less positive affect when with their maternal caregivers than do less victimized girls. Boys, however, do not show much change in the emotional quality of their relationships as a function of their exposure to violence. Taken in combination, these findings suggest that children exposed to high levels of community violence feel unsure about themselves and their relationships with others.

Social Cognition

Community violence may affect children's social cognition and processing of interpersonal information. For example, children who have been exposed to high levels of community violence appear to have negative perceptions of their mothers' behavior. In one study, children who had either witnessed or been victimized by high levels of community violence reported significantly more negative behavior in their mothers than did children who had been exposed to less violence (Lynch & Cicchetti, 2002). Interestingly, there was no difference in the levels of positive maternal behavior reported by the two groups of children. Actual maternal behavior was not observed in this study. Regardless of whether these children's perceptions of maternal behavior were accurate, it is clear that high-exposed children were vigilant to negative maternal behavior, as indicated by their self-reports.

Community violence may affect the processing of interpersonal information about caregivers in different ways for different children. In a free recall task of positive and negative maternal attributes, nonmaltreated children who had been victimized by community violence recalled significantly more negative attribute words than did less victimized children (Lynch & Cicchetti, 1998b). Surprisingly, however, maltreated children showed the opposite pattern. Maltreated children who had been victimized recalled significantly *fewer* negative maternal attribute words than did less victimized maltreated children. It appears that nonmaltreated children who were victimized by high levels of violence may have been able to process negative information about their mothers more openly than maltreated children. In contrast, acknowledging the negative attributes of their mothers may have been difficult (if not painful) for victimized maltreated children, thus negatively affecting their recall.

Witnessing violence, as opposed to victimization, may have specific effects on other aspects of social cognition. For example, witnessing violence has been linked to social cognitive biases among urban children in grades 4 through 6. Children who have witnessed violence are more likely to have tolerant attitudes toward violence, positive expectations about the efficacy of aggressive strategies, and aggressive fantasies (Guerra et al., 2003; Schwartz & Proctor, 2000).

Peer Relations

A number of studies have demonstrated evidence of problematic peer relations among children who have been exposed to violence as a result of feelings of insecurity and alterations in social cognition. For example, college students who reported having been exposed to high levels of community violence also reported experiencing a range of interpersonal problems (Scarpa et al., 2002). More specifically, exposure to community violence has been associated with higher levels of peer-nominated aggression (Attar, Guerra, & Tolan, 1994; Schwartz & Proctor, 2000). In addition, the peers of children who have been victimized by violence report that these children are more likely to engage in bullying behavior and are more likely to be rejected by their peers than are less victimized children (Schwartz & Proctor, 2000).

Educational Outcomes

There have been mixed findings on the impact of exposure to community violence on educational outcomes in children. Some studies report that community violence is unrelated to academic achievement and social competence in school (Attar, Guerra, & Tolan, 1994; Hill & Madhere, 1996). Other researchers have reported declines in academic performance associated with violence exposure (e.g., Warner & Weist, 1996). At a basic level, reports of exposure to danger in the neighborhood and danger in school predicted declines in school attendance and increases in school behavior problems in a sample of sixth through twelfth graders (Bowen & Bowen, 1999). Perhaps as a partial explanation for declines in attendance and increased behavior problems, exposure to violence in school *per se* has been linked to students' fear of assault at school in a national sample of students between the ages of 12 and 19 years (Alvarez & Bachman, 1997). Perceptions of the school as being dangerous may undermine children's psychological and behavioral engagement in school.

With respect to academic performance, witnessing violence has been linked to lower levels of academic achievement in urban middle school students (Henrich, Schwab-Stone, Fanti, Jones, & Ruchkin, 2004), while perceptions of neighborhood and school danger have predicted declines in grades among middle school and high school students (Bowen & Bowen, 1999).

Overstreet and Braun (2000) reported a weak relationship between exposure to community violence and academic functioning in their cross-sectional study of 45 urban African American children in grades 6 through 8. Overall exposure to community violence (including violent events that children witnessed or were personally victimized by) was negatively correlated with an index of academic functioning based on children's grade point average (GPA). The relationship between exposure to community violence and academic functioning in this study was intensified under certain circumstances. Family achievement expectations moderated the effects of exposure to community violence such that violence-exposed children who perceived very high achievement expectations were most at risk for poor academic functioning. Overstreet and Braun (2000) suggested that families that are exposed to high levels of community violence may be too overwhelmed to provide the support and structure needed to back up high expectations for achievement. As a result, children may get frustrated and fall behind in their schoolwork.

In perhaps the most thorough study to date on the relationship between community violence and academic performance, Schwartz and Gorman (2003) examined the potential mediating role of both depression and disruptive behavior in their cross-sectional study of 237 urban children in grades 3 through 5. The investigators reported that personal victimization by community violence was associated with poor academic performance as indicated by low GPA and standardized math achievement test scores. In addition, self-reports of victimization were associated with multi-informant ratings of depressive symptoms and disruptive behavior problems, both of which in turn were associated with poor academic functioning. It appears that depression and disruptive behavior served a mediating role, at least partially accounting for the negative association between victimization and academic functioning.

Additional research has shed light on other aspects of the relationship between exposure to community violence and performance in school. For example, community violence exposure may be related to the development of general academic skills necessary for school achievement. In a study of urban first-grade children, exposure to community violence was negatively correlated with IQ and reading ability (Delaney-Black et al., 2002). In this study, trauma-related distress predicted additional decrements in IQ and reading achievement. It appears that the combination of violence exposure and subsequent symptoms of traumatic stress may create particular challenges for academic achievement (Delaney-Black et al., 2002; Saltzman, Pynoos, Layne, Steinberg, & Aisenberg, 2001). For example, stress-related problems with memory and concentration, sleep disturbance, and intrusive thoughts all would likely interfere with performance in school. In fact, among adolescents exposed to violence, severe PTSD has been associated with impaired school functioning (Saltzman et al., 2001), and interventions that focused on the reduction of PTSD symptoms were associated with improved academic performance.

Juvenile Justice Outcomes

Two studies have shown links between exposure to community violence and juvenile justice outcomes. Victimization by community violence was positively associated with juvenile offenses in a sample of 12- to 18-year-old African Americans, particularly among males (McGee & Baker, 2002). In addition, in a sample of youth who were detained in the juvenile justice system, those who had been exposed to community violence were four times more likely to have committed serious criminal behaviors (Preski & Shelton, 2001).

MEDIATING VARIABLES

It is important for researchers to move beyond a main effects approach to understanding the consequences of community violence. A number of studies have begun to outline some of the processes and mechanisms that mediate the link between community violence and children's development, although more research is needed.

Characteristics of Child

Factors within children themselves may account for the influence of community violence on subsequent development. In particular, as children react to community violence, their adaptation versus maladaptation is likely to influence their subsequent development and adjustment. The emergence of stress symptomatology in children as a response to community violence may account (at least in part) for links between community violence and children's poor educational outcomes. Subsequent traumatic stress and intrusive thoughts may also partially mediate the relation between violence exposure and substance use (Kilpatrick et al., 2000) as well as internalizing symptomatology (Kliewer et al., 1998).

Exposure to community violence may shape developmental trajectories in other ways, as well. For example, the ability to regulate emotion and process social information is critical for the formation of successful peer relationships. Schwartz and Proctor (2000) found that exposure to community violence was linked to problems with emotion regulation and social information processing; these problems then mediated the negative effects of violence exposure on subsequent interpersonal difficulties with peers. Likewise, changes in children's beliefs and attitudes about aggression resulting from their exposure to violence appear to partially mediate the relationship between witnessing violence and aggressive behavior (Guerra et al., 2003; Schwartz & Proctor, 2000).

More generally, there is evidence that children's *perceptions* of their exposure to community violence may mediate the impact of *actual* exposure on social and emotional adjustment (Hill & Madhere, 1996). In a similar vein, decreased feelings of safety in the neighborhood may mediate the impact of violence exposure on distress symptoms (Overstreet & Braun, 2000).

Characteristics of Social Environment

It is possible that community violence exerts at least some of its influence on children's development through its effect on the family. There is evidence that increased conflict in the family partially accounts for the impact of violence exposure on children's PTSD symptoms (Overstreet & Braun, 2000). In general, there is growing evidence that exposure to community violence is associated with compromised parenting, and maternal distress appears to be a crucial factor (Aisenberg, 2001; Linares et al., 2001). In an important study, Linares and her colleagues (2001) demonstrated that exposure to community violence had an effect on problem behavior among preschool-age children, even when the effects of more proximal family violence were controlled. However, maternal distress partially mediated the link between exposure to community violence and young children's behavior problems, reducing the direct effect of community violence by about 50%. More global family distress also appears to play a role, and it has been shown to mediate the link between neighborhood characteristics (including violence) and externalizing problems in urban 8- to 12-years-olds (Plybon & Kliewer, 2001).

These findings point out the importance of assessing the impact of community violence on the entire family and on the system of relationships within the family. Parents living in dangerous communities may feel overwhelmed and distressed. These feelings may diminish their ability to be responsive to their children during times when their children feel threatened. As a result, when children and their families are exposed to community violence, children may feel threatened themselves, they may perceive threat through social referencing of distressed caregivers (Linares et al., 2001), and they may be unable to derive feelings of safety and security from distressed and possibly traumatized caregivers. All of these factors may play a role in children's response to violence and their risk for poor developmental outcomes.

MODERATING FACTORS

Not all children respond to community violence in the same way. Researchers have identified a number of factors that may moderate children's responses to community violence.

Characteristics of Exposure

Characteristics of exposure to violence influence its impact. Chronic exposure to violence, events that are in close proximity to the child, and events involving persons with whom the child is familiar all have been associated with more negative outcomes (Martinez & Richters, 1993; Pynoos, 1993).

Characteristics of Child

Individual differences in temperament may moderate and shape children's particular responses to community violence (e.g., Pynoos, 1993), although we know little about whether there are more fundamental individual differences in children's biological vulnerability to violence. Perhaps, partially related to temperament, the coping strategies that children use also may moderate children's responses to community violence. Differences in the use of avoidant coping strategies such as cognitive distraction and behavioral avoidance have been linked to different levels of cognitive and behavioral arousal among children exposed to high levels of violence (Dempsey, Overstreet, & Moely, 2000). Gender is another potential moderator, although this is still unclear. A number of studies have shown that males and females may be at increased risk for different outcomes as a result of exposure to community violence. However, other studies have shown similar effects of violence across both genders (e.g., Schwab-Stone et al., 1999). Not much is known about the role of ethnicity in how children respond to community violence, although the few studies that have examined ethnicity report similar effects across ethnic groups (e.g., Schwab-Stone et al., 1999).

Characteristics of Social Environment

Exposure to other traumatic experiences—such as child maltreatment—may moderate children's responses to community violence. For example, although *nonmaltreated* children who have been victimized by violence express a greater desire for closeness to their caregivers than do less victimized children (Lynch & Cicchetti, 2002), *maltreated* children who have been victimized by community violence do not, especially as they get older (Lynch & Cicchetti, 1998b). More generally, consistent with a cumulative risk model, there is evidence that child maltreatment in combination with exposure to community violence creates additive effects that increase children's risk for a variety of behavioral and emotional problems (Lynch & Cicchetti, 1998a).

Along these lines, there is evidence that family conflict and domestic violence moderate (and exacerbate) the relationship between community violence and poor outcomes in children (Buka, Stichick, Birdthistle, & Earls, 2001). In contrast, family support and cohesion may have ameliorative effects on the influence of community violence (Buka et al., 2001; Plybon & Kliewer, 2001). Fewer externalizing problems have been reported among children living in violent neighborhoods who live in highly cohesive homes (Plybon & Kliewer, 2001). There also is evidence that family support (assessed in a number of ways) moderates the relationship between violence exposure and internalizing problems such as anxiety, depression, and intrusive thoughts (Kliewer et al., 1998; Overstreet et al., 1999). Children exposed to community violence who experience little social support from their families manifest the highest levels of internalizing symptoms. Moreover, harsh parenting and the increasing use of restrictive management strategies (especially for adolescents) intensify the behavioral and academic difficulties experienced by children exposed to community violence (Gutman, Friedel, & Hitt, 2003; Krenichyn et al., 2001). However, the protective function of family support may be overwhelmed in some cases. For example, family support did not lessen problem behavior among a clinically referred sample of urban adolescents who had been victimized by violence (Youngstrom, Weist, & Albus, 2003).

Parental education and parental monitoring also have been shown to influence the impact of community violence. Martinez and Richters (1993) found that children reported higher levels of stress associated with exposure to violence when their mothers had less than a high school education. Pettit, Bates, Dodge, and Meece (1999) reported that children living in dangerous neighborhoods demonstrated fewer externalizing behavior problems when their parents monitored what they were doing and whom they were with. Finally, the availability of supportive relationships and the opportunity to talk with a supportive adult appears to play an important role in lessening the negative impact of exposure to community violence (Boney-McCoy & Finkelhor, 1995; Kliewer et al., 1998).

RESILIENT OUTCOMES

Although the risk for problematic outcomes in development is elevated among children who have been exposed to community violence, the majority of those exposed to violence do not have diagnosable conditions. Many of the moderating factors just discussed may act as protective factors for children, buffering them from the adverse effects of community violence. Studies that have looked specifically at resilient functioning among children exposed to community violence have identified three key factors as being important: parent support, school support, and peer support (Hill & Madhere, 1996; O'Donnell, Schwab-Stone, & Muyeed, 2002). In an important study by O'Donnell and her colleagues (2002), parent support was a powerful predictor of resilient functioning in several do-

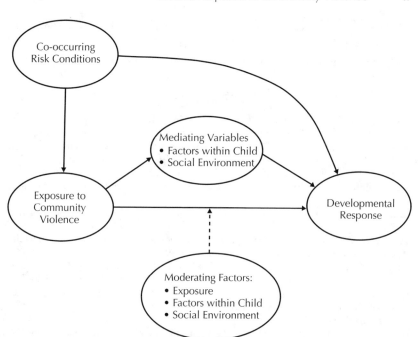

Figure 2.1. A possible model of the relationship between exposure to community violence and its consequences.

mains among sixth, eighth, and tenth graders, but became significantly less important over time. In contrast, support from school increased over time in its ability to predict resilient functioning, particularly in domains related to substance use and school misconduct. Peer support had the weakest positive impact on resilient functioning, and it actually had a negative impact on substance abuse and misconduct. Taken together, these findings suggest that parents, schools, and peers may play different roles in promoting adaptive functioning among children exposed to community violence.

Figure 2.1 presents a possible model of the relationship between exposure to community violence and its consequences. Researchers have identified a number of factors that are associated with increased risk for both exposure to community violence and developmental difficulty, but further articulation of the complex links between violence exposure and developmental outcomes is needed. In addition, future research needs to increase our understanding of the unique effects of exposure to community violence over and above the effects of other co-occurring risk factors. A number of studies have begun to outline some of the factors that mediate and moderate the link between community violence and children's development. However, more precise identification is needed in order to create more focused and effective approaches to intervention, thus increasing the likelihood of resilient functioning in the face of serious environmental adversity.

REFERENCES

Aisenberg, E. (2001). The effects of exposure to community violence upon Latina mothers and preschool children. *Hispanic Journal of Behavioral Sciences, 23,* 378–398.

Alvarez, A., & Bachman, R. (1997). Predicting the fear of assault at school and while going to and from school in an adolescent population. *Violence and Victims, 12,* 69–86.

Attar, B., Guerra, N., & Tolan, P. (1994). Neighborhood disadvantage, stressful life events, and adjustment in urban elementary-school children. *Journal of Clinical Psychology, 23,* 391–400.

Bell, C.C., & Jenkins, E.J. (1993). Community violence and children on Chicago's southside. *Psychiatry, 56,* 46–54.

Berton, M.W., & Stabb, S.D. (1996). Exposure to violence and post-traumatic stress disorder in urban adolescents. *Adolescence, 31,* 489–498.

Boney-McCoy, S., & Finkelhor, D. (1995). Psycho-social sequelae of violent victimization in a national youth sample. *Journal of Consulting and Clinical Psychology, 63,* 726–736.

Bowen, N., & Bowen, G. (1999). Effects of crime and violence in neighborhoods and schools on the school behavior and performance of adolescents. *Journal of Adolescent Research, 14,* 319–342.

Bronfenbrenner, U. (1977). Toward an experimental ecology of human development. *American Psychologist, 32,* 513–531.

Buka, S., Stichick, T., Birdthistle, I., & Earls, F. (2001). Youth exposure to violence: Prevalence, risks and consequences. *American Journal of Orthopsychiatry, 71,* 298–310.

Cicchetti, D. (1987). Developmental psychopathology in infancy: Illustration from the study of maltreated youngsters. *Journal of Consulting and Clinical Psychology, 55,* 837–845.

Cicchetti, D., & Lynch, M. (1993). Toward an ecological/transactional model of community violence and child maltreatment: Consequences for children's development. *Psychiatry, 56,* 96–118.

Cicchetti, D., & Rizley, R. (1981). Developmental perspectives on the etiology, intergenerational transmission, and sequelae of child maltreatment. *New Directions for Child Development, 11,* 32–59.

Cooley-Quille, M., Boyd, R.C., Frantz, F., & Walsh, J. (2001). Emotional and behavioral impact of exposure to community violence in inner-city adolescents. *Journal of Community Psychology, 30,* 199–206.

Crouch, J.L., Hanson, R.F., Saunders, B.E., Kilpatrick, D.G., & Resnick, H.S. (2000). Income, race/ethnicity, and exposure to violence in youth: Results from the national survey of adolescents. *Journal of Community Psychology, 28,* 625–641.

Delaney-Black, V., Covington, C., Ondersma, S.J., Nordstrom-Klee, B., Templin, T., Ager, J., et al. (2002). Violence exposure, trauma, and IQ and/or reading deficits among urban children. *Archives of Pediatric and Adolescent Medicine, 156,* 280–285.

Dempsey, M., Overstreet, S., & Moely, B. (2000). "Approach" and "avoidance" coping and PTSD symptoms in inner-city youth. *Current Psychology: Developmental, Learning, Personality, Social, 19,* 28–45.

DuRant, R., Cadenhead, C., Pendergrast, R., Slavens, G., & Linder, C. (1994). Factors associated with the use of violence among urban black adolescents. *American Journal of Public Health, 84,* 612–617.

Esbensen, F., & Huizinga, D. (1991). Juvenile victimization and delinquency. *Youth and Society, 23,* 202–228.

Evans, G.W. (2004). The environment of childhood poverty. *American Psychologist, 59*, 77–92.

Farrell, A., & Bruce, S. (1997). Impact of exposure to community violence on violent behavior and emotional distress among urban adolescents. *Journal of Clinical Child Psychology, 26*, 2–14.

Federal Interagency Forum on Child and Family Statistics. (2002). *America's Children: Key National Indicators of Well-Being, 2002.* Washington, DC: U.S. Government Printing Office.

Fehon, D., Grilo, C., & Lipschitz, D. (2001). Correlates of community violence exposure in hospitalized adolescents. *Comprehensive Psychiatry, 42*, 283–290.

Fitzpatrick, K.M. (1993). Exposure to violence and presence of depression among low-income, African-American youth. *Journal of Consulting and Clinical Psychology, 61*, 528–531.

Fitzpatrick, K.M., & Boldizar, J.P. (1993). The prevalence and consequences of exposure to violence among African-American youth. *Journal of the American Academy of Child & Adolescent Psychiatry, 32*, 424–430.

Freeman, L., Mokros, H., & Poznanski, E. (1993). Violent events reported by normal urban school-age children: Characteristics and depression correlates. *Journal of the American Academy of Child & Adolescent Psychiatry, 32*, 419–423.

Frost, R., & Stauffer, J. (1987). The effects of social class, gender, and personality on physiological responses to filmed violence. *Journal of Communication, 37*, 29–45.

Garbarino, J., Dubrow, N., Kostelny, N., & Pardo, C. (1992). *Children in danger: Coping with the consequences of community violence.* San Francisco: Jossey-Bass.

Gershoff, E., Pedersen, S., Ware, A., & Aber, J.L. (2004, March). Violence exposure and parenting impacts on behavior problems and risk behaviors: Moderation by neighborhood context. In E. Gershoff (Chair), *Advances in measurement, trajectory, and multilevel analyses of violence exposure and adolescent problem behaviors and achievement.* Symposium conducted at the biennial meeting of the Society for Research in Adolescence, Baltimore, MD.

Gladstein, J., Rusonis, E.S., & Heald, E.P. (1992). A comparison of inner-city and upper-middle class youths' exposure to violence. *Journal of Adolescent Health, 13*, 275–280.

Gorman-Smith, D., & Tolan, P. (1998). The role of exposure to community violence and developmental problems among inner-city youth. *Development and Psychopathology, 10*, 101–116.

Guerra, N.G., Huesmann, L.R., & Spindler, A. (2003). Community violence exposure, social cognition, and aggression among urban elementary school children. *Child Development, 74*, 1561–1576.

Guterman, N.B., Hahm, H.C., & Cameron, M. (2002). Adolescent victimization and subsequent use of mental health counseling services. *Journal of Adolescent Health, 30*, 336–345.

Gutman, L., Friedel, J., & Hitt, R. (2003). Keeping adolescents safe from harm: Management strategies of African-American families in a high-risk community. *Journal of School Psychology, 41*, 167–184.

Henrich, C.C., Schwab-Stone, M., Fanti, K., Jones, S.M., & Ruchkin, V. (2004). The association of community violence exposure with middle school achievement: A prospective study. *Journal of Applied Developmental Psychology, 25*, 327–348.

Hill, H., & Madhere, S. (1996). Exposure to community violence and African-American children: A multidimensional model of risks and resources. *Journal of Community Psychology, 24*, 26–43.

Horowitz, K., Weine, S., & Jekel, J. (1995). PTSD symptoms in urban adolescent girls: Compounded community trauma. *Journal of the American Academy of Child and Adolescent Psychiatry, 34*, 1353–1361.

Ingoldsby, E., & Shaw, D. (2002). Neighborhood contextual factors and early-starting antisocial pathways. *Clinical Child and Family Psychology Review, 5,* 21–55.

Kilpatrick, D.G., Acierno, R., Resnick, H.S., Saunders, B.E., & Best, C. (1997). A 2-year longitudinal analysis of the relationships between violent assault and substance use in women. *Journal of Consulting & Clinical Psychology, 65,* 834–847.

Kilpatrick, D.G., Acierno, R., Saunders, B.E., Resnick, H.S., Best, C., & Schnurr, P.P. (2000). Risk factors for adolescent substance abuse and dependence: Data from a national sample. *Journal of Consulting & Clinical Psychology, 68,* 19–30.

Kilpatrick, D.G., Saunders, B.E., & Smith, D.W. (2003). Youth victimization: Prevalence and implications. *NIJ Research in Brief.* Washington, DC: U.S. Department of Justice.

Klaus P., & Rennison, C.M. (2002). *Age patterns in violent victimization, 1976–2000* (NCJ 190104). Washington, DC: U.S. Department of Justice, Office of Justice Programs, Bureau of Justice Statistics.

Kliewer, W., Lepore, S., Oskin, D., & Johnson, P. (1998). The role of social and cognitive processes in children's adjustment to community violence. *Journal of Consulting & Clinical Psychology, 66,* 199–209.

Krenichyn, K., Saegert, S., & Evans, G.W. (2001). Parents as moderators of psychological and physiological correlates of inner-city children's exposure to violence. *Applied Developmental Psychology, 22,* 581–602.

Linares, L.O., Heeren, T., Bronfman, E., Zuckerman, B., Augustyn, M., & Tronick, E. (2001). A mediational model for the impact of exposure to community violence on early child behavior problems. *Child Development, 72,* 639–652.

Lynch, M. (2003). Consequences of children's exposure to community violence. *Clinical Child and Family Psychology Review, 6,* 265–274.

Lynch, M., & Cicchetti, D. (1998a). An ecological-transactional analysis of children and contexts: The longitudinal interplay among child maltreatment, community violence, and children's symptomatology. *Development and Psychopathology, 10,* 235–257.

Lynch, M., & Cicchetti, D. (1998b). Trauma, mental representation, and the organization of memory for mother-referent material. *Development and Psychopathology, 10,* 739–759.

Lynch, M., & Cicchetti, D. (2002). Links between community violence and the family system: Evidence from children's feelings of relatedness and perceptions of parent behavior. *Family Process, 41,* 519–532.

Margolin, G., & Gordis, E.B. (2000). The effects of family and community violence on children. *Annual Review of Psychology, 51,* 445–479.

Martinez, P., & Richters, J. (1993). The NIMH community violence project: II. Children's distress symptoms associated with violence exposure. *Psychiatry, 56,* 22–35.

McGee, Z., & Baker, S. (2002). Impact of violence on problem behavior among adolescents: Risk factors among an urban sample. *Journal of Contemporary Criminal Justice, 18,* 74–93.

Miller, L., Wasserman, G., Neugebauer, R., Gorman-Smith, D., & Kamboukos, D. (1999). Witnessed community violence and anti-social behavior in high-risk urban boys. *Journal of Clinical & Child Psychology, 28,* 2–11.

Muller, R.T., Goebel-Fabbri, A.E., Diamond, T., & Dinklage, D. (2000). Social support and the relationship between family and community violence exposure and psychopathology among high risk adolescents. *Child Abuse and Neglect, 24,* 449–464.

O'Donnell, D.A., Schwab-Stone, M.E., & Muyeed, A.Z. (2002). Multidimensional resilience in urban children exposed to community violence. *Child Development, 73,* 1265–1282.

Osofsky, J.D. (1995). The effects of exposure to violence on young children. *American Psychologist, 50,* 782–788.

Osofsky, J.D., Wewers, S., Hann, D.M., & Fick, A.C. (1993). Chronic community violence: What is happening to our children? *Psychiatry, 56,* 36–45.

Overstreet, S., & Braun, S. (2000). Exposure to community violence and post-traumatic stress symptoms: Mediating factors. *American Journal of Orthopsychiatry, 70*, 263–271.

Overstreet, S., Dempsey, M., Graham, D., & Moely, B. (1999). Availability of family support as a moderator of exposure to community violence. *Journal of Clinical Child Psychology, 28*, 151–159.

Perry, B. (2001). The neurodevelopmental impact of violence in childhood. In D. Schetky & E.P. Benedek (Eds.), *Textbook of child and adolescent forensic psychiatry* (pp. 221–238). Washington, DC: American Psychiatric Press.

Pettit, G., Bates, J., Dodge, K., & Meece, D. (1999). The impact of after-school peer contact on early adolescent externalizing problems is moderated by parental monitoring, perceived neighborhood safety, and prior adjustment. *Child Development, 70*, 768–778.

Plybon, L., & Kliewer, W. (2001). Neighborhood types and externalizing behavior in urban school-age children: Tests of direct, mediated, and moderated effects. *Journal of Child and Family Studies, 10*, 419–437.

Preski, S., & Shelton, D. (2001). The role of contextual, child and parent factors in predicting criminal outcomes in adolescence. *Issues in Mental Health Nursing, 22*, 197–205.

Pynoos, R.S. (1993). Traumatic stress and developmental psychopathology in children and adolescents. In J.M. Oldham, M.B. Riba, & A. Tasman (Eds.), *American Psychiatric Press review of psychiatry, Vol. 12* (pp. 205–238). Washington, DC: American Psychiatric Press.

Richters, J.E., & Martinez, P.E. (1993). The National Institute of Mental Health Community Violence Project: I. Children as victims of and witnesses to violence. Children and violence [Special issue]. *Psychiatry, 56*, 7–21.

Saltzman, W., Pynoos, R., Layne, C., Steinberg, A., & Aisenberg, E. (2001). Trauma- and grief-focused intervention for adolescents exposed to community violence: Results of a school-based screening and group treatment protocol. *Group Dynamics, 5*, 291–303.

Salzinger, S., Feldman, R.S., Stockhammer, T., & Hood, J. (2002). An ecological framework for understanding risk for exposure to community violence and the effects of exposure on children and adolescents. *Aggression and Violent Behavior, 7*, 423–451.

Scarpa, A., Fikretoglu, D., Bowser, F., Hurley, J., Pappert, C., Romero, N., et al. (2002). Community violence exposure in university students: A replication and extension. *Journal of Interpersonal Violence, 17*, 253–272.

Scarpa A., & Ollendick, T.H. (2003). Community violence exposure in a young adult sample: III. Psychopathology and victimization interact to affect risk for aggression. *Journal of Community Psychology, 31*, 321–338.

Schwab-Stone, M., Ayers, T., Kasprow, W., Voyce, C., Barone, C., Shriver, T., et al. (1995). No safe haven: A study of violence exposure in an urban community. *Journal of the American Academy of Child and Adolescent Psychiatry, 10*, 1343–1352.

Schwab-Stone, M., Chen, C., Greenberger, E., Silver, D., Lichtman, J., & Voyce, C. (1999). No safe haven: II. The effects of violence exposure on urban youth. *Journal of the American Academy of Child and Adolescent Psychiatry, 38*, 359–367.

Schwartz, D., & Gorman, A. H. (2003). Community violence exposure and children's academic functioning. *Journal of Educational Psychology, 95*, 163–173.

Schwartz, D., & Proctor, L. (2000). Community violence exposure and children's social adjustment in the school peer group: The mediating roles of emotion regulation and social cognition. *Journal of Consulting & Clinical Psychology, 68*, 670–683.

Selner-O'Hagan, M.B., Kindlon, D.J., Buka, S.L., Raudenbusch, S.W., & Earls, F.J. (1998). Assessing exposure to violence in urban youth. *Journal of Child Psychology and Psychiatry and Allied Disciplines, 39*, 215–224.

Singer, M.I., Anglin, T.M., Song, L., & Lunghofer, L. (1995). Adolescents' exposure to violence and associated symptoms of psychological trauma. *Journal of the American Medical Association, 273*, 477–482.

Slovak, K., & Singer, M.I. (2002). Children and violence: Findings and implications from a rural community. *Child & Adolescent Social Work Journal, 19*, 35–56.

Sroufe, L.A. (1979). The coherence of individual development: Early care, attachment, and subsequent developmental issues. *American Psychologist, 34*, 834–841.

Stein, B.D., Jaycox, L.H., Kataoka, D., Rhodes, H.J., & Vestal, K.D. (2003). Prevalence of child and adolescent exposure to community violence. *Clinical Child and Family Psychology Review, 6*, 247–264.

Terr, L. (1991). Childhood traumas: An outline and overview. *American Journal of Psychiatry, 48*, 10–20.

Trickett, P.K., Duran, L., & Horn, J.L. (2003). Community violence as it affects child development: Issues of definition. *Clinical Child and Family Psychology Review, 6*, 223–236.

U.S. Department of Justice. (2002). *Violent victimization rates by age, 1973–2001.* Washington, DC: Bureau of Justice Statistics.

Vermeiren, R., Ruchkin, V., Leckman, P.E., Deboutte, D., & Schwab-Stone, M. (2002). Exposure to violence and suicide risk in adolescents: A community study. *Journal of Abnormal Child Psychology, 30*, 529–537.

Warner, B., & Weist, M. (1996). Urban youth as witnesses to violence: Beginning assessment and treatment efforts. *Journal of Youth and Adolescence, 25*, 361–377.

Weist, M.D., Acosta, O.M., & Youngstom, E.A. (2001). Predictors of violence exposure among inner-city youth. *Journal of Clinical Psychology, 30*, 187–198.

Wilson, D., Kliewer, W., Teasley, N., Plybon, L., & Sica, D. (2002). Violence exposure, catecholamine excretion, and blood pressure non-dipping status in African-American male versus female adolescents. *Psychosomatic Medicine, 64*, 906–915.

Youngstrom, E., Weist, M.D., & Albus, K.E. (2003). Exploring violence exposure, stress, protective factors and behavioral problems among inner-city youth. *American Journal of Community Psychology, 32*, 115–129.

3

CHILDREN EXPOSED
TO WAR AND TERRORISM

Paramjit T. Joshi, Deborah A. O'Donnell,
Lisa M. Cullins, and Shulamit M. Lewin

There are few human tragedies that stir sympathy and concern more deeply than seeing children suffer during war and the other increasingly frequent epidemics of violence around the world. After looking at the death and destruction that has been wrought over the past century, one cannot help but be sobered by the pain that people inflict on each other. While total deaths have drastically decreased since the great wars of the early to mid-20th century, it is difficult to make the assertion that the world is a safer place now. After all, any instance of conflict, regardless of whether it results in death, affects the surrounding populace in numerous ways. In our current age of bioterrorism, far greater numbers of people experience psychological distress at the threat of release of toxic agents, leading to states of terror and anxiety among millions. Falling witness or victim to acts of war and terrorism stirs an array of powerful human emotions. Conflict essentially stops the growth of society wherever and whenever it occurs and becomes a smoldering fire that continues to burn and take lives in distant places. Regardless of the specific character of any particular war or act of terror, such circumstances by definition involve destruction, pain, and death. Although these physical losses can be reconstructed or replaced and the accompanying pain and sorrow gradually diminish, the psychological scars—the trauma, and the horrifying images and memories—do not heal as easily.

Wartime survival is perhaps most challenging and complex for children, whose age and psychological immaturity render them more vulnerable to the effects of overwhelming and inescapable stressors. It has generally been found that

Adapted from Joshi, P., & O'Donnell, D.A. (2003). Consequences of exposure to war and terrorism among youth. *Clinical Child and Family Psychology Review, 6*(4), 275–292. With kind permission of Springer Science and Business Media.

the psychological effects related to war and terrorism are similar to those associated with natural and human-initiated disastrous events. However, the often-intertwined psychosocial, economic, political, cultural, religious, and community variables have an enormous psychological impact.

Until recent times, very little attention had been paid to the psychological well-being of children as victims of war and terrorism. The resulting paucity of psychological interventions has given rise to spirits of hopelessness and helplessness, increased incidences of alcohol and drug use, and delinquency and conduct problems among children. These factors have all been shown to have a negative impact on society at large. In an environment characterized by such suffering, deprivation, and violence, children—who are still developing—are severely affected. Sometimes survivors of war and/or torture transmit trauma to the next generation. They endure and relive their trauma for years to come, frequently in the wake of recurring terrifying events such as terrorist attacks.

This chapter focuses on the consequences of childhood trauma secondary to war and terrorism and summarizes some of the experiences of children who have traumatic stress. These include children, for example, who have been exposed to random gun fire; those victimized by human-made disasters such as the 9/11 terrorist attacks in New York City, Washington, D.C., and Pennsylvania; those present during the Oklahoma bomb blast; those forced to become part of school shootings such as Columbine; and those terrorized by the 2002 sniper attacks in Washington, D.C.

HOW MANY CHILDREN ARE AFFECTED BY WAR AND TERRORISM?

Each year, hundreds of thousands of children around the world are exposed to direct war activities (air raids, shellings, and bombings) and their consequences (traumatization, multiple losses, abrupt changes in family structure and patterns, living with highly distressed adults, prolonged displacement, and dissolving communities). According to a 1996 UNICEF report, approximately 2 million children died in wars between 1986 and 1996, and an additional 10 million were traumatized by war. As many as 4 million children have been rendered with physical handicaps or disabilities as a result of war- or terrorism-related wounds (Shaw, 2000). The United Nations High Commission for Refugees (UNHCR; 2002) estimated that, as of 2002, there were 22 million refugees in the world. Approximately half of these refugees were children. The child-to-adult refugee ratio varied depending on world region. The majority of refugees in Central Africa were children (57%); child refugees in Central and Eastern Europe accounted for approximately one fifth of the refugee population (UNHCR, 2002). Twelve million children have been made homeless, and one million have been orphaned or separated from parents as a result of war and terrorism (de Jong, 2002). A study done by UNICEF during the war in the Balkans showed that 27.5% of displaced children spent more than a month in a bomb shelter, and many of them (28.6%) stayed in shelters without their parents or other family members (Kuterovac, Dyregrov, & Stuyland, 1994).

Any war or act of terror, as a sudden, unpredictable, and dramatic event, has a tremendous negative impact at various levels including the community, family, and individual. War encompasses exposure to trauma-related events, which may become chronic, often leading to marked disruptions in the contextual and social fabric within which one lives. Children are usually affected most by these experiences. Yet, relatively few studies have examined the effects of war and terrorism on children. From the studies done during and after World War II (Winnicott, 1992) and the Yom Kippur War (Milgram, 1982) to those documenting psychological outcomes from more recent wars (Baker, 1991), it is evident that war experiences can hinder the psychosocial development of children and their expectations regarding future life. The traumas of war and terrorism share many similar features but are also marked by important differences. Terrorism is, by definition, a tactic of psychological manipulation revolving around the development and maintenance of societal states of fear, terror, and lack of control (DiGiovanni, 1999). As such, children existing in situations of terrorism may appear to be functioning adequately in day-to-day life, but exist in a state of chronic underlying anxiety, sleep deprivation, and dysphoria (Gurwitch, Sitterle, Young, & Pfefferbaum, 2002). During wartime, children not only deal with the traumas associated with violence exposure, displacement, and death of loved ones, but they also struggle with malnutrition and disease. Most children who die in wartime are the victims of starvation or illness, not bombs or bullets (Allwood, Bell-Dolan, & Husain, 2002).

In the naturalistic conditions of war, displacement, and terrorism, accurate prevalence estimates are often difficult to obtain. Methodological obstacles and lack of access to accurate exposure data necessitate reliance on retrospective and single-method data and lead to difficulties in accessing representative samples of victims (Reid, 1990). Collection of accurate data regarding psychological adjustment during and following acts of war and terrorism comes with additional challenges, such as difficulty in specifying pre-exposure adjustment and the multiple threats to accurate and comprehensive self-reporting brought about by the negative impact of trauma exposure on memory, perception, and cognition. Children exposed to the traumas of war and terrorism may be poor reporters on their mental states due to increased incidence of dissociation, depression, and physiological dysregulation (Robins, 1983).

CONSEQUENCES OF EXPOSURE
TO WAR AND TERRORISM FOR CHILDREN

In the 1990s and early 2005, a more or less circumscribed body of research about the various aspects of trauma developed. The wars in the Balkans, Afghanistan, and the Middle East provide good examples of the array of trauma victims who are displaced from their homes and communities and forced to live in refugee camps or in exile. The situations in other parts of the world such as South Africa and Southeast Asia also illustrate the strife, war, and trauma many young lives come to know too well. Similarly, in the United States, terrorist attacks, random gunfire, acts of mass violence, and school shootings are becoming increasingly prevalent. Because children who grow up in war zones and other communities of chronic aggression are exposed to persistent violence and danger, they are at high risk for developing mental illness. In addition to the expected posttraumatic stress reactions, traumatic stress can have an even more insidious impact on children and adolescents, affecting many domains of child development, including pro-social behavior and citizenship at school, in the home, and in the community. Children exposed to war and terrorism simultaneously face both the tasks of growing up and confronting numerous losses and traumas. Often, they get pulled in many different directions, which distorts or stagnates the developmental process. Ideas and knowledge have changed and expanded dramatically since the 1950s. Accordingly, so has our ability to make children's lives better. The ultimate goal of this work is to diminish and ease the psychological impact of war and terrorism.

In our modern age, the threat of harm by acts of bioterrorism and other weapons of mass destruction has become increasingly salient. With this threat comes unique challenges and consequences to children, their families, and society. Mass sociogenic illness and surges in anxiety have been described in the literature even when no agent has been released or when no exposure has taken place (DiGiovanni, 1999; Hall & Norwood, 2002). Research indicates that the psychological consequences of such exposure, or threats thereof, may exert a more profound impact than even the physical effects. For instance, during the 1991 scud missile attacks in Israel, approximately 1,000 people presented for emergency care—more than 78% for behavioral and psychiatric emergencies (Kartensky et al., 1991). When Tokyo experienced the release of Sarin gas in 1995, close to 4,000 people sought emergency care believing they had been exposed to the gas, yet they had no signs of exposure. Only 11 people actually died as a result of the Sarin release, but 1,000 were treated for varying levels of toxic symptoms (Ohbu et al., 1997). Shortly after the 2001 terrorist attacks in the United States, as rumors of bio-terrorism spread in Manila, Philippines, more than 1,000 students showed up at health clinics with flu-like symptoms. States of mass panic merit further examination as communities are called upon to deal constructively and collaboratively with acts of biological, chemical, nuclear, or radiological terrorism (Hall & Norwood, 2002).

Children exposed to war and/or terrorism often experience repeated, uncontrollable, and unpredictable affronts to their sense of safety, well-being, and bodily integrity. Such disruptions to the normal developmental trajectories of childhood can set into motion a cascade of effects on development. Because children's brains, minds, and bodies change and grow over the course of their young lives, reactions to trauma typically vary by age and developmental level. It is important to view these reactions within the context of the social-cognitive processes occurring during each developmental stage to best understand how and why specific trauma reactions appear.

The developmental course of childhood renders the unfolding of reactions to war and terrorism a dynamic process reflecting the interplay between risk and protective factors that change over time. This unfolding may take different forms over the course of development, and symptoms may wax and wane over time and across situations. As such, some children exposed to wartime trauma may experience immediate symptom onset, while others may not manifest symptoms of distress until weeks or months later (Terr, 1983). It is only when such emotional responses persist for extended periods of time or are accompanied by significant functional impairment that concern is warranted.

Consequences During the Preschool Years (Younger than 6 Years)

Children in the preschool years often have the most vague and somatic responses to terror, even though their lack of well-integrated and developed cognitive, social, and emotional selves make them particularly vulnerable to the insidious effects of wartime violence and destruction (Arroyo & Eth, 1996; Pynoos & Nader, 1993). Cognitively, children younger than the age of 6 have a difficult time taking others' perspectives. As a result, they often focus their attention too narrowly, and sometimes ignore important information. When a child of this age experiences a traumatic event, he or she may mistakenly think that the event is his or her fault. This can lead to magical thinking to fill in gaps in understanding, resulting in ideas like, "If I had just been a better kid by picking up my toys when my mother asked me to, this event wouldn't have happened."

Often, information about the traumatic event that is presented in the media and talked about among adults in the child's life is too complicated and cognitively advanced for a child of this age to comprehend, particularly when the media coverage involves complex discussions of political and social issues. This leads to further confusion in the child. These feelings of self-blame and confusion are sometimes unintentionally reinforced by adults in the child's environment. When adults become over-extended and stressed in the face of a traumatic event, they may be more likely to yell and lose their tempers. When this is done in front of a young child, even if the yelling is not directed at the child, a young child may think that the adult is yelling at him or her.

Another key characteristic of children of this age is an inability to understand death as permanent. Children of this age often manifest their emotional responses to trauma in the form of sleep difficulties. Worry and anxiety manifest as clinging behavior in the form of refusing to leave the caregiver's side, worrying that something bad might happen to the caregiver, fearing going to sleep, or fearing leaving the house. In addition, increased temper tantrums may surface (Cooley-Quille, Turner, & Beidel, 1995; Osofsky, 1995).

Consequences during School Age (7 to 11 Years)

Children ages 7 to 11 have acquired the ability to take other points of view, but they remain very concrete in their thinking, making many traumatic experiences difficult for them to accurately and fully comprehend. As a result, children of this age will often become fearful, confused, and anxious following a trauma. A common response is regression, or acting younger than one's age. Regressive behaviors include bed-wetting, thumb sucking, baby talk, and wanting to carry a transitional object like a teddy bear or blanket (Osofsky, 1995). Children of this age may also develop physical symptoms (e.g., loss of appetite, stomachaches, headaches, dizziness). School-related issues are also common, such as inability to concentrate, refusal to attend school, or increased defiance, aggression, and hyperactivity (Dodge, 1993). Prolonged fear of being alone, feelings of responsibility and guilt, safety concerns, and preoccupation with danger may surface. These fears often become exacerbated during times of prolonged war/terrorism, resulting in chronic states of alarm and hyper-reactivity or dissociative states (Perry, 2001).

Becoming less egocentric and more in tune with the thoughts and feelings of those around them, children of this age tend to pay particularly close attention to parents' anxieties. Children are aware of their parents' worries most of the time, but they are particularly sensitive to their parents' reactions during a crisis. Looking to their parents for cues on how to act and react helps children to know how to behave in the face of danger. It is especially important for parents to be honest with their school-age children about their fears and concerns and to stress their abilities to cope with the situation. School-age youth may also experience loss of interest in activities and repetitious traumatic play and retelling of the trauma (James, 1994).

Consequences during the Teenage Years (Older than 12 Years)

Teenagers have developed the ability to think abstractly. With this capacity for abstract thought comes an increased focus on religion, morality, and ethics, which can impact a teenager's understanding of, and response to, acts of war and terrorism. More than at any other stage of development, a pre-teen or teenager is likely to keep his or her feelings about the trauma inside, making him or her more prone to developing depressed feelings. A teenager may begin to withdraw from family and friends. Or, a teenager may minimize concerns following a trauma in an attempt to appear as if everything is okay. In such instances, a teenager may increase his or her activity level and involvement with others as a means of managing inner fear and anxiety. Irritability and defiance may appear, as well as a wish for revenge and action-oriented responses to trauma. In addition, it is important to consider that teenagers who feel particularly alienated and/or disenfranchised due to these trauma-related processes may be especially susceptible to the influence of terrorist organizations.

MULTI-LEVEL DEVELOPMENTAL EFFECTS OF EXPOSURE TO WAR AND TERRORISM

States of warfare and terrorism encompass multiple, often chronic, traumatic events that affect and are affected by the contextual and interpersonal processes in which a developing organism exists (Bronfenbrenner, 1988). Such events threaten optimal development either through a direct impact on the child or via the impact of the war or terrorism on the family and community within which the child lives. In his bioecological systems theory, Bronfenbrenner (1988) articulated that the complex and mutually reinforcing interactions among factors in the child's maturing biology, the immediate family and community environment, and the societal framework energize and help to steer development. Changes or conflicts in any one layer, as occurs in states of war and terrorism, will ripple throughout other layers. War and terrorism, unfortunately, exact their impact in several of these ecological domains simultaneously. What follows is a discussion of the effects on each ecological layer.

Environmental and Family Consequences

Loss of Loved One   Many children lose their family members, close relatives, and friends; many are orphaned. It is estimated that in the 1990s a million children around the world were orphaned as a result of war and acts of terrorism (Shaw, 2000). In many cases, children directly witness violence directed at, and the death of, their own family members. Sadly, it is even more difficult when the family members are listed as missing for long periods of time, such as when fathers or mothers are taken as prisoners of war or there are unidentified bodies following a tragedy. In a war situation, parents are often called away to fight and are absent from their families for long periods of time.

Even a horrifying event experienced from a remote and relatively safe distance (distant trauma) conveyed repetitively by the media may have a psychological impact on children. For example, even 2 years after the Oklahoma City bombing, 16% of youngsters living within 100 miles of Oklahoma City were still experiencing symptoms of posttraumatic stress. These youth were not directly exposed to the trauma itself and were not related to either the killed or injured victims (Pfefferbaum et al., 1999). In a study of prior stressors among youth in New York City following 9/11, 51% reported experiencing a prior trauma, 5% had lived previously in a country at war, and 1% reported a prior loss of at least one family member, rendering these youth more vulnerable to the effects of repeated loss (Columbia University Mailman School of Public Health, 2002).

Family Stress and Change   Findings have indicated that the amount of time spent with family during the Holocaust predicted recollection of both positive and negative emotional memories among survivors. While half of all victims interviewed in one study were unable to recall any memories of the trauma, survivors who lived through most of the war with parents/family recalled more positive and negative emotional memories than those who had experienced the war mostly on their own (Chaitin & Bar-on, 2002). Other research with Holocaust survivors has indicated that family relationships are impaired in a number of ways following trauma, with effects including emotional unavailability among family members, problematic family communication patterns, and parent overinvolvement in children's lives (Chaitin, 2000; Solomons, 1998). Many of these altered family dynamics appear to persist for multiple generations (Rosenthal, 1998). In addition, some of the exigencies of wartime situations necessitate the passing on of age-inappropriate responsibilities to children. For instance, hiding one's ethnicity, lying about one's age, and having to memorize addresses of relatives and friends are common activities that even very young children are forced to do in the face of persecution, displacement, or terrorism (Amir & Lev-Wiesel, 2001; Bugner, 2000).

Displacement   The majority of victims of war around the world are displaced children who are forced into exile and have to flee from their homes, often separated from their parents and/or living without parental supervision and care. Although home plays an important role in the identity formation and development of children, many displaced children are driven from their homes with only very few personal belongings, and they often have no homes to return to because of the destruction and damage. Even several years later, some displaced children, and many adolescents, continue to be separated from their parents because their educational needs can not be met in their communities of origin. Research has shown that children who have poor coping capacities and lack supportive family environments display high levels of stress-related symptomatology throughout the entire refugee period and are at special risk for the development of further psychological difficulties (Ajdukovic & Ajdukovic, 1998).

Displacement often leaves children and their families in a state of alienation from their cultures (Minkowski, 2000). In addition, displaced families often deeply miss their hometowns, referring frequently to their hometowns with a sense of despair and grief. This pattern has been termed Vukovar syndrome, after the Croatian refugees from Vukovar who were forced from their homes to barracks in a suburb of Zagreb. The town of Vukovar was completely destroyed and considered a part of Serbian territory, rendering it impossible for these refugees to return to their homes (Minkowski, 2000).

Living with Distressed Adults   Adult members of displaced families are themselves exposed to multiple stressors and trying challenges. Often, fathers and mothers returning home at the end of a war are themselves injured and unable to find jobs, or they are not able to work on account of their injuries. This leads to increased family stress, marital discord, alcohol and substance use, and domestic violence. In many traditional cultures and societies in which the father has been the breadwinner, the mother is placed in a new role, changing the family hierarchy and creating a source of conflict within families. Studies suggest that during warfare displaced adults frequently display anxiety, depression, anger, aggression, alcohol abuse, distrust, somatization or illness, and sleep disturbances (Moro & Vidovic, 1992). Often, these adults lose their jobs and no longer have access to employment, which results in declines in their social status. They feel degraded and demoralized having become financially dependent and helpless. These cumulative negative effects produce high levels of stress among the adults and have disturbing consequences for their children (Ajdukovic, 1996).

Loss of Traditional Ways of Living   Many children, especially those from rural areas, go through an acculturation process during which they lose contact with traditional values and ways of living in their communities. These losses can leave a big emptiness in the lives of many children. At the same time, change in traditional ways of living has a two-fold negative impact on children when they have to adapt to an urban environment or when they return to their communities of origin. Often, children go through a very stressful and painful period of reintegration if they return to their original towns, villages, and cities (Druzic, Grl, Kletecki, & Ajdukovic, 1997). Similarly, cultural and religious practices get disrupted. Spirituality and religion often serve as anchors to help both adults and children get through difficult times. In a survey done 3–5 days after the 9/11 events in New York City, 90% of the adults turned to religion to help them cope, and another 98% were helped by talking to others (Schuster et al., 2001). Unfortunately, wars and acts of terror are often motivated by religious differences and/or intolerance of a particular way of life, allowing less opportunity for individuals to freely turn to religion as a source of support and comfort.

Lack of Educational Structure   With school interruptions and the quality of education decreased, youth often become bored, with few opportunities to spend their time in any enjoyable or useful ways. Although extensive efforts to organize schooling for displaced children are often undertaken, fewer than half of these children are enrolled immediately after their arrival, often in whatever educational setting is available given the circumstances. This is often because parents do not want their children to start at new schools, as they hope to soon go back to their original homes. Over time, many students begin to display numerous difficulties in adapting to new educational environments because they continue to long for their old schools (Dzepina et al., 1992).

Poor Physical Environments   During a war or act of terrorism when thousands are affected, many displaced persons are accommodated in collective centers. In many cases, two or even three families have to share one room, and many children do not have beds of their own. In most collective centers there is often no place for play activities or for learning. Most children who come from rural areas are accommodated in high-rise refugee centers in cities and, not surprisingly, find limited possibilities for playing and using their free time in these new settings. Even those accommodated with host families experience a lack of space. They are faced with high social density, lack of privacy, and, often, poor-quality housing. Alongside them, children of the host families are also affected by the long-term displacement (Ajdukovic & Ajdukovic, 1998).

Community-Level Changes   Destruction forces uprooting of hundreds of thousands of people, leading to increased unemployment, poverty, and overall changes in the complexion of the community. The most pronounced of these community-level changes include shifted priorities of the social welfare, health, and educational systems; loss of community balance and distortion of typical community value systems; and increased prejudice and social rigidity toward other groups. Community-level disappearances of, or significant reductions in, prevention efforts in the areas of juvenile delinquency, child abuse, neglect, and alcohol and drug abuse are also problematic.

Finally, it is important to note that providers of health care are also impacted by these changes. Research shows high levels of traumatization of professionals and para-professionals during times of warfare and trauma (Ajdukovic & Zic,

1997; Galea et al., 2002). These changes in community often translate into problems integrating into new social environments for children, their parents, and other community adults.

Children Socialized to Violence   Three phenomena have been identified in children exposed to persistent and extreme violence: fear, aggression, and desensitization. Fear has the potential to paralyze children and negatively affect their emotional growth. Increases in aggressive behavior and/or changes in attitudes and values unfortunately favor the use of aggression to solve conflicts, especially among adolescents. There is some evidence suggesting that exposure to increased levels of violence leads to decreased sensitivity to violence and a greater willingness to tolerate increasing levels of aggression and violence in society. Social learning theorists view violence as a largely learned phenomenon, developing through both direct and observational learning. Reinforcement for aggressive acts, in the form of both material and non-material rewards, also serves to increase the probability of aggressive responding among youth (Bandura, 1978). In adolescence, advances in abstract thought and self-focus facilitate feelings of disenchantment and a sense of being unappreciated and unwanted. This type of cognitive and affective state often leaves adolescents quite vulnerable to the influence of militant adults and governments that recruit them as pupils of war, glorifying their acts of terror. Such youth are made to feel important with a purpose in life—albeit destructive and dangerous.

Children living in transitional societies in which war and violence are commonplace often become both victims and aggressors simultaneously, losing their youthfulness in the process. In such states of violence, children are sometimes armed to fight in insurgent or counter-insurgency forces, exploited in the labor force, and thrust into political and social spheres not intended for the young (Feldman, 2002). In such situations, these children are sometimes forbidden from contacting family and school for fear of reprisals against their families and schools or for fear of being found by the police. Sadly, many of these children socialized to violence remain violent and unaccepted by society long after wars have ended. For example, in post-war South Africa, now-grown children who in the 1980s entered into sustained military action not only must suddenly shed their political military past, upon which so much of their identities have formed, but they also face lost educational and career opportunities, estranged family, and high risk for substance abuse and criminal activity (Feldman, 2002).

Physical Effects

Loss of Physical Capacity   Survivors of physically disfiguring trauma experience a series of assaults on the mind and body that present extraordinary and complex challenges to human resilience. The injurious event itself is traumatic, but additional traumas can also occur from painful and frightening medical treatments. The physical changes in the survivor's body are permanent reminders of the fear, horror, sadness, and pain experienced. The real and imagined reactions of others to their disfigured bodies present survivors with the additional and ongoing trauma of feeling rejected, isolated, unworthy, and humiliated. It is estimated that in the 1990s approximately 2 million children alone were killed in war-related events. Twice as many children develop physical handicaps or disabilities after they have been wounded (Shaw, 2000). In the majority of cases, these injuries result from explosions and shootings during artillery and air force bombing, exposure to land mines in the case of war, and direct or indirect injuries sustained during a terrorist act. Many injured children become permanently disabled. This seriously incapacitates the child, resulting in prolonged suffering, hospitalizations, and rehabilitation (Ajdukovic & Ajdukovic, 1998).

Disfigurement   Children who are disfigured by traumatic insults must recreate themselves, adapting their previous self-concepts and world views. Cognitively, they must accommodate to their altered bodies and new life experiences. The children must overcome pain to discover new ways of functioning in order to accomplish tasks that were once easily completed. They must develop new interpersonal skills to assist their negotiations as disfigured people in societies in which even very young children place a premium on physical attractiveness (Bordlieri, Solodky, & Mikos, 1985; Cash, 1990). Severe burn injury, for example, is horrifying by any measure. Beyond the acute fear and pain experienced by the victim, such an injury inevitably results in disfigurement. Sometimes the scars can be hidden, but more often the bodies of burned children are noticeably marked. Frequently, burn survivors have lost body parts. They may also have lost family members, family pets, homes, and personal treasures in the same terrible events that altered their bodies. Victims sometimes blame themselves and, while enduring painful treatments and bereavement, may also struggle with feelings of self-recrimination and guilt (Blakeney et al., 1996; Dell Orto, 1991).

Malnutrition   Both during pre-flight and displacement, many children do not have access to adequate nutrition. With the growth of the displaced and refugee populations, the financial possibility for providing adequate food decreases. Studies of the nutritional status of school-age children during war situations have shown a significant degree of malnutrition. In one study, a third of the children had clinical symptoms secondary to nutritional deficiency. Further, one of every two children who lived in displacement longer than 6 months was found to be malnourished (Grguric & Hirsl-Hecej, 1993).

Neurodevelopmental Effects

Intelligence, Cognition, Memory, and Attention   Neuroanatomical and neurophysiological changes secondary to trauma may directly decrease a child's ability to express feelings in words. Cognitive and academic impairments among traumatized children have been consistently documented in a number of studies (Coster, Gersten, Beeghly, & Cicchetti, 1989; Fox, Long, & Anglois, 1988; McFadyen & Kitson, 1996). Language delays have been reported in abused children (Fox et al., 1988). Studies of preschoolers exposed to trauma suggest that such children demonstrate significantly decreased intelligence (Vondra, Barnett, & Cicchetti, 1990). Wodarski, Kurtz, Gaudin, and Howing (1990) studied a group of physically abused youth, finding that 60% of the neglected and 55% of the abused youth had repeated at least one grade, compared with 24% of the comparison group.

To date, no studies have examined the intellectual effects of war and terrorism on children. However, these outcomes need to be considered, especially when the trauma is chronic. A traumatic event overwhelms the child, disrupting homeostasis and creating a compensatory response that leads to a less functional new state of equilibrium (Perry, 2001). All parts of the brain are affected—cortex, limbic system, midbrain, and brainstem—with different types of traumatic memories created in each brain region. Altered cortical homeostasis results in dysregulation of cognitive and narrative memory, disruptions to the limbic system result in emotional memory impairments, disruptions to the midbrain region are implicated in motor memory impairments, and traumatic activation of the brainstem is involved in the creation of physiological state memories (Castro-Alamancos & Connors, 1996; Perry & Pollard, 1998; Phillips & LeDoux, 1992). This altered brain equilibrium and resulting "memories" are the foundation of abuse-related neuropsychiatric signs and symptoms. Consolidation of long-term memory involves gene expression, new protein synthesis, and growth or pruning of synaptic connections. Memory is based on changes at the cellular level. A cascade of intracellular events takes place, allowing for short-term memory to be converted into long-term memory. Before memories can be stored at any location in the brain, they must be processed in the hippocampus. With sufficient damage to the hippocampus, most types of new memories cannot be stored, but old memories remain intact.

Two properties of memory, use-dependent storage and state-dependent recall, are important to consider in relation to the effects of violent culture on cognition. Use-dependent storage, a form of mental economizing, refers to the process by which experience appears to create a "processing template" through which new environmental input is filtered. In this way, if many of a child's experiences are characterized by violence or danger, as is the case in situations of war or terrorism, future experiences—whether objectively violent or not—will likely be viewed through a "template" expectant of violence and danger. State-dependent recall is the process through which memory is triggered through exposure to sensory or affective stimuli similar to stimuli present when a memory is formed (Gilligan & Bower, 1983; Godden & Baddeley, 1975). In trauma survivors, state-dependent recall can be seen when internal and/or external cues that symbolize or resemble an aspect of the traumatic event (i.e., sights, smells, sounds, or emotional experiences present during the trauma) result in re-experiencing of the traumatic event. Memory formation and consolidation become impaired in such a way that some memories are enhanced, detailed, and intrusive, while other significant items are forgotten (Kopelman, 2000).

Similarly, the chronic violence present in states of war and terrorism can give rise to a variety of cognitive distortions and attribution and expectancy biases. Research indicates that youth exposed to chronic violence are more likely to expect violence, hostility, and aggression in their environments and to perceive these traits to exist even when they objectively do not. A hostile attribution bias, the attribution of hostile intent to others when no such intent exists, is common among individuals exposed to chronic violence (Dodge, 1993). It may be that the "processing templates" present in violence-exposed individuals predispose them to perceive violence, danger, and hostility. In a dangerous and violent world, these mechanisms can be helpful and serve to protect an individual. Unfortunately, though, such cognitive biases and distortions also serve to deplete brain and body resources, allowing a person to only narrowly focus on, and sometimes even misperceive, threatening cues, denying them the opportunity to attend to other environmental cues and serving to push others away.

The effects of violent culture on cognition, memory, and attention have also come to encompass neuro-psychiatric effects of chemical and biological agents. Unfortunately, little is known about these effects. Preliminary research indicates that disorders of mood, cognition, and behavior are the most common outcomes of biological weaponry, accompanied by uncertainty, fear, and panic—particularly when the agents are spread silently from person to person. Nerve agents have great potential to cause confusion, while blister agents may produce delirium. Acute intoxication from organophosphate pesticides can produce long-term neuropsychiatric effects including drowsiness, memory impairment, depression, fatigue, and increased irritability (DiGiovanni, 1999). These neuro-psychiatric effects of chemical and biological agents often mirror the after-effects of psychological trauma, making it difficult to distinguish between them.

Central Nervous System Structure and Function Human behavior, including aggression and violence, is the outcome of complex brain processes. Exposure to violence can be emotionally arousing and may have a lasting influence. Studies suggest that neurobiological changes occur in the brain following exposure to trauma and violence in children (Kandel, 2001). A number of important findings concerning changes in brain function have been identified in individuals with posttraumatic stress disorder (PTSD), such as smaller brain volumes and reduced hippocampal size. This may explain, in part, the memory impairments seen in victims of trauma (Bremner, Randall, Scott, & Bronen, 1997; Bremner et al., 1995; DeBellis, 2002). Other victims have shown decreased activity of the anterior cingulate area of the brain that inhibits the amygdala and other regions of the brain involved in the fear response (Bremner et al., 1997; DeBellis, 2002; Shin et al., 1999). Studies have shown that the hypothalamic pituitary axis (HPA) and autonomic nervous system can both over- and under-react as a result of early traumatic experiences (McEwen & Magarinos, 1997; Yehuda, Spertus, & Golier, 2001). Further, pituitary adrenocortical hyperresponsivity has been reported in trauma survivors (Heim, Newport, & Heit, 2000). In general, trauma activates victims' stress-response systems with heightened physiological arousal when confronted with cues of the trauma (Keane, Kolb, & Kaloupek, 1998). There is concern that neural systems that are repeatedly activated via the PTSD stress response cycle undergo permanent changes in synaptic architecture and neurotransmitter receptors (Perry, 1999; Perry & Pollard, 1998; Perry, Pollard, Blakely, Baker, & Vigilante, 1995).

Metabolic and Endocrine Function Hyperarousal, a primary human response to trauma, involves activation of the sympathetic nervous system via the midbrain norepinephrine neuron-containing locus coeruleus. Arousal, startle responses, vigilance, irritability, and sleep are all affected by this activation. Traumatized youth exhibit impaired sleep efficiency with prolonged sleep latency and increased activity during sleep (Glod, Teicher, & Hartman, 1997). In addition, the locus coeruleus interacts with the HPA, with a resulting increase in the release of adrenocorticotropin and cortisol, preparing the body for defense (Perry & Pollard, 1998). Chronic activation of the HPA may have negative consequences, including hippocampal/limbic damage and abnormalities (Sapolsky, 1996). The amygdala and the hippocampus are areas of the brain involved in arousal, attention, detection of threat, and possible long-term memory storage of threatening events, with potentially significant emotional processing of violent material. Studies of abused children have found abnormalities in these brain regions, which in turn predispose to memory deficits and emotional dysregulation. Following the acute fear response, the brain creates a set of memories that can be triggered by reminders of the trauma. Cortisol likely mediates this process (Nelson & Carver, 1998). Some studies have found abused children to have elevated cortisol levels.

Adults with PTSD who have been abused as children also possess higher cortisol levels than those who are abused and do not develop PTSD (DeBellis, 2002; Lemieux & Coe, 1995). Areas of the brain involved in threat perception, such as the amygdala, have altered metabolism in adult trauma survivors with PTSD (Bremner et al., 1997; Yehuda et al., 2001). It is postulated that children exposed to the traumas of war and terrorism may have similar findings.

Genetic Effects   Both hereditary and acquired illnesses have a genetic component (Kandel, 2001). Hereditary illnesses result from the expression of altered genes or allelic variants that lead to the production of abnormal proteins, giving rise to the disease state. An acquired condition such as PTSD involves the modulation of gene expression by environmental stimuli as a result of learning, leading to the transcription of a previously inactive gene. Terrifying experiences can cause defects in gene regulation that can lead to mental disorder. The ongoing modification of synapses throughout life means that all behavior of an individual is produced by genetic and developmental mechanisms acting on the brain.

Behavioral geneticists have begun to explore why stressful experiences lead to depression in some people but not in others. Findings indicate that individuals with a certain type of brain chemistry gene are more vulnerable to depression after exposure to traumatic events. The 5-HTT gene has been specifically implicated in helping to control how individuals respond to stress. This gene, which plays a role in regulating the neurotransmitter serotonin, can exist in two forms— long and short. Individuals may inherit two copies of the long form of the gene, two copies of the short form, or one copy of each. A study conducted by Caspi et al. (2003) analyzed the form of 5-HTT gene carried by 847 adults in New Zealand. The participants had experienced a stressful life event, such as a death in the family, marriage break-up, or job loss, over the preceding 5-year period. Adults who carried at least one copy of the short form of the 5-HTT gene were more at risk for depression after stressful life events than were those who carried a long form. This suggests that the short form of the gene may predispose individuals to heightened sensitivity to emotional stress. Those with even one copy of the short 5-HTT gene were almost three times more likely to consider or attempt suicide than were those with only one long form. Individuals with two copies of the long 5-HTT gene were the most resistant to depression following stressful events and appeared to tolerate stress better. Following exposure to four traumatic events, of those with two copies of the long form of 5-HTT, only 17% were diagnosed with depression whereas 33% of those with one copy of the short form developed depression. These striking findings are important as they emphasize the crucial role that advances in genetic technology have and the potential for improved and refined traumatic stress reaction prevention efforts.

Psychological and Emotional Effects

Diagnostic Considerations, Clinical Findings, and Comorbidity   There is increasing evidence that children who are victims of trauma are prone to behavioral and emotional difficulties. Cicchetti and Toth (1995) noted a wide range of effects in abused children including affect dysregulation, disruptive and aggressive behaviors, insecure and atypical attachment patterns, impaired peer relationships with either increased aggression or social withdrawal, and academic underachievement. The same authors also found a high rate of other co-morbid psychiatric disorders including major depressive disorder (MDD), conduct disorder (CD), attention-deficit/hyperactivity disorder (ADHD), oppositional defiant disorder (ODD), and PTSD. Others have reported abuse to be significantly associated with global impairment, poor social competence, MDD, CD, ODD, agoraphobia, generalized anxiety disorder, ADHD, and substance abuse (Flisher, Kramer, Hoven, & Greenwald, 1997; Kaplan et al., 1998; Livingston, Lawson, & Jones, 1993).

Posttraumatic Stress Disorder   Not all youth exposed to traumatic events will develop PTSD. The stressfulness of an event depends in part upon the psychobiological surface upon which it strikes. Research has provided us with insight into some of the factors that likely mediate the relation between stressful events and the development of PTSD. An important issue that remains is whether we can effectively measure and change the psychobiological surface upon which stressful events impact.

The presentation of posttraumatic stress symptomatology, which often arises as a child begins to understand that something terrible has happened and he or she is in danger, may initiate a process of encoding and storage of implicit and/or explicit traumatic memories. These processes in children differ in several important ways from adult responses (Terr, 1996). First, research indicates that children often display disorganized or agitated behavior rather than the fear, helplessness, and horror described in adults (Talbot, 2001). Such disorganized behavior may manifest itself in the form of sleep disturbances, nightmares with vague content often not about the trauma itself, increased autonomic arousal, and psychosomatic complaints (Green, 1997). It is also quite common for traumatized children to reveal the effects of their trauma exposure through repetitive play expressing themes of abuse, flashbacks, constriction of affect, or avoidance of events associated with the abuse (Pelcovitz, Kaplan, Goldenberg, & Weinblatt, 1994). This traumatic play may eventually develop into more clearly defined intrusive thoughts, fears, and repeated nightmares with specific trauma content (Terr, 1996). A foreshortened sense of the future, with accompanying reckless risk-taking behavior, is also common.

The epidemiology of PTSD among children following trauma exposure has been the subject of debate. Some research indicates that as many as 39% of maltreated children develop PTSD (Green, 1997); other studies suggest that behavioral, emotional, and social difficulties are more likely outcomes than clear PTSD (Pelcovitz et al., 1994). Diagnostic considerations are often clouded by a delay in onset of PTSD symptoms and developmental issues. Traumatic stress reactions often do not manifest themselves until days, weeks, or even months after trauma exposure, and they may present differently depending on the child's developmental level at the time of the exposure. Thus, children who at one assessment point may appear to be functioning adaptively may present as very troubled at another assessment point. For instance, in his classic trauma studies, Krystal (1968) reported that Holocaust survivors frequently did not manifest PTSD symptoms until years after leaving the concentration camps. In a study examining refugee children in Croatia, older children reported more posttraumatic stress symptoms than younger children, with significant increases in symptoms among children of all ages 6 months following displacement. By maternal report, although child symptoms decreased at 12 months post-displacement, more than half of the children were reported to still manifest at least one indicator of adjustment difficulty, with 10% continuing to experience five or more symptoms. Symptom manifestations encompassed physiological (e.g., eating and sleep disturbances, increased sweating, concentration difficulties), behavioral (e.g., defiance, aggression, hyperactivity, withdrawal), and emotional (e.g., fears of separation, despondency, general fearfulness, weeping, nightmares) domains. A significant correlation was found between the number of stress symptoms manifest during the 6- and 12-month assessments, indicating that displacement was more damaging for some children than others (Ajdukovic & Ajdukovic, 1998).

Depression   Major depressive disorder (MDD), across all developmental levels, may be a consequence of trauma. Traumatized infants are prone to affective withdrawal, diminished capacity for pleasure, and a tendency to exhibit negative affects such as sadness and distress (Green, 1997). MDD and/or dysthymia were reported in 27% of elementary school-age children who had been traumatized (Green, 1997). Studies also reported an association between trauma in childhood and subsequent suicidal behavior and risk-taking (Kaplan, Pelcovitz, & Labruna, 1999).

Symptoms of depression were studied in refugee children in Croatia using the Child Depression Inventory (CDI) (Kovacs, 1981). Children with high scores on the CDI were characterized by higher rates of both depression and anxiety. Scores for refugee children were significantly higher in school children than before the war. Scores did not differ, however, between the refugee children and a clinical sample of children who were treated before the war in a mental health institution for psychosomatic problems, school failure, depression, or anxiety. Moreover, 22% of refugee children, compared with 18% of children from the clinical sample, had scores considered to be clinically significant (Zivcic, 1993).

A comparison of refugee children with a group of school children that had not been displaced during the war revealed interesting findings. While the displaced children had slightly higher scores on the CDI, there was no significant difference between the two groups, corroborating the findings of Zivcic (1993). Both groups showed more depressive symptoms compared to children of the same age who were assessed before the war (Ajdukovic & Ajdukovic, 1998). The war stressors clearly had a negative impact on the emotional functioning of all children. A study done 2 years later found no significant differences between displaced children and a comparable group of non-displaced children. However, the overall level of depression was lower than in 1992 and close to the pre-war time (Ajdukovic & Ajdukovic, 1998). In the same study, at 6-month follow-up there was a significant decrease in depressive symptoms among refugee children. Correlational analyses revealed that the level of refugee children's depression was not related to the number of traumatic events experienced but rather to the family situation, child's age, and the child's poor coping abilities during displacement, especially school difficulties. Deteriorating relations among family members, mother's poor relationship with the child since becoming a refugee, and the child's perception of rejection by the mother were significant correlates of the child's depression.

Dissociative States   During times of trauma, fight or flight is rarely an option for children who are often physically unable to defend themselves or escape. The most readily accessible response to the pain of trauma may be to activate dissociative mechanisms, involving disengagement from the external world through the use of primitive defenses such as depersonalization, derealization, numbing, and, in extreme cases, catatonia (Perry & Pollard, 1998). Dissociation is protective, allowing the child to psychologically survive the trauma. Over time, however, it often becomes maladaptive, emerging at inappropriate times, especially during situations that may trigger verbal or non-verbal/bodily memories of earlier trauma. During dissociative episodes, the child may stare off briefly and appear as if he or she is daydreaming. Such children may be misdiagnosed as suffering from ADHD, inattentive type. Other children may freeze in response to certain activating stimuli. Caregivers or teachers may misinterpret this type of reaction as an act of defiance. If confronted, more anxious children can quickly escalate to feeling threatened and freeze, ultimately resorting to a classic fight or flight response by becoming aggressive or combative over relatively minor events. According to Perry (2001), males tend to utilize hyperarousal responses while females are more likely to dissociate. Other children may react to stressors by dissolving into re-gressed, dissociative states that may contain micro-psychotic episodes, including auditory command hallucinations. It is relatively common for severely trauma-tized children to hear voices commanding them to harm themselves or others. Consequently, they can be erroneously misdiagnosed as suffering from a primary psychotic disorder such as schizophrenia. At other times, a dissociating child may be misdiagnosed as having an externalizing disorder (i.e., a child with ADHD, ODD, or an impulse control disorder).

Behavioral Disorders   A frequent outcome of trauma is aggression. Patho-logical defense mechanisms, including identification with the aggressor, may play a role. Preschool children who have been traumatized engage in more frequent ag-gressive behavior than their peers (Klimes-Dougan & Kistner, 1990) and more often attribute hostile intent to their peers (Dodge, Bates, & Pettit, 1990). Trau-matized children have also been reported to be at risk for violent criminal behav-ior in adolescence (Herrenkohl, Egolf, & Herrenkohl, 1997) and adulthood (Widom, 1989). Lewis summarized how traumatic experiences can beget violence:

> In short, whatever increases impulsivity and irritability, engenders hypervigi-lance and paranoia, diminishes judgement and verbal competence, and curtails the ability to recognize one's own pain and the pain of others, also enhances the tendency toward violence. In a resilient child, maltreatment . . . may not engen-der aggression. In an already vulnerable child with tendencies toward impulsiv-ity, hypervigilance, expressive difficulties, and dissociation from painful feelings, maltreatment is often sufficient to create a very violent individual. (Lewis, 1992, pp. 388–389)

It is known that the repeated infliction of pain can lead to aggression. Lewis (1996) wrote that aggressive and violent experiences provide a model for violence, teach aggression through reinforcement, inflict pain, and cause central nervous system injuries associated with impulsivity, emotional lability, and impaired judg-ment. Further, this creates a sense of being endangered and thus increases para-noid feelings and diminishes the child's capacity to recognize feelings, put them into words, and inhibit aggressive behavioral impulses.

Alcohol and Substance Use   Children may resort to behaviors that fa-cilitate opioid-mediated dissociation, such as rocking, head banging, and self-mutilation, with these painful stimuli activating the brain's endogenous opiates. Traumatized children are also more prone to develop substance abuse, likely in a self-medicating fashion. Alcohol serves to reduce anxiety, opiates trigger soothing dissociation, and stimulants such as cocaine activate dopaminergic and mesolim-bic areas of the brain (Perry & Pollard, 1998).

MEDIATING VARIABLES IMPACTING THE PSYCHOSOCIAL WELL-BEING OF CHILDREN EXPOSED TO WAR AND TERRORISM

Most experts agree that there are a number of mediating variables that affect how a child will respond when exposed to the traumas of war and terrorism.

Type and Degree of Exposure

Two categories of trauma have been described by Terr (1991). Type I trauma produces typical PTSD symptoms after a one-time, sudden traumatic event. Type II trauma is the result of long-term repeated exposure to trauma, similar to what many physically abused youth experience. Type II trauma often results in an array of dysfunctional coping mechanisms, such as denial and dissociation, rather than symptoms characteristic of PTSD. Terr also noted conduct disorder, ADHD, depression, and dissociative disorders as common in children with histories of Type II trauma. In examining children's symptoms of distress in a wartime situation as measured by the Impact of Events Scale, Horowitz, Wilner, and Alvarez (1979) found that among the high-risk children, 39% were refugees, 35% were displaced, and 16% were from parts of the country where there were no crises. The high level of distress among this last group of children originated from indirect exposure to the war. The results of this study clearly indicated that children with varying degrees of exposure to the traumas of war were affected, although the risk for poor outcome was related to the level of exposure to the destruction caused by war.

Family Support Structures

Several studies have indicated that when a child is faced with multiple cumulative war-related stressors, especially in the absence of appropriate support from the family and community, problems with psychosocial functioning are to be expected (Garbarino, Kostelny, & Dubrow, 1991; McCallin & Fozzard, 1990). Special attention should be directed toward the adaptation of mothers and fathers to displacement and the changes in their relationships with their children. In a Croatian study, the number of adjustment difficulties in children correlated with the mother's posttraumatic stress reactions and decreases in maternal gentleness. There was also a significant correlation between the number of children's symptoms and separation from other members of the family. Such findings are in keeping with the research of McCallin and Fozzard (1990) who reported a correlation between the intensity of psychosocial difficulties in mothers' adjustment to displacement and stress-related reactions in children of Mozambique. Again, the number of stress-related symptoms significantly correlated with mothers' posttraumatic stress reaction scores. These findings emphasize the significance of a stable emotional relationship between parents and children in strengthening a child's ability to cope with unfavorable circumstances (Ajdukovic, 1996). There was also a moderately high, significant correlation among the number of stress symptoms manifested by a child at each longitudinal assessment point. Therefore, children who manifested a higher number of difficulties after the first 6 months of displacement continued to manifest such difficulties after 12 months, and even after 4 years. Exposure to chronic refugee stress likely exacerbated pre-existing developmental propensities toward maladjustment in these children (Ajdukovic & Ajdukovic, 1998). Child treatment following trauma exposure also appears to be affected by parental stress reactions. Following 9/11, children ages 4-18 living in Manhattan were more likely to present for psychological treatment when their parents were experiencing posttraumatic stress reactions (Stuber et al., 2002).

In a study of burn patients, Blakeney and Meyer (1995) found somewhat surprisingly that neither age at injury nor characteristics of the injury (i.e., extent of injury, depth of burn, area of the body scarred, amputations) served as determining factors of good psychosocial recovery (Meyer, Blakeney, LeDoux, & Herndon, 1995; Meyer et al., 1997). The immediate emotional response of the patient and/or the patient's family also did not predict adjustment (Blakeney & Meyer, 1995), as virtually all patients and their families evidenced severe distress during the early days or weeks following a traumatic injury. However, a lack of family cohesion and frequent, unresolved conflict within the family were correlated with poor adjustment (Blakeney, Portman, & Rutan, 1990; LeDoux, Blakeney, Meyer, & Herndon, 1994). Indices of parental stress, parental depression, and parental guilt beyond the first year post-trauma also appeared to be strongly related to a child's poor adjustment (Blakeney & Meyer 1995; Meyer et al., 1997).

Post-injury, a supportive family environment, and the patient's willingness to take social risks appear to play critical roles in the adaptation process, together accounting for most of the variance in adjustment (Blakeney, Robert, & Meyer, 1989; LeDoux et al., 1994; Moore et al., 1993). Many parents also report high levels of stress extending several years following the war-related injuries of their children (Blakeney, Herndon, Desai, Beard, & Wales-Sears, 1988).

Family support is also crucial to healthy development during the infant years. Gunnar (1998) suggested that the security of attachment between an infant and caregiver buffers stress by down-regulating the HPA. When compared with insecurely attached infants, decreased cortisol levels have been found in 18-month-old children with secure attachments to their mothers who were frightened by a clown (Nachmias, Gunnar, Mangelsdorf, & Parritz, 1996). Numerous studies have identified the key role of a responsive, predictable, and nurturing caregiver in the development of a healthy neurobiological stress-response (Perry & Pollard, 1998). During the first 2 years of life, there is a genetically programmed over-production of axons, dendrites, and synapses in the brain, with subsequent pruning of those not used (Singer, 1995). The environment thus regulates which synaptic connections survive (Glaser, 2000), possibly explaining the power of physical abuse, war, or other stressful situations in derailing attachment and developmental outcomes, and of nurturance in sustaining secure attachments and healthy outcomes.

Child Variables

Child factors associated with poor prognosis for psychosocial adjustment include shyness or other impediments to socialization, such as phobias or anxiety disorders, and family interaction patterns that foster overdependence, creating a learned helplessness (Blakeney et al., 1988). Individuals who make good psychosocial recoveries tend to be extroverted social risk takers with good impulse control and capacity for self-regulation, who reach out to others for support. They live with a family group that places value on reciprocal support in times of need, representing high levels of family cohesion. Such well-adjusted families value and encourage individual autonomy within their groups, as well as organization that facilitates functioning. Expressiveness of individual ideas is encouraged, and conflict is resolvable.

Healthy infant-parent attachment promotes optimal development in the face of adversity and protects against negative outcomes such as low self-esteem, poor social skills, and maladaptive adjustment. Kagan (1984, 1998) suggested that secure attachment patterns in infants are due more to a child's temperament than to the environment, although he conceded that a negative environment can worsen an inhibited/anxious temperament.

Other research reveals a more variable pattern of attachment-trauma interaction. In a study examining attachment patterns and trauma responses among 176 Palestinian males from the Gaza Strip, all of whom had been detained or imprisoned during the Intifada, different attachment patterns appeared most protective, depending upon whether the torture experienced was physical or psychological. Among insecurely attached participants, exposure to a high level of physical torture was associated with increased levels of PTSD, while secure attachment was predictive of PTSD in the face of exposure to high levels of psychological torture (Kanninen, Punamaki, & Qouta, 2003). The authors interpret these findings in terms of the different meanings that physical and psychological torture convey to individuals who are securely versus insecurely attached.

A study of Vietnam War combat veterans found that individuals who developed post-war PTSD, as compared to those combat veterans who did not, reported more childhood neurodevelopmental problems and childhood ADHD symptoms and had lower IQs. This suggests that neurological compromise may constitute a risk factor for the development of PTSD following exposure to trauma (Gurvits et al., 2000). Similar neurological soft signs have been shown to reflect an underlying genetic predisposition for the development of other psychiatric conditions including schizophrenia and OCD (Aronowitz et al., 1992; Garver, 1997).

Resilience, successful coping in specific domains despite adversity, including both behavioral and emotional arenas, has become a more frequently researched construct as the field has come to recognize that many youth exposed to chronic violence achieve adaptive success (Luthar, 1993; Luthar & Zigler, 1991). One empirically supported conceptualization of resilience among youth exposed to violence separated resilience into seven dimensions: adaptive success in future expectations, self-reliance, interpersonal relations, substance abuse, delinquent behavior, depression/anxiety, and somatization. In this longitudinal study of 2,600 middle school students exposed to chronic violence, perceived parent and school support predicted resilient outcomes in multiple domains, while peer support decreased resilience in the domains of substance abuse and delinquent behavior (O'Donnell, Schwab-Stone, & Muyeed, 2002). A study of resilient outcomes in children of depressed mothers found that high levels of perceived maternal warmth and acceptance, low levels of perceived maternal psychological control, and low levels of emotional overinvolvement were associated with resilient outcomes in adolescent children (Brennan, Le Brocque, & Hammen, 2003).

In a study of Cambodian refugee youth, adolescents whose families were more highly exposed to political violence reported more positive social adjustment and fewer mental health symptoms than those less exposed (Rousseau, Drapeau, & Rahimi, 2003). Some of these Khmer youth reported perceiving that their parents would sacrifice their lives for them, leading these researchers to hypothesize that such perceptions of high family investment may have engendered resilient outcomes (Rousseau, Drapeau, & Platt, 1999). In a study of Bosnian adolescents, self-efficacy levels among traumatized males were higher than those of non-traumatized peers, suggesting the possibility of a "steeling effect" of surviving traumatic experiences (Ferren, 1999). Other professionals have sometimes observed a phenomenon wherein the stresses of war, especially in developing countries, are associated with stimulation and improvement in the mental condition of children (Minkowski, 2000). Children orphaned as the result of war and other traumas often develop strong support systems among themselves, creating a powerful community identity (Minkowski, 2000).

CONCLUSION

A common consensus that children should not suffer because of adult inability to live in peace has become part of a global commitment to human rights. The General Declaration on Human Rights adopted by the United Nations General Assembly reads "mothers & children have the right to special care and assistance." Further, the International Covenant on Civil and Political Rights was adopted by the United Nations in December 1966 and made operative in March 1976. Article 6 reads "all human beings have the natural right to live, which should be protected by laws, and which they are not to be deprived of." Article 2 reads "a family is a natural and basic social unit enjoying the right of being protected by society and a state" and Article 24 reads "every child, regardless of race, color, gender, language, religion, national or social origin, is entitled to protective measures provided by his family, society and state, as required by his condition of a minor."

Yet, much compelling evidence exists informing us that children exposed to acts of war and terrorism are placed at risk for the development of multiple and sometimes protracted forms of biopsychosocial maladjustment. Children, as the unwitting and innocent recipients of these horrific consequences, are best understood as possessing normal, expected reactions to horribly abnormal events. Full recovery often involves living through a very difficult process of re-learning, on physiological, psychological, and social levels, how to understand the world without the constant threat of fear, hostility, and danger. As such, childhood trauma may be associated with an allostatic load, with continuing deleterious derivative effects on the CRF stress response and catecholaminergic systems that may have lasting and enduring effects, as well as an impact on the structures of the central nervous system. The most challenging times for this re-learning appear to occur during the first two years post-trauma.

This knowledge brings with it an imperative to learn more about how such trauma, from one generation to the next, causes illness and behavioral disorders, lying dormant in the psyche and later spreading as destructively as a latent virus. It may be neither necessary nor beneficial to wait for the development of PTSD in children to be cared for more positively, or to become a generation with less hatred. Children and parents who learn resilience in the face of psychological trauma and PTSD can become effective peace builders working directly in their communities.

Peace building is perhaps the central effort in preventing the irrational violence that plagues our children all around the world. The urgency now is to vastly enhance the means both to prevent future conflicts and to better support victims. Today's problems of poverty and violence will never subside unless we invest in the physical, mental, and emotional development of the next generations. Concern for children is also a way to address today's violence. In many of today's chronic disputes, violence does not cease; it merely subsides. Averting future conflicts will require not just caring for the youngest victims of war but also educating them for peace.

REFERENCES

Ajdukovic, M. (1996). Mothers' perception of their relationship with their children during displacement: A six month follow-up. *Child Abuse Review, 5*, 34–49.

Ajdukovic, M., & Ajdukovic, D. (1998). Impact of displacement on the psychological well being of refugee children. *International Review of Psychiatry, 10*, 186–195.

Ajdukovic, M., & Zic, V. (1997, September). *Prevention of delinquent experience in childhood: Croatian experience.* Paper presented at the 7th European Conference on Psychology and Law, Stockholm.

Allwood, M.A., Bell-Dolan, D., & Husain, S.A. (2002). Children's trauma and adjustment reactions to violent and nonviolent war experiences. *Journal of the American Academy of Child and Adolescent Psychiatry, 41*, 450–457.

Amir, M., & Lev-Wiesel, R. (2001). Does everyone have a name? Psychological distress and quality of life among child Holocaust survivors with lost identities. *Journal of Traumatic Stress, 14*, 859–869.

Aronowitz, B., Hollander, E., Mannuzza, S., Davis, J., Chapman, T., & Fyer, A. (1992). Familial transmission of OCD. *American Psychiatric Association Meeting: New Research Program and Abstracts.* Washington, DC: American Psychiatric Association.

Arroyo, W., & Eth, S. (1996). Traumatic stress reactions and post-traumatic stress disorder (PTSD). In R. Apfel & B. Simon (Eds.), *Minefields in the heart: The mental health of children in war and communal violence.* New Haven: Yale University Press.

Baker, A. (1991). Psychological response of Palestinian children to environmental stress associated with military occupation. *Journal of Refugee Studies 4*, 237–247.

Bandura, A. (1978). Social learning theory of aggression. *Journal of Communications, 28*, 12–29.

Blakeney, P., Herndon, D., Desai, M., Beard, S., & Wales-Sears, P. (1988). Long-term psychological adjustment following burn injury. *Journal of Burn Care and Rehabilitation, 9*, 661–665.

Blakeney, P., & Meyer, W. (1995). Psychosocial recovery of burned patients and reintegration into society. In D.N. Herndon (Ed.), *Total burn care* (pp. 569–563). London: W.B. Saunders.

Blakeney, P., Meyer, W., Levin, H., Ledoux, J., Moore, P., Robert, R., et al. (1996). Psychosocial resilience may require extraordinary family effort: A comparison of pediatric burn survivors, head injured children, and their families. *Proceedings of the American Burn Association, 28*, 29–37.

Blakeney, P., Portman, S., & Rutan, R. (1990). Familial values as factors influencing long-term psychological adjustment of children following severe burn injury. *Journal of Burn Care and Rehabilitation, 11*, 472–475.

Blakeney, P., Robert, R., & Meyer, W.J. (1989). Psychological and social recovery of children disfigured by physical trauma: Elements of treatment supported by empirical data. *International Review of Psychiatry, 10*, 196–200.

Bordlieri, J.E., Solodky, M.L., & Mikos, K.A. (1985). Physical attractiveness and nurses: Perceptions of pediatric patients. *Nursing Research, 34*, 24–26.

Bremner, J.D., Randall, P., Scott, T.M., & Bronen, R.A. (1997). MRI-based measurement of hippocampal volume in PTSD related to childhood physical and sexual abuse: A preliminary report. *Biological Psychiatry, 41*, 23–32.

Bremner, J.D., Randall, P., Scott, T.M., Capelli, S., Delaney, R., McCarthy, G., et al. (1995). Deficits in short-term memory in adult survivors of childhood abuse. *Psychiatry Research, 59*, 97–107.

Brennan, P.A., Le Brocque, R., & Hammen, C. (2003). Maternal depression, parent-child relationships, and resilient outcomes in adolescence. *Journal of the American Academy of Child and Adolescent Psychiatry, 42*, 1469–1477.

Bronfenbrenner, U. (1988). Interacting systems in human development: Research paradigms: Present and future. In N. Bolger & A. Caspi (Eds.), *Persons in context: Developmental processes* (pp. 25–49). London: Cambridge University Press.

Bugner, N. (2000). *Stolen identity: Jewish children hiding in Poland.* Jerusalem: Yad Vashem.

Cash, T.F. (1990). The psychology of physical appearance: Aesthetics, attributes, and images. In T.F. Cash, & I.T. Pruzinsky (Eds.), *Body images: Development, deviance, and change* (pp. 51–79). New York: Guilford Press.

Caspi, A., Sugden, K., Moffitt, T.E., Taylor, A., Craig, I.W., Harrington, H., McClay, J., Mill, J., Martin, J., Braithwaite, A., & Poulton, R. (2003). Influence of life stress on depression: Moderation by a polymorphism in the 5-HTT gene. *Science, 301*, 386–389.

Castro-Alamancos, M.A., & Connors, B.W. (1996). Short-term plasticity of a thalamocortical pathway dynamically modulated by behavioral state. *Science, 272*, 274–276.

Chaitin, J. (2000). Facing the Holocaust in generations of families of survivors: The case of partial relevance and interpersonal values. *Contemporary Family Therapy, 22*, 289–313.

Chaitin, J., & Bar-on, D. (2002). Emotional memories of family relationships during the Holocaust. *Journal of Loss and Trauma, 7*, 299–326.

Cicchetti, D., & Toth, S.L. (1995). A developmental psychopathology perspective on child abuse and neglect. *Journal of the American Academy of Child and Adolescent Psychiatry, 34*, 541–565.

Columbia University Mailman School of Public Health. (2002). *Effects of the World Trade Center attack on NYC public school students.* New York: Applied Research and Consulting, LLC.

Cooley-Quille, M., Turner, S., & Beidel, D. (1995). Emotional impact of children's exposure to community violence: A preliminary study. *Journal of the American Academy of Child and Adolescent Psychiatry, 34*, 1362–1368.

Coster, W.J., Gersten, M.S., Beeghly, M., & Cicchetti, D. (1989). Communicative functioning in maltreated toddlers. *Developmental Psychology, 25*, 777–793.

DeBellis, M.D. (2002). Abuse and ACTH response to corticotropin releasing factor. *American Journal of Psychiatry, 159*, 157–161.

Dell Orto, A.E. (1991). Coping with the enormity of illness and disability. In R.P. Marinelli, & A.E. Dell Orto (Eds.), *The psychological and social impact of disability* (pp. 333–335). Berlin: Springer.

DiGovanni, C. (1999). Domestic terrorism with chemical or biological agents: Psychiatric aspects. *American Journal of Psychiatry, 156*, 1500–1505.

Dodge, K.A. (1993). Social-cognitive mechanisms in the development of conduct disorder and depression. *Annual Review of Psychology, 44*, 559–584.

Dodge, K.A., Bates, J.E., & Pettit, G.S. (1990). Mechanisms in the cycle of violence. *Science, 250*, 1678–1683.

Druzic, O., Grl, M., Kletecki, M., & Ajdukovic, M. (1997). Meeting the needs of children in resettlement process in Hvatska Kostajnica. *Proceedings of the International Conference on Trauma Recovery Training: Lessons Learned, Croatia, 61*, 97–104.

Dzepina, M., Prebeg, Z., Juresa, V., Bogdan-Matjan, K., Brkljacic, D., Erdelj-Stivicic, B., et al. (1992). Suffering of Croatian school children during war. *Croatian Medical Journal, 33*, 40–44.

Feldman, A. (2002). X-children and the militarization of everyday life: Comparative comments on the politics of youth, victimage and violence in transitional societies. *International Journal of Social Welfare, 11*, 286–299.

Ferren, P.M. (1999). Comparing perceived self-efficacy among adolescent Bosnian and Croatian refugees with and without posttraumatic stress disorder. *Journal of Traumatic Stress, 12*, 405–420.

Flisher, A.J., Kramer, R.A., Hoven, C.W., & Greenwald, S. (1997). Psychosocial characteristics of physically abused children and adolescents. *Journal of the American Academy of Child and Adolescent Psychiatry, 36*,123–129.

Fox, L., Long, S.H., & Anglois, A. (1988). Patterns of language comprehension deficit in abused and neglected children. *Journal of Speech and Hearing Disorders, 53*, 239–244.

Galea, S., Ahern, J., Resnick, H., Kilpatrick, D., Bucuvalas, M., Gold, J., et al. (2002). Psychological sequelae of the September 11 terrorist attacks in New York City. *New England Journal of Medicine, 346*, 982–987.

Garbarino, J., Kostelny, K., & Dubrow, N. (1991). *No place to be a child: Growing up in a war zone.* Lexington, MA: Lexington Books.

Garver, D.L. (1997). The etiologic heterogeneity of schizophrenia. *Harvard Review of Psychiatry, 4*, 317–327.

Gilligan, S.G. & Bower, G.H. (1983). Reminding and mood-congruent memory. *Bulletin of the Psychonomic Society, 21*, 431–434.

Glaser, D. (2000). Child abuse and neglect and the brain: A review. *Journal of Child Psychology and Psychiatry, 41*, 97–116.

Glod, C.A., Teicher, M.H., & Hartman, C.R. (1997). Increased nocturnal activity and impaired sleep maintenance in abused children. *Journal of the American Academy of Child and Adolescent Psychiatry, 36*, 1236–43.

Godden, D.R., & Baddeley, A.D. (1975). Context-dependent memory in two natural environments: On land and underwater. *British Journal of Psychology, 66*, 325–331.

Green, A.H. (1997). Physical abuse of children. In J. Weiner (Ed.), *American Academy of Child and Adolescent Psychiatry Textbook of Child and Adolescent Psychiatry* (pp. 17–38). Washington, DC: American Psychological Association.

Grguric, J., & Hirsl-Hecej, V. (1993). *Program for providing minimum nutritional and health care requirements for children in Croatia.* Zagreb: Committee for Coordination of Relief and Health Care for Children in Exceptional Circumstances.

Gunnar, M. (1998). Quality of early care and buffering of neuroendocrine stress reactions: Potential effects on the developing human brain. *Preventative Medicine, 27*, 208–211.

Gurvits, L.V., Gilbertson, M.W., Lasko, N.B., Tarhan, A.S., Simeon, D., Macklin, M.L., Orr, S.P., & Pitman, R.K. (2000). Neurologic soft signs in chronic posttraumatic stress disorder. *Archives of General Psychiatry, 57*, 181–186.

Gurwich, R.H., Sitterle, K.A., Young, B.H., & Pfefferbaum, B. (2002). The aftermath of terrorism. In A.M. La Greca (Ed.), *Helping children cope with disasters and terrorism* (pp. 327–357). Washington, DC: American Psychological Association.

Hall, M.J., & Norwood, A.E. (2002). Preparing for bioterrorism at the state level: Report of an informal survey. *American Journal of Orthopsychiatry, 72*, 486–491.

Heim, C., Newport, D.J., & Heit, S. (2000). Pituitary-adrenal and autonomic responses to stress in women after sexual and physical abuse in childhood. *Journal of the American Medical Association, 284*, 592–597.

Herrenkohl, R.C., Egolf, B.P., & Herrenkohl, E.C. (1997). Preschool antecedents of adolescent assaultive behavior: A longitudinal study. *American Journal of Orthopsychiatry, 67*, 422–432.

Horowitz, M., Wilner, N., & Alvarez, W. (1979). Impact of Event Scale: A measure of subjective stress. *Psychosomatic Medicine, 41*, 209–218.

James, B. (1994). *Handbook for treatment of attachment-trauma problems in children.* New York: The Free Press.

Kagan, J. (1984). *The nature of the child.* New York: Basic Books.

Kagan, J. (1998). *Three seductive ideas.* Boston: Harvard University Press.

Kandel, E.W. (2001). The molecular biology of memory storage: A dialogue between genes and synapses. *Science, 294*, 1030–1038.

Kanninen, K., Punamaki, R.L., & Qouta, S. (2003). Personality and trauma: Adult attachment and posttraumatic distress among former political prisoners. *Peace and Conflict: Journal of Peace Psychology, 9*, 97–126.

Kaplan, S.J., Pelcovitz, D., & Labruna, V. (1999). Child and adolescent abuse and neglect research: A review of the past 10 years: Part I. Physical and emotional abuse and neglect. *Journal of the American Academy of Child and Adolescent Psychiatry, 38*, 1214–1222.

Kaplan, S.J., Pelcovitz, D., Salzinger, S., Weiner, M., Mandel, F.S., Lesser, M.L., et al. (1998). Adolescent physical abuse: Risk for adolescent psychiatric disorders. *American Journal of Psychiatry, 155*, 954–959.

Kartensky, E., Shemer, J., Alshech, I., Cogocaru, B., Moscovitz, M., Shapiro, Y., et al. (1991). Medical aspects of the Iraqi missile attacks on Israel. *Israel Journal of Medical Sciences, 27*, 603–607.

Keane, T.M., Kolb, L.C., & Kaloupek, D.G. (1998). Utility of psychophysiology measurement in the diagnosis of posttraumatic stress disorder: Results from a department of Veteran's Affairs cooperative study. *Journal of Consulting and Clinical Psychology, 66*, 914–923.

Klimes-Dougan, B., & Kistner, J. (1990). Physically abused preschoolers' responses to peers' distress. *Developmental Psychology, 26*, 599–602.

Kopelman, M.D. (2000). Fear can interrupt the continuum of memory. *Journal of Neurology, Neurosurgery, and Psychiatry, 69*, 431–432.

Kovacs, M. (1981). Rating scale to assess depression in school-aged children. *Acta Peadopsychiatrica, 46*, 305–315.

Krystal, H. (1968). *Massive psychic trauma.* New York: International Universities Press.

Kuterovac, G., Dyregrov, A., & Stuvland, R. (1994). Children in war: A silent majority under stress. *British Journal of Medical Psychology, 67*, 363–375.

LeDoux J., Blakeney, P., Meyer, W., & Herndon, D. (1994). Relationships between parental emotional states, family environment, and the behavioral adjustment of pediatric burn survivors. *Proceedings of the American Burn Association, 26*, 96–107.

Lemieux, A.M., & Coe, C.L. (1995). Abuse-related posttraumatic stress disorder: Evidence for chronic neuroendocrine activation in women. *Psychosomatic Medicine, 57*, 105–115.

Lewis, D.O. (1992). From abuse to violence: Psychophysiological consequences of maltreatment. *Journal of the American Academy of Child and Adolescent Psychiatry, 31*, 383–391.

Lewis, D.O. (1996). Development of the symptom of violence. In M. Lewis (Ed.), *Child and adolescent psychiatry: A comprehensive textbook.* Baltimore: Williams and Wilkins.

Livingston, R., Lawson, L., & Jones, J.G. (1993). Predictors of self-reported psychopathology in children abused repeatedly by a parent. *Journal of the American Academy of Child and Adolescent Psychiatry, 32*, 948–953.

Luthar, S.S. (1993). Methodological and conceptual issues in research on childhood resilience. *Journal of Child Psychology and Psychiatry, 34*, 441–453.

Luthar, S.S., & Zigler, E. (1991). Vulnerability and competence: A review of research on resilience in childhood. *American Journal of Orthopsychiatry, 61*, 6–22.

McCallin, M., & Fozzard, S. (1990). *The impact of traumatic events on the psychological well-being of Mozambican refugee women and children.* Geneva: International Catholic Child Bureau.

McEwen, B.S., & Magarinos, M. (1997). Stress effects on morphology and function of the hippocampus. In R. Yehuda & A.C. McFarlane (Eds.), *Psychobiology of posttraumatic stress disorder* (pp. 271–284). New York: New York Academy of Sciences.

McFadyen, R.G., & Kitson, W.J.H. (1996). Language comprehension and expression among adolescents who have experienced childhood physical abuse. *Journal of Child Psychology and Psychiatry, 37*, 551–562.

Meyer, W., Blakeney, P., Ledoux, J., & Herndon, D.N. (1995). Diminished adaptive behaviors among pediatric survivors of burns. *Journal of Burn Care and Rehabilitation, 16*, 511–518.

Meyer, W., Doctor, M., Robert, R., Murphy, L., McShan, S., & Blakeney, P. (1997). Psychosocial outcome of 327 pediatric burn survivors. *Proceedings of the American Burn Association, 29*, 2–13.

Milgram, N.A. (1982). War related stress in Israeli children and youth. In L. Goldberg & S. Brenitz (Eds.), *Handbook of stress: Theoretical and clinical aspects* (pp. 656–676). New York: The Free Press.

Minkowski, A. (2000). Protection of the young child's brain: Personal observations and thoughts in postwar stress syndrome and in natural catastrophes. *Acta Paediatrica, 89*, 378–385.

Moore, P., Blakeney, P., Broemeling, L., Portman, S., Herndon, D.N., & Robson, M. (1993). Psychological adjustment following childhood burn injuries predicted by personality traits. *Journal of Burn Care and Rehabilitation, 14*, 80–82.

Moro, L.J., & Vidovic, V. (1992). Psychological changes in displaced children and adults. In E. Klain (Ed.), *War psychology and psychiatry* (pp. 171–192). Zagreb: Committee for Coordination of Relief and Health Care for Children in Exceptional Circumstances.

Nachmias M., Gunnar, M., Mangelsdorf, S., & Parritz, R.H. (1996). Behavioral inhibition and stress reactivity: The moderating role of attachment security. *Child Development, 67*, 508–522.

Nelson, C.A., & Carver, L.J. (1998). The effects of stress and trauma on brain and memory: A view from developmental cognitive neuroscience. *Development and Psychopathology, 10*, 793–809.

Ohbu, S., Yamashina, A., Takasu, N., Yamaguchi, T., Murai, T., Nakano, K., et al. (1997). Sarin poisoning on Tokyo subway. *Southern Medical Journal, 90*, 587–593.

O'Donnell, D.A., Schwab-Stone, M.E., & Muyeed, A. (2002). Multidimensional resilience in urban children exposed to community violence. *Child Development, 73*, 1265–1282.

Osofsky, J. (1995). The effects of exposure to violence on young children. *American Psychologist, 50*, 782–788.

Pelcovitz, D., Kaplan, S., Goldenberg, B., & Weinblatt, M. (1994). Post-traumatic stress disorder in physically abused adolescents. *Journal of the American Academy of Child and Adolescent Psychiatry, 33*, 305–312.

Perry, B.D. (1999). The memories of states: How the brain stores and retrieves traumatic experience. In J. Goodwin & R. Attias (Eds.), *Splintered reflections: Images of the body in trauma* (pp. 9–38). New York: Basic Books.

Perry, B.D. (2001). The neurodevelopmental impact of violence in childhood. In D. Schetky & E. Benedek (Eds.), *Textbook of child and adolescent forensic psychiatry* (pp. 221–238). Washington, DC: American Psychiatric Press.

Perry, B.D., & Pollard, R. (1998). Homeostasis, stress, trauma and adaptation—a neurodevelopmental view of childhood trauma. *Child and Adolescent Psychiatric Clinics of North America, 7*, 33–51.

Perry, B.D., Pollard, R.A., Blakley, T.L., Baker, W.L., & Vigilante, D. (1995) Childhood trauma, the neurobiology of adaptation, and "use-dependent" development of the brain: How "states" become "traits." *Infant Mental Health Journal, 16*, 271–291.

Pfefferbaum, B., Nixon, S.J., Tucker, P.M., Tivis, R.D., Moore, V.L., Gurwitch, R.H., et al. (1999). Posttraumatic stress responses in bereaved children after the Oklahoma

City bombing. *Journal of the American Academy of Child and Adolescent Psychiatry, 38,* 1372–1379.

Phillips, R.G., & LeDoux, J.E. (1992). Differential contribution of amygdala and hippocampus to cued and contextual fear conditioning. *Behavioral Neuroscience, 106,* 274–285.

Pynoos, R., & Nader, K. (1993). Issues in the treatment of posttraumatic stress in children and adolescents. In J. Wilson & B. Raphael (Eds.), *International handbook of traumatic stress syndromes.* New York: Plenum Press.

Reid, J.B. (1990). A role for prospective longitudinal investigations in the study of traumatic stress and disasters. *Journal of Applied Social Psychology, 20,* 1695–1703.

Robins, L.N. (1983). Some methodological problems and research issues in the study of the effects of stress on children. In N. Garmezy & M. Rutter (Eds.), *Stress, coping, and development in children* (pp. 335–346). New York: McGraw Hill.

Rosenthal, G. (1998). *The Holocaust in three generations: Families of victims and perpetrators of the Nazi regime.* London: Kassel.

Rousseau, C., Drapeau, A., & Platt, R. (1999). Family trauma and its association with emotional and behavioral problems and social adjustment in adolescent Cambodian refugees. *Child Abuse and Neglect, 23,* 1263–1273.

Rousseau, C., Drapeau, A., & Rahimi, S. (2003). The complexity of trauma response: A 4-year follow-up of adolescent Cambodian refugees. *Child Abuse and Neglect, 27,* 1277–1290.

Sapolsky, R. (1996). Why stress is bad for your brain. *Science, 273,* 749–750.

Schuster, M.A., Stein, B.D., Jaycox, L.H., Collins, R.C., Marshall, G.N., Elliott, M.N., et al. (2001). A national survey of stress reactions after the September 11, 2001, terrorist attacks. *New England Journal of Medicine, 345,* 1507–1512.

Shaw, J.A. (2000). Children, adolescents and trauma. *Psychiatric Quarterly, 71,* 227–243.

Shin, L.M., McNally, R.J., Kosslyn, S.M., Thompson, W.L., Rauch, S.L., Alport, N.M., et al. (1999). Regional cerebral blood flow during script-driven imagery in childhood sexual abuse related PTSD: A PET investigation. *American Journal of Psychiatry, 156,* 575–584.

Singer, W. (1995). Development and plasticity of cortical processing architectures. *Science, 270,* 758–764.

Solomons, Z. (1998). Transgenerational effects of the Holocaust. In Y. Danieli (Ed.), *International handbook of multigenerational legacies of trauma* (pp. 69–83). New York: Plenum.

Stuber, J., Fairbrother, G., Galea, S., Pfefferbaum, B., Wilson–Genderson, M., & Vlahov, D. (2002). Determinants of counseling for children in Manhattan after the September 11 attacks. *Psychiatric Services, 53,* 815–822.

Talbot, J.A. (2001, October 26). Look behind classic symptoms to spot PTSD in affected kids. *Clinical Psychiatry News,* p. 12.

Terr, L.C. (1983). Chowchilla revisited: Post-traumatic child's play. *Journal of the American Academy of Child and Adolescent Psychiatry, 20,* 741–760.

Terr, L.C. (1991). Childhood traumas: an outline and overview. *American Journal of Psychiatry 148,* 10–20.

Terr, L.C. (1996). Acute responses to external events and posttraumatic stress disorder. In M. Lewis (Ed.), *Child and adolescent psychiatry: A comprehensive textbook.* Baltimore: Williams and Wilkins.

United Nations High Commission for Refugees. (2002). *Refugees by numbers 2002.* New York: Oxford University Press.

UNICEF. (1996). *The state of the world's children.* New York: Oxford University Press.

Vondra, J.I., Barnett, D.E., & Cicchetti, D. (1990). Self-concept, motivation, and competence among preschoolers from maltreating and comparison families. *Child Abuse and Neglect, 14,* 525–532.

Widom, C.S. (1989). Child abuse, neglect, and adult behavior. *Criminology, 27*, 251–271.

Winnicott, D.W. (1992). *Deprivation and delinquency.* London: Routledge.

Wodarski, J.S., Kurtz, P.D., Gaudin, J.M., Jr., & Howing, P.T. (1990). Maltreatment and the school age child: Major academic, socioemotional, and adaptive outcomes. *Social Work, 35*, 581–589.

Yehuda, R., Spertus, I., & Golier, J. (2001). Relationship between childhood traumatic experiences and PTSD in Adults. In S. Eth (Ed.), *PTSD in children and adolescents* (pp. 117–146). Washington, DC: American Psychiatric Publishing.

Zivcic, I. (1993). Emotional reactions of children to war stress in Croatia. *Journal of the American Academy of Child and Adolescent Psychiatry, 32*, 709–713.

II

INTERVENTIONS
AND SERVICES
FOR CHILDREN
EXPOSED TO VIOLENCE

4

CHILD-PARENT PSYCHOTHERAPY AND THE EARLY TRAUMA TREATMENT NETWORK

Collaborating to Treat Infants, Toddlers, and Preschoolers

Patricia Van Horn and Alicia F. Lieberman

This chapter describes a collaborative effort to improve the way that mental health services are delivered to traumatized young children and their families. This collaboration, the Early Trauma Treatment Network[1] (ETTN), was developed among four institutions that share the philosophy that relationships are central to young children's mental health. The ETTN has four central missions:

1. To design and disseminate a universal assessment protocol that can be used to evaluate the impact of traumatic events on infants and young children and those who care for them and on the child's caregiving environment

2. To test the effectiveness of a relationship-based psychotherapy model to intervene with very young traumatized children and their caregivers

3. To create, pilot, and disseminate a uniform training protocol to use for training mental health professionals to assess and treat traumatized young children and their families

4. To share with one another the expertise that we have developed over the years in working with the various systems with which traumatized young children and their families interact

---

[1]The Early Trauma Treatment Network is a member of the National Childhood Traumatic Stress Network funded by the Substance Abuse and Mental Health Services Administration (SAMHSA) of the United States Department of Health and Human Services.

In this chapter, we consider the essential factors in understanding the impact of trauma on young children and their families and describe child-parent psycho-therapy (CPP), a relationship-based model of intervention that was developed at one of the ETTN sites (the University of California, San Francisco Child Trauma Research Project, located at San Francisco General Hospital) and is currently being evaluated with a diverse population of young children and their caregivers at all four sites of the ETTN. Finally, we analyze relationships as they exist and are supported in community systems. We describe the programs of the ETTN and demonstrate the ways in which this network of researchers and clinicians has joined forces to share their intervention expertise to enhance young children's mental health.

UNDERSTANDING THE IMPACT
OF TRAUMA ON YOUNG CHILDREN

We, as a society, prefer to turn away from the idea that infants and very young chil-dren suffer traumas. Many people assume that traumatic life events have no impact on the youngest of our children. Many rationales are offered for this stance: Young children won't understand what is happening; they will forget; they are resilient; if not reminded of frightening events they will put the events out of their minds. We repeat these refrains to deny the impact of trauma on very young children.

The work of both clinicians and researchers in the fields of infant mental health and child trauma, however, has taught us that traumatic experiences have a lasting effect on many young children (Osofsky, 2004). Kitzman, Gaylord, Holt, and Kenny (2003) demonstrated that children across a variety of developmental stages respond differently to witnessing domestic violence, with preschool-age children being somewhat more vulnerable to the effects of violence exposure than older children. Although there is no published research to date focusing specifi-cally on the impact of violence exposure on infants and toddlers, we presume that some of these very young children will develop well in spite of their exposure to violence. We understand, however, that infants and toddlers exposed to violence are at increased risk for a range of problems, including increased irritability, dis-turbances in appetite and sleeping, increased crying and emotional distress, in-creased aggression, temper tantrums, fearfulness, inability to separate from their parents or caregivers, and regression in newly acquired skills such as toileting and language (Drell, Siegel, & Gaensbauer, 1993; Zeanah & Scheeringa, 1996).

As knowledge of the impact of childhood trauma has increased, we have be-come more sensitive to the complex factors that moderate children's responses to traumatic events (Bosquet, 2004; Groves, Lieberman, Osofsky, & Fenichel, 2000; Pynoos, Steinberg, & Piacentini, 1999). These can be divided into four categories:

- Factors related to the child: age, developmental status, functioning before the trauma, and history of past trauma

- Factors related to the trauma: type of trauma, duration of the trauma, the child's proximity to the traumatic event, the emotional salience of the people involved in the trauma to the child, whether the trauma was a natural disaster or an intentional human act, and the level of caregiving support during and immediately after the trauma

- Factors related to the child's overall caregiving environment: the past trauma history of caregivers, whether the caregivers were involved in the trauma, the pre-trauma quality of the caregiving relationships, and the caregiver's mental health

- Contextual and posttrauma variables: other stresses such as poverty, racism, substance abuse, or mental illness in the family; level of support for the family from the larger community; the presence of traumatic reminders following the trauma; and the presence of secondary adversities (such as placement in foster care after an incident of substantiated child abuse) after the trauma

Underlying all of these factors is the child's and family's culture, which "phenomenologically shapes the lived experience of both children's development and their experience of trauma" (Lewis & Ghosh Ippen, 2004, p. 14). Culture plays a part in defining the meaning of the traumatic experience for the child. It may also provide rituals, customs, and traditions that dictate reactions to the trauma, which are instrumental in the child's healing. Because all of these factors are intertwined, the impact of trauma on young children is complex, involving not only the child and the trauma but also the entire network of relationships and systems in which the child is embedded. This is particularly true when a trauma befalls a very young child.

Infants, toddlers, and preschoolers do not have well-developed coping mechanisms. They rely on the adults who care for them to support their cognitive development by engaging them in exploring the world, emotional development by helping them regulate affective experience and expression, and social development by teaching them what to expect from relationships (Klapper, Plummer, & Harmon, 2004; Marans & Adelman, 1997). When young children are overwhelmed by trauma, either because their caregivers have turned from nurturing figures to dangerous ones or because their caregivers have failed, sometimes in spite of their best efforts, to protect them from overwhelming fear, all of these lines of development are derailed. Traumatized young children must then rely on caregivers and on the systems that surround them to restore their development to a more positive trajectory. Many parents of traumatized children are able, on their own and without help from mental health professionals, to offer the reassurance and support that children need to heal. Often, however, either due to the parent's own traumatic experiences or due to the emotional and behavioral challenges of these children, caregivers need help. We believe that to help a traumatized child heal, we must support all of the relationships and systems on which the child depends.

CHILD–PARENT PSYCHOTHERAPY

In 2001, in recognition of the increasing numbers of traumatized children in our society, the U.S. Department of Health and Human Services announced the National Childhood Traumatic Stress Initiative (NCTSN). The Initiative had as its mission to fund a network of researchers and treatment providers (NCTSN) that could develop and disseminate evidence-based models of assessment and treatment of childhood trauma. The ETTN was established to bring to the NCTSN an awareness of the needs of the youngest traumatized children. The ETTN's goals include evaluating CPP to determine whether it is an effective way to treat a diverse population of young children who have suffered a variety of interpersonal traumas.

The ETTN is made up of four very diverse programs that have in common a primary mission of advancing the mental health of infants and young children: the Child Trauma Research Project in San Francisco, California; the Child Witness to Violence Project in Boston, Massachusetts; the Infant Team at the Tulane University Medical Center; and the Early Trauma Treatment Program at the Louisiana State University Health Sciences Center in New Orleans, Louisiana. All four agencies strive to attain that mission, in part, by offering direct mental health services to young children and their families. They also have in common the belief that young children are most likely to be mentally healthy when they are surrounded by systems that understand and support their need for sustaining relationships; with that belief in mind, each of the programs has formed ties to other systems that are integral to the way they do their work.

History and Goals

CPP is a modification of infant–parent psychotherapy (Fraiberg, Adelson, & Shapiro, 1980; Lieberman, 2004; Lieberman & Pawl, 1993) for children in the first 6 years of life. Infant-parent psychotherapy, a form of intervention developed by Selma Fraiberg to address mental health problems in children from birth to age 3, has as its theoretical target the web of mutually constructed meanings in the infant-parent relationship (Lieberman, Silverman, & Pawl, 2000; Pawl & St. John, 1998). When an infant is the target of the intervention, the primary therapeutic focus involves uncovering the unconscious links between the parent's psychological conflicts and parenting that is not attuned to the baby's needs. When an older child is the target of the intervention, the treatment focuses on the growing child's agency and internal world and less on uncovering the parent's early conflicts (Lieberman, 2004).

In CPP, the parent and child attend the therapy sessions together. Close observation of the child's behavior and translation of the meaning of the behavior to the parent, in the context of the child's developmental stage, is central to CPP. Infants and young children often cannot express their wishes and intentions in words. They rely upon crying, reaching, facial expressions, tantrums, running away, and infinite other behaviors to express what they need and the intensity with which they need it. Parents who cannot decipher the meaning of their young children's behavior are often unable to respond effectively to their children and find themselves trapped with their children in a cycle of miscommunication and mutual alienation, in which neither party understands the intentions of the other. In such cases, the therapist guides the parent in observing the child and reflecting on the child's behavior. When the parent is stuck, the therapist may offer explanations that are framed in the context of the child's developmental stage.

The ability to carefully observe, an understanding of early childhood development, and the ability to translate the child's behavior to the parent are core skills demanded of the child-parent psychotherapist, as they are in other forms of relationship-based treatment for infants and young children such as early family intervention (Heinicke, Fineman, Ponce, & Guthrie, 2001), interaction guidance (McDonough, 2000, 2004), and "watch, wait, and wonder" (Cohen et al., 1999; Muir, Lojkasek, & Cohen, 1999). In all of these relationship-based treatments, the hallmark of the intervention is the therapist's ability to accurately observe the child, place the child's behavior in developmental context, and translate the meaning of the behavior for the individual child to the parent in order to increase the parent's competence in responding to the child.

CPP is set apart by the addition of layers of mutuality in the therapeutic process. The child-parent psychotherapist examines the meaning of the child's behavior not only for the child, but also for the parent. The therapist also helps the child understand the meaning of the parent's behaviors so that the child can understand the parent's motivations and enter into a cooperative and collaborative relationship with the parent.

Although CPP is a suitable intervention for any young child whose development is impeded by conflicts in the parent-child relationship, it was developed with the specific aim of helping young children who had suffered traumatic life experiences—specifically, witnessing the battering of their mothers by father figures. Under such circumstances, the trauma itself interferes with the child's development in a number of ways. First, it subjects the child to overwhelming negative affect at a time when the child has not yet learned to self-regulate affect but still relies upon caregivers for help. Second, but inextricably intertwined with the first, the children's view of their attachment figures as safe havens and protectors is disrupted. When children are terrified by the sights and sounds of violence and most need their caregivers' protection, their caregivers are least able to provide it, involved as they are in their own intense feelings of anger, fear, and hurt (Lieberman & Van Horn, 1998; Osofsky, 1995). Third, even after the traumatic event ends, its effects continue to reverberate, as the child and his or her caregivers are exposed to traumatic reminders and secondary adversities and as their expectations of the ways in which people will behave in relationships are changed by the trauma (Pynoos et al., 1999). CPP was developed to address all of these effects of trauma in the lives of young children.

CPP has much in common with other trauma treatments and shares many of their basic goals (Marmar, Foy, Kagan, & Pynoos, 1993), including

- Encouraging a return to normal development, adaptive coping, and engagement with present activities and future goals. This is the overarching goal of treatment for traumatized children and adults, and all of the goals that follow can be seen as serving this goal

- Fostering a realistic response to threat

- Maintaining regular levels of affective arousal

- Rebuilding the capacity for trust and reciprocity in intimate relationships

- Lending an understanding that the intrusive thoughts, nightmares, numbing, avoidance and hyperarousal that follow trauma are normative responses to an overwhelming situation

- Encouraging a differentiation between reliving and reenacting the trauma in the present and remembering it as something that happened in the past

- Placing the traumatic event in perspective by encouraging integration of the experience with other life experiences so that it doesn't remain a central preoccupation of the traumatized person

With CPP, careful assessment precedes the treatment and informs the goals of intervention for the particular parent and child. Informal assessment continues throughout the treatment as the therapist and parent work together to understand what goals have been met and what new needs have arisen. Always, the child-parent relationship is used as the vehicle for the realization of the treatment goals. Using a variety of modalities, the therapist helps both caregiver and child reestablish a sense of safety and trust in their own feelings, in their relationship, and in the world. Using the parent-child relationship in therapy requires the therapist to understand the overwhelming emotional responses of trauma from a developmental perspective, including recognizing that different kinds of events will be traumatic for people at different developmental phases and translating the meaning of overwhelming events across developmental stages.

The child-parent psychotherapist makes use of several discrete treatment modalities to achieve the goal of helping the parent and child to negotiate their different developmental agendas and to create solutions to conflicts in their relationship, whether those conflicts are instigated by trauma, by "ghosts in the nursery" that find their source in difficulties in the parent's childhood caregiving relationships, or by other hardships.

Treatment Modalities

Case Management and Assistance with Concrete Problems of Living
Case management and assistance with concrete problems is often the modality of choice in the early phase of CPP following trauma. For example, a family that has experienced domestic violence may need immediate help negotiating the legal system to obtain restraining orders, locating shelters or other safe housing, and finding work or some other source of income. This kind of assistance has benefits beyond provision of food, shelter, and income. The therapist, in supporting the family members in meeting these basic needs, models the stance that safety is an important goal and that they are worthy of protection, beliefs that may have been shattered by the experience of trauma.

Play and Putting Feelings into Words Play and putting feelings into words are central to all psychotherapies with children. Play is the child's primary mode of symbolic expression. In play, children can repeat anxiety-provoking situations in order to master them and alter the outcomes of frightening events to make them more palatable. Because the parent is the most important organizer of a young child's feelings and experiences, it is important for the parent to understand the meaning of the child's play in order to respond to the message that it contains. In joint sessions, the child-parent psychotherapist translates the play for the parent so that the parent can understand the meaning of the child's symbolic language.

Physical Contact Physical contact is an essential way that love and intimacy are expressed between parent and child. Trauma, however, exposes both parent and child to overwhelming sensory stimulation, which may live on in the body (van der Kolk, 1994) and be re-experienced without conscious awareness of its roots in the trauma. This problem is compounded when the child and parent serve as traumatic reminders for one another. Affectionate touch, one of the hallmarks of parent-child intimacy, can become threatening. Child-parent psychotherapy encourages touch between parent and child as a way of restoring a sense of protection and safety and restoring the knowledge that bodily experiences can be pleasurable.

Providing Unstructured Developmental Guidance Providing unstructured developmental guidance is often the simplest and most effective intervention that a child-parent psychotherapist initiates. This guidance doesn't follow a prescribed curriculum but is offered as particular struggles or conflicts emerge in the course of the intervention. The obvious aim of developmental guidance is to help the parent understand the child's behavior. A less frequently considered secondary benefit, developmental guidance also helps children understand that they are like other children and that their feelings, which may seem unmanageable, are a normal part of childhood.

After trauma, another kind of developmental guidance may be needed: guidance to help both parent and child understand their strong feelings and responses. Trauma produces horror, helplessness, and terror. It may be followed by shame about these feelings and by a sense of unreality in which the parent or the child doubts the accuracy of his or her own recollections of what happened, even as he or she seems caught in a trap of vivid and intrusive memories from which he or she cannot escape. Reassurance that these are normative expectable responses to trauma is helpful to both mother and child.

Modeling Appropriate Protective Behavior Modeling appropriate protective behavior is particularly important after trauma, when both parents and children may have distorted perceptions of what is safe and what is dangerous as a result of their experiences. Their distortions may lead them to minimize real danger or to see frightening risk in relatively safe situations. CPP interventions emphasize the importance of safety, restoring the parent to a protective role, and limit setting as essential components of a young child's sense of safety.

Interpretation Interpretation presents special problems in CPP because of the disparate developmental stages of parent and child, yet it is often a critical modality. Interpretations can help parents become aware of the unconscious repetition of destructive past relationships in the care of their children, correct distortions—sometimes trauma based—in their perceptions of their children, and free them to engage in more flexible and developmentally appropriate parenting practices. Interpretations can also help children become aware of unconscious beliefs and defenses that may have been appropriate in the face of trauma but that no longer serve them well and free them to experiment with new ways of coping with anxiety.

When both parent and child are present in the session, interpretation calls for great tact and delicate timing on behalf of the therapist. Too deep exploration of a parent's history to understand what past patterns are being repeated in the present may expose a child to developmentally inappropriate information. This impasse is sometimes best managed by scheduling separate sessions with the parent or by dividing the child-parent session into separate segments: one for play that includes child, parent, and therapist and one for more "grown-up" conversation that takes place between the adult and the therapist while the child plays on his or her own. At times, these conversations may take place privately between the adult and the therapist. At other times, however, when the content of the adult conversation will not be overwhelming for the child, the child may find it reassuring to play quietly and listen to adults grapple with and attempt to resolve adult problems.

All CPP treatment modalities are delivered in a strong atmosphere of *emotional support* for both parent and child. Emotional support is an indispensable component of all effective therapeutic interventions. But in CPP, a parallel process occurs in which the child benefits from observing the caring way in which the therapist relates to the parent, and the parent learns and benefits as well from observing how the therapist behaves toward the child. As in all therapies, the therapist's supportive stance is a corrective experience for the client. In CPP, there is an additional benefit as the therapist acts as a role model of benevolent, protective behavior for both parent and child. In CPP, it is not a particular way of talking or behaving toward the child that is modeled for the parent. Rather, the therapist models an attitude of supportive collaboration for both parent and child.

PROGRAMS OF THE
EARLY TRAUMA TREATMENT NETWORK

Although all of the ETTN programs provide child-parent psychotherapy, they have broader goals and philosophies. Each of the four programs was born of an understanding that in order to truly support children who have suffered traumatic experiences and their families, mental health professionals must form collaborative relationships with other systems with which the families are involved. Each ETTN program has approached the challenge of collaboration in a unique way.

The Child Trauma Research Project

The Child Trauma Research Project (CTRP) at San Francisco General Hospital has as its mission to develop and evaluate ecologically valid, culturally competent interventions for children younger than the age of 6 who have experienced interpersonal traumas. CTRP's underlying philosophy is that it cannot accomplish its research mission without first establishing deep collaborative roots within the community, because without such community engagement it would not be credible with the agencies that refer children for intervention. Since its establishment in 1996, CTRP has formed partnerships with a variety of community agencies that serve young children and their families.

Like other agencies in the ETTN, CTRP recognizes that collaboration with the child protection system is essential to understanding the lives of children traumatized by physical and sexual violence. CTRP's director, Alicia F. Lieberman, has provided mental health consultation to child welfare workers and their supervisors in the San Francisco Department of Human Services for more than 20 years. This consultation is collaborative and case specific and depends on the formation of a trusting relationship with the child welfare worker as well as on an understanding of the special demands that the worker faces in making placement and reunification recommendations for children and their families (Lieberman, 1999, 2000). The consultation forms the bedrock upon which a network of trusting relationships between CTRP clinicians and child welfare workers rests. In addition to the child welfare system, CTRP provides consultation to a variety of other agencies that serve children, including a network of family resource centers, child care centers, domestic violence shelters, and the family court (Lieberman, 2000; Van Horn & Hitchens, 2004).

With firm relationships in the community, CTRP has been able to recruit a diverse group of preschool-age children and their mothers who had experienced domestic violence. Initially, CTRP offered treatment to all of the participating mother-child dyads. After the CPP had taken form, CTRP initiated a randomized trial to test its efficacy (Lieberman & Van Horn, in press). Although data collection from the randomized trial is not complete, the pre- and post-treatment data from the first 85 dyads to complete treatment demonstrates the promise of this relationship-based treatment model.

The assessment protocol includes measures, some of which are described more fully below, that examine the mother's individual functioning, the child's individual functioning, the nature of traumas experienced by both mother and child, and the quality of the parent-child relationship. Before treatment, mothers were interviewed about their lifetime history of exposure to major stressful events using the Life Stressor Checklist–Revised (Wolfe, Kimerling, Brown, Chrestman, & Levin, 1996). Both during the initial assessment and the post-treatment assessment, mothers were assessed for posttraumatic stress disorder using the Clinician-Administered PTSD Scale (CAPS) (Blake et al., 1990). Children were assessed for their cognitive functioning and readiness to learn using the Wechsler Preschool and Primary Scales of Intelligence–Revised. The quality of the mother–child relationship was rated using the Parent-Infant Relationship Assessment Scale (PIRGAS) (Zero to Three, 1994) on the basis of the assessor's observations of mother-child interaction; and the child's symptoms were elicited from the mother using the Child Behavior Checklist (Achenbach, 1991). These measures have robust psychometric properties, and they assess critical areas of functioning known to be affected by trauma.

Consistent with reports that domestic violence often gets transmitted across generations and co-occurs with child maltreatment and community violence (Kitzman et al., 2003), the mothers sampled had experienced many traumatic stressors in their lifetimes in addition to domestic violence: 51% reported that they witnessed domestic violence in their families of origin, 36% reported childhood physical abuse, and 36% reported sexual molestation or rape before age 16. Their adult lives also showed a high frequency of interpersonal violence and loss, with 56% reporting the traumatic death of someone close to them, 36% reporting coerced intercourse, and 37% reporting having been robbed or mugged.

Not surprising, initial assessment showed that both mothers and children were quite distressed and that this distress manifested itself across domains. Children's performance on the WPPSI was below the norm on the full scale (mean IQ = 92), verbal scale (mean IQ = 90), and performance scale (mean IQ = 97). Fifty-four percent of the mothers met full diagnostic criteria for posttraumatic stress disorder. The mean PIRGAS score for quality of the mother-child relationship was 44, which, according to the scoring criteria, ranks as "disturbed" and placing the dyad at "significant risk for dysfunction."

The assessments following 1 year of weekly treatment indicated substantial improvements. Children's IQ scores improved significantly in the performance ($p < .001$), verbal ($p < .05$), and total ($p < .001$) scales. There was also a statistically significant decrease in children's total behavioral problem scores ($p < .01$). The percentage of mothers who met criteria for PTSD diagnosis declined to 23%, with significant decreases in the frequency and intensity of re-experiencing ($p < .001$), avoidance ($p < .05$), and arousal symptoms ($p < .01$). Finally, the quality of the mother–child relationship improved by 18 points ($p < .01$), to become "strained in some way but still largely adequate and satisfying to the partners" according to the PIRGAS criteria.

CPP was developed at CTRP before the ETTN was formed. With the formation of the ETTN, because CPP is such a promising modality, CTRP proposed that clinicians at all ETTN sites be trained to deliver it and that the ETTN sites gather data to determine whether CPP is effective to treat children and parents from the diverse populations that they serve. Because all of the sites have clinicians with experience treating young children and an abiding belief in the central place that relationships hold in the healing of traumatized children, the ETTN seemed to be a natural venue to further test CPP. Since 2004, 97 children from birth to age 6 (42% girls and 53% boys) have been treated at the ETTN sites using CPP. The children are ethnically diverse (36% Latino, 28% African

American, 21% mixed race, 13% European-American, and 2% Asian-American), and 25% of the children or their mothers are monolingual Spanish speakers. The children have also experienced a wide variety of traumas. Sixty-nine percent have been exposed to domestic violence, and 9% have been exposed to violent incidents in their communities. A number of them have been exposed to child abuse and neglect: 18% physical abuse, 15% neglect, and 12% sexual abuse. Thirteen percent have experienced the death of someone close to them, and 26% have been separated from their primary caregivers at some point in their lives.

Because many of these children are still in treatment, outcome data is not yet available. The ETTN, in line with its belief in the importance of relationships in the healing of young children, will continue to treat them and their caregivers using CPP.

The Child Witness to Violence Project

The Child Witness to Violence Project (CWVP) opened its doors in 1992. Its roots extend deep into pediatrics and child care. Betsy McAlister Groves, the Director of CWVP, was the clinical director of the Family Development Center, a child care center at Boston Medical Center, when two cataclysmic events opened her eyes to the particular needs of very young children who witness violent events. First, a busload of children being taken home from the center at the end of the day witnessed a bleeding and injured man being pursued by his attacker who was armed with a knife. The injured man collapsed in front of the bus, and his assailant escaped. Second, the mother of two young children enrolled in the center was murdered in her home, in front of her children, by burglars (Groves, 2002). These two events inspired the teachers at the center to struggle with the best way to deal with the children's fears and questions in a classroom setting. They also inspired a study of families with children younger than 6 who used the pediatric services at Boston Medical Center. Mothers of young children were approached in the waiting room. If they agreed to participate in the study, they completed a questionnaire and were interviewed about their children's exposure to violence. In all, 115 mothers agreed to take part; the average age of their children was 2.7 years. Forty-seven percent of the mothers said that their children had heard gunshots, with 94 of these mothers reporting more than one episode. Ten percent of the children had directly witnessed an assault with a knife or gun, and nearly 20% had witnessed an episode of hitting, kicking, or shoving (Groves, Zuckerman, Marans, & Cohen, 1993).

From the beginning, CWVP was a collaboration between mental health and pediatrics: Its co-founders are a clinical social worker and a pediatrician. It is housed in the Pediatrics Department of the Boston Medical Center. One of its early projects was the creation of a curriculum to help early childhood educators cope with the classroom needs of violence-exposed children (Boyle, Groves, Bernard, Thompson, & Tittnich, 1998). A central tenet of CWVP has been that mental health counseling is but one service that traumatized children need to help them heal and to heal completely children need support from all of their relationships. Helping pediatricians learn to screen for the impact of violence and to talk to traumatized young children and their parents as well as helping child care providers and early childhood educators listen to and support traumatized children in their classrooms is as critical to CWVP's mission as is the direct provision of mental health services.

CWVP has extended its reach to other disciplines in its annual summer training institutes. Co-sponsored by CWVP and the Massachusetts Attorney General's Office, the institutes have reached police officers and other first responders, child welfare workers, mental health providers, educators, and medical providers. The institutes articulate five basic principles of support for young children traumatized by exposure to violence (Groves & Gannon, 2000, p. 36):

- Healing begins with relationships.
- No matter what our role is, we must do what we can to stabilize environments for children and families and to provide safety and security for them.
- In general, the best way to help children is to help their parents.
- We cannot do this work alone. We must create effective partnerships with other systems.
- We must learn to be comfortable with the limits of our professions.

Although these principles were first articulated by CWVP, they, together with a belief in the importance of good supervision and peer support and in the importance of examining our own attitudes toward violence as we seek to understand and inform the attitudes of others, are core beliefs of the ETTN and of all of the agencies that comprise it (Groves et al., 2000).

The Infant Team at the Tulane University Medical Center

The Infant Team at the Tulane University Medical Center is a multidisciplinary team that works intensely with infants in the child welfare system and their families, both biological and foster. The Infant Team is located in the Institute of Infant and Early Childhood Mental Health at Tulane University. It is made up of mental health professionals, developmental psychologists, pediatricians, and paraprofessionals, all of whom have expertise in early childhood development. The Infant Team's mandate is to assess infants taken into foster care and their families and to recommend requirements for the safe reunification of the children with their biological parents. In performing its assessments, the Team works with a variety of specialty care providers, public agencies, child care and Early Head Start centers, and treatment providers (Larrieu, 2002).

The Infant Team has developed an assessment protocol that allows it to understand the strengths and vulnerabilities in the parent–child relationship and to understand the multiple stressors that each child and family faces. Most families with which the Infant Team works have endured multiple chronic stressors including poverty, unemployment, lack of education, parental histories of child maltreatment, parental depression and PTSD, histories of substance abuse, and involvement in violent relationships and communities (Bellow & Larrieu, 2004; Larrieu & Zeanah, 1998). The initial assessment investigates the family's cultural and childrearing values as well as the stressors that impinge upon it but focuses particularly on the parent-child relationship. The Infant Team looks at the following domains of parent–child interaction as critical to understanding how the relationship functions and what the treatment goals for the relationship should be (Bellow & Larrieu, 2004):

- How emotionally available is the parent? How capable is the child of regulating the expression of affect? Can the parent help the child modulate affect?

- Is the parent nurturing, empathic, and contingently responsive to the child? Does the child behave in a secure, trusting way toward the parent?

- Can the child rely upon the parent for protection, or does he or she seem vigilant and on guard or overly preoccupied with self-protection or with protecting the parent?

- Is the parent able to provide comfort when the child needs it? Does the child approach the parent for comfort?

- Does the parent encourage and support the child in exploring and learning from the environment? Does the child demonstrate curiosity about the world and a desire to master the environment?

- Can the parent and child play together? Does the parent support the child's imaginative play?

- Does the parent set limits on the child's behavior? Is the child developing the capacity for self-control and cooperation with the parent's wishes?

- Does the parent provide the child with the structure and routine in daily living that allows the child to make reasonable predictions about the world?

Its careful attention to the parent–child relationship and to the complexities of the family's life allows the Infant Team to establish an empathic and supportive relationship with the biological parents. Without such a relationship, the Infant Team could not carry out the second vital part of its mandate: to give collaborative feedback to the child's biological family and to provide treatment that will help the biological parents reach their reunification goals (Larrieu, 2002). Parents whose children have been removed and placed in foster care can be expected to be angry, suspicious, and defensive. The Infant Team's mandate requires it to assess, recommend, and treat, which is an enormous task with such challenging families. In carrying out its complicated mandate, the Infant Team demonstrates the ETTN's belief that relationships are the source of healing. It uses its healing relationship with the biological parents to model the quality of relationship that it hopes the parents will be able to form with the child.

The Early Trauma Treatment Program at Louisiana State University Health Sciences Center

The Early Trauma Treatment Program at Louisiana State University Health Sciences Center is the early childhood program within the Violence Intervention Program (VIP) for children and families. VIP was developed in 1992 in response to the sharp increase in violence in New Orleans and to the growing awareness that more and more children were being exposed to violence, either as victims or as witnesses, and an early childhood focus within VIP, the Early Trauma Treatment Program, inherited the philosophy of broad-based community collaboration that is VIP's hallmark. VIP's approach to violence reduction and amelioration is systemic: It works with the whole community, and in particular with parent groups, police, mental health professionals, and schools to help solve the problems of youth violence and of violence that affects children. VIP also works at several levels of prevention and intervention, including campaigns to raise public awareness of the problems of violence, education and training of stakeholders, consultation and referral, and provision of direct services (Osofsky, 2000; Osofsky, Hammer, Freeman, & Rovaris, 2004).

Because of its philosophy that early referral and intervention can greatly ameliorate the impact of trauma on young children, VIP has developed a close collaboration with the New Orleans Police Department. This collaboration has included cross-training, the establishment of a hotline that police officers or family members can use to call for consultation and referrals, patrol ride-alongs, and stress reduction groups for police officers (Osofsky et al., 2004). In keeping with the philosophy that a helping professional, regardless of his or her role, should stabilize environments for children and families and provide safety and security for them, VIP's training for police officers goes beyond recognizing symptoms in children, using the hotline, and making referrals: It emphasizes the unique opportunity that police officers, as first responders, have to calm and support children and offer them information after establishing order at the scene. VIP has learned that a few words of concern from a police officer at the scene can make a difference in restoring a sense of calm to a traumatized child.

VIP has extended its collaborative reach well beyond New Orleans. In a unique collaboration with Cindy Lederman, a juvenile dependency court judge in Miami, Florida, VIP's director, Joy D. Osofsky, helped conceptualize and organize a service court for infants in the dependency system. A mental health professional is available on site at the court to perform developmental and parent–child relationship assessments for every infant and young child whose case comes to the court. Information from the assessment is available to the judge to help her craft appropriate orders for reunification. Dyadic psychotherapy (Fraiberg et al., 1980) is available for some mother–child dyads, and using funds from a Safe Start grant from the Office of Juvenile Justice and Delinquency Prevention, the court and its consultants have formed a Head Start classroom designed specifically to meet the needs of foster children (Lederman & Osofsky, 2004; Osofsky & Lederman, 2004).

Although police officers and judges are not typically thought of as part of the network of relationships that sustains young children, children who have suffered traumas (e.g., witnessing domestic or community violence, suffering physical or sexual abuse) are likely to come into contact with these systems at times when the children are especially vulnerable. As they interact with the child and family shortly after the trauma, judges and police officers have an opportunity to help restore order to the lives of traumatized children and to begin the healing process. VIP has maximized this opportunity through its collaborative work with police officers and the courts.

CONCLUSION

CPP is based on the deep conviction that young children's mental health and sound development are best assured when parents are empathic, flexible, supportive, and joyful in their interactions with their children. The helplessness and horror that accompany trauma can undermine a parent's trust in his or her own sense of what is safe in the world and in relationships. It can make both parent and child rigid and defended in their interactions with one another. CPP uses the parent–child relationship to restore to each partner the ability to trust in bodily sensations, to express seemingly unmanageable emotions in words and play, and to understand and collaborate with one another's agendas.

The child-parent psychotherapist understands, however, that in an environment of continuing fear and distrust, the parent–child relationship cannot be effectively restored. Intervention in all of the systems in which parents and children are embedded, of the sort practiced by all of the ETTN partners, is crucial so that the parents can feel secure in taking their place as their children's protectors, teachers, and guides in the complex enterprise of development.

Working together, the agencies that make up the ETTN have come much closer to the goal of assuring that clinicians, child care providers, police officers, and courts understand the complex needs of traumatized young children than we could possibly have come working alone. The ETTN has created a preliminary assessment protocol, described by Bosquet (2004). Providers are delivering CPP in all four ETTN sites to children from a variety of cultural and caregiving environments who have experienced many different kinds of traumas. We have developed a three-phase training protocol to teach clinicians about the assessment and treatment of traumatized young children and have piloted it in several NCTSN sites. We have received funding[2] to develop guidelines that will help preschool teachers and child care providers work more effectively with the traumatized children that they encounter in their classrooms. Most powerfully, we have learned from one another and supported one another in the difficult and sometimes painful work of intervening with traumatized infants, toddlers, and preschoolers. Our reliance on our own relationships as we do this work reminds us every day of the importance of relationships in the lives of the children and families we serve.

REFERENCES

Achenbach, T.M. (1991). *Manual for the Child Behavior Checklist 4-18 and 1991 Profile.* Burlington: University of Vermont Department of Psychiatry.

Bellow, S.M., & Larrieu, J.A. (2004). Relationship assessment for young traumatized children. In J.D. Osofsky (Ed.), *Young children and trauma: Intervention and treatment* (pp. 155–172). New York: Guilford Press.

Blake, D.D., Weathers, F., Nagy, L., Kaloupek, D.G., Klauminzer, G., Charney, D., et al. (1990). Clinician-administered PTSD scale. *The Behavior Therapist, 18,* 12–14.

Bosquet, M. (2004). How research informs clinical work. In J.D. Osofsky (Ed.), *Young children and trauma: Intervention and treatment* (pp. 301–325). New York: Guilford Press.

Boyle, E., Groves, B.M., Bernard, A., Thompson, A., & Tittnich, E. (1998). *The Safe Havens training project: Helping teachers and child care providers support children and families who witness violence in their communities.* Pittsburgh, PA: Family Communications, Inc.

Cohen, N.J., Muir, E., Lojkasek, M., Muir, R., Parker, C.J., Barwick, M., et al. (1999). Watch, wait, and wonder: Testing the effectiveness of a new approach of mother-infant psychotherapy. *Infant Mental Health Journal, 20,* 429–451.

Drell, M.J., Siegel, C.H., & Gaensbauer, T.J. (1993). Post-traumatic stress disorders. In C. Zeanah (Ed.), *Handbook of infant mental health* (pp. 291–304). New York: Guilford Press.

Fraiberg, S., Adelson, E., & Shapiro, V. (1980). Ghosts in the nursery: A psychoanalytic approach to the problem of impaired infant-mother relationships. *Journal of the American Academy of Child Psychiatry, 14,* 387–342.

Groves, B.M. (2002). *Children who see too much.* Boston: Beacon Press.

[2]We gratefully acknowledge the generosity of the Mailman Foundation in making possible the development of these guidelines.

Groves, B.M., & Gannon, J. (2000). Building community capacity to protect young children and families: The Massachusetts Child Witness to Domestic Violence Project. In J.D. Osofsky & E. Fenichel (Eds.), *Protecting young children in violent environments: Building staff and community strengths* (pp. 34–41). Washington, DC: Zero to Three.

Groves, B.M., Lieberman, A.F., Osofsky, J.D., & Fenichel, E. (2000). Protecting young children in violent environments: A framework to build on. In J.D. Osofsky & E. Fenichel (Eds.), *Protecting young children in violent environments: Building staff and community strengths* (pp. 9–13). Washington, DC: Zero to Three.

Groves, B.M., Zuckerman, B., Marans, S., & Cohen, D. (1993). Silent victims: Children who witness violence. *Journal of the American Medical Association, 269,* 262–264.

Heinicke, C.M., Fineman, N.R., Ponce, V.A., & Guthrie, D. (2001). Relation-based intervention with at-risk mothers: Outcome in the second year of life. *Infant Mental Health Journal, 22,* 431–462.

Kitzman, K., Gaylord, N., Holt, A., & Kenny, E. (2003). Child witnesses to domestic violence: a meta-analytic review. *Journal of Consulting and Clinical Psychology, 71,* 339–352.

Klapper, S.A., Plummer, N.S. & Harmon, R.J. (2004). Diagnostic and treatment issues in cases of childhood trauma. In J.D. Osofsky (Ed.), *Young children and trauma: Intervention and treatment* (pp. 139–154). New York: Guilford Press.

Larrieu, J.A. (2002). Treating infant-parent relationships in the context of maltreatment: Repairing ruptures of trust. *Zero to Three, 22*(5), 16–22.

Larrieu, J.A., & Zeanah, C.H. (1998). Intensive intervention for maltreated infants and toddlers in foster care. *Child and Adolescent Psychiatric Clinics of North America, 7*(2), 357–371.

Lederman, C., & Osofsky, J.D. (2004). Infant mental health interventions in juvenile court: Ameliorating the effects of maltreatment and deprivation. *Psychology, Public Policy, and the Law, 10*(1), 162–177.

Lewis, M.I., & Ghosh Ippen, C. (2004). Rainbows of tears, souls full of hope: Cultural issues related to young children and trauma. In J.D. Osofsky (Ed.), *Young children and trauma: Intervention and treatment* (pp. 11–46). New York: Guilford Press.

Lieberman, A.F. (1999). The trials and rewards of being a clinical consultant to child protective services. *Zero to Three, 19*(3), 14–18.

Lieberman, A.F. (2000). Using a mental health perspective to educate and support community partners. In J.D. Osofsky & E. Fenichel (Eds.), *Protecting young children in violent environments: Building staff and community strengths* (pp. 27–28). Washington, DC: Zero to Three.

Lieberman, A.F. (2004). Child-parent psychotherapy: A relationship-based approach to the treatment of mental health disorders in infancy and early childhood. In A.J. Sameroff, S.C. McDonough, & K.L. Rosenblum (Eds.), *Treating parent-infant relationship problems* (pp. 97–122). New York: Guilford Press.

Lieberman, A.F., & Pawl, J.H. (1993). Infant-parent psychotherapy. In C.H. Zeanah (Ed.), *Handbook of infant mental health* (pp. 427–442). New York: Guilford Press.

Lieberman, A.F., Silverman, R., & Pawl, J.H. (2000). Infant-parent psychotherapy: Core concepts and current approaches. In C.H. Zeanah (Ed.), *Handbook of infant mental health* (2nd ed., pp. 472–484). New York: Guilford Press.

Lieberman, A.F., & Van Horn, P. (1998). Attachment, trauma, and domestic violence: Implications for child custody. *Child and Adolescent Psychiatric Clinics of North America, 7,* 423–444.

Lieberman, A.F., & Van Horn, P. (in press). *"Don't hit my mommy!": A manual for child-parent psychotherapy with young witnesses of family violence.* Washington, DC: Zero to Three Press.

Marans, S., & Adelman, A. (1997). Experiencing violence in a developmental context. In J.D. Osofsky (Ed.), *Children in a violent society* (pp. 202-222). New York: Guilford Press.

Marmar, C., Foy, D., Kagan, B., & Pynoos, R.S. (1993). An integrated approach for treating posttraumatic stress. In J.M. Oldman & A. Talman (Eds.), *American Psychiatric Association review of psychiatry* (Vol. 12, pp. 238–272). Washington, DC: American Psychiatric Press.

McDonough, S. (2000). Interaction guidance: An approach for difficult-to-engage families. In C.H. Zeanah (Ed.), *Handbook of infant mental health* (2nd ed., pp. 485–493). New York: Guilford Press.

McDonough, S. (2004). Interaction guidance: Promoting and nurturing the caregiving relationship. In A.J. Sameroff, S.C. Mc Donough, & K.L. Rosenblum (Eds.), *Treating parent-infant relationship problems* (pp. 79–96). New York: Guilford Press.

Muir, E., Lojkasek, M., & Cohen, N.J. (1999). *Watch, wait, wonder: A manual describing a dyadic infant-led approach to problems in infancy and early childhood.* Toronto, Ontario: Hincks-Dellcrest Institute.

Osofsky, J.D. (1995). The effects of exposure to violence on young children. *American Psychologist, 50,* 782–788.

Osofsky, J.D. (2000). The Violence Intervention Program for Children and Families: New Orleans, Lousiana. In J.D. Osofsky & E. Fenichel (Eds.), *Protecting young children in violent environments: Building staff and community strengths* (p.7). Washington, DC: Zero to Three/National Center for Clinical Infant Programs.

Osofsky, J.D. (Ed). (2004) *Young children and trauma: Intervention and treatment.* New York: Guilford Press.

Osofsky, J.D., Hammer, J.H., Freeman, N., & Rovaris, J.M. (2004). How law enforcement and mental health professionals can partner to heal traumatized children. In J.D. Osofsky (Ed.), *Young children and trauma: Intervention and treatment* (pp. 285–298). New York: Guilford Press.

Osofsky, J.D., & Lederman, C. (2004). Healing the child in juvenile court. In J.D. Osofsky (Ed.), *Young children and trauma: Intervention and treatment* (pp. 221–232). New York: Guilford Press.

Pawl, J.H., & St. John, M. (1998). *How you are is as important as what you do.* Washington, DC: Zero to Three/National Center for Clinical Infant Programs.

Pynoos, R.S., Steinberg, A.M., & Piacentini, J.C. (1999). A developmental psychopathology model of childhood traumatic stress and intersection with anxiety disorders. *Biological Psychiatry, 46,* 1542–1554.

Van der Kolk, B.A. (1994). The body keeps the score: Memory and the evolving psychobiology of posttraumatic stress. *Harvard Review of Psychiatry, 1,* 253–265.

Van Horn, P., & Hitchens, D.J. (2004). Partnerships for young children in court: How judges shape collaborations serving traumatized children. In J.D. Osofsky (Ed.), *Young children and trauma: Intervention and treatment* (pp. 242–259). New York: Guilford Press.

Wolfe, J.W., Kimerling, R., Brown, P.J., Chrestman, K.R., & Levin, K. (1996). Psychometric review of The Life Stressor Checklist-Revised. In B.H. Stamm (Ed.), *Measurement of stress, trauma, and adaptation.* Lutherville, MD: Sidran Press.

Zeanah, C., & Scheeringa, M. (1996). Evaluation of posttraumatic symptomatology in infants and young children exposed to violence. In J.D. Osofsky & E. Fenichel (Eds.), *Islands of safety: Assessing and treating young victims of violence* (pp. 9–14). Washington, DC: Zero to Three.

Zero to Three: National Center for Clinical Infant Programs (1994). *Diagnostic Classification: 0-3. Diagnostic Classification of Mental Health and Developmental Disorders of Infancy and Early Childhood.* Washington, DC: Author.

5

INTERVENTIONS AND PROMISING APPROACHES FOR CHILDREN EXPOSED TO DOMESTIC VIOLENCE

Betsy McAlister Groves and Abigail Gewirtz

As domestic violence has become a widely acknowledged social and public health problem, there has been increasing recognition of the particular risks for the children who are affected. Since the 1990s, a large body of research has accumulated on the effects of children's exposure to domestic violence (see Chapter 1). Programs to respond to children's needs have been established across the country in a variety of settings, including courts, health/mental health settings, shelters, police departments, and schools. This chapter considers the goals for intervention and proposes core principles for good practice with children. It highlights the most common settings in which interventions occur, discussing important elements of programming in each setting. It distinguishes between evidence-based programs developed for children exposed to violence (those few programs for which there is strong empirical support) and promising approaches developed for these children (a larger group of programs, in a variety of contexts, which show promise for addressing children's and families' different needs).

CHILDREN'S EXPOSURE TO DOMESTIC VIOLENCE: A HISTORICAL OVERVIEW

In order to appreciate the progress that has been made in recognizing the needs of children exposed to domestic violence, it is important to consider both the historical and political contexts. The growth in programming for children can be attributed both to the substantial research about the effects of trauma on children and the evolution of the battered women's movement.

History of the
Battered Women's Movement

The recognition of children's issues is intertwined with the history of the battered women's movement and a sometimes uneasy tension between women's issues and children's needs. The first battered women's shelters in the United States opened in the mid-1970s. The National Coalition against Domestic Violence was formally organized in January 1978 with a meeting of 100 battered women's advocates from all parts of the nation. The Child Advocacy Task Force of the National Coalition against Domestic Violence was established in 1982, with its mission "To provide a voice for children/youth within the battered women's movement; to promote the value of children's/youth's experiences; to work toward empowerment of children/youth and those who care for them; and to challenge the battered women's movement in its accountability to children/youth and their advocates" (Schechter, 1981). This mission statement seems to imply that the battered women's movement did not see itself as including children and youth.

According to early activists, the movement struggled over whether to assume that women should be independently responsible for their children (and thus outside of the scope of service provision for shelters) or whether to directly assist them with their children (E. Roberts, personal communication, September, 1999; Schechter & Edleson, 1999). This debate reflected one of the central questions the larger feminist movement sought to address: How can women define their identities as separate from those of wife, mother, or homemaker? As shelters sprang up across the country, questions about children's services emerged. There were heated arguments about whether to offer parenting groups in shelters. Was this an assumption that these women were bad mothers? Was this not another form of victim blaming? Shouldn't the focus be on helping the woman to be safe and to understand that she does not deserve to be hurt and terrorized? Where do children fit into the picture?

This reluctance to recognize the needs of women as mothers extended to programming. Few shelters had children's programs. There were no budgets for toys or supplies and no designated spaces for children. This stemmed in part from the pressure of limited resources. Advocates had fought hard for the gains they made in setting up shelters, and most operated on shoestring budgets. The reluctance to divert money to children's programming was understandable both from practical and political standpoints. The tension between women's and children's needs was also influenced by the failures of two larger systems to respond to the unique and pressing needs of women and children who were victims of violence: child protection services and the mental health system.

Battered Women and the Child Protection System

In most states, the rise of the state-mandated child protection system in the late 1960s and 1970s paralleled the rise of the shelter movement for battered women. Many advocates distrusted and resented this system with its mandatory reporting requirements. Children's advocates sometimes saw signs of child abuse or of harsh parenting in the shelters. However, many advocates had no training about how to appropriately identify or respond to child abuse or neglect, and they were reluctant to involve the child protection system. There was deep concern about how this system would respond. Acknowledging child abuse at the hands of the perpetrators was not difficult. However, to view women as perpetrators of child abuse was a troubling and controversial issue. There were strong concerns about blaming the victims for their failure to protect their children and revictimizing the mothers by accusing them or by removing their children. Vestiges of the tension between the needs and rights of battered women and issues related to children's safety are still evident and perhaps best exemplified in the 1998 lawsuit brought against New York City's child protection agency on behalf of battered women. This suit alleged that the city's child protection agency engaged in unjustified removal of children from their mothers' custody, solely because the mothers had been victims of domestic violence (Sengupta, 2000). This case was heard on appeal in Federal District Court in 2001, ruling in favor of the women and directing reforms within the New York City's child protection system.

Battered Women and the Mental Health System

Battered women's advocates also struggled with the mental health system, which was notoriously slow to recognize the existence or the prevalence of domestic violence. Women were treated, hospitalized, and medicated, without apparent regard for the existence of violence in their lives (Carmen, Rieker, & Mills, 1984). The majority of psychiatrists and psychologists were men, and the advocacy community saw this established mental health system as a patriarchal system that should be avoided if possible because it was not responsive to the perspectives of women. In addition, there was much less recognition of the impact of trauma on children, particularly young children. The diagnosis of posttraumatic stress disorder (PTSD) was not thought to be relevant for children and was not found in the diagnostic nomenclature for children. Their responses to terror were thought to be more transitory and short lived and therefore not appropriate for such a diagnosis. There was even less awareness that very young children could be affected by violent events in their environments.

Recognition of the Impact of Trauma on Children

Children of Battered Women was the first book devoted to this topic (Jaffe, Wolfe, & Wilson, 1990). In their preface, the authors noted that although there was a growing body of research on domestic violence and its effects on women, few researchers had considered the impact of wife abuse on children. They then wrote about their clinical experiences in London, Ontario. This book made an important contribution to the field by focusing interest on child witnesses in a scholarly way, and also, perhaps more importantly, by writing about the issue in a way that did not blame mothers. The authors wrote thoughtfully about the role of trauma in women's lives and about how to work with women and children in ways that acknowledged and supported mothers.

A 1999 review of research on this topic cites more than 100 articles that were published in the previous decade (Edleson, 1999). Extensive research demonstrates very young children's vulnerability to trauma in their environments. Infants are remarkably aware of and shaped by their early environments, and even very young children show symptoms associated with PTSD (Perry, 1997; Scheerenga & Zeanah, 1995).

As the prevalence of domestic violence has been better documented and as research has well established the risks of trauma to children, particularly young children, programmatic interventions for children affected by domestic violence have multiplied. In 1998, following a national survey, the National Council of Juvenile and Family Court Judges published a guide, *Emerging Programs for Battered Women and their Children,* that described the best programs in the country. These programs existed in a number of settings, had different goals, and operated with a range of professionals (National Council of Juvenile and Family Court Judges, 1998).

INTERVENTION WITH CHILDREN EXPOSED TO DOMESTIC VIOLENCE: PROGRAMMATIC GOALS

Programs for children affected by domestic violence now exist in a variety of settings, with varied services, staffing patterns, and budgets. These programs generally serve one or more of the following goals: identifying children at risk, increasing safety and protection of children and families, and/or providing therapeutic intervention for a range of behavioral and emotional problems associated with children's exposure to violence.

Identifying Children at Risk

Estimates of the number of children exposed to domestic violence vary widely, depending on the sampling method and definition of domestic violence. In one study of young children's exposure to violence, it was estimated that 28% of children had witnessed moderate to severe violence by the age of 6. Half of the parents reported that their children had seen violence in the home (Taylor, Harik, Zuckerman, & Groves, 1994). Although there is general consensus as to the importance of early identification of these children, this goal presents a challenge because children may not be physically harmed and their symptoms are rarely obvious (Groves, Zuckerman, Marans, & Cohen, 1993).

Courts, schools, police departments, child protection services, and child and family health settings have struggled to improve their capacities to identify children at risk. Of these settings, child health agencies and schools are the most likely settings for comprehensive screening of children. All families pass through these systems at various points throughout their children's lives, and thus, these systems offer an important potential avenue for identifying children at risk. However, there may be unintended negative consequences for the implementation of comprehensive screening for exposure to domestic violence in these settings. In school settings, confidentiality may not be guaranteed; parents may be particularly reluctant to disclose family trouble for fear of being negatively judged or becoming involved with the child protection system. Health settings may offer more privacy and greater comfort to parents who wish to disclose family violence. Such inquiry belongs within the scope of child health, and parents are generally not offended if a provider asks (Zink, 2000). However, there are obstacles to screening in health settings, including lack of time, lack of resources for services, and inadequate training of medical staff (Groves, Augustyn, Lee, & Sawires, 2002). Some efforts are being made to implement screening in pediatric health settings.

Increasing Safety and Protection of Children

It can be argued that children affected by domestic violence need safety, and until they and their caregivers are safe, it is difficult to address their longer-term mental health problems. A primary goal of shelters, courts, child protection services, and police departments is to address this basic goal of safety. Many shelters have expanded their services to include children's advocates, implement screening and assessment protocols for children, and offer legal advocacy that includes children's needs. Many police departments have instituted training to increase officers' awareness of children's needs. Police, who are first on the scene of many domestic calls, are in a unique position to identify children and make referrals for services.

Courts have also become more responsive to children, both by offering programs specifically for victims and their children and by offering legal remedies designed to increase safety. The most widely used remedy is the protective or restraining order available to victims of intimate partner violence. However, some states have also implemented enhanced penalties for the commission of violent acts in front of children and custody/visitation guidelines that make it more difficult for an abuser to have unsupervised access to his children. Court systems in several states have improved the coordination of court responses to domestic violence by unifying civil, criminal, and family court proceedings for families involved with domestic violence. By coordinating the different court proceedings and improving the communication between branches of the court, safety considerations for families are more expediently addressed (Lemon, 1999).

Child protection services by mandate have the safety of children as their primary mission. They play an important (and at times controversial) role in determining when children are at risk and directly intervening to protect children. The most effective child protection interventions are those that strive to maintain a mother's safety in pursuit of their primary goal of child safety.

Providing Therapeutic Intervention

As awareness of the impact of domestic violence on children's emotional, social, and cognitive development has grown, there has also been an increase in the number of therapeutic intervention services for these children. These services may exist in shelters, mental health agencies, or hospitals or as community-based programs. In general, these interventions strive to alleviate trauma-related symptoms in children and address the associated behavior problems that arise. Because children may be affected in a range of ways and some children appear to be more vulnerable than others, therapeutic programs are challenged to develop sensitive assessment protocols and interventions that build on the child's and family's strengths (Silvern, Karyl, & Landis, 1995). Many programs recognize that an essential element to stabilizing children is assisting the non-abusing parent (Groves, Roberts, & Weinreb, 2000). The parent may be transitioning to single parenting and/or may have had her parenting undermined by the batterer's controlling and abusive behavior. Assistance may include assessing and treating the parent for trauma or other psychological distress, providing advocacy and case management services, and/or improving parenting skills and parent understanding of the impact of domestic violence on children. Similarly, learning parenting skills might be an important treatment goal for a father who has completed batterer treatment and who continues to be involved or becomes re-engaged in his child's life (Fleck-Henderson & Arean, 2004).

GUIDING PRINCIPLES FOR INTERVENTION WITH CHILDREN EXPOSED TO DOMESTIC VIOLENCE

In this chapter, we propose four essential principles for intervention with children, regardless of the setting or primary intervention goal. These principles are implicit, if not explicit, in the interventions and promising approaches described later in this chapter. They have evolved, in part, through the recognition that, in this field, integrative work is essential in order to address the diverse needs of children and families who are in contact with so many different systems. These principles are also consistent with developmental systems theory (Ford & Lerner, 1992) and ecological theories (e.g., Bronfenbrenner, 1992), as well as a resilience framework (Masten & Coatsworth, 1998; Yates & Masten, 2004). This section discusses these principles and provides brief examples of best practices in different settings.

Interventions should be conceptualized within an ecological framework, considering the child and family in the context of the other systems that affect the family.

Children do not live in a vacuum; and any intervention will also affect the child's family and other support systems. Therefore, interventions should be conceived with multiple systems in mind. Children attend schools and have health providers. They may have active court cases or be involved with the child protection sytem. Ideally, an intervener is aware of these systems and is skilled at using resources from them. For example, if a child is being evaluated at a mental health clinic for behavioral problems associated with exposure to domestic violence, the clinician should actively work with the school and perhaps the health provider to make sure that there is a common understanding of the behavior problems and a mutually agreed-upon approach to working with the problems. If a health provider identifies domestic violence as an issue within the family, it is crucial to ask the parent about previous attempts to get help. Knowledge of a parent's use of law enforcement, the legal system, and community supports will help the provider make a better decision about referral and support. Families are best helped when service providers collaborate with each other in an attempt to provide complementary services.

The active involvement of the non-abusing parent, usually the mother, is an essential component of intervention with a child.

Strengthening the parent–child relationship is ultimately the most potent and valuable intervention for the child (Lieberman & Van Horn, 1998). However, active engagement of the mother may be challenging because her acknowledgment of the impact of domestic violence on her children may produce intense shame and fear. Some mothers experience guilt about their failure to protect their children. They may fear that their children will be removed from their care or that authorities will judge them negatively as parents. Other mothers may deny or minimize the impact of violence on their children. The denial may be associated with shame, with the mother's trauma, or with a lack of knowledge about child development and child trauma. Interveners must keep in mind that a mother's experiences with trauma and her feelings of inadequacy shape her willingness to seek help and her readiness to give information and to enter into a therapeutic relationship. These dynamics affect a mother's comfort with disclosing domestic violence to her child's pediatrician, her willingness to have her child see a counselor, her ability to give her child permission to talk about the domestic violence, and her interactions with police. Regardless of the setting, interveners should engage the mother in a respectful partnership, communicating either directly or indirectly that the mother's role is essential in helping her child, that she has special knowledge about her child, and that her aspirations for her child are important.

In some settings, such as courts and law enforcement, attempting to provide safety for the mother is the best way to help a child. Children, especially young children, depend on their parents for physical and emotional safety and protection. If a parent is unsafe, the child is vulnerable. Research on young children has shown that their subjective appraisal of the vulnerability of their caregivers is strongly associated with their level of trauma. In fact, one study of children ages 4 and younger demonstrated that a child's perception of the threat to his or her caregiver was a stronger risk factor for the development of PTSD than was his or her history of direct abuse (Lyons, 1987; Scheerenga & Zeanah, 1995). Children must be able to trust that their parents are reliable protectors. Regardless of setting, interveners must acknowledge the primacy of the parental role and the potential impact of the domestic violence on a mother's functioning and self-image, as well as the importance of advocacy in order to increase safety for the mother and child.

Interventions should aim to reduce risk and promote resilience in children, using approaches that are flexible and tailored to meet the contextual (cultural and community) needs of families.

A significant body of research investigates threats to children's development (risk factors) and ways in which children may be protected from risk or the positive resources in children's lives (protective factors and assets). The interplay between these factors within the child and between the child and his or her environment is dynamic and evolving. After several decades of study, much is known about both protective factors and child-related risk factors for disorder, development gone awry, and a variety of poor outcomes (Luthar, Cicchetti, & Becker, 2000; Masten & Gewirtz, in press).

Similarly, an increasing body of knowledge is developing about resilience, children's ability to function adequately despite significant adversity. Masten

(2001) suggested that resilience is "ordinary magic," more common than previously thought and a function of the remarkable human propensity to survive and thrive. The complex interplay between child and environment means that children may be vulnerable at some points and resilient at others. In the wake of crisis, we would not expect resilience from children exposed to domestic violence. However, there are clearly differences among children weeks and months after such an event; these differences are associated with the relevant risk and protective factors in a child's life.

Children are affected by domestic violence in different ways. Vulnerability may be associated with younger age, more severe and chronic violence, a concurrent history of child abuse or neglect, lack of support from caregivers, and a more difficult temperament.[1] Evidence from longitudinal studies suggests that there are common protective factors that support adaptive functioning in high-risk circumstances: intelligence, supportive and consistent parenting, and good extra-familial support (Werner & Smith, 1982). It seems reasonable to assume that these same factors are also protective for children exposed to domestic violence. Because of the variability of children's reactions, flexible strategies for assessing their needs are essential. Screening and assessment protocols must inquire about strengths, protective factors, and areas of competence in children and families. Children who appear resilient also need to be supported, even though they may not require specialized or continuing services. Likewise, vulnerable children may need extra support, clinical intervention, and an ongoing therapeutic relationship.

A family's culture also plays an important role in how it seeks and accepts help, how children's symptoms are understood, and how children make meaning out of the domestic violence they experience. For example, if a family's cultural experience or understanding of the role of police officers is shaped by experiences in other countries in which police are brutal, corrupt, or unresponsive, its comfort with seeking help from police in the United States may be limited. Children may be told not to talk about personal matters with anyone outside of the family. In some cultures, the practice of taking a child to talk with a counselor is unheard of. The recognition of trauma symptoms may also vary by culture. Interventions must be culturally sensitive. Depending on the culture, interventions may be more family focused and may include the abuser in the interventions.

---

[1]Difficult temperament is a standard term used to describe children who are slow to adapt to new experiences and who demonstrate intense negative emotional expressions. About 10% of infants can be classified as having a difficult temperament. For a review, see Chess and Thomas (1996). While difficult temperament is not in itself a diagnostic category (although it is included in the Zero to Three diagnostic classification system [National Center for Infant Study Programs, 1994]), it does represent a risk factor for children, particularly in combination with other contextual stressors such as exposure to violence.

**Interventions should be informed by an understanding
of child development, the developmental impact of
trauma on children, and the dynamics of domestic violence.**

Although the depth of expertise required in particular areas will vary according to
the professional and the program, all professionals who work with children affected by domestic violence need a basic knowledge of child development, child
trauma, and domestic violence. For example, it is important that a police officer
have some understanding of the impact of a child's age on his or her ability to report events or to understand what has happened. If a health provider is inquiring
about domestic violence, he or she should have a working knowledge of the dynamics of violence within a family, the obstacles that may exist to a parent disclosing the violence, and typical symptoms of child trauma. A mental health clinician
should have a thorough knowledge of the dynamics of domestic violence; otherwise the intervention may be ineffectual or may increase risk to a family member.

The most effective interventions for children are those that are informed by
child development, the impact of trauma, and domestic violence. This has implications for training and preparation for professionals who work with children and
families affected by domestic violence. It is rare that any professional would have
equal preparation in all areas. Mental health clinicians may be well versed in child
trauma but know less about domestic violence. Shelter advocates may have thorough knowledge of domestic violence, but know less about child development.
Resources for cross-training are thus essential.

PROMISING APPROACHES:
THERAPEUTIC INTERVENTIONS

Using these four principles as guidelines, we review current approaches in a variety of settings that provide services to children exposed to domestic violence. We
describe specific, innovative, and evidence-based programs that provide examples
of these principles. These programs do not reflect a comprehensive listing of innovative programs, but rather, were selected for one of two reasons: There is strong
empirical support for the effectiveness of the program, or the program represents
an innovative approach to working with children exposed to domestic violence. A
listing of contact information for each program is found in the chapter appendix.

Clinical/Trauma-Focused Interventions

Various authors have suggested that, to be effective, clinical interventions with
children and families affected by domestic violence must include both interven-

tions to address the trauma and intervening to improve access to concrete support for families (variably described as advocacy or case management). These may include addressing issues related to transportation, housing, finances, and the legal system. This is particularly true for families in shelters who universally face many challenges beyond exposure to domestic violence. Hence, although the focus of the interventions listed below is clinical, aiming for the amelioration of behavioral and emotional problems, it is recognized that for many families, a key component in their engagement in, and successful completion of, such services is the provision of supportive and concrete interventions.

The *Child Trauma Research Project (CTRP)* *CTRP* at San Francisco General Hospital has conducted research and provided clinical services since 1996 to children younger than the age of 6 who have been exposed to domestic violence or other interpersonal traumas. Children are referred by family courts, child welfare, advocacy programs for battered women, pediatricians, child care providers, and preschool teachers. Children are seen with their primary caregivers, most typically their mothers. Both mothers and children are offered intensive assessments before treatment begins. Mothers and children are seen together in child-parent psychotherapy, a theoretically based, multi-modal approach that focuses on restoring children to positive developmental trajectories by intervening to improve their relationships with their caregivers (see Chapter 4). The intervention also includes parent support, developmental guidance, and advocacy. The intervention has been manualized and is being used at three additional sites (see Chapter 4).

The *Child Witness to Violence Project (CWVP)* *CWVP* is located in the Department of Pediatrics at Boston Medical Center and provides outpatient counseling services to children ages 8 and younger (and their families) who have witnessed significant violence. Services are offered at no cost to the families. Approximately 80% of referrals are for children who have witnessed domestic violence. Families are referred to the project from courts, domestic violence shelters, health centers, early childhood programs, and schools. Approximately 25% of referrals come from victims of domestic violence who are concerned about their children. The project is staffed by mental health clinicians with training in early childhood development, trauma, and domestic violence. Children are usually evaluated with the non-offending parent and are seen in individual and/or dyadic treatment. Parents are always involved in the treatment; they are seen directly with the child or meet separately with the child's therapist. The general goal of intervention is to restore equilibrium for the child and family, to allow the child a safe place to talk about what has happened, to help the child gain a better perspective on the traumatic event, to help the parent better understand the child's behavior, and to equip the parent with strategies to help the child (Groves, 2002). The project uses an ecological model of intervention, working actively with the child's and family's network of caregivers (see Chapter 4).

Project SUPPORT   *Project SUPPORT*, developed by Jouriles and his colleagues (2001), is a targeted, home-based, rigorously evaluated intervention, designed to reduce behavior problems in children and enhance parenting effectiveness in battered mothers. This program recruits mothers leaving battered women's shelters, whose 4- to 9-year-old children meet criteria for oppositional defiant and/or conduct disorder. Participating families receive a thorough assessment of the child and the family, which provides direction for treatment goals. Services include weekly 1½-hour parenting coaching sessions with a therapist, advocacy (including concrete case management services), and mentoring for children. Services are provided in the home over an average of 8 months. Service providers are trained graduate students (therapists) and undergraduates (child mentors).

In Project SUPPORT's original efficacy study, families participated in an average of 23 sessions each. Participant mothers' child management skills were enhanced as a result of the program and children showed a more rapid decrease in behavior problems than control children (Jouriles et al., 2001).

Psychoeducational and
Supportive Group Interventions for Children

Arguably the most prevalent interventions for children of battered women are support groups for school-age children exposed to domestic violence. These have been documented in the literature with several manualized curricula available (e.g., End Violence Alliance, 2000; Peled & Davis, 1995; Peled & Edleson, 1995; Wilder Community Assistance Program, 1997). Few, however, have been rigorously evaluated.

The Kids Club   *The Kids Club* is a 10-week, empirically validated, group psychoeducational program for 5- to 13-year-old children of battered women (Graham-Bermann, 2001; Graham-Bermann & Hughes, 2003). The group aims to foster resilience and promote recovery from traumatic exposure to domestic violence. Mothers of group members also receive parenting support. In the original evaluation study, children in the intervention group showed the highest decrease in both externalizing and internalizing problems (including PTSD) compared with control group and child-intervention only groups. The program follows a manual, and group leaders receive weekly supervision. The Kids Club has been offered in both community and shelter settings, with a range of ethnically diverse participant families.

Advocacy Interventions Aimed at Improving Mother and Child Outcomes

The Community Advocacy Program (CAP) *CAP* is an empirically validated program designed to address the advocacy needs of battered women and their children (Sullivan & Bybee, 1999; Sullivan, Bybee, & Allen, 2002). This 12- to 16-week program offers intensive home-based advocacy from trained undergraduate students who spend 6-10 hours per week with families, assessing and addressing housing, legal, social support, employment, education, and other needs of families. Children receive mentoring and participate in the Learning Club, a 10-week group educational intervention designed to improve self-competence. A study of this program indicated that at 22-month follow-up, mothers who participated in the intervention showed increased social support and psychological well-being, children had enhanced self-competence, and fewer children were abused by a parent as compared to the control group (Sullivan & Bybee, 1999).

PROMISING APPROACHES: INTERVENING WITH CHILDREN EXPOSED TO DOMESTIC VIOLENCE IN OTHER CONTEXTS

Shelter Settings

Child residents of battered women's shelters have often been exposed to significant degrees of trauma and upheaval, related both to domestic violence and homelessness. Not surprising, these children may demonstrate a range of traumatic stress symptoms, as well as behavior and adjustment difficulties (Gewirtz & Edleson, 2004; Jouriles et al., 2001). Shelters, then, provide a valuable opportunity to screen children for developmental, cognitive, emotional, and behavioral problems. The challenges for shelters include the variable and often short stay lengths of families, and the lack of funding resources that force many shelters to restrict services to "three hots and a cot." Despite these meager resources, the opportunity to provide screening, triage, and referral for child clients is compelling.

Tubman Family Alliance At the *Tubman Family Alliance's* three shelters, with 128 beds serving the Minneapolis/St. Paul metropolitan area, a family advocate meets with every child and mother entering the shelters to undertake a basic intake/screening and to complete a child and family safety plan. The intake may incorporate the use of an evidence-based child assessment tool, such as the Ages & Stages Questionnaires (Bricker & Squires, 2001). This is a screening tool in use in several shelters across the nation, which is completed by the mother (or by shelter staff, with the mother's help) in less than a half hour, and which gives valuable information to parents and staff about young children's development across various domains. At *Harriet Tubman Shelter* in Minneapolis, on-site licensed child care affords further opportunity to assess the development of infant and preschool shelter residents (whose mothers are encouraged to use the child care on a regular, rather than a drop-in, basis). Trained child care staff screen young children about whom there are concerns for developmental lags, using the Denver Development Screening Test (Frankenburg, Goldstein, & Camp, 1971). These results may be used to refer children as eligible for Birth to 3 and/or other voluntary prevention and intervention services, without the added need for outside referrals or eligibility assessment (Gewirtz & Menakem, 2004).

At the Tubman Family Alliance shelters in Minnesota, advocates also offer structured recreational family activities 1 or 2 nights per week, as well as individual parenting guidance when requested by clients. Recreational activities include cultural and religious heritage celebrations (e.g., for Cinco de Mayo, Kwanzaa, Chinese New Year). As part of these activities, mothers have the opportunity to cook communal meals for shelter residents that reflect and celebrate their cultural traditions.

Pro Bono Children's Mental Health Project at Women's Center and Shelter of Greater Pittsburgh   In a few shelters, clinical intervention for children is offered by in-house child therapists who provide individual and group therapy. For example, the *Pro Bono Children's Mental Health Project* offers individual therapy for children from the time they are in shelter at least through their transition to permanent housing. The project utilizes the expertise of in-house therapists as well as volunteer mental health professionals from the community. A weekly "moms and kids" night affords mothers the opportunity to play in structured activities with their children, with parenting support available from facilitators.

The Homeless Children's Network (HCN)   *HCN* in San Francisco offers no-cost mental health services to any child in any shelter in the city. Funded largely by the city, HCN offers individual and family therapy without preset time limits to battered mothers and their children. Mental health professionals continue working with children through their transition to a stable living environment and act as mental health case managers for children with more complex problems. Therapists conduct both office- and home-based treatment and offer consultation to childcare providers and schools.

Court Settings

Children exposed to domestic violence may be involved with the courts in several ways: as victims of child abuse or neglect, as the subject of court hearings on visitation or custody, or as petitioners listed on restraining orders. The courts offer opportunities for specialized assessments of children and linkages with other needed services, as well as enhanced protection of children from additional exposure to violence. Battered women's advocates have been vocal critics of the court's failure to adequately address issues of domestic violence within the family court system (Cuthbert et al., 2002; Jaffe, Lemon, & Poisson, 2003). These criticisms focus on numerous cases in which a child may be ordered to have visitation with an abusive father or cases in which custody decisions do not adequately consider the existence of domestic violence.

The Domestic Violence/Guardian ad Litem Project (DV/GAL Project)
DV/GAL Project was established as a joint program with the Child Witness to Violence Project and the Family Advocacy Program at Boston Medical Center. This program combines the expertise of lawyers and mental health clinicians to offer specialized evaluations to the court in cases involving questions of visitation or custody of children. Staff from the DV/GAL Project are appointed by the courts to conduct evaluations of children and families in order to make specific recommendations to the courts about visitation or custody. Each member of the family is interviewed; extensive collateral reports are gathered. The evaluators are well trained in child development, domestic violence, and child trauma. The lawyer/mental health partnership ensures that the final report and recommendations meet legal standards and are presented in ways that offer maximum guidance to the courts.

The Miami Safe Start Project   *The Miami Safe Start Project* located within the Miami-Dade County Court system offers direct evaluations of children between the ages of 1 and 5 who are under the court's jurisdiction for child maltreatment and/or family violence. All children are screened for developmental, emotional, and cognitive functioning. Written reports are made to the judges to assist them in determining the legal goals of the case (family reunification or placement in care outside the family) and to order appropriate treatment. This program has created an Early Head Start program that is linked with the court system. Located a few blocks from the courthouse, the center provides child care and early education as well as opportunities for non-custodial parents to visit with their children in a supervised setting. In order to enhance the quality of services offered to these high-risk children and families, the court also offers training to child welfare workers and all court staff on early child development and mental health issues for infants and toddlers.

Police Collaborations

Police are key figures for children, particularly those exposed to violence. The role of the police officer is to ensure the safety of those who have requested help and to enforce the law, and in their everyday doings, officers have the potential to be powerful symbols of benign authority to children. This is particularly significant for vulnerable, high-risk children, who may be seeking authoritative, non-violent adult role models. Programs that partner police officers with mental health professionals and domestic violence advocates offer ways to enhance police response to children exposed to domestic violence, as well as earlier identification, acute response, and referrals for traumatized children and families, and education to caregivers about the effects of exposure to domestic violence on children.

Yale Child Development-Community Policing Program (CD-CP) CD-CP offers a 24-hour-per-day, 7-day-per-week consultation service to New Haven Police officers, who can call child mental health professionals to the scenes of violent incidents involving children (Marans et al., 1995). Training on child development is offered to police officers at all ranks within the police department, beginning in the Police Academy. Federal funding has enabled the program to provide training and technical assistance for replication to a further ten communities developing police-mental health partnerships.

The Minnesota Child Response Initiative (MCRI) MCRI is a broad partnership of police, community social service agencies, and schools, aimed at identifying and intervening with children exposed to violence via intervention and community/system change. In addition to training, and a 24/7 on-call consultation service for police, MCRI intervention partners family violence detectives or patrol supervisors from the Minneapolis Police Department in squad cars with child mental health professionals and advocates during peak evening times for domestic violence incidents. The clinical-advocacy teams are staffed both by paid and volunteer staff from mental health, family violence, and culturally specific agencies across the Twin Cities Metro area. The development of a community-based and volunteer infrastructure offers both local community "ownership" of such a program, and a sustainable program infrastructure. This is particularly important in cities with large or highly diverse non-majority communities and in cities with a history of community suspicion toward police, or conflict between police and community.

The Violence Intervention Program (VIP) at Louisiana State University VIP offers extensive training to police officers as well as a direct referral linkage. VIP offers brief, role-call training on children and trauma to patrol officers of the New Orleans Police Department, as well as more intensive training through the police academy. Officers refer families to a 24-hour hotline staffed by child mental health clinicians who are also available to respond to the scenes of violent trauma. About 25% of calls to the hotline come from police officers requiring consultation or making referrals at the scene of an incident (Osofsky et al., 2004; see also Chapter 4).

Health Settings

Health settings offer important opportunities to identify children who are living with domestic violence. In 1998, the American Academy of Pediatrics Committee on Child Abuse and Neglect published a position statement entitled *The Role of the Pediatrician in Recognizing and Intervening on Behalf of Abused Women*. The first sentence of that statement was, "The abuse of women is a pediatric issue" (p. 1091). The statement presented information about the impact of domestic violence on women and children and the obstacles women face in disclosing that they are victims of domestic violence. One of the recommendations was that "pediatricians should attempt to recognize evidence of family or intimate partner violence" (p. 1091). The statement made a strong case for recognizing domestic violence but did not offer specific guidelines for screening or provide discussion about the policy and practice dilemmas that arise when providers implement screening protocols for exposure to domestic violence.

Since that time, several articles have appeared in the medical literature about the challenges and efficacy of universal screening for domestic violence in pediatric or family health settings (Erickson, Hill, & Siegel, 2001; Ganetsky, Giardino, Grosz, & Christian, 2002; Parkinson, Adams, & Emerling, 2001; Siegel, Hili, Henderson, Ernst, & Boat, 1999). There have also been articles about the reactions of mothers to being asked sensitive questions in the presence of their children (Zink, 2000). In 2002, the Family Violence Prevention Fund published guidelines for screening mothers for domestic violence in pediatric, family, and adolescent health settings (Groves et al., 2002). These guidelines were developed with input from the American Academy of Pediatrics, the American Association of Family Practitioners, the National Pediatric Nurse Practitioner Association, and the American College of Obstetrics and Gynecology. They include specifics about who and how often to screen, what questions to ask, how to provide basic safety planning, and how to respond if a child discloses that he or she is living with domestic violence. The guidelines highlight several dilemmas that are unique to child health settings, including when to report a child's exposure to domestic violence to child protection services, how to document findings in the child's medical chart while protecting the privacy of the parent, and whether to ask about domestic violence in the presence of a child. These guidelines have been widely disseminated and are available through the Family Violence Prevention Fund.

Children's Mercy Hospital Researchers at the Children's Mercy Hospital in Kansas City, Missouri, have developed and evaluated a domestic violence screening protocol for use in a pediatric emergency department. This project had six goals: 1) to identify barriers and opportunities for screening in a pediatric setting; 2) to design and pilot test a screening protocol; 3) to develop and pilot test an educational program for health providers on using the screening protocol; 4) to implement the educational program and the screening protocol; 5) to evaluate effectiveness of the protocol; and 6) to disseminate the screening model to other sites. The protocol was implemented and evaluated after 1 year. During the first year, approximately 97% of families using the Pediatric Emergency services were screened; 1% answered yes to at least one of the questions about intimate partner violence; 38% did not answer. Interventions were offered to all who said yes. Compared to referrals made prior to the use of the screening protocol, there was a three- to fourfold increase in referrals. An educational model was designed and made available as a training CD-ROM (Dowd, Knapp, Kennedy, Stallbaumer-Royer, & Henderson, 2004).

The Community Advocacy Program (CAP) *CAP* at the Center for Community Health Education, Research, and Services has placed a family advocate at each of six community health centers located in Boston, to expand health and social services for domestic violence victims. These advocates provide adult victims with case management services, support groups, and referrals for services. The family advocate is generally from the community, reflecting the culture and language of the population that uses the health center. The family advocate works closely with adult and pediatric providers to ensure that screening occurs and to provide on-site direct counseling services, linkage with legal or housing assistance, and victim compensation services. This program is based on the premise that community-based health services for women and their children are the ideal setting for identification of families experiencing domestic violence and for long-term intervention. This model of recruiting advocates directly within a community health practice is praised by health providers; it increases their comfort with screening for domestic violence because they have immediate access to resources that provide specialized help to families.

PATCHES The Arizona chapter of the American Academy of Pediatrics, along with a local health center, sponsored a statewide initiative to provide training to each of the state's regional mental health centers on clinical intervention with children affected by domestic violence. Two-day trainings were offered at three locations throughout the state, using the Child Witness to Violence Project's curriculum *Shelter from the Storm: Clinical Intervention with Young Children Affected by Violence* (Groves et al., 2000). The goal of this project, *PATCHES*, was to build expertise and capacity in the mental health system for responding to children's needs. Referral partnerships were then established with local battered women's shelters. A 1-year follow-up of participants in the training found that the training had a moderate to high impact on their interventions with children affected by violence and that the training prepared them to train others on issues related to child exposure to domestic violence. The number of children identified in counseling as having histories of exposure to domestic violence remained the same (Crimi, 2003).

AWAKE *AWAKE* is an innovative program that provides advocacy to battered women in conjunction with pediatric services for children. In the mid-1980s, staff at Children's Hospital in Boston realized that interventions that focused exclusively on abused or neglected children missed the larger context of violence within the home. Knowing that they could better protect children by helping their mothers, staff designed a hospital-based outreach, identification, and intervention model to assist battered women. Services include individual counseling, risk assessment and safety planning, assistance in securing emergency shelter, legal representation, and a walk-in support group. They also offer groups for mothers and children. *AWAKE* works regularly with health care professionals and social workers in the hospital and in its affiliated neighborhood health centers, both on individual cases and on training and policy development.

Child Welfare/Child Protection Settings

The challenge of maintaining a balance between women's rights and children's rights as they intersect with concerns about child abuse and neglect is enormous. In a few states, legislation now mandates that a child's exposure to domestic violence be defined as child maltreatment. In most states, however, more discretion is left to the mandated reporter to decide when exposure to violence is child maltreatment. While there is general agreement that exposure to violence poses risks for children's emotional (and sometimes physical) well-being, there is disagreement over whether the appropriate response should include mandated reporting.

Both mandated and non-mandated child welfare programs may provide support to children and families exposed to domestic violence. The documented overlap between child maltreatment and domestic violence has led to several initiatives, both at the federal and state levels, to increase collaborations between domestic violence and child protection service systems. They include systems reform efforts and family-focused initiatives. Perhaps the best-known systems reform initiative is the federally funded *Greenbook* initiative. This initiative implements guidelines released in 1999 by the National Council of Juvenile and Family Court Judges in *Effective Interventions in Domestic Violence and Child Maltreatment: Guidelines for Policy and Practice*, known as "*The Greenbook*" (National Council of Juvenile and Family Court Judges, 1998). *The Greenbook* offers a comprehensive set of policy recommendations designed to increase safety for mothers and children experiencing both domestic violence and child maltreatment. These guidelines target three systems—battered women's advocates, child protection services, and family court judges—with the goal of keeping mothers and children safe and together and avoiding unnecessary out-of-home placement. Federal partners supporting the demonstration initiative, which was launched in January 2001, include the U.S. Department of Health and Human Services and the Department of Justice. Private partners supporting related efforts include the David and Lucile Packard Foundation, the Edna McConnell Clark Foundation, the Annie E. Casey Foundation, the National Council of Juvenile and Family Court Judges, the Family Violence Prevention Fund, and the American Public Human Services Association (see the chapter's Appendix).

After 3 years of implementation, there are still major challenges in meeting the needs of children exposed to domestic violence. To serve these children, the community must have appropriate resources to treat children and families and must work out procedures for effectively helping families access these services.

The Institute for Safe Families An example of a family-focused initiative is found in the work of the *Institute for Safe Families* in Philadelphia. They have launched a 5-year collaborative project bringing together the child welfare system, domestic violence services, battered women services, children's treatment providers, legal aid, and substance abuse providers in order to provide more integrated and comprehensive services to families affected by domestic violence and child maltreatment. In this collaboration, the Philadelphia Department of Human Services has identified 15–20 cases each year to be followed by this multidisciplinary collaborative team. The cases received family preservation services, in addition to a variety of other domestic violence, mental health, batterers intervention, and substance abuse services.

Each case was discussed at length at monthly team meetings. A key focus of the monthly meetings was to provide information and support for the actual providers of service for each case. While discussion was primarily focused on planning and intervention strategies, attention was also paid to policy and practice issues inherent in the work, in order to develop specific recommendations for comprehensive and integrative services for families with child welfare and domestic violence service involvement.

An interim evaluation of this project yielded interesting results. Nearly half the families received housing services and one third required medical attention, a reminder of the underlying stressors of poverty and health issues for many families involved in the child protection system. Seven fathers remained actively engaged with their families; they were referred for services, including batterers intervention, drug or alcohol treatment, or parenting classes. Eleven of the fifteen mothers were referred for support services, including counseling, battered women's support groups, or drug/alcohol treatment. However, only 4 of the 44 children found in these 15 families received referrals for counseling. Reasons for the low referral rate for children included the lack of specialized services available, reluctance on the part of parents to acknowledge that their children were in need of services, and the tendency of the team to focus on the priorities of the parents (Coffey, 2003). The findings of this multi-disciplinary team document the significant need for non-mandated public services that offer support to women and children leaving abusive environments.

Families First   Home-based services designed to provide valuable support in the transition from shelter to permanent housing also address the overlap of domestic violence and child abuse. In Michigan, the *Families First* program has successfully offered in-home help for families at risk from an assailant or from domestic violence-related homelessness, and for those making the transition from shelter to permanent housing. Advocates, funded through *Families First* and working out of domestic violence shelters, visit the home from 5 to 20 hours a week, and are available 24 hours per day to help parents with safety and concrete needs, advocacy, and parenting. Funded by Temporary Assistance to Needy Families (TANF) dollars, the program has successfully demonstrated a decreased involvement with child protective services by participating families.

CONCLUSIONS AND RECOMMENDATIONS

Despite a growing body of evidence indicating the risks to children of exposure to domestic violence, tools for identifying and intervening with these children remain relatively scarce. The few evidence-based interventions developed and/or tailored for children exposed to domestic violence have not been widely disseminated. Broad community dissemination is a common problem for evidence-based interventions (Shonkoff & Phillips, 2000). Barriers to dissemination include lack of resources and the traditional suspicion of grassroots organizations (which characterize most domestic violence programs/shelters) toward research and system/government interventions. In addition, the broad diversity of children and families exposed to domestic violence often requires that adaptations be made to standardized, evidence-based programs in order to meet different cultural and community needs and contexts. The current emphasis in intervention and mental health services research on understanding the process of dissemination, and the shift from effectiveness research to broad-based dissemination, offers promise for future direction and for narrowing the oft-described "15-year gap" between science and practice. *The National Child Traumatic Stress Network* is an example of this emphasis on dissemination of best practices for child trauma services. Funded by the Substance Abuse and Mental Health Services Administration (SAMHSA), this initiative funds a large and comprehensive network of trauma-focused research and intervention programs with a core mission of developing and disseminating effective evidenced-based practices throughout the country.

Exposure to domestic violence does not affect all children in the same way. There is a range of child functioning as well as wide variability in the risk and protective factors in a child's life. Similarly, while many battered mothers are competent, consistent, and nurturing parents, some may struggle with the sequelae of violence (e.g., depression, PTSD) that render them less emotionally available to their children. Some children—those who have fewer risk factors and/or more protective factors in their lives—may need temporary, crisis-driven/acute interventions for a single traumatic incident. However, other children, particularly those with a chronic history of exposure to violence—those who live with more risks and/or fewer protective factors—may need more intensive interventions. Effective clinical assessment of children and families that addresses risk and protective factors and a range of interventions that are calibrated to the needs of individual children and families are desperately needed. These interventions might be short- or long-term; focused on the parent(s) and/or the child(ren); and implemented in the home, community, clinic, or school by paraprofessionals or professionals.

Although the focus in this chapter is on interventions for children exposed to domestic violence, it is critical to consider the broader context of the child's and family's life. Many children who live with domestic violence also face poverty, homelessness, and other forms of violence (e.g., child abuse, exposure to community violence). In addition, their exposure to domestic violence is rarely a single-event phenomenon. Data from the *Minnesota Child Response Initiative* indicate that 87% of battered women calling 911 for domestic violence had a self-reported and/or police reported history of at least one prior domestic violence incident. Several researchers have documented the high rates of conduct problems among children of battered women resident in shelters: Up to two thirds of school-age children may meet criteria for oppositional defiant disorder and/or conduct disorder (Jouriles et al., 2001), and child conduct problems are themselves risk factors for a variety of poor outcomes, regardless of etiology (Patterson, Reid, & Dishion, 1992).

We need to assess children's exposure to violence within a cumulative risk perspective and to ensure that interventions are tailored appropriately. Intervention researchers have suggested that for children living with multiple, cumulative risk factors, and relatively few assets and protective factors, interventions must be comprehensive, multi-level, and multi-focused (Coie et al., 1993; Masten & Coatsworth, 1998; Wyman, Sandler, Wolchik, & Nelson, 2000).

There is a burgeoning literature on comprehensive interventions, and plenty of data on their effectiveness. The classic example of such an intervention is the *Head Start* program (Zigler & Muenchow, 1992), which targets the cognitive, social, and emotional development of young children at risk due to poverty and related chronic stressors. Other examples include nurse home visitation (Olds, Henderson, Tatelbaum, & Chamberlin, 1998), which targets young families at high risk for abuse and neglect and affects a wide range of child/youth outcomes, including academic achievement, adjustment, substance use, and juvenile delinquency. A specific programmatic example is the *Triple P Program*, a multi-level program developed in Australia that focuses on improving parenting skills. *Triple P* is a comprehensive program that has a universal prevention component (parent education via public service messages and television programs) and four more intensive components, ranging from as-needed telephone consultation and support to parents, to individual home-based interventions for families at high risk for abuse, neglect, and problem behaviors (Sanders, Turner, & Markie-Dadds, 2002).

These programs are targeted toward children and families facing multiple risk factors who are at risk for a variety of poor outcomes. They address some of the root causes of family violence. However, there is evidence to suggest that these interventions are not as effective for families exposed to domestic violence (Duggan et al., 1999; Eckenrode et al., 2000). Given the complicated dynamics of these families and the lack of training that child service providers generally receive in domestic violence, this is not surprising. In addition, several researchers have documented the challenges to engaging families struggling with domestic violence, including stigma about help-seeking, concerns about system/child protection involvement, safety concerns, and transportation/economic barriers. However, rather than "throwing the baby out with the bathwater," we propose that efforts to address the needs of families dealing with domestic violence within these comprehensive interventions (i.e., adapting the delivery systems to meet the unique needs of this population) would broaden the range of effective interventions available to children and families exposed to domestic violence. While there is utility to developing specific clinical interventions aimed at children exposed to domestic violence, there is also a critical need to build the capacity of comprehensive, multi-level interventions to meet the needs of families exposed to domestic violence, toward the goal of enhancing children's development across multiple domains of functioning.

CONCLUSIONS

In summary, although a range of effective interventions and promising approaches has been developed to meet the needs of children exposed to domestic violence, the field is still at a formative stage. Capacity building for child professionals in a variety of different fields (e.g., police, early childhood, child welfare, mental health) is necessary in order to offer sensitive, timely, and appropriate interventions that enhance children's safety and promote their resilience. Evidence-based practices and promising approaches that target the emotional and social wellness of children exposed to domestic violence should be disseminated more broadly, in order to benefit larger numbers of children. Finally, the significant numbers of children exposed to this stressor, and the recognition of domestic violence as a public health problem, require that comprehensive interventions pay attention to and adapt programs to meet the unique needs of this group of children and families. Ultimately, all those intervening with children exposed to domestic violence, in whatever setting they may meet children, have as their common goal the reduction of risks and/or the promotion of resilience for children and their families.

REFERENCES

American Academy of Pediatrics Committee on Child Abuse and Neglect. (1998). The role of the pediatrician in recognizing and intervening on behalf of abused women. *Pediatrics, 101*(6), 1091–1092.

Bricker, D., & Squires, J. (1999). *Ages & Stages Questionnaires (ASQ): A parent-completed, child-monitoring system* (2nd ed.). Baltimore: Paul H. Brookes Publishing Co.

Bronfenbrenner, U. (1992). Ecological systems theory. In R. Vasta (Ed.), *Six theories of child development: Revised formulations and current issues* (pp. 187–249). London: Jessica Kingsley.

Carmen, E.H., Rieker, P.P., & Mills, T. (1984). Victims of violence and psychiatric illness. *American Journal of Psychiatry, 141*(3), 378–383.

Chess, S., & Thomas, A. (1996). Temperament. In M. Lewis (Ed.), *Child and adolescent psychiatry: A comprehensive textbook* (pp. 170–181). Baltimore: Williams & Wilkins.

Coie, J.D., Watt, N.F., West, S.G., Hawkins, J.D., Asarnow, J.R., Markman, H.J., et al. (1993). The science of prevention: A conceptual framework and some directions for a national research program. *American Psychologist, 48*(10), 1013–1022.

Coffey, D.S. (2003). *DHS Domestic Violence Collaborative Project, July 1, 2002–June 30, 2003.* Unpublished annual report, Institute for Safe Families, Philadelphia.

Crimi D. (2003). *Evaluation of training to serve child witnesses of domestic violence.* Unpublished paper, Arizona State University West, School of Social Work.

Cuthbert, C., Slote, K., Driggers, M.G., Mesh C.J., Bancroft, L., & Silverman, J. (2002). *Battered mothers speak out: A human rights report on domestic violence and child custody in the Massachusetts family courts.* Wellesley, MA: Wellesley Centers for Women.

Dowd, M.D., Knapp, J., Kennedy, C., Stallbaumer-Rouyer, J., & Henderson, D. (2004). *It's time to ask: An instructional program for identifying and intervening in intimate partner violence in the pediatric setting.* Kansas City, MO: Children's Mercy Hospital.

Duggan, A.K., McFarlane, E.C., Windham, A.M., Rhode, C.A., Salkever, D.S., Fuddy, L., et al. (1999). Evaluation of Hawaii's Healthy Start Program. *The Future of Children, 9,* 66–90.

Eckenrode, J., Ganzel, B., Henderson, C., Smith, E., Olds, D., Powers, J., et al. (2000). Preventing child abuse and neglect with home visitation: The limiting effects of domestic violence. *Journal of the American Medical Association, 284*(1), 1385–1391.

Edleson, J.L. (1999). Children's witnessing of adult domestic violence. *Journal of Interpersonal Violence, 14*(8), 839–870.

End Violence Alliance. (2000). *End Violence: A manual for group leaders* (2nd ed.). Scarborough, Ontario, Canada: Aisling Discoveries Child and Family Center.

Erikson, M.J., Hill, T.D., & Siegel, R.M. (2001). Barriers to domestic violence screening in the pediatric setting. *Pediatrics, 108*(1), 98–102.

Fleck-Henderson, A., & Arean, J.C. (2004). *Breaking the cycle: Fathering after violence: Curriculum guidelines and tools for batterer intervention programs.* San Francisco: Family Violence Prevention Fund.

Ford, D.H., & Lerner, R.M. (1992). *Developmental systems theory: An integrative approach.* Thousand Oaks, CA: Sage.

Frankenburg, W.K., Goldstein, A.D., & Camp, B.W. (1971). The revised Denver Development Screening Test: Its accuracy as a screening instrument. *Journal of Pediatrics, 79,* 988–995.

Ganetsky, M., Giardino, A., Grosz, & Christian, C. (2002, May). *General pediatricians' approaches to domestic violence in the office setting.* Presented at the annual meeting of the Pediatric Academic Society, Baltimore.

Gewirtz, A., & Edleson, J. (2004). Young children's exposure to adult domestic violence: Towards a developmental risk and resilience framework for research and intervention. In S. Schechter (Ed.), *Domestic violence, poverty and young children* (pp. 141–167). Iowa City: University of Iowa.

Gewirtz, A., & Menakem, R. (2004). Working with young children and their families: Recommendations for domestic violence agencies and batterer intervention programs. In S. Schechter (Ed.), *Domestic violence, poverty and young children* (pp. 113–140). Iowa City: University of Iowa.

Graham-Bermann, S.A. (2001). Designing intervention evaluations for children exposed to domestic violence: Applications of research and theory. In S. Graham-Bermann & J. Edleson. (Eds.), *Domestic violence in the lives of children: The future of research, intervention, and social policy* (pp. 237–267). Washington, DC: American Psychological Association.

Graham-Bermann, S., & Hughes, H. (2003). Intervention for children exposed to interparental violence (IPV): Assessment of needs and research priorities. *Clinical Child and Family Psychology Review, 6,* 189–204.

Groves, B.M. (2002). *Children who see too much: Lessons from the Child Witness to Violence Project.* Boston: Beacon Press.

Groves, B.M., Augustyn, M., Lee, D., & Sawires, P. (2002). *Identifying and responding to domestic violence: Consensus recommendations for child and adolescent health.* San Francisco: Family Violence Prevention Fund.

Groves, B.M., Roberts, E., & Weinreb, M. (2000). *Shelter from the storm: Clinical intervention with young children affected by domestic violence.* Boston: Boston Medical Center.

Groves, B., Zuckerman, B., Marans, S., & Cohen, D. (1993). Silent victims: Children who witness violence. *Journal of the American Medical Association, 269*(2), 262–264.

Jaffe, P., Lemon, N.K.D., & Poisson, S.E. (2003). *Child custody and domestic violence: A call for safety and accountability.* Thousand Oaks, CA: Sage.

Jaffe, P.G., Wolfe, D.A., & Wilson, S.K. (1990). *Children of battered women.* Newbury Park, CA: Sage.

Jouriles, E.N., McDonald, R., Spiller, L., Norwood, W.D., Swank, P.R., Stephens, N., et al. (2001). Reducing conduct problems among children of battered women. *Journal of Consulting & Clinical Psychology, 69,* 774–785.

Lemon, N.K.D. (1999). The legal system's response to children exposed to domestic violence, *The Future of Children, 9,* 21–32.

Lieberman, A.F., & Van Horn, P. (1998). Attachment, trauma, and domestic violence. *Child Custody, 7,* 423–443.

Luthar, S.S., Cicchetti, D., & Becker, B. (2000). The construct of resilience: A critical evaluation and guidelines for future work. *Child Development, 71,* 543–562.

Lyons, J.A. (1987). Post traumatic stress disorder in children and adolescents: A review of the literature. In S. Chess & A. Thomas (Eds.), *Annual progress in child psychiatry and development* (pp. 451–467). New York: Bruner Mazel.

Masten, A.S. (2001). Ordinary magic: Resilience processes in development. *American Psychologist, 56*(3), 227–238.

Masten, A.S., & Coatsworth, J.D. (1998). The development of competence in favorable and unfavorable environments: Lessons from research on successful children. *American Psychologist, 53*(2), 205–220.

Masten, A., & Gewirtz, A. (in press). Vulnerability and resilience. In D. Philips & K. McCartney (Eds.), *Blackwell handbook of early childhood development*. Malden, MA: Blackwell, Ltd.

Marans, S., Adnopoz, J., Berkman, M., Esserman, D., MacDonald, D., Nagler, S., et al. (1995). *The Police-Mental Health Partnership: A community-based response to urban violence.* New Haven, CT: Yale University.

National Center for Infant Study Programs. (1994). Diagnostic classification: 0–3. Arlington, VA: Author.

National Council of Juvenile and Family Court Judges. (1998). *Family violence: Emerging programs for battered women and their children.* Reno, NV: Author.

Olds, D.L., Henderson, C.R., Tatelbaum, R., & Chamberlin, R. (1998). Improving the life-course development of socially disadvantaged mothers: A randomized trial of nurse home visitation. *American Journal of Public Health, 78,* 1436–45.

Osofsky, J.D., Rovaris, M., Hammer, J.H., Dickson, A., Freeman, N., & Aucoin, K. (2004). Working with police to help children exposed to violence. *Journal of Community Psychology, 32*(5), 593–606.

Parkinson, G.W., Adams, R.C., & Emerling, F.G. (2001). Maternal domestic violence screening in an office-based pediatric practice [Electronic version]. *Pediatrics, 108*(3), e43.

Patterson, G.R., Reid, J.B., & Dishion, T.J. (1992). *A social learning approach: IV. Antisocial boys.* Eugene, OR: Castalia.

Peled, E., & Davis, D. (1995). *Group work with children of battered women: A practitioner's manual.* Thousand Oaks, CA: Sage.

Peled, E., & Edleson, J.L. (1995). Process and outcome in small groups for children of battered women. In E. Peled, P. Jaffe, & J. Edleson (Eds.), *Ending the cycle of violence: Community responses to children of battered women* (pp. 77–96). Thousand Oaks, CA: Sage.

Perry, B.D. (1997). Incubated in terror: Neurodevelopmental factors in the "Cycle of Violence." In J. Osofsky (Ed.), *Children, youth and violence: The search for solutions* (pp. 124–148). New York: Guilford.

Sanders, M.R., Turner, K.M.T., & Markie-Dadds, C. (2002). The development and dissemination of the Triple P—Positive Parenting Program: A multilevel, evidence-based system of parenting and family support. *Prevention Science, 3*(3), 173–189.

Schechter, S. (1981). *For shelter and beyond.* Boston: Massachusetts Coalition of Battered Women's Service Groups.

Schechter, S., & Edleson, J. (1999). *Effective intervention in domestic violence and child maltreatment cases: Guidelines for policy and practice.* Reno, NV: National Council of Juvenile and Family Court Judges.

Scheerenga, M.S., & Zeanah, C. (1995). Symptom expression and trauma variables in children under 48 months of age. *Infant Mental Health Journal, 16,* 259–270.

Sengupta, S. (2000, July 8). Tough justice: Taking a child when one parent is battered. *New York Times,* pp. B1.

Shonkoff, J.P., & Phillips, D.A. (2000). *From neurons to neighborhoods: the science of early childhood development.* Washington, DC: National Academies Press.

Siegel, R.M., Hill, T.D., Henderson, V.A., Ernst, H.M., & Boat, B.W. (1999). Screening for domestic violence in the community pediatric setting. *Pediatrics, 104*(4), 874–877.

Silvern, L., Karyl, J., & Landis, T.Y. (1995). Individual psychotherapy for the traumatized children of abused women. In E. Peled, P.G. Jaffe, & J.L. Edleson (Eds.), *Ending the cycle of violence: Community responses to children of battered women* (pp. 43–76). Thousand Oaks, CA: Sage.

Sullivan, C.M., & Bybee, D.I. (1999). Reducing violence using community-based advocacy for women with abusive partners. *Journal of Consulting and Clinical Psychology, 67,* 43–53.

Sullivan, C.M., Bybee, D.I., & Allen, N.E. (2002). Findings from a community-based program for battered women and their children. *Journal of Interpersonal Violence, 17*(9), 915–936.

Taylor, L., Harik, V., Zuckerman, B., & Groves, B. (1994). Exposure to violence among inner city children. *Developmental and Behavioral Pediatrics, 15,* 120–123.

Werner, E.E., & Smith, R.S. (1982). *Vulnerable but invincible: A study of resilient children.* New York: McGraw-Hill.

Wilder Community Assistance Program. (1997). *Children Domestic Abuse Program: Group manual.* St. Paul, MN: Amherst H. Wilder Foundation.

Wyman, P.A., Sandler, I., Wolchik, S., & Nelson, K. (2000). Resilience as cumulative competence promotion and stress protection: Theory and intervention. In D. Cicchetti, J. Rappaport, I. Sandler, & R.P. Weissberg (Eds.), *The promotion of wellness in children and adolescents* (pp. 133–184). Thousand Oaks, CA: Sage.

Yates, T.M., & Masten, A.S. (2004). Fostering the future: Resilience theory and the practice of positive psychology. In P.A. Linley & S. Joseph (Eds.), *Positive psychology in practice.* Hoboken, NJ: Wiley.

Zigler, E., & Muenchow, S. (1992). *Head Start: The inside story of America's most successful educational experiment.* New York: Basic Books.

Zink, T. (2000). Should children be in the room when the mother is screened for partner violence? *The Journal of Family Practice, 49*(2), 130–136.

Appendix: Contact Information for Programs

Child Development–Community Policing Program
Yale University School of Medicine
Yale Child Study Center
230 South Frontage Road
New Haven, CT 06520
203-785-7047 or 1-877-496-2238

Child Trauma Research Project
University of California at San Francisco
San Francisco General Hospital
Building 20, Suite 2100, Room 2122
1001 Potrero Avenue
San Francisco, CA 94110
415-206-5328

The Child Witness to Violence Project
Boston Medical Center, MAT 5
Boston, MA 02118
617-414-4244
http://www.childwitnesstoviolence.org

Children's Mercy Hospital
Division of Emergency Medicine
2401 Gilliam Rd.
Kansas City, Missouri 64108
816-234-3450
Denise Dowd, M.D., or Jennifer Stallbaumer-Rouyer, LCSW

The Community Advocacy Program
Center for Community Health, Education Research and Services
c/o Northeastern University
716 Columbus Avenue, Room 398 CP
Boston, MA 02115
http://www.cchers.org

Families First, Michigan
Michigan Family Independence Agency
P.O. Box 30037
Lansing, MI 48909
517-373-2035
http://www.michigan.gov/fia/1,1607,7-124-5452_7124_7210-15373--,00.html

Homeless Children's Network
3265 17th Street, Suite 404
San Francisco, CA 94110
415-437-3990
http://www.hcnkids.org

Institute for Safe Families
3502 Scotts Lane, Building 1, Suite 4
Philadelphia, PA 19129
215-843-2046

Miami Safe Start Project
C/o Linda Ray Intervention Center
750 NW 15th Street
Miami, FL 33136
305-325-1818
http://miamisafestart.org

Minnesota Child Response Initiative
C/o Tubman Family Alliance
3111 1st Avenue South
Minneapolis, MN 55408
612-821-4740
http://www.childresponse.org

National Child Traumatic Stress Network
NCCTS - University of California, Los Angeles
11150 W. Olympic Blvd., Suite 650
Los Angeles, CA 90064
(310) 235-2633
Fax: (310) 235-2612
http://www.nctsn.org

Tubman Family Alliance/Harriet Tubman Shelter
3111 1st Avenue South
Minneapolis, MN 55408
612-825-3333
http://www.tubmanfamilyalliance.org

Violence Intervention Program
Louisiana State University Health Sciences Center
1542 Tulane Avenue
New Orleans, LA 70112
504-568-4450
http://www.futureunlimited.org

Women's Center and Shelter of Greater Pittsburgh
P.O. Box 9024
Pittsburgh, PA 15224
412-687-8017
http://www.wcspittsburgh.org

6

CRISIS INTERVENTION

Secondary Prevention for Children Exposed to Violence

Steven J. Berkowitz and Steven Marans

Exposure to violence—whether it occurs in their homes, schools, neighborhoods, or communities—affects children's development. Witnessing parents' brutal interactions, street crimes, or the destruction and death of terrorist attacks leaves children vulnerable to a host of symptoms and adaptations that compromise their ability to grow and feel secure (Bolton, O'Ryan, Udwin, Boyle, & Yule, 2000; Horn & Trickett, 1998; Margolin & Gordis, 2000; Schwab-Stone et al., 1999). Researchers and clinicians have recognized that high rates of violence exposure and their subsequent risks to mental health are a public health problem that requires a range of responses/interventions (Cohen, Berliner, & Mannarino, 2000, 2003; Ruggiero, Morris, & Scotti, 2001). Neither the types of exposure nor the factors that mediate clinical outcome are uniform. As a result, some efforts to investigate associated phenomena have been organized around attempts to categorize violence exposure by type. The spectrum of categorization captures both the settings in which violence occurs and the scope of those directly affected—from violence involving interpersonal victimization that occurs in the home (from physical and sexual abuse to spousal abuse), neighborhoods (from shootings to assaults on neighborhood streets), and schools (from bullying to assaults to life-threatening attacks with weapons), to mass casualties that occur as a result of attacks on the broader population. This spectrum runs from the most to least catastrophic exposures; however, in its inverse it moves from the most to least common manners in which children are exposed to violence.

Despite the inordinate number of children victimized by violence, far more are exposed as witnesses or secondary victims. It is estimated that as many as 10 million children per year are exposed to domestic violence (Centers for Disease Control and Prevention, 1999), and 9 million are exposed to violence in their communities and neighborhoods (Kilpatrick, 1997). For many, these exposures are unrelenting.

THE IMPACT OF TRAUMA

Although most single episodes of violence or potentially traumatic events (PTEs) have only temporary effects (Harvey & Bryant, 1999; McFarlane, 2000), even temporary posttraumatic symptomatology may have profound effects on school performance and peer relationships, depending on timing and contextual features. Furthermore, given an inopportune combination of risk factors, single episodes may lead to psychosocial difficulties and posttraumatic disorders in some individuals. Many children also suffer effects from chronic exposure to violence, experiencing a broad range of associated difficulties.

Exposure to episodes of violence may have severe disabling effects on children's development and has been correlated to functional and emotional difficulties as well as psychiatric disorders. Violence exposure has been linked to depression and depressive symptoms, posttraumatic stress, anxiety, and somatization disorders (Campbell & Schwarz, 1996; Freeman, Mokros, & Poznanski, 1993). For example, Campbell and Schwarz (1996) found a positive correlation between levels of violence exposure and psychiatric symptomatology in a group of sixth graders. Low school achievement and high levels of anger, anxiety, aggression, anti-social behaviors, and alcohol and drug use have also been associated with violence exposure (Boney-McCoy & Finkelhor, 1995; DuRant, Getts, Cadenhead, Emans, & Woods, 1995; Hill & Madhere, 1996; Schwab-Stone et al., 1995).

There is still much to learn, however, about the extent of enduring impact on cognitive capacities, dose and other event-related factors, and the role of gender, socioeconomic status, and developmental phases in children's responses to exposure to violent events. In addition, while the focus of research has been on the effects of violence on the individual child, there are broader implications for the community. For example, exposure to violence may have an impact on school classrooms when children's symptomatic responses include learning difficulties and behavioral problems. It also has an impact on the criminal justice system, with high correlations between violence exposure and juvenile arrests and incarceration (Dodge, Pettit, & Bates, 1997; Ford, 2002; Hill & Madhere, 1996).

APPLYING A PUBLIC HEALTH MODEL

One may conclude that the large numbers of children who are exposed to violence and the subsequent transitory or chronic effects of such exposure suggest that a public health model is indispensable. While primary prevention strategies are an essential public health response, they are unlikely to eliminate violence as an aspect of the human condition. Children will continue to be subject to both primary and secondary violence exposure at unacceptable rates. Treatments, or tertiary prevention strategies, have improved substantially for children with post-traumatic symptoms (Pine & Cohen, 2002). Trauma-focused cognitive behavioral therapy (CBT) (Cohen, Perel, De Bellis, Friedman, & Putnam, 2002) and abuse-focused CBT (Kolko, 1998) have demonstrated efficacy in clinical trials. However, regardless of advances in treatment approaches, there will never be a sufficient number of practitioners or systems of care in place to respond to the enormous number of children and families requiring intervention. This discrepancy between need and capacity challenges us to explore innovative approaches to secondary prevention that may offer alternatives for ameliorating the effects of violence exposure on children and adolescents.

Current approaches to secondary prevention typically involve various forms of crisis intervention and early intervention programs. However, few of these models have been sufficiently studied to demonstrate their effectiveness. Due to the variability of situation and subject intervention models, such interventions are difficult to evaluate, and longitudinal studies have been inconclusive (Hendricks, McKean, & Hendricks, 2003). When they have been thoroughly studied, programs that have been the most highly promoted and previously heralded, such as the Critical Incident Stress Debriefing or Management (CISD or CISM) strategies, have not demonstrated effectiveness and, in some studies, have proven detrimental (Gist & Devilly, 2002; van Emmerik, Kamphuis, Hulsbosch, & Emmelkamp, 2002). Some researchers have even called for the cessation of CISD/M's use (Rose, Bisson, & Wessely, 2001). Given the possibility that certain models may be more appropriate for specific situations or populations, evaluation approaches may be most productive when they address the question, "What intervention for whom?"

Although the research remains unclear, many agree that early identification, intervention, and continued follow-up are valuable methods to prevent or decrease post-exposure responses (Creamer, 1996; Gordon, Farberow, & Maida, 1999). These methods were frequently applied in crisis response approaches following the terrorist attacks of 9/11 and continue to be considered optimal practice for children and adults exposed to PTEs (Creamer, 1996; Gordon et al., 1999).

SECONDARY PREVENTION AND TYPES OF EXPOSURES

The types of violence exposure children experience have significant ramifications for the nature of the crisis intervention provided and for establishing desired outcomes. For example, because events involving disaster and mass casualties affect a broad part of the population, the challenges for intervention are equally broad. In addition to the immediate traumatic impact on the most proximal victims, these events destabilize community infrastructures and often lead to demoralization, confusion, and chaos in the wider community. In these circumstances, strategies for providing individualized clinical responses need to be complemented by multi-level responses that address the psychological needs of the broader community.

Clinicians involved in crisis response must be prepared to work closely and collaborate with professionals from a number of agencies in order to address these concerns. Perhaps most important, mental health providers must be able to work in close partnerships with first responders and be an integral part of the Incident Command System (ICS) that directs and dictates all activities during these events. Consequently, preparation of mental health providers for crisis and early intervention mental health response not only requires training in specific clinical models of intervention but also in the structure, operation, and practices of the ICS, if providers are to apply their psychological expertise as full partners in the system's response to catastrophic events. Without this level of engagement in both planning and response, the ability of mental health professionals to adequately respond to the affected population may be limited (Harris, Putnam, & Fairbank, in press).

In considering approaches to intervening in violent events involving mass casualties, it may be useful to look to similarities in crisis intervention strategies for children and families exposed to domestic and community violence. Although large-scale events often necessitate more general and broad-based approaches, appropriate interventions directed at individual children and families share many of the same elements and considerations. One of the common features may be the necessity of collaborating with first responders, especially law enforcement and emergency medical personnel; this is essential if mental health professionals are to identify, let alone gain access to, affected children and families in order to assess them and provide them with a range of therapeutic interventions. Although episodes of violence in homes and neighborhoods may be more circumscribed in terms of the numbers of affected children than mass casualty events, the resulting experiences and vulnerability to their untoward effects are no less severe or potentially overwhelming.

While familial and domestic violence are the most common ways in which children are exposed to violence, they also may be the most complex. Children in these situations are more likely to be chronically exposed to violence and confronted with the threat of harm and death to loved ones. In addition, when family violence erupts, children are often forced into highly confused and ambivalent states as their fathers, mothers, sisters, and brothers are combatants who threaten the safety of their homes. Young children, typically the most vulnerable witnesses to events involving parents (Margolin & Gordis, 2000; Osofsky, 2003), are more likely to be bystanders than any other age group (Osofsky, 1999). Although there may be a clear primary aggressor (typically a male), it is not unusual for a child to be completely distraught if that parent is arrested and removed from the home. The ambivalence the child might feel about the perpetrator may be an additional cause of complex symptoms and behaviors. Furthermore, parents who are victims are often too overwhelmed to support the needs of their fragile children. Their worry and anxiety may also greatly exacerbate the children's difficulties.

All of these complications inherent in familial violence require modifications to typical secondary prevention strategies. First, providers need to recognize that familial and domestic violence often are chronic situations, even though this may not be apparent during initial screening and assessment (Tjaden & Thoennes, 2000). Second, mental health services are of limited use if they are not part of more comprehensive interventions, including programs for perpetrators, housing, and provision of safety and security. Third, whereas all early interventions for children must include a parental component, domestic violence may require a specific focus on the perpetrator, and it certainly requires a specific focus on the non-offending parent and her relationship with her children. It is not unusual for domestic violence advocates to be unaware of children's needs as they focus on the drama of the adults. In many cases, the non-offending parent's probable traumatization requires evaluation and crisis response coincident with treatment of her children or together as a family. Collaboration with domestic violence advocates, court personnel, and others is frequently vital, especially as these situations often require multiple ecological interventions in order to be stabilized and to permit the opportunity to make use of psychological treatments. In our experience, crisis providers must be prepared to reintroduce interventions time and time again until something evolves that allows treatment interventions to take hold.

SECONDARY PREVENTION AND RISK FACTORS
Categorizing Risk Factors

Effective crisis intervention strategies share the ability to identify the most vulnerable, potential psychological casualties and to address risk factors for poor outcome/adaptation soon after an event of violence exposure. In order for crisis intervention models to provide effective secondary prevention strategies, their first task is to identify who is at greatest risk. While access to potential psychological victims is the first essential step to intervening, recognizing risk factors is crucial to moving from crisis response to secondary prevention roles and functions.

Although much of the research literature on children's developmental course and risk factors following exposure to violence has been performed in the aftermath of single episodes or mass exposures including disaster, war, and terrorism, increasingly there are studies evaluating the effects of chronic violence exposure (Margolin & Gordis, 2000; Masten, Neemann, & Andenas, 1994). Although these studies have found that children manifest a wide range of posttraumatic symptoms and disorders, the vast majority of research has focused on the course and outcome of posttraumatic stress disorder (PTSD) and posttraumatic symptoms. Nevertheless, these studies have much to teach us about the course of and risk factors for poor outcomes after violence exposure.

Risk factors for poor response after violence exposure or PTEs have been categorized in various ways. Some researchers have delineated three categories along an environmental or ecological model: pretraumatic factors, peritraumatic factors, and posttrauma lifespan (King, King, Fairbank, Keane, & Adams, 1998). Others have divided the risk factors into the categories of event factors, individual factors, and peritraumatic response factors (Pfefferbaum, 1997). However, a developmental approach consistent with theories of developmental psychopathology leads to a classification matrix that essentially merges these categories into event factors and individual factors that include innate, environmental, and peritraumatic response factors. Only relatively recently has exposure to PTEs been considered not to be the sole risk factor for PTSD and other posttraumatic symptoms (Litz, Gray, Bryant, & Adler, 2002). In fact, this premise likely created the framework for most early intervention strategies and formed the basis for most of the earliest debriefing models that are now being called into question (Everly, Flannery, Eyler, & Mitchell, 2001). Unfortunately, this initial emphasis on the type of violence exposure or victimization as the sole risk factor for the development of PTSD may have led to the neglect of other risk factors in the provision of crisis intervention. Now that it has become clear that there are many other essential factors that contribute to the development of posttraumatic responses, more comprehensive crisis intervention models need to be implemented.

CRISIS INTERVENTION GOALS

The following review of and recommendations for early intervention strategies are based on our current knowledge concerning the typical patterns of response after exposure to violence, the range of children likely to be encountered, and the known risk factors that affect posttraumatic outcomes. The proposed recommendations presume that crisis intervention strategies that are responsive to an individual child's presentation and risk factors will decrease his/her immediate distress and may prove beneficial in the long term. In addition, the appropriate early intervention strategies will improve access to care for those who require ongoing treatment and will identify those who require continued monitoring.

Risk Factors: Event Factors

There are innumerable types and settings in which individuals may be exposed to violence and PTEs. Different forms of exposures may be more likely to cause trauma-related symptoms and sequelae than others. Physical and emotional proximity during specific types of events appears to be a key factor in determining outcomes (Campbell & Schwarz, 1996; Foy & Goguen, 1998; Pfefferbaum, Call, & Sconzo, 1999; Richters & Martinez, 1993a). For instance, individuals who are injured, tortured, or raped appear to be at highest risk for psychiatric and psychological difficulties and disorders (Finkelhor & Dzuiba-Leatherman, 1994; Foy & Goguen, 1998; Yehuda, McFarlane, & Shalev, 1998). Children who witness the injury or death of a parent also are at increased risk for posttraumatic sequelae (Pynoos et al., 1987). Unquestionably, traumatic grief can have especially devastating responses. However, in other circumstances, individual factors and vulnerabilities appear to be equally salient in determining clinical outcomes (Lonigan, Shannon, Taylor, Finch, & Sallee, 1994; Yehuda et al., 1998).

Most child mental health professionals concur that development is determined by the interaction of experience and biological or innate factors (Pynoos, Steinberg, & Piacentini, 1999). Nowhere is this more evident than in the individual's response to a PTE (McFarlane, 2000; Yehuda et al., 1998). Thus, the same event experienced by two different children might lead to very dissimilar reactions and psychosocial outcomes as a result of their different individual risk and protective factors.

Risk Factors: Individual Factors

The recognition that children's responses to similar violence exposures will not be uniform must be a core principle in the provision of crisis response. While identifying event factors is key in the identification of risk for children exposed to violence, it should not be the primary principle of crisis intervention. In fact, the objective facts of an event may have little to do with a particular child's subjective experiences and his or her subsequent reactions. When crisis interventions do not recognize this phenomenon, they may be at best ineffective and at worst harmful.

Individual risk factors include innate and environmental factors, as well as peritraumatic response factors—that is, the immediate and early postviolence exposure symptoms and responses, including dissociation, hyperarousal, and acute depression (Morgan, Krystal, & Southwick, 2003). Clearly, crisis response providers are well positioned to identify and assess these peritraumatic responses. In most cases, the appearance of these acute symptoms calls for immediate trauma-focused psychotherapy.

Innate factors include age, gender, previous and current psychiatric history, intellectual functioning, and any existing disabilities. Not all of these factors should or can be assessed at the time of an initial crisis intervention, but some situations may require more information about these innate factors in order to inform the immediate intervention. In addition, many of these innate factors will become crucial aspects in understanding the child's long-term response to trauma.

Individual environmental factors are frequently more accessible in the initial response and may be easier to address in early stages of intervention. The most well-researched environmental risk factors are the child's history of exposure to previous violent events and his or her prior traumatic reactions (King, King, Foy, Keane, & Fairbank, 1999; Stretch, Knudson, & Durand, 1998). There is clear evidence that exposure to earlier violent events, such as physical or sexual abuse, heightens the likelihood of a traumatic response after a current PTE (Bremner et al., 1992; Breslau et al., 1998; Green et al., 2000). Without evaluating violence exposure and trauma history, it is difficult to respond effectively in the immediate and follow-up periods.

Social support is also essential to recovery from a PTE (McFarlane, 2000; Pynoos & Eth, 1986). An initial assessment of who is available to the family to support the child and the facilitation of social support should be determined by crisis mental health providers.

Risk Factors: A Developmental Approach

It is imperative that responders assess the specific child's developmental level. While individuals of all ages share many typical symptoms in response to violence exposure, children display symptomatology that is grounded in phase-specific developmental processes. Throughout development, children have particular concerns and psychological issues that come to prominence at different times. As a result, depending on their developmental level, children may be more or less vulnerable to similar events. In general, younger children are more likely to have difficulty with the disappearance of a caregiving adult, while older children and adolescents are more likely to have difficult reactions to the details and nature of a violent event (Marans, 1996; Marans, Berkman, & Cohen, 1996; Marans, Berkowitz, & Cohen, 1998; Martinez & Richters, 1993).

It is not atypical for younger children to lose recently achieved developmental milestones such as bowel and bladder control in the face of a PTE (Marans, 1996; Marans & Adelman, 1997). Toddlers and preschoolers are prone to becoming clingy or displaying a lower threshold for tantrums, with an accompanying increase in tantrum frequency (Marans & Adelman, 1997). Pynoos and Eth (1986) found that preschool children were often more withdrawn and less communicative than older children and adults. These children experienced more separation anxiety and required more corroboration about events from adults.

In addition to difficulties with affect regulation and irritability, school-age children and adolescents may experience diminutions in attention and concentration skills, which in turn may bring about problems with learning, decreased school attendance, or disruptive behaviors in the classroom (Marans, 1996; Marans & Adelman, 1997; Marans et al., 1998). In general, children often try to compensate for their increased sense of vulnerability and helplessness with revenge fantasies or more oppositional and aggressive behaviors (Marans, 1996).

School-age children are especially attentive to their physical prowess or intellectual success and may react to feelings of vulnerability by assuming some responsibility for their inaction; this, in turn, may lead them to compensate for vulnerable feelings by becoming more demanding or aggressive (Marans, 1996; Marans et al., 1996; Marans et al., 1998; Martinez & Richters, 1993).

Risk Factors: The Role of Neuromaturation

Exposure to violence may have an especially devastating impact on both children's short- and long-term functional and psychological outcomes due to the relatively immature state of their central nervous system (CNS). Children's developing brains appear to be especially responsive to the impact of experience. While there is a great deal of scientific evidence that appropriate experiential stimulation is necessary for optimal brain development, overwhelming frightening or dangerous experiences can have harmful effects. Many neurotransmitters that are released at times of fear and anxiety affect the brain. If these neurotransmitters become dysregulated during periods of neurodevelopment, they may be responsible for the brain abnormalities seen in children with PTSD, as well as more subtle brain abnormalities (De Bellis, Baum, et al., 1999; De Bellis, Keshavan, et al., 1999; Laor, Wolmer, Mayes, & Gershon, 1997). However, the relative plasticity of the child's brain is also cause for hope. It is quite possible that children's brains are more amenable to interventions and treatment and recover from traumatic symptoms more readily.

Basic knowledge of developmental traumatology also helps in crafting crisis intervention protocols for children (Berkowitz, 2003), especially if one understands that interrupting and preventing the dysregulation of neurotransmitters is a priority for crisis intervention. Because of these factors, the development and evaluation of interventions for children exposed to violence is a priority for the mental health field (Berkowitz, 2003).

SECONDARY PREVENTION:
CRISES AND EARLY INTERVENTION

A useful way to conceptualize traumatic responses to violence is in terms of the general loss of control an individual experiences. This sense of loss occurs in the internal experience of body, emotion, and cognition, as well as the way in which an individual experiences the external environment. If this is the case, then the goal of crisis interventions is to help the child establish the best possible organization and structure in his or her external environment and internal world in the aftermath of a violent event. The proposed recommendations rely on this precept and recommend not to explore the violent event but to help the exposed child reestablish a sense of control, utilizing developmental principles and the assessment of risk factors.

There are several reasons to consider the implementation of early intervention strategies for children exposed to violence. The first is based on the premise that early intervention may ameliorate or diminish the child's immediate distress. The second is the conviction that the intervention may enhance the child's innate coping mechanisms to process the event effectively, with the goal of preventing later psychiatric and functional disability. Increasingly, crisis intervention models have recognized these goals and mechanisms, although they have not typically been targeted at children. Currently employed crisis intervention models designed for children have generally been centered on school events; few have been developed specifically for children exposed to violence in the home and community.

Part 1: Engagement, Assessment, and Monitoring

Obviously, a clear benefit of crisis intervention is the ability to engage children and families prior to the onset or at the initiation of traumatic symptoms and before they crystalize. Early engagement increases the likelihood of developing a preventative individualized intervention plan. Such a plan may include the ongoing follow-up contact and monitoring of children and their families and of the unfolding ecologically relevant issues that may impact symptom formation and functioning. The many risk factors that have been identified as predicting poor outcomes are not guarantees of poor posttraumatic responses. Rather, early identification and engagement in a therapeutic process may interrupt a propensity toward the development of traumatic symptoms and disorders.

In addition, it does little good for a clinician to evaluate a child's various risk factors after a child has developed a posttraumatic disorder. Only secondary prevention models have the promise of effectively utilizing information about risk and protective factors. Optimal early intervention strategies not only allow for engagement and follow-up monitoring for initial signs of difficulty, but they also allow providers to identify children who have existing vulnerabilities. In this manner, crisis response providers may place special emphasis on intervening with those risk factors that are amenable to modification and change, by identifying those children and families who require more intensive follow-up monitoring for symptom development and functional impairment.

Follow-up monitoring of children and families affected by violence is the third ingredient in the optimal crisis response. While this approach may be controversial, symptoms related to traumatic events may appear unexpectedly after an event and may be triggered by secondary reminders that were previously unrecognized or simply unavoidable (Davidson, 2001; McFarlane, 2000; North et al., 2002). Continued monitoring allows for the early identification of symptoms and for treatment of traumatic symptoms to be instituted when such symptoms may be most amenable to improvement. Follow-up monitoring may take multiple forms, such as direct contact, telephone communication, and administration of information flyers. Thus, interventionists must determine the mode of follow-up that will best meet the requirements of the particular child and family.

Part 2: Specific Risks and Intervention Recommendations

Although little can be done by crisis responders about actual events or innate risk factors, much can be done to prevent deterioration and support recovery by addressing salient environmental issues.

Social Support and Parents   Social support has been identified as one of the most salient features involved in an individual's recovery. Early intervention strategies should systematically evaluate the nature of the child's familial and social support. The two most important support areas are parents, or caregivers, and school. No individuals or institutions are more central to the life of a child. In some instances, other people or activities may also be equally important, for example, coaches, clergy, or an extra-curricular activity such as boy or girl scouts.

Regardless of the age of a child, at times of distress parents assume primary and essential roles in the lives of their children. Child mental health professionals have long recognized that parents are principal therapeutic agents in children's lives. Increasingly, treatment models have focused on parents and parent-child interactions as central ingredients in therapeutic endeavors. In general, throughout the course of normal development, children seek their parents' aid when encountering developmental challenges. Early in a child's life, many experiences are novel and seem threatening. Such things as new sounds or new people may cause alarm and arouse responses. Parents mediate these new occurrences and help children discern what previously unknown experiences are safe or threatening, in large part by ensuring safety and order. This parental mediation interacts with neuromaturation and creates increasing competence in cognitive and psychological resources.

At no time is the role of parenting more important than when a child experiences overwhelming and threatening experiences. The role of parents as mediators of experience and the guarantors of safety and structure is especially vital at moments of real threat and danger. At such times, parents are thrust into complex roles, where they have to secure their own safety and psychological well-being as well as those of their children. Parents' difficulties in recognizing their children's distress and in supporting their needs may be a consequence of their own traumatic reactions and distress (Marans et al., 1996), or they may reflect a lifelong style of inattentive or inadequate parenting.

Appropriate parental attention and support may be one of the most essential ingredients open to early intervention efforts (Richters & Martinez, 1993b). Crisis interventionists are well positioned to identify any issues that are compromising a parent's ability to support his or her child. If parents are struggling with their own reactions to an event, interventionists may help them understand the normalcy of their responses and help them to associate their reactions to how their children are feeling. Lack of parental knowledge about violence exposure and traumatic responses may be dealt with by supplying developmentally informed psychoeducational information and literature about the typical reactions of children and adults to upsetting and overwhelming events. In addition, helping parents understand what behaviors are worrisome and learn parenting and stress management techniques is essential. Assisting parents to cope with their own difficulties and providing information that will help them attend to their children's needs may improve and hasten children's recovery and resilience. Parents can become important therapeutic allies in providing safety and support and monitoring their children's responses and difficulties.

In the aftermath of familial and domestic violence, children's confidence in their parents may be quite damaged, and parents may be psychologically incapable of aiding their children. At these times, direct work with parents around their own needs as well as their children's needs is needed. However, it may also be necessary to recruit other known adults to help facilitate children's coping, such as their teachers. Daily involvement in schooling can be an essential support. However, all too often violence exposure results in children's missing or changing schools. When this occurs, children lose many of the resources that may help mediate the effects of their exposure to violence. In addition, for many children, the known structure and organization of school may be a psychologically safe place. As they mature, school-age children and adolescents increasingly depend on peers and adults outside the home for guidance and support. Disruption from the school community may have especially devastating effects on this age group.

Crisis and early interventions should try to ensure a child's continuation in school when appropriate. They can help parents understand the important role that schools can play in their children's recovery and can help parents work with schools to provide needed support.

Physical Displacement and Social Disruption Longitudinal studies after large-scale events have identified key issues in the social support environments surrounding displacement and social disruption (Laor, Wolmer, & Cohen, 2001; Laor et al., 1997; Laor et al., 1996; Lonigan et al., 1994). The risk factors identified in these studies are especially important elements for consideration for early intervention models.

Displacement from homes and communities and the accompanying loss of social supports may strain even the most resilient individuals. In fact, dislocation may cause more psychological distress than the event itself. Although children may appear to be more adaptive to changes in their surroundings, the burden that displacement may place on their parents and families can contribute a great deal to children's distress. In addition to the potential loss of the comforts of home and the support of school and neighborhood friends, children are endangered by their parents' focus on the basic issues of securing a new living situation. Early intervention responders may identify this risk and either help to slow down the process, when it is voluntary, or to ease the transition by helping the family maintain emotional ties.

Other familial stressors include economic hardship due to job loss or leave of absence, legal procedures, and medical issues. Crisis responders, in coordination with other community resources and agencies, may lessen the burden of these secondary effects of violence exposure. In fact, without intervention these secondary effects may become so stressful and overwhelming that they become primary factors leading to psychosocial dysfunction. Providers may be able to use their professional positions and psychological expertise to intercede with employers, school officials, housing agencies, and court or legal personnel to prevent misunderstandings or punitive responses to a parent's or child's apparent poor performance or unexplained absences.

Continuing Threat One very salient issue for children exposed to violence that is often overlooked by crisis providers is the assessment of ongoing threat and the attempt to secure safety. Law enforcement personnel and domestic violence advocates are the most aware of this concern and frequently offer mothers and children placement in shelters if the perpetrators are not incarcerated. When safety is a valid concern, the continued threat may cause tremendous psychological distress as fear overtakes the child. When threats are real, psychotherapeutic interventions are insufficient. Although one may provide useful stress reduction techniques, the individual's biological imperative is to remain vigilant in the face of danger. Thus, it is irrational to think that psychotherapeutic or psychopharmacological treatments for psychiatric and psychological symptoms that are a direct response to real external danger will be of much utility.

Early assessment and identification of the nature, degree, and validity of a presumed threat allows providers to help children and families appropriately deal with such situations. When danger is exaggerated, factual information may help relieve fear and anxieties; if a threat is imagined, psychotherapeutic treatments may be very useful. When the child's and family's fears are realistic, crisis providers should collaborate with law enforcement, court personnel, and others to communicate the family's concerns and put a safety plan into operation. For instance, crisis responders may help officials increase the bond for a perpetrator or inform officials of a perpetrator's prior offenses. They may also convince law enforcement to provide extra patrols in a geographic area or furnish families with special emergency mobile phones or provide use of safe houses. These are effective tools that should be employed in the face of actual threats to diminish the impact of such threats on children's mental health and functioning (Marans, Berkowitz, & Murphy, 2002). Without appropriate interventions of this kind, concerns about real or imagined threats can be a primary cause of depressive and anxiety symptoms. In addition, these fears can lead to misperceptions of environmental stimuli, as children perceive threats where none exist, resulting in oppositional and aggressive behaviors in an attempt to preempt an anticipated attack (Ford, 2002; Wood, Foy, Layne, Pynoos, & James, 2002).

Part 3: Collaboration

Experts suggest that given the many aspects of children's development that are affected by violence exposure, it is a mistake to initially address psychological issues. Instead, they suggest that the first step should be to ensure safety and environmental stability (Resnick, Acierno, Holmes, Dammeyer, & Kilpatrick, 2000). With this in mind, it becomes apparent that the provision of crisis mental health services cannot be performed in isolation. Most crisis providers generally have close relationships with mental health clinics or practitioners. However, although such relationships are easy to establish, they may not necessarily be the most productive. Rather, relationships need to be forged with law enforcement, courts, schools, local governments, and child protective and social service agencies such as the Red Cross. Depending on the particular jurisdiction in which the crisis intervention providers operate, not all of these collaborations need to be direct. For instance, courts and local governments may be best accessed via law enforcement, and schools may be the best manner to access governmental resources.

Perhaps the best way to create relationships with the various agencies involved in crisis response is to establish a presence within the Incident Command System (ICS). Although most jurisdictions have had an ICS for many years, concerns about terrorism and mass violence have increased the prominence of these projects, and most states, counties, and municipalities now have regular meetings of their ICS members. Crisis intervention programs should be included in the ICS in preparation for deployment in cases of mass violence, and the special needs of children exposed to violence should also be considered as episodes of violence that may require the same coordination of responses, albeit on a much smaller scale.

MODELS OF RESPONSE

The range of events that constitutes exposure to violence requires flexibility in how professionals manage treatment for individuals or groups. For example, some forms of exposure may be recurrent but only recently identified; others may be acute experiences that may not have been anticipated. The result is a set of possible approaches—one that focuses on immediate responses to an event or set of events and another that acknowledges the necessity for responses that may be delayed. In some circumstances, such as those that occur in a prolonged event, a combination of delayed responses and acute intervention or prevention efforts may be employed.

Crisis Intervention: Acute Response

Some crisis intervention programs may be deployed within hours of an episode of violence exposure. This is an opportunity to perform assessments of peritraumatic responses, develop safety plans, and provide basic psychoeducational materials about typical responses to danger to both parents and children. In addition to conducting an assessment of the child, it is an opportunity to help engage in a brief session that involves the child's communicating concerns either through play, drawing, or talking. This should be a time for the child to take the lead and, whether by engaging motor and cognitive skills through drawing or play or simply by talking and questioning, it provides an opportunity for the child to reestablish some sense of control in the presence of an adult. If the child wishes, it may be useful to both the child and parent for the parent to be present at this time. As always, families should know how to contact the service provider at any time and be encouraged to do so.

While an acute response may be helpful in decreasing a child's immediate distress, there is no evidence that one-time interventions have a positive longitudinal impact (van Emmerik et al., 2002). In addition to diminishing immediate distress, perhaps the most important goal of an acute response is the engagement with the child and family that can set the stage for future interactions.

Crisis Response: Peri-exposure Interventions

In many, if not most, situations, immediate responses are either unwarranted or not possible, and the initial crisis response does not occur until sometime later. When this is the case, the same procedures as in an acute response should be followed with some additions. Given that more time has elapsed, there is more information that can be gathered and shared. First, the child's and family's symptomatic responses can and should be evaluated more fully. A review of potential risk factors, especially focusing on previous histories of PTE, psychiatric history, and developmental history, is essential. Learning about the child's and family's immediate concrete concerns such as schooling, housing, and safety issues should also be a priority. Telephone calls to governmental, law enforcement, and other social service agencies may help address some of these concerns. If a child or family member is significantly distressed or has acute dissociative, hyperarousal, or depressive symptoms, he or she should be linked with trauma-focused treatment providers immediately. If an acute response has occurred prior to this meeting, it obviously may be shortened; regardless, it seems prudent that a series of approximately three meetings occur over several weeks to support recovery and continued monitoring.

In the next meeting, hopefully occurring within a week, many of the same activities will need to occur. Follow-up assessments of psychological symptoms and environmental concerns as well as linkages to resources and information sharing are requisite. A review with parents of their and their children's symptoms, if any, lays the groundwork for the goal of this second meeting. Parents should be provided with techniques in verbal and written form to help them effectively manage and support their child's behavior and symptoms. These may include such techniques as nurturing limit setting for oppositional behavior, responding to nightmares and sleep disturbance, performing relaxation techniques for anxiety, and diminishing any self-blame. Often, it is useful to practice these techniques in an interactive manner with the affected child or children.

The third meeting should review and address earlier issues and concerns, review psychological, behavioral, and functional difficulties, and provide a booster for parent management related to child behavior. In addition, a plan should be made for next steps, whether this involves a recommendation for treatment, continued monitoring, or nothing substantial. By this time, typically 3 weeks post-event, the need for psychotherapeutic services should be known, and the crisis provider is in the best position to make this linkage, perhaps even accompanying the child and family to a first session to ease this difficult transition. If continued monitoring seems sufficient, the provider and family will need to agree on the mechanism and time interval for contact. Providers cannot forget that the natural tendency to avoid and minimize internal difficulties requires that providers make the effort to ensure further contact and do not rely on families to check in or acknowledge new psychological issues.

Potential Hazards of Crisis Intervention

The provision of crisis intervention is not without potential dangers. While it is important to be humble about the preventative and curative effects of these strategies, it is also important to recognize that if not carefully performed they have potential to do harm. Because many individuals tend to recover from their initial distress, it is important that during the practice of intervening, early responders do not derail a child's innate coping abilities. It is possible that children who otherwise would recover without aid may be harmed by inappropriately applied techniques or overzealous interventions (Gist & Devilly, 2002; Mayou, Ehlers, & Hobbs, 2000).

There are a number of ways that crisis providers could inadvertently do harm. Perhaps the most frequent mistake that occurs is when an episode of violence involves a group of children. It often seems that this would be a reasonable opportunity to provide services in a group format, especially when resources are limited. However, an inherent danger in the use of groups is the potential for a contamination effect. Children or adults who are more distraught and symptomatic may have a negative psychological impact on mildly symptomatic or previously resilient children. In a treatment study conducted after the 1998 earthquakes in Turkey, children were provided a series of classroom-based interventions. Children who were asymptomatic faired worse and developed new symptoms, while symptomatic children improved (Laor, 2002). If it is necessary to provide group intervention for children exposed to violence, it is essential that individuals first be assessed and that symptomatic children are treated separately from asymptomatic children (Berkowitz, 2003). Homogeneity among group members based both on developmental phase and symptom presentation appears essential (Berkowitz, 2003). It may be the case that the only time that a group format should be used during a crisis intervention phase is for informational and administrative processing.

Second, in the process of providing a crisis intervention, one may unnecessarily re-expose children to the details of the event before they are prepared to psychologically process them. It is rarely appropriate to ask children to review what occurred. Typically, at some point they will report their experience of the incident, but it is essential that it be on their terms. Otherwise, providers are in the position of potentially being perceived as forcing them to re-experience the event and children may feel re-victimized by the very people attempting to help them. Exposure to internal and external stimuli, without clear and obvious symptomatology, may interfere with a natural recovery process and working through events by the individual child and his or her family (Mayou et al., 2000). Although exposure therapies are an appropriate treatment for children with posttraumatic symptoms, they are probably contraindicated for crisis interventions if children are not clearly symptomatic (Berkowitz, 2003).

A third issue is the danger of "pathologizing" events that may not be understood or experienced as unusual or causing distress (Mayou et al., 2000). Although most crisis intervention providers attempt to normalize persons' reactions to violence exposure, the fact that others believe that they require professional help may increase children's and family's feelings of inadequacy and inability to support recovery among themselves. Again, it is essential that crisis providers carefully explain their role to children and families and ensure that they allow them to take the lead when appropriate.

CONCLUSIONS

As more research and evaluation has been accomplished regarding the outcomes, risk and protective factors, and treatment interventions for children exposed to violence, the provision of crisis intervention has become more complex. If we are hoping to create paradigms of secondary prevention, then the research must guide the development of and training in these models. For instance, we now know that single interventions do not seem to have much effect; therefore, crisis intervention models must provide multiple sessions. We also have a much better understanding of risk and protective factors, and it has become requisite that these factors be evaluated and addressed when appropriate and possible. The importance of using a developmental framework when evaluating and intervening with children exposed to violence is clear. Debriefing models should be used rarely, if at all, and providing intervention in a group setting may be contraindicated. The inordinate variability of presentations of exposed children in conjunction with variability of factors and situations calls for a remarkable amount of expertise and a wide array of collaborating partners.

All of these findings and recommendations require a great deal of training and practice for those providing crisis intervention; yet frequently, crisis intervention providers are trained to follow specific protocols or scripts (McGee & Jennings, 2002), which may be inadequate to the complexity of the situations and tasks at hand. Crisis intervention for children exposed to violence must be viewed as it truly is: a complex task that requires thoughtful and well-trained providers (Berkowitz, 2003).

REFERENCES

Berkowitz, S.J. (2003). Children exposed to community violence: The rationale for early intervention. *Clinical Child & Family Psychology Review, 6*(4), 293–302.

Bolton, D., O'Ryan, D., Udwin, O., Boyle, S., & Yule, W. (2000). The long-term psychological effects of a disaster experienced in adolescence: II. General psychopathology. *Journal of Child Psychology & Psychiatry & Allied Disciplines, 41*(4), 513–523.

Boney-McCoy, S., & Finkelhor, D. (1995). Psychosocial sequelae of violent victimization in a national youth sample. *Journal of Consulting & Clinical Psychology, 63*(5), 726–736.

Bremner, J., Southwick, S., Brett, E., Fontana, A., Rosenheck, R., & Charney, D.S. (1992). Dissociation and posttraumatic stress disorder in Vietnam combat veterans. *American Journal of Psychiatry, 149*(3), 328–332.

Breslau, N., Kessler, R.C., Chilcoat, H.D., Schultz, L.R., Davis, G.C., & Andreski, P. (1998). Trauma and posttraumatic stress disorder in the community: The 1996 Detroit Area Survey of Trauma. *Archives of General Psychiatry, 55*(7), 626–632.

Campbell, C., & Schwarz, D.F. (1996). Prevalence and impact of exposure to interpersonal violence among suburban and urban middle school students. *Pediatrics, 98* (3 Pt 1), 396–402.

Centers for Disease Control and Prevention. (1999). *Co-occurrence of intimate partner violence against mothers and abuse of children.* Atlanta, GA: National Center for Injury Prevention and Control.

Cohen, J.A., Berliner, L., & Mannarino, A. P. (2000). Treating traumatized children: A research review and synthesis. *Trauma, Violence & Abuse, 1*(1), 29–46.

Cohen, J.A., Berliner, L., & Mannarino, A. (2003). Psychosocial and Pharmacological Interventions for Crime Victims. *Journal of Traumatic Stress, 16*(2), 175–186.

Cohen, J.A., Perel, J.M., DeBellis, M.D., Friedman, M.J., & Putnam, F.W. (2002). Treating traumatized children: Clinical implications of the psychobiology of posttraumatic stress disorder. *Trauma, Violence & Abuse, 3*(2), 91–108.

Creamer, M. (1996). The prevention of posttraumatic stress. In P. Cotton & H. Jackson (Eds.), *Early intervention & prevention in mental health* (pp. 229–246). Australia: Australian Psychological Society.

Davidson, J.R. (2001). Recognition and treatment of posttraumatic stress disorder. *JAMA, 286*(5), 584–588.

De Bellis, M.D., Baum, A.S., Birmaher, B., Keshavan, M.S., Eccard, C.H., Boring, A. M., et al. (1999). Developmental traumatology: I. Biological stress systems. *Biological Psychiatry, 45*(10), 1259–1270.

De Bellis, M.D., Keshavan, M.S., Clark, D.B., Casey, B., Giedd, J.N., Boring, A.M., et al. (1999). Developmental traumatology: II. Brain development. *Biological Psychiatry, 45*(10), 1271–1284.

Dodge, K.A., Pettit, G.S., & Bates, J.E. (1997). How the experience of early physical abuse leads children to become chronically aggressive. In D. Cicchetti & S.L. Toth (Eds.), *Developmental perspectives on trauma: Theory, research, and intervention (Rochester symposium on developmental psychopathology)* (Vol. 8, pp. 263–288). Rochester, NY: University of Rochester Press.

DuRant, R.H., Getts, A., Cadenhead, C., Emans, S.J., & Woods, E.R. (1995). Exposure to violence and victimization and depression, hopelessness, and purpose in life among adolescents living in and around public housing. *Journal of Developmental Behavioral Pediatrics, 16*(4), 233–237.

Everly, G.S., Flannery, R.B., Eyler, V., & Mitchell, J.T. (2001). Sufficiency analysis of an integrated multicomponent approach to crisis intervention: Critical incident stress management. *Advanced Mind Body Medicine, 17*(3), 174–181.

Finkelhor, D., & Dzuiba-Leatherman, J. (1994). Victimization of children. *American Psychologist, 49*(3), 173–183.

Ford, J.D. (2002). Traumatic victimization in childhood and persistent problems with oppositional-defiance. *Journal of Aggression, Maltreatment & Trauma, 6*(1), 25–58.

Foy, D.W., & Goguen, C. (1998). Community violence-related PTSD in children and adolescents. *PTSD Research Quarterly, 9*, 1–6.

Freeman, L.N., Mokros, H., & Poznanski, E. (1993). Violent events reported by normal urban school-aged children: Characteristics and depression correlates. *Journal of the American Academy of Child & Adolescent Psychiatry, 32*(2), 419–423.

Gist, R., & Devilly, G.J. (2002). Post-trauma debriefing: the road too frequently travelled. *Lancet, 360*, 741–742.

Gordon, N.S., Farberow, N.L., & Maida, C.A. (1999). *Children and disasters*. Philadelphia: Brunner/Mazel.

Green, B.L., Goodman, L.A., Krupnick, J.L., Corcoran, C.B., Petty, R.M., Stockton, P., et al. (2000). Outcomes of single versus multiple trauma exposure in a screening sample. *Journal of Traumatic Stress, 13*(2), 271–286.

Harris, W., Putnam, F., & Fairbank, J. (in press). *Mobilizing trauma resources for children*. Manuscript submitted for publication.

Harvey, A.G., & Bryant, R.A. (1999). The relationship between acute stress disorder and posttraumatic stress disorder: 2-year prospective evaluation. *Journal of Consulting & Clinical Psychology, 67*(6), 985–988.

Hendricks, J.E., McKean, J., & Hendricks, C.G. (2003). *Crisis intervention: Contemporary issues for on-site interveners* (3rd ed.). Springfield, IL: Charles C Thomas Publishers, Ltd.

Hill, H.M., & Madhere, S. (1996). Exposure to community violence and African American children: A multidimensional model of risks and resources. *Journal of Community Psychology, 24*(1), 26–43.

Horn, J.L., & Trickett, P.K. (1998). Community violence and child development: A review of research. In P.K. Trickett & C.D. Schellenbach (Eds.), *Violence against children in the family and the community* (pp. 103–138). Washington, DC: American Pscyhological Association.

Kilpatrick, D.S.B. (1997). *The prevalence and consequences of child victimization: Summary of a research study*. Washington, DC: U.S. Department of Justice, National Institute of Justice.

King, D.W., King, L.A., Foy, D.W., Keane, T.M., & Fairbank, J.A. (1999). Posttraumatic stress disorder in a national sample of female and male Vietnam veterans: Risk factors, war-zone stressors, and resilience-recovery variables. *Journal of Abnormal Psychology, 108*(1), 164–170.

King, L.A., King, D.W., Fairbank, J.A., Keane, T.M., & Adams, G.A. (1998). Resilience-recovery factors in post-traumatic stress disorder among female and male Vietnam veterans: Hardiness, postwar social support, and additional stressful life events. *Journal of Personal and Social Psychology, 74*(2), 420–434.

Kolko, D. (1998). Treatment and intervention for child victims of violence. In P.K. Trickett & C.D. Schellenbach (Eds.), *Violence against children in the family and the community* (pp. 213–249). Washington, DC: American Psychological Association.

Laor, N. (2002). *Community reactivation after war and disaster: The role of child mental health professionals*. Paper presented at the 49th Annual Meeting of the American Academy of Child and Adolescent Psychiatry, October 25, San Francisco, CA.

Laor, N., Wolmer, L., & Cohen, D.J. (2001). Mothers' functioning and children's symptoms 5 years after a SCUD missile attack. *American Journal of Psychiatry, 158*(7), 1020–1026.

Laor, N., Wolmer, L., Mayes, L.C., & Gershon, A. (1997). Israeli preschool children under scuds: A 30-month follow-up. *Journal of the American Academy of Child Psychiatry, 36*(3), 349–356.

Laor, N., Wolmer, L., Mayes, L.C., Golomb, A., Silverberg, D.S., Weizman, R., et al. (1996). Israeli preschoolers under Scud missile attacks: A developmental perspective on risk-modifying factors. *Archives of General Psychiatry, 53*(5), 416–423.

Litz, B.T., Gray, M.J., Bryant, R.A., & Adler, A.B. (2002). Early intervention for trauma: Current status and future directions. *Clinical Psychology-Science & Practice, 9*(2), 112–134.

Lonigan, C.J., Shannon, M.P., Taylor, C.M., Finch, A.J., Jr., & Sallee, F.R. (1994). Children exposed to disaster: II. Risk factors for the development of post-traumatic symptomatology. *Journal of the American Academy of Child and Adolescent Psychiatry, 33*(1), 94–105.

Marans, S. (1996). Psychoanalysis on the beat: Children, police, and urban trauma. *Psychoanalytic Study of the Child, 51*, 522–541.

Marans, S., & Adelman, A. (1997). Experiencing violence in a developmental context. In J.D. Osofsky & P. Scharf (Eds.), *Children in a violent society* (pp. 202–222). New York: Guilford.

Marans, S., Berkman, M., & Cohen, D. (1996). Child development and adaptation to catastrophic circumstances. In R.J. Apfel & B. Simon (Eds.), *Minefields in their hearts: The mental health of children in war and communal violence* (pp. 104–127). New Haven, CT: Yale University Press.

Marans, S., Berkowitz, S.J., & Cohen, D.J. (1998). Police and mental health professionals: Collaborative responses to the impact of violence on children and families. *Child and Adolescent Psychiatric Clinics of North America, 7*(3), 635–651.

Marans, S., Berkowitz, S.J., & Murphy, R.A. (2002). Police-mental health responses to children exposed to violence: The Child Development-Community Policing program. In M. Lewis (Ed.), *Child and adolescent psychiatry: A comprehensive textbook* (3rd ed., pp. 1406–1416). Baltimore: Williams and Wilkins.

Margolin, G., & Gordis, E.B. (2000). The effects of family and community violence on children. *Annual Review of Psychology, 51*, 445–479.

Martinez, P., & Richters, J.E. (1993). The NIMH Community Violence Project: II. Children's distress symptoms associated with violence exposure. *Psychiatry, 56*(1), 22–35.

Masten, A.S., Neemann, J., & Andenas, S. (1994). Life events and adjustment in adolescents: The significance of event independence, desirability, and chronicity. *Journal of Research on Adolescence, 4*(1), 71–97.

Mayou, R., Ehlers, A., & Hobbs, M. (2000). Psychological debriefing for road traffic accident victims: Three-year follow-up of a randomised controlled trial. *British Journal of Psychiatry, 176*, 589–593.

McFarlane, A.C. (2000). Posttraumatic stress disorder: A model of the longitudinal course and the role of risk factors. *Journal of Clinical Psychiatry, 61*(Suppl 5), 15–20.

McGee, R.K., & Jennings, B. (2002). Ascending to "lower" levels: The case for nonprofessional crisis workers. In D. Lester (Ed.), *Crisis intervention and counseling by telephone* (2nd ed., pp. 231–241). Springfield, IL: Charles C Thomas.

Morgan, C.A., III, Krystal, J.H., & Southwick, S.M. (2003). Toward early pharmacological posttraumatic stress intervention. *Biological Psychiatry, 53*(9), 834–843.

North, C.S., Tivis, L., McMillen, J.C., Pfefferbaum, B., Spitznagel, E.L., Cox, J., et al. (2002). Psychiatric disorders in rescue workers after the Oklahoma City bombing. *American Journal of Psychiatry, 159*(5), 857–859.

Osofsky, J.D. (1999). The impact of violence on children. *Future of Children, 9*(3), 33–49.

Osofsky, J.D. (2003). Prevalence of children's exposure to domestic violence and child maltreatment: Implications for prevention and intervention. *Clinical Child & Family Psychology Review, 6*(3), 161–170.

Pfefferbaum, B. (1997). Posttraumatic stress disorder in children: A review of the past 10 years. *Journal of the American Academy of Child and Adolescent Psychiatry, 36*(11), 1503–1511.

Pfefferbaum, B., Call, J.A., & Sconzo, G.M. (1999). Mental health services for children in the first two years after the 1995 Oklahoma City terrorist bombing. *Psychiatric Services, 50*(7), 956–958.

Pine, D.S., & Cohen, J.A. (2002). Trauma in children and adolescents: risk and treatment of psychiatric sequelae. *Biological Psychiatry, 51*(7), 519–531.

Pynoos, R., & Eth, S. (1986). Witness to violence: The child interview. *The Journal of the American Academy of Child and Adolescent Psychiatry, 25*, 306–319.

Pynoos, R.S., Frederick, C., Nader, K., Arroyo, W., Steinberg, A., Eth, S., et al. (1987). Life threat and posttraumatic stress in school-age children. *Archives of General Psychiatry, 44*(12), 1057–1063.

Pynoos, R.S., Steinberg, A.M., & Piacentini, J.C. (1999). A developmental psychopathology model of childhood traumatic stress and intersection with anxiety disorders. *Biological Psychiatry, 46*(11), 1542–1554.

Resnick, H., Acierno, R., Holmes, M., Dammeyer, M., & Kilpatrick, D. (2000). Emergency evaluation and intervention with female victims of rape and other violence. *Journal of Clinical Psychology, 56*(10), 1317–1333.

Richters, J.E., & Martinez, P. (1993a). The NIMH Community Violence Project: I. Children as victims of and witnesses to violence. *Psychiatry, 56*(1), 7–21.

Richters, J.E., & Martinez, P.E. (1993b). Violent communities, family choices, and children's chances: An algorithm for improving the odds. *Development & Psychopathology, 5*(4), 609–627.

Rose, S., Bisson, J., & Wessely, S. (2001). Psychological debriefing for preventing posttraumatic stress disorder (PTSD), *Cochrane Review,* Cochrane Library.

Ruggiero, K.J., Morris, T.L., & Scotti, J.R. (2001). Treatment for children with posttraumatic stress disorder: Current status and future directions. *Clinical Psychology-Science & Practice, 8*(2), 210–227.

Schwab-Stone, M., Chen, C., Greenberger, E., Silver, D., Lichtman, J., & Voyce, C. (1999). No safe haven: II. The effects of violence exposure on urban youth. *Journal of the American Academy of Child and Adolescent Psychiatry, 38*(4), 359–367.

Schwab-Stone, M.E., Ayers, T.S., Kasprow, W., Voyce, C., Barone, C., Shriver, T., et al. (1995). No safe haven: A study of violence exposure in an urban community. *Journal of the American Academy of Child and Adolesccent Psychiatry, 34*(10), 1343–1352.

Stretch, R.H., Knudson, K.H., & Durand, D. (1998). Effects of premilitary and military trauma on the development of post-traumatic stress disorder symptoms in female and male active duty soldiers. *Military Medicine, 163*(7), 466–470.

Tjaden, P., & Thoennes, N. (2000). Prevalence and consequences of male-to-female and female-to-male intimate partner violence as measured by the National Violence Against Women Survey. *Violence Against Women, 6*(2), 142–161.

van Emmerik, A.A., Kamphuis, J.H., Hulsbosch, A.M., & Emmelkamp, P.M. (2002). Single session debriefing after psychological trauma: a meta-analysis. *Lancet, 360*, 766–771.

Wood, J., Foy, D.W., Layne, C., Pynoos, R., & James, C. (2002). An examination of the relationships between violence exposure, posttraumatic stress symptomatology, and delinquent activity: An "ecopathological" model of delinquent behavior among incarcerated adolescents. *Journal of Aggression, Maltreatment & Trauma, 6*(1), 127–147.

Yehuda, R., McFarlane, A.C., & Shalev, A.Y. (1998). Predicting the development of posttraumatic stress disorder from the acute response to a traumatic event. *Biological Psychiatry, 44*(12), 1305–1313.

7

MENTAL HEALTH INTERVENTIONS FOR CHILDREN AFFECTED BY WAR OR TERRORISM

B. Heidi Ellis, Audrey Rubin,
Theresa Stichick Betancourt, and Glenn Saxe

The effects of war on the lives of children are many and far-reaching. Children who witness or experience combat are directly exposed to violence. Even those who never see war suffer losses of family members, their country, or their sense of safety. Children lose fundamental experiences of childhood, such as a continuous education and a social and economic infrastructure that can support their basic health and other developmental needs. All of these disruptions have profound implications for the mental health and development of children (Ajdukovic & Ajdukovic, 1993). Viewed from a social ecological framework (Bronfenbrenner, 1979; Elbedour, ten Bensel, & Bastien, 1993), war affects all levels of the social ecology: the individual child, the family, the community, the school infrastructure, and the broader culture.

Such a complex and far-reaching experience as war demands a comprehensive intervention response. Unfortunately, the science of mental health interventions for war-affected children is fraught with methodological and ethical difficulties, and it lags far behind the need. Where does one begin in treating a child affected by war?

As a first step, it is necessary to determine where the intervention is taking place, who the intervention is for, and what the intervention seeks to address. Is the intervention in the field, where war is likely to have devastated basic infrastructure? Is the intervention in response to a single act of violence or to a pattern of chronic violence and unrest? Is the intervention provided by Western clinicians for children of another culture, or is it a community-based response led by local paraprofessionals? Is the intervention addressing posttraumatic stress symptoms,

cultural bereavement, or another symptom cluster? Each of these questions significantly impacts the type of intervention, the outcomes targeted by the intervention, and the methods of both implementation and evaluation.

Children who experience war in their own countries are sometimes resettled
as refugees in, or flee as asylum seekers to, other countries. These children often
carry with them horrific stories of trauma and years of development spent within
the suboptimal, and at times chronically dangerous and depriving, environments
of refugee camps. After resettlement within the host country, children must further confront loss of their own culture and country, loss of past community and
family members, and all of the challenges associated with acculturation.

This chapter focuses on interventions provided for war-affected children
within the United States of America, but also draws on innovative international
examples. The United States has a highly developed and well-functioning infrastructure; as a result, these interventions are different from those provided else-
where. Because the United States is seen as a comparatively safe and stable country, interventions tend to focus on healing and moving beyond past trauma;
interventions provided in places of ongoing danger tend to focus on supporting
the broader social community that protects a child (Boothby, 1994).

ISSUES IN RESEARCH ON INTERVENTIONS
FOR CHILDREN EXPOSED TO WAR AND TERRORISM

War versus Terrorism

Although war and acts of terrorism share many basic elements, including willful
violence with socio-political roots, the effects may differ significantly, requiring
significantly different interventions. Prolonged terrorism within a country or region, such as the Middle East, may result in a war-like state for citizens of that
country or region. Single or limited acts of terrorism, such as those that occurred
within the United States on September 11th (hereafter referred to as 9/11), have
very different implications for intervention. Children exposed to the 9/11 attacks
remained in their communities. Within a short period of time, basic infrastructure such as schools and medical facilities were functioning again, affording these
children access to more sophisticated interventions.

Levels of Intervention

Mental health responses to war and terrorism must be understood as embedded
within a complex, interrelated system influenced by cultural, community, familial, and individual factors. An ecological developmental model is very useful for

understanding the many interrelated contributing layers. This chapter uses the different levels of the social ecology as a framework for providing intervention in order to take a broad perspective on how to provide mental health interventions to war-affected children and include concepts from public health and community mental health. Some refugee children experience acute mental health problems such as posttraumatic stress disorder (PTSD) and depression and require individual interventions; other children do not seek individual treatment, perhaps because of the high stigmatization of mental illness within certain cultures, because their symptoms do not reach such acute levels, or because their family's priority is on returning to "normal life" rather than seeking treatment (Geltman, Augustyn, Barnett, Klass, & Groves, 2000). Apfel and Simon (1996) argued that interventions that focus on a larger number of seemingly unaffected children are as important as those providing intensive interventions to children with the greatest need. Interventions at different levels of the social ecology address different needs and outcomes of war-affected children.

Methodological Challenges to Research with War-Affected Children

Approximately 20 million youth have been displaced due to war. Many more continue to live in environments where they are surrounded by violence and political strife (United Nations High Commission for Refugees [UNHCR], 2002). There is unquestionably a great need to understand the mental health needs of these children and to develop and offer effective interventions. However, the literature examining specific interventions and their effectiveness is sparse. Methodological challenges create barriers to empirical testing of interventions. Differences in languages and a lack of instruments validated for specific cultures can lead to difficulties in evaluation. Interventions developed for one culture may not be readily transferable to another culture, leading to problems in replicability. In addition, all of the standard challenges of conducting intervention research within a community exist, including identifying appropriate control groups, maintaining treatment fidelity in a changing environment, identifying a group of children with similar treatment needs, and mustering resources for both intervention and evaluation (Rousseau, 1993; Stein et al., 2002).

Despite these challenges, research on interventions for war-affected children is essential. There are few resources directed toward refugee children, although by virtue of their exposure to war and resettlement stressors, refugee children are at high risk for the development of mental health problems (Howard & Hodes, 2000) and in great need of effective interventions.

Culture and Children's Mental Health

Culture and mental health are intrinsically linked, particularly in the context of war, which can magnify tensions between different cultures or result in people fleeing to new countries. The cultural and historical meanings given to violent experiences have important implications for both mental health consequences and interventions (Honwana, 1998). Although many definitions of culture exist, the classic features are well summarized in the definition provided by Helman:

> A set of guidelines (both explicit and implicit) which individuals inherit as members of a particular society, and which tells them how to view the world, how to experience it emotionally, and how to behave in relation to other people, to supernatural forces or gods, and to the natural environment. (1994, p. 2)

Culture plays a central role in how trauma, mental health, and healing are conceptualized. Cross-cultural perspectives on medicine can inform discussions of mental health and mental health responses. As in the relationship between culture and illness as described by Kleinman, Eisenberg, and Good (1978), culture is the lens through which experience is understood, labeled, and given meaning. These processes are intrinsically linked to both physical and mental health. Many cultures, particularly non-Western cultures, do not draw distinctions between the mind and body. In many refugee populations, mental health distress may be expressed through somatic as well as emotional complaints and symptoms.

Spiritual or religious systems of understanding trauma and healing may be important to explore when working with multicultural populations. As a whole, when responding to mental health issues across vast cultural differences, assessment must consider issues of meaning and the cultural perspective through which experience is interpreted and understood.

Furthermore, mental health responses to war and terrorism are intrinsically linked to the social systems in which they occur and must be understood at the level of the family, society, and the larger culture. As Honwana (1998) underlined, in some non-Western settings the locus of emotional distress or disorder is not always ascribed to the individual. Entire families and communities may be conceptualized as in need of healing.

INTERVENTIONS FOR WAR-AFFECTED
CHILDREN ACROSS THE SOCIAL ECOLOGY:
INDIVIDUAL AND FAMILY INTERVENTIONS

At the center of the social ecological model is the individual child, the locus of intervention most traditionally targeted under Western models of mental health care. Emphasizing the psychopathology of an individual has received due criticism, however, from those who assert that the problem is better localized within the warring society and not the individual child (Berman, 2001); still, there remains a great need for interventions that aid individual children and their families (Barenbaum, Ruchkin, & Schwab-Stone, 2004; Howard & Hodes, 2000). Children at high risk for dangerous or suicidal behaviors need closer monitoring than may be afforded by group interventions. In addition, the family unit can be an important protective factor for children; by involving the family in therapy, the child's most central support system may be bolstered and strengthened.

Unfortunately, there is very little empirical examination of individual and family intervention approaches for war-affected children. Some of the very complexities that make post-war adjustment difficult for children—being forced to relocate to a foreign country, lack of knowledge of health care systems in the area of resettlement, and a paucity of resources—create challenges for conducting empirical research on the effectiveness of different treatment models. Evaluation of treatment models is complicated by a lack of instruments validated for different cultural groups. Thus, while many groups have developed innovative and culturally sensitive treatment approaches for war-affected children (Ellis, 2004; Miller & Billings, 1994; Rousseau, Singh, Lacroix, Bagilishya, & Meacham, 2004), there is very limited empirical evaluation of these treatment models.

Trauma-Focused Interventions

Research on other traumatized populations provides a starting point for developing theoretically driven treatment approaches for refugees and other war-affected children. There is some evidence that cognitive-behavioral therapy (CBT) is an effective treatment for traumatized children and adolescents (Cohen, 1998; Deblinger, McLeer, & Henry, 1990; Saigh, Yasik, & Oberfield, 1999). According to a review of treatments for children and adolescents with PTSD, clinical consensus identifies the following elements as key dimensions of trauma treatment: direct exploration of the trauma, stress-management techniques, addressing inaccurate attributions about trauma, and including parents in the treatment (Cohen, 1998).

Short-term trauma-focused therapy has been described as a model of family intervention for use with war-related trauma (Nieves-Grafals, 2001). This model proposes four phases of treatment: building the alliance, strengthening coping skills, reprocessing the trauma, and terminating the treatment. However, viewing the mental health of war-affected children only through a trauma lens may obscure other important targets of treatment such as grief, loss, and post-war stressors (Layne, Pynoos, & Saltzman, 2001). Furthermore, PTSD is frequently not the presenting problem (Mueke, 1992; Sveaass & Reichelt, 2001). Despite high rates of exposure to violence, many children remain resilient (Apfel & Simon,

1996; Rousseau, Said, & Gagné, 1998; Sack, Him, & Dickason, 1999). Within individual treatment, recognizing the variability of individual responses to war is essential.

In addition, cultural differences may affect the appropriateness of using a trauma-focused treatment approach. For refugees from some cultures, treatment that focuses on discussing the past may be in contradiction to cultural values of focusing on the present and future. Furthermore, the meaning ascribed to symptoms or events may be quite different from Western understanding. For instance, a Somali family who experienced trauma in the war might view mental health symptoms of a child, and indeed events of the war itself, as a result of the family's own failure in God's eyes. Challenging the family's understanding of the problem would effectively be challenging a cultural belief system. A more appropriate and culturally sensitive intervention might demand focusing on positive coping skills or decreasing current stressors.

Interventions that Address the Social Ecology

Many families do not present with trauma and related symptoms as the primary problem. Rather, they may identify social issues such as economic stability or threat of deportation as more pressing than psychological well-being. Until these basic needs are attended to, psychotherapy may not be perceived as useful to a family (Geltman et al. 2000; Sveaass & Reichelt, 2001; Watters, 2001). In fact, environmental factors such as unemployment may precipitate or contribute to PTSD symptomatology (Westermeyer, 1989). Clinical consensus among the refugee mental health field points toward a need to both assess and address the broader socio-ecological needs of families (Kinzie, 1989; Lustig, Weine, Saxe, & Beardslee, 2004; Watters, 2001).

In a preliminary study of school-based mental health services for refugee children, O'Shea, Hodes, Down, and Bramley (2000) evaluated a model of intervention that included CBT as well as attention to socio-environmental factors, such as support for asylum or housing applications. The intervention was individualized according to each child's needs and involved family therapy or individual therapy accordingly. By locating the services at the school and involving the teachers in engaging families, the program circumvented critical problems of service access that may prevent refugee families from seeking mental health care in more traditional settings (Howard & Hodes, 2000). Fourteen refugee children with significant exposure to war and violence, ages 7–11, were enrolled in the program. Length of treatment appeared to be individualized. A Strengths and Difficulties Questionnaire was implemented pre- and post-intervention. For the seven children for whom pre- and postassessments were available, scores showed improvement. Several methodological problems limit this study, including small sample size, a brief outcome measure that does not specifically capture psychopathology, and hetero-geneity of intervention design. Nonetheless, this study is one of few that provides some evaluation and incorporates theoretically supported components of interven-tion such as CBT and support for socio-environmental needs.

Trauma Systems Therapy for Refugees is an intervention approach that specifically addresses the social ecology. This intervention is based on the premise that posttraumatic symptoms of a child exposed to trauma are the result of both a child's dysregulated emotional system and a social environment that is unable to contain the child's dysregulation. Interventions seek to bolster the individual child's regulation skills and stabilize the child's social environment. Social environ-mental interventions can include legal advocacy for basic needs such as safe hous-ing, legal status in a new country, financial or nutritional resources, or appropriate educational placements. Community-based or home-based care is also frequently implemented, in an effort to strengthen the family functioning and better support the child's mental health needs (Ellis, 2004; Saxe, Ellis, & Kaplow, 2004).

Use of Play and Narrative in Interventions

Apfel and Simon (1996) proposed that rather than focusing on pathology, inter-ventions should focus on leveraging strengths and resilience in war-affected chil-dren. As an illustration of this, play—a child's natural resource—can be used in therapy to help the child express experiences related to past traumatic events. Art therapy has been used widely cross-culturally and may serve as a bridge between clients and therapists who do not share common languages or experiences (Miller & Billings, 1994; Rousseau et al. 2004).

Testimonial psychotherapy has been used with adult survivors of political atrocities and is premised on the idea that refugees experience healing through giving a testimony of the persecution they experienced. The testimony can then be used for the purposes of education and advocacy (Agger & Jensen, 1990; Mol-lica, 2001; Neuner, Schauer, Klaschik, Karunakara, & Elbert, 2004; van der Veer, 1998; Weine, Kulenovic, Pavkovic, & Gibbons, 1998; Weine & Laub, 1995). Re-duced rates of depression and PTSD were seen in adult Bosnian refugees who par-ticipated in testimonial therapy (Weine et al., 1998). Although this model has not been evaluated on adolescents, a pilot study with Sudanese adolescents suggests its safety and feasibility in this age group (Lustig et al., 2004).

Family Therapy

Because war often affects whole families, family therapy may be indicated. Nieves-Grafals (2001) suggested that only rarely does just one member of a family expe-rience distress. Barenbaum and colleagues (2004) identified the primary goals of family therapy with war-affected children to be reducing family distress while promoting parental stability, both of which impact child well-being. Boothby (1994) suggested that particularly when children are faced with ongoing instability in the environment, as might be seen with refugee families facing significant resettlement stressors, interventions that provide direct assistance to parents may be of great benefit to children. However, although parents are critical supports to children, even the most prepared parent cannot protect a child from the effects of war, and care must be taken not to communicate blame or unrealistic expectations of parents (Barenbaum et al., 2004).

Several approaches to therapy with war-affected families have been described, although none have been empirically evaluated. Woodcock (1995) proposed that cultural rituals be incorporated into treatment, helping families to acknowledge and move beyond atrocities by drawing on existing cultural means for doing so. Bemak (1989) emphasized the importance of incorporating Eastern healing principles into more traditional family work with Southeast Asians, and he noted the flexibility required of a therapist depending on the phase of acculturation of a particular family. Work with Central American refugee families has similarly noted the importance of maintaining flexibility, acknowledging the variation of families within a given culture, and being sensitive to traditional models of family and healing (Arrendondo, Orjuela, & Moore, 1989).

Early Psychological Intervention

Very little is known about the effectiveness of early psychological intervention for youth affected by war and terrorism. However, following the attacks of 9/11 there has been increased urgency to evaluate and understand how best to respond to incidents of mass violence. In 2003, a National Advisory Committee on Children and Terrorism (NACCT) report, issued to the U.S. Department of Health and Human Services, provided recommendations regarding developing a comprehensive public health strategy for responding to children's needs in the wake of terrorism. Specific recommendations regarding children's mental health and psychosocial well-being included a community-based approach involving pediatric mental health training for a range of providers who come into contact with children, including emergency responders and teachers. The report further emphasized early intervention and the importance of supporting parents and families (NACCT, 2003).

A report by the National Institute of Mental Health (NIMH) issued several recommendations based on current literature, including observing a hierarchy of needs by addressing key safety issues first and fostering innate resilience and recovery (NIMH, 2002). Based on a review of current literature, there was some evidence for the effectiveness of early, brief, and focused interventions for reducing distress in children, as well as for the effectiveness of cognitive-behavioral interventions. Notably, there was no support for debriefing or the use of individual recitation of emotional events, and there was some concern that these might put some children at higher risk for the development of later problems (NIMH, 2002). It is essential that any high-risk interventions such as retelling of the trauma be carefully evaluated and monitored.

Psychopharmacology

Psychopharmacology has come to play an increasingly prominent role in the treatment of mental health difficulties in children and adolescents. Clinical practice, which has been based largely on extrapolation from adult data as well as clinical observation and experience, has proceeded more quickly than empirical validation of the use of psychopharmaceuticals. Nevertheless, there is now good evidence for the safety and efficacy of pediatric psychopharmacological treatments targeting a number of psychiatric symptoms and disorders, including some that war- and terrorism-affected youth may experience (Martin, Scahill, & Charney, 2003; McClellan & Werry, 2003). Although medication cannot heal a child's spirit, make meaning of the trauma she has experienced, or repair the social ecology that war disrupts, it can modify symptoms such as depressed mood or panic attacks (Kaufman & Blumberg, 2003; Koda, Charney, & Pine, 2003). Sometimes ameliorating even a single symptom such as insomnia or nightmares can significantly improve a child's functioning (Donnelly, 2003).

Two medication trials have suggested that agents used in the immediate aftermath of a traumatic experience may prevent or minimize the subsequent development of PTSD. Adults started on a 10-day course of propanolol (a medication that blocks adrenergic transmission) within 6 hours of a traumatic event developed fewer symptoms of PTSD 3 months later as compared with those given a placebo (Pitman et al., 2002). Opiates, including morphine, are also known to inhibit the adrenergic system in areas of the brain hypothesized to be responsible for the consolidation of traumatic memories. A naturalistic study of medically hospitalized children given morphine as part of routine care for severe burns showed a correlation between higher morphine doses and fewer symptoms of PTSD 6 months later, independent of the child's subjective experience of pain (Saxe et al., 2001). It has been speculated that, should these findings be replicated in more methodologically robust studies, medications such as propanolol (which is safe for most individuals and not habit-forming) could be used to secondarily prevent PTSD in individuals or small groups exposed to a single acute trauma (Marmar, Neylan, & Schoenfeld, 2002). However, issues of cost, logistics, and the manpower that would be necessary to conform to safe clinical practice make it difficult to imagine that prophylactic medication use could become the standard of care in experiences of mass trauma, such as war or terrorist attacks, in the developed world. Mass administration seems even less feasible in the developing world, where the public health infrastructure, even in politically stable times, is far more limited (Barenbaum et al., 2004) and cultural barriers to the preventive use of medications may be significant.

There is growing empirical evidence that once PTSD symptoms develop in children and adolescents, a variety of pharmacological agents can reduce at least some of them (Arroyo & Eth, 1996; Donnelly, 2003; Friedman, Davidson, & Mellman, 2000; Marmar et al., 2002; McClellan & Werry, 2003). There have been neither empirical studies nor case reports focusing specifically on the use of psychotropic medications in war-affected children or adolescents, although such treatment is occurring in specialty clinics for refugees and torture survivors and probably more widely (Westermeyer & Wahmanholm, 1996). A small number of anecdotal reports and open trials have supported the use of psychotropic medications (as a part of a multimodal mental health treatment program) in refugee adults in the United States. Dating from the 1980s to early 1990s, before the widespread use of selective serotonin reuptake inhibitors (SSRIs), these reports indicated that the use of tricyclic antidepressants (Boehnlein, Kinzie, Ben, & Fleck, 1985; Moore & Boehnlein, 1991; Westermeyer, 1989), as well as tricyclics combined with clonidine (Kinzie & Leung, 1989), could ameliorate the symptoms of depression and PTSD in refugees from Southeast Asia. However, in general, patients were found to be more sensitive to the side effects of these medications than Caucasian patients and to have very high levels of noncompliance (Kinzie, Leung, & Boehnlein, 1987; Kroll, Linde, & Habenicht, 1990; Moore & Boehnlein, 1991).

Since the early 1990s, the emerging field of ethnopharmacology has begun to explore ways in which culture and ethnicity may influence medication use and effects (Lin, Poland, & Nakasaki, 1993; Ruiz, 2001). For example, pharmacogenetic investigations have shown substantial differences across ethnic groups (as well as among individuals) in the distribution of gene variants that code for the enzymes that regulate the metabolism of psychoactive medications (most important, the cytochrome P450 isoenzymes). Thus, in some ethnic groups there is a much higher proportion than in others of individuals who metabolize medications either extremely rapidly or extremely slowly (Lin, Smith, & Ortiz, 2001). These pharmacokinetic variations help to explain clinical observations that patients from different ethnic backgrounds sometimes require somewhat different dosages and vary in their tendency to develop side effects (Lin, Anderson, & Poland, 1995). There also appear to be genetically based ethnic variations in the activity of receptor and transporter proteins that modulate and mediate the action of neurotransmitters and are the presumed targets of many psychotropic medications; the clinical implications of these so-called pharmacodynamic variations are just beginning to be investigated (Lin et al., 2001).

In addition to genetics, environment and culture may also have a large impact on pharmacokinetics and on medication effect. Diet (e.g., the ratio of proteins to carbohydrates; the presence of particular foods such as brussel sprouts, cabbage, or grapefruit juice), cooking practices (e.g., charcoal-broiling beef), and the use of tobacco and alcohol have all been shown to cause changes in the activity level of some of the P450 isoenzymes. Traditional medications, including herbal preparations that are widely used by some adults and children, even after resettlement in a western country, can affect the very sensitive P450 system as well (Lin et al., 2001). It has been suggested that experiences associated with warfare, such as chronic stress, incarceration, starvation, and untreated infections, might also have pharmacokinetic effects (Kroll, Linde, & Habenicht, 1990).

Culture is also important in determining the meaning of psychopharmacological intervention for a particular child and family, and it will affect the way side effects are experienced and understood, the way medication is utilized, and ultimately the degree of compliance to a prescribed regimen (Lin et al., 1993). In some cultures, western medicines are seen as the most powerful type of intervention available and may either be welcomed (sometimes at the expense of other treatments) or dreaded as an indication of the most serious and stigmatizing conditions. Some patients fear that western medications will be harmful to their bodies and especially to their children's more vulnerable bodies. If they experience unpleasant side effects that are not consistent with their traditional ideas of safe and effective treatment, they take them as proof that these medications are indeed too strong for them. In some cultural systems, health is seen as a balance of opposing energies in the body, for example, hot and cold, or ying and yang. Patients may believe that psychotropic medications, generally because of their side effects, have too much of one energy or the other and discontinue treatment (Lin et al., 2001).

In most traditional societies, parents use medications for their children for rapid symptom relief on a short-term basis. In many parts of the world, medications may be purchased from pharmacies without a prescription and may also be obtained from untrained vendors in village markets or from black markets in refugee camps. For this reason, adults are accustomed to using their own judgment about how and when to medicate themselves and their children. Unless clinicians specifically indicate otherwise, patients and parents may alter dosages, stop treatment as soon as some relief is experienced, or share prescriptions with family members or others. In addition, issues of fear and mistrust, cultural styles requiring absolute respect and politeness toward those in positions of authority, or indirect communication styles often inhibit non-western or refugee individuals from being straightforward with clinicians regarding negative side effects from, lack of response to, or desire to discontinue medication. It appears that when clinicians raise the issue of potential noncompliance proactively in an open and non-threatening way and explain why adherence to prescribed treatment is important, compliance improves substantially (Kinzie et al., 1987).

GROUP TREATMENTS

Moving out a layer from the individual and family levels of the social ecology, group intervention is a promising means for providing mental health services to war-affected children. Practically, groups are a cost-effective way of providing services in resource-poor settings and providing an opportunity for individuals who have been through a common or similar situation of trauma or loss to connect. Group members may share coping strategies and provide supportive feedback. For refugee children, meeting in groups can decrease feelings of stigma and offer opportunities to celebrate traditions that are part of their identity, while exploring common challenges in the process of adjustment.

For adolescents growing up in western cultures or adjusting to resettlement in the west, groups may be an ideal intervention from a developmental standpoint (Berkovitz, 1972). During adolescence, connections with peers are of paramount importance, and some youth find it difficult to trust or feel understood by adults. Symbolically, groups can create a space and culture of structure, order, and predictability that challenges chaos and terror. By emphasizing support and trust and strengthening the bonds between members, groups begin to rebuild community and repair the social fabric damaged by war.

In studies of traumatized adults, groups have been empirically shown to be effective (Foy, Glynn, & Schnurr, 2000). Studies in children have been too limited to demonstrate a benefit of group over individual treatment or vice versa, or of any particular type of group intervention. However, CBT-based groups have received the most empirical validation within the limited number of studies reported (Cohen, Berliner, & March, 2000).

Despite the theoretical strengths of group interventions, and our impression that they are occurring in field and clinical settings, we were able to locate less than a dozen published or circulated papers describing group interventions for war- or terrorism-affected children and adolescents (Dybdahl, 2001; Fisher, Sanderson, & Chew, 2003; Layne et al., 2001; Miller & Billings, 1994; Rousseau et al., 2004; Rubin, 1995; Tsui & Sammons, 1988). These interventions were designed to serve a variety of purposes ranging from prevention to treatment, from supporting the general well-being and appropriate development of children in the midst of warfare to offering specific treatments to torture victims and refugees with symptoms of PTSD. The reports describe diverse approaches to group intervention; some of the interventions are unstructured and flexible in content; others are manualized approaches that focus on building specific skills. Although publications describing the former approach offer rich clinical observations and hypotheses about therapeutic factors in the group process, most do not include any evaluation of the interventions' effectiveness other than leaders' subjective assessments or reports of participants' comments. Interventions that have been empirically evaluated are a very recent development and limited in number.

A survey of interventions with war-affected youth concludes that there is inadequate evidence to support any particular type of group treatment over another or to indicate that a particular degree of structure is optimal (Barenbaum et al., 2004). Different circumstances may require different approaches. It is essential that any intervention incorporate local understanding and values into both program development and evaluation. Incorporating local community knowledge of child development, styles of offering support, and ideas about how success is to be recognized and measured into the development, implementation, and evaluation of group treatment is likely to greatly enhance perceived relevance of groups and participation.

Cultural Considerations in Group Interventions

Children from traditional cultures that rely on a variety of group activities to bring families, clan, and tribal groups together for social, cultural, and religious activities may find group interventions more natural than individual approaches (Ho, 1992). Some scholars have suggested that children coming from cultures that place a high value on interdependence and cooperation may be even more capable of becoming cohesive in a group than those who come from more individualistic cultures (Yamaguchi, 1986). Group therapy, as it has been developed in western clinical settings, however, may conflict with some cultures' norms about communication styles, role hierarchies, and appropriate degrees of self-disclosure. In many Asian cultures, for example, negative affect is rarely expressed, humility and modesty are emphasized, and it is considered shameful to discuss private or family matters publicly. Individuals in a position of leadership are shown deference and expected to guide others in the proper course of action because they have superior knowledge (Ho, 1992). Successful groups for traumatized Asian refugee adults have been structured in such a way as to honor these norms yet still meet therapeutic goals, for example, by focusing on activities such as cooking traditional meals, gardening, or carpentry, during which personal and psychological discussions may arise unobtrusively. In such groups, the leader adopts a role and language more typical of a teacher than a therapist (Kinzie, Leung, & Bui, 1988).

When a group requires an interpreter, the logistics of translating each speaker's comments can be cumbersome and awkward for the group process. However in groups for refugees, leadership by two co-therapists representing both the participants' birth culture and the resettlement culture, can facilitate members' explorations of their developing bicultural identities (Kinzie et al., 1988; Rubin, 1995). Groups that contain refugee children from more than one ethnic group can model positive interethnic contact and expose members to different norms in problem-solving, adding flexibility to their coping strategies (Ho, 1992).

School-Based Groups

In communities where schools are functioning, school-based groups may be a particularly effective method of reaching children who would otherwise find psychosocial services difficult or impossible to access. In the United States, schools are the major provider of mental health services, especially for poor and minority youth (Stein et al., 2003). School personnel are generally sensitive to children's mental health needs and have a stake in serving them. Locating services in schools diminishes concrete barriers such as transportation and symbolic barriers such as stigma (Kataoka, Stein, & Jaycox, 2003). In addition, school-based services are consistent with the United Nations International Children's Emergency Fund's (UNICEF) best-practice recommendation that intervention with traumatized youths take place in a stable environment by caregivers who have an ongoing relationship with the child (Layne et al., 2001). Delivering services in schools tends to increase their sustainability, particularly if school mental health personnel are trained to offer and supervise the interventions (Miller & Billings, 1994).

Stein and colleagues (2003) published the first randomized controlled trial of a psychosocial treatment for youth traumatized by community violence using a school-based group intervention. Although the majority of Los Angeles sixth graders who benefited from this intervention were Latino immigrants, and some of their exposure to violence occurred prior to or during migration, the authors implied that most of their trauma occurred after arrival in the United States. Thus, the effectiveness of this intervention for war-affected children remains to be demonstrated.

Layne and colleagues (2001) developed and empirically validated a group intervention targeting Bosnian adolescents with chronic symptoms of PTSD, depression, and complicated grief. The authors were invited by UNICEF to consult with Bosnian government agencies in designing and implementing a project that would meet local need, be sustainable, and the effectiveness of which could be measured. They based their program on CBT, incorporating the specific components of this model that have the greatest empirical support in the treatment of youth traumatized by other mechanisms (e.g., disasters, sexual abuse, community violence). Over a 4-year period, the 20-session, manualized, semistructured protocol was piloted in secondary schools and adapted to local conditions. In the evaluation 4 years after the end of the war, youth from 13 schools, who had been screened at baseline for the presence of moderate to severe symptomatology, showed reduced symptom levels of all disorders and improved psychosocial functioning. The results, however, are considered preliminary because the evaluation design did not use a control group, only self-report measures were used, and students from schools that were able to implement only about half of the total number of sessions showed as much improvement as students receiving the full course of treatment.

Group Interventions for Parents

Dybdahl (2001) described a preventive intervention developed toward the end of the war in Bosnia that attempted to help young children by helping their mothers. The intervention reflects lessons learned from two arenas: 1) the model of early childhood care and education programs in developed and developing countries that have demonstrated sustained positive benefits to children during peace time; and 2) repeated observations from the trauma literature that the mental health of children depends on the well-being of the adults around them. Five-year-olds and their mothers who had been internally displaced by the war were randomly assigned to either a 5-month psychosocial intervention group along with basic medical care or to a control group receiving medical care only. The manualized, semistructured intervention was provided by nursery school teachers who were specially trained and supervised. Each weekly meeting began with a psycho-educational presentation about a topic, such as child development, mother-child interactions, or children's responses to trauma. Following this, mothers shared their experiences and feelings about the topic. Children were evaluated pre- and postintervention using a variety of subjective and objective measures by multiple raters, including their mothers, professionals blind to the randomization, and self-reports; mothers' mental health was assessed in a more limited way. On follow-up, children in the intervention group showed significant improvements on several measures of mental health and psychosocial functioning as compared to controls. They also had greater weight gain; their mothers' mental health improved as well. Dybdahl (2001) was only able to speculate on possible mechanisms of change and noted that although changes were modest, they may be considered impressive given the simple, inexpensive, and short-term nature of the intervention.

Pre-adolescent Groups

Several authors have described expressive arts workshops in which pre-adolescent children engage in activities such as drawing, collage, games, drama, storytelling, and other creative activities that stem from local cultures in order to express ideas and feelings related to the overwhelming experiences they have lived through. Miller and Billings (1994) noted that children in situations of extreme adversity and war have diminished opportunities and capacity to engage in play, which is the primary, developmentally appropriate way in which children explore and understand themselves and the world. Rousseau et al. (2004) described creative expression workshops offered to immigrant and refugee children in Montreal schools as "transitional spaces" that provide a bridge between the past and the present, the home and the school, and the child's internal and external worlds. These formats allow children to disclose their histories at their own pace and indirectly, if they wish, through the use of metaphor. They encourage children to use their talents and competencies to feel some mastery over their experiences, and they help them and their teachers to see their strengths and resilience. Rousseau et al. (2004) emphasized that nonverbal activities should always be paired with verbal ones in order to engage the maximum amount of processing and insight.

Adolescent Groups

Adolescence has been recognized as an especially vulnerable time for refugee youth because they need to transition to both adulthood and a new culture simultaneously and to both the mainstream culture and the alternative culture of adolescence (Tobin & Friedman, 1984). Two papers have described group interventions with refugees in the United States navigating through the transitions of adolescence. Tsui and Sammons (1988) described groups designed to support the psychosocial adjustment of recently arrived unaccompanied minors from Vietnam living with American foster parents. The stated goal of the groups was to coach these youth in assertiveness and other social skills that were not part of their birth culture's behavioral repertoire but considered necessary to get their needs met in the United States. Meetings were cast as "classes" with mini-lectures, discussions, and role-playing, which were felt to be congruent with traditional values of education and learning and far more acceptable and comprehensible than therapy or mental health treatment is in Vietnamese culture. Working through this formal structure, members discovered opportunities to grieve their losses and thus make space for new values and ideas alongside the old.

Rubin (1995) reported on a year-long peer discussion and support group for Cambodian adolescent girls in Seattle, Washington. Born a few years before or after their families' arrival in the United States, each young woman had a parent with severe chronic medical or mental illness as a consequence of the Cambodian genocide. Despite cultural inhibitions against airing personal or family troubles, once these girls felt safe in the group and recognized common struggles, they were able and willing to share intimate and often painful material, sometimes putting it into words for the first time. In time, the group became a place where these teens could safely explore their Cambodian identity together without getting entangled in the web of guilt and sorrow that arose for many when they discussed the same issue with their parents. By anecdotal report of both the participants and their parents, intergenerational conflict diminished.

The Center for Multicultural Human Services (CMHS) in Falls Church, Virginia, developed a group intervention for Sierra Leonean youth that built on the community's high regard for education and Sierra Leonean culture (CMHS, 2002; Fisher et al., 2003). This summer program incorporated study of heroic figures from Sierra Leone and used traditional art forms, such as mask-making, to help the children develop a sense of pride in their heritage and to express and share their experiences.

COMMUNITY-BASED INTERVENTION AND PREVENTION

At the outermost level of the social ecology are layers of influence rooted in the cultural, political, and community systems. Interventions that operate at this level of the social ecology hold great promise for ameliorating mental health problems in war-affected youth. As war affects whole communities in multiple ways throughout the social ecology, community-level interventions are particularly appropriate. For example, the after-effects of war and terrorism commonly interrupt the delivery of basic medical and social services as well as undermine family and extended social networks.

Community-based intervention and prevention models of mental health draw heavily from a public health perspective by taking larger populations as their unit of focus. They often involve interventions at several levels and can include policy and legal initiatives combined with prevention and intervention programs targeting large numbers of affected people (Wandersman & Florin, 2003). Community interventions are defined by their aims to both prevent disorders and dysfunction and to promote health and well-being among defined subgroups within the larger population. However, the implementation of such programs is complicated, and very few evaluations of their efficacy are yet available.

Community-level programs often seek to reach their target population by building on strengths and resources that are already present in the communities being served, such as social networks, religious institutions, cultural groups, and community organizations. As Boothby (1996) argued, community-based models are more cost-effective and flexible than interventions based in mental health centers or the offices of mental health professionals, and they are able to reach larger numbers of affected populations. Community-based interventions for war-affected children often involve the training and involvement of paraprofessionals, aid workers, teachers, social service professionals, and religious leaders who serve children through community social service agencies, religious institutions, schools, and nongovernmental organizations (Boothby, 1996). For example, many field-based mental health programs for war-affected populations utilize a "train the trainer" model to build on local agency through training of local paraprofessionals to assist in psychosocial responses, and ultimately, to have broader reach.

Community-based interventions often address variables that are theorized to *moderate* the impact of violence on child and family mental health. For instance, many community interventions focus on bolstering social support networks, enriching parenting and/or coping skills, raising awareness, advocating for public policy, and organizing support and self-help groups for those affected by violence due to war and/or terrorism. As an example of this, initiatives for Bantu refugees in the United States have integrated participation with agricultural programs. Helping Bantu elders return to farming and agriculture practices is believed to be important to their sense of identity and, ultimately, supportive of their overall adjustment and healthy integration into life in the United States (Van Lehman & Eno, 2002). Similarly, programs run by the International Rescue Committee to assist the psychosocial adjustment and community reintegration of former child soldiers in Sierra Leone involve participation in skills training and work apprenticeships in tailoring, farming, and carpentry.

Intervention strategies that build on local capacities, social capital, and other informal social resources are a powerful means of enhancing the value of limited funding for mental health in resource-poor environments, such as impoverished post-conflict environments or the lower income communities where many refugees are resettled. However, the pursuit of locally driven community strategies must be characterized by meaningful participation of community members and genuine support of local initiatives. Furthermore, care must be taken not to shift the burden of mental health promotion onto communities whose resources are already limited.

Education programs and systems present an exciting venue for the integration of multi-systemic mental health promotion and intervention programs. Awareness of the importance of education systems in addressing the mental health of children affected by war and terrorism has recently grown both internationally and in the United States in the response to the terrorist attacks of 9/11.

Emergency Education

Emergency education involves the restoration of learning and recreational activities very early on in humanitarian emergencies. These interventions are often employed in refugee camps and other situations where numerous children and adolescents of school age have been displaced. Often these programs begin with informal activities such as basic literacy and math skills and are developed into formal education programs as time and politics will allow. (For a complete discussion of education as an emergency response, see Aguilar & Retamal, 1998.) There are a number of theorized mechanisms by which involvement in emergency educational interventions are linked to promoting mental health in war-affected youth. Among these are the restoration of structure, predictability, and a safe place, allowing children to return to age-appropriate activities; the enrichment of social support networks via contact with peers, teachers, and program youth leaders; the meaningful engagement of youth in activities important to their sense of a positive future; and the ability to screen and refer violence-affected youth to a higher level of mental health care (Stichick-Betancourt, 2002).

Integrated Mental Health Services for Refugees in Schools

In addition to providing direct mental health services, school settings create an environment for introducing activities to raise awareness and build sensitivity to the mental health needs of children affected by violence. Some school-wide interventions of note have combined psychoeducation directed at parents, teachers, and school staff, and changes in school policies to support student mental health, in addition to more standard group and individual intervention. The work of Stein and colleagues (2002) described a participatory intervention and research project targeting immigrant children exposed to violence. The intervention involved psychoeducation for parents and teachers as well as the training of school social workers to administer eight cognitive-behavioral sessions for students in groups in the school setting. Of particular note in this project was the emphasis on participation from important stakeholders—in this case, the school and academics collaborating on the research.

In the international world of intervention for war-affected children, participatory interventions have been given a great deal of emphasis. Programs and evaluations of this sort aim to involve stakeholders at many levels, from those designing and implementing interventions and evaluations to the youth and families who are the direct beneficiaries of these efforts. Theorists such as Summerfield (1999) have argued that participatory interventions are essential for working with war-affected populations as they allow local realities and meaning to be valued from the beginning, and they avoid stereotyping.

Peace Education

Peace education is a community intervention that addresses issues related to intergroup hatred and that builds skills in conflict resolution and leadership for peace. Very little data exists to support or refute the efficacy of peace education in terms of child and adolescent attitudes for constructive problem-solving and attitudes toward peace and conflict resolution. However, these programs have been very popular in addressing issues of co-existence facing communities divided by war and terrorist attacks. Seeds of Peace (2004) is one example of a community intervention aimed at peace resolution and peace education. The program began in 1993 with activities aimed at bringing together children and youth from both sides of the Israeli-Palestinian conflict. The program has now expanded its work to numerous war-affected regions such as Afghanistan and India/Pakistan and the Balkans. This program features an international camp each year in Maine, follow-up programming at the Seeds of Peace Center for Coexistence in Jerusalem, youth conferences in many international sites, as well as regional workshops, educational and professional opportunities, and an adult educator program. Activities center on building empathy and respect among young people as well as the development of conflict resolution and negotiation skills. Cohorts of young people are able to engage in exchange and relationship-building over a period of several years. Children involved in these interventions report greater ability to understand the perspective of their peers on the other side of the conflict's ethnic divide.

Schools and the U.S. Response to September 11, 2001

• • • The United States' response to the terrorist attacks of September 11, 2001, involved several integrated, community interventions that centered on school-based interventions. As Marshall and Suh (2003) noted, because the primary goals of terrorism are to create fear and uncertainty and to demoralize populations, a focus on mental health from a public health perspective is a well-suited response. The theoretical basis for some of these interventions has been described by Laor, Wolmer, Spirman, and Weiner (2003).

Although no formal program evaluations are yet available in the published literature, anecdotal reports indicate a range of creativity in the design of community-based mental health interventions following the 9/11 attacks. For example, Project Liberty (Felton, 2002) was launched with support from the federal government as well as the New York State Office of Mental Health and New York's city and county mental health departments. The intervention involved providing public education regarding reactions to traumatic stress and appropriate coping strategies, outreach to affected communities, and short-term counseling interventions for affected populations. The rationale for this response was to respond to and provide information and supports to address the expected range of "normative" stress reactions to the traumatic event. This type of front-line response encourages people to draw upon already existing coping strategies and social supports in their lives. In addition to media campaigns, a toll-free crisis counseling and referral line was established and operated by the New York City Department of Health. Television and radio public service announcements were created in English and Spanish involving well-known local celebrities. The media campaign also featured placards in bus and subway stations featuring New Yorkers sharing their own coping strategies employed following the terrorist attacks.

The second phase of the intervention involved specialized treatment to individuals whose trauma symptoms met criteria for a diagnosed mental health disorder, most commonly PTSD. This phase of the intervention involved new contracts to be negotiated to allow mental health funds to be disbursed from state to local governments and to establish new mechanisms for insurance claims and reimbursements for service providers responding to the increased demand. Like train-the-trainer models used in war-affected environments, Project Liberty involved the training of thousands of mental health professionals and paraprofessionals in skills of basic community outreach and disaster mental health counseling. In a stunning marshalling of resources, the main components of Project Liberty were able to be implemented 4-6 weeks following the terrorist attacks. Initial process data from the Project Liberty intervention indicated that Project Liberty staff provided more than 42,000 mental health service encounters. Twenty-six percent were crisis interventions, although 60% of those involved had come into care via group education initiatives. Eighty-seven percent of service encounters were delivered in community environments. Project Liberty counselors also referred 9% of those they served to further mental health services. Although this program did not target children and adolescents, it is presented as a compelling model by which to conceptualize immediate responses to terrorist attacks or other such broad-scale traumatic events (Felton, 2002). • • •

Traditional Healing Practices in Community Interventions

In many war-affected environments, there is a growing awareness of the need to incorporate traditional healing practices into community-based mental health interventions. In recognizing the role of culture in healing and coping with the hardships of war, some of the most innovative examples of interventions at the community level come from programs that support cultural traditions and build upon already-existing community strengths (Stichick, 2001). In any one context in which populations are responding to the effects of violence, it is important to recognize community processes that have traditionally helped to guide the care and support of children.

For example, a program in Zimbabwe has involved traditional healers in mental health intervention. As one component of a comprehensive intervention program, the *n'anga,* as they are called, perform ritual cleansing and healing ceremonies for children who have participated in armed conflict or have emotional difficulties as a result (Resseler, Tortocini, & Marcelino, 1993). Community-based healing ceremonies have also formed a central part of the work of some nongovernmental organizations (NGOs) working to integrate former child soldiers from Sierra Leone. In some cases, NGOs have been able to use mental health program funding to support families to host a feast or ceremony to welcome a demobilized former combatant into the community and make a symbolic transition from the time of warring to a new phase of life as a returned member of the community. In another example from the Khmer refugee camps in Thailand, health services were designed to integrate traditional healers and traditional medicines into the care provided. The treatment derived its strength from the familiarity of cultural practices long known to the child, family, and community. The potential value of traditional practices should be given important attention in the design of community-level mental health programs in war-affected contexts. Some scholars have argued that interventions involving traditional practices may have much greater potency than mental health treatment models imported to war-affected countries from Western mental health traditions (Summerfield, 1999).

Another example of rethinking mental health interventions in war-affected environments comes from the work of Mollica and colleagues. In Cambodia, the Pol Pot regime had deliberately sought to destroy religious networks by "derobing" and demoralizing Buddhist monks (Mollica, 1989). Knowledgeable of how this practice had disrupted the tradition of teaching youth the spiritual practices and stories of their peoples, the team centered their psychosocial intervention on returning safety and support to the monks working with Cambodian refugees. Once empowered to return to their work, the monks were able to revive traditional practices and provide an important source of support and healing to war-affected children as well as the entire community.

CONCLUSIONS AND RECOMMENDATIONS

Interventions provided for children affected by war and terrorism are incredibly diverse, ranging from adaptations of CBTs for individual PTSD treatment, to expressive group interventions, to community-based initiatives that support the well-being of whole populations. Ultimately, a combination of intervention strategies may prove most effective in responding to the diverse needs of both individuals and communities affected by war.

Sadly, the need for interventions for children affected by war and terrorism is unlikely to diminish in coming years. The effects of political violence reach deeply into all communities, via the presence of refugees in schools, the fear of terrorism within one's community, or the ravages of war within one's country. The need for theoretically driven, culturally sensitive, and empirically supported treatments is great.

As the field moves forward in developing and evaluating interventions, several key principles can be drawn from past experience: 1) the importance of involving local communities in development and evaluation of interventions; 2) the necessity of providing and integrating interventions at all levels of the social ecology; and 3) the role of research and evaluation in helping to understand the safety and efficacy of different interventions:

1. **Local communities and stakeholders must be involved in the development of intervention and research projects.** Programs developed overseas have long recognized the necessity of incorporating local value systems, knowledge, skills, and goals in the development of intervention programs. Community participatory research has begun to gather momentum in the United States as well, where schools, refugee communities, youth, and other local groups frequently have strong interests in the development of intervention programs and research. Only through involving all key participants can a program be developed in a way that acknowledges and values the complexity of different needs, strengths, and goals within a specific community.

2. **A socio-ecological approach is essential.** War and terrorism affect all levels of a child's social-ecological environment. Interventions must similarly seek to repair damage to each of these levels. Broad-based community initiatives to support the well-being of youth affected by war and terrorism have great potential to magnify innate resiliencies, capitalize on limited resources, and promote a holistic approach to children's mental health. Although more traditional interventions such as individual therapies are often the easiest to implement and evaluate, the mental health field must stretch beyond traditional bounds and seek to develop and evaluate those approaches that are theoretically the most promising. These include interventions at all levels of the social ecology: individual and family, group, and community-based prevention/intervention programs.

3. **Programs must be evaluated scientifically for efficacy.** Regardless of the type of intervention, in order to move the field of mental health for war-affected children, more attention to evaluating outcomes of programs is essential (Rousseau, 1995). It is ethically imperative that interventions be evaluated for their safety and, in a time of limited resources, effectiveness. Engaging in research with war-affected populations is itself ethically challenging. War-exposed children are a particularly vulnerable group and any research conducted within this population must be extremely mindful of not doing harm or taking unnecessary risks. Many innovative interventions by necessity depend upon temporary funding sources; in this situation, the potential harm of initiating treatment that may later need to be withdrawn must be considered (Jablensky et al., 1994). At other times, programs must make the difficult choice between allocating resources to evaluation or using those resources to provide more intervention. Despite these challenges to developing careful

evaluations, policy makers and mental health practitioners must recognize the value of understanding an intervention's effects, the potential for replication and dissemination, and the opportunity to advance the science of mental health intervention for war-affected children afforded by research.

Despite the complexity of developing and evaluating interventions for children affected by war and terrorism, efforts to do so have been gathering momentum. In 2001 the Substance Abuse and Mental Health Services Administration (SAMHSA) funded the National Child Traumatic Stress Network (NCTSN), a federal initiative to improve the care of traumatized children and their families across the United States. As part of this network, 15 sites from around the United States have coalesced into a task force that is actively seeking to improve and evaluate services for refugee children. In addition, a Terrorism and Disaster branch of the NCTSN has been formed "to promote the well-being of children and families by strengthening our nation's preparedness and response to terrorism and disaster" (NCTSN, 2004). The NCTSN provides an excellent example of raising the task of helping war- and terrorism-affected children to a national level. Through this and other continued efforts to develop and provide empirically supported, culturally sound interventions, we, as a society, can begin to make amends for the tragedy of allowing children to be exposed to war.

REFERENCES

Agger, I., & Jensen, S.B. (1990). Testimony as ritual and evidence in psychotherapy for political refugees. *Journal of Traumatic Stress, 3*(1), 115–130.

Aguilar, P., & Retamal, G. (1998). *Rapid educational response in complex emergencies: A discussion document.* Geneva: International Bureau of Education.

Ajdukovic, M., & Ajdukovic, D. (1993). Psychological well being of refugee children. *Child Abuse and Neglect, 17*(6), 843–854.

Apfel, R.J., & Simon, B. (1996). Psychosocial interventions for children of war: The value of a model of resiliency. *Medicine and Global Survival, 3*(A2), 1–20.

Arrendondo, P., Orjuela, E., & Moore, L. (1989). Family therapy with Central American war refugee families. *Journal of Strategic and Systemic Therapies, 8*(2), 28–35.

Arroyo, W., & Eth, S. (1996). Post-Traumatic Stress Disorder and other stress reactions. In R. Apfel & B. Simon (Eds.), *Minefields in their hearts: The mental health of children in war and communal violence* (pp. 52–74). New Haven: Yale University Press.

Barenbaum, J., Ruchkin, V., & Schwab-Stone, M. (2004). The psychosocial aspects of children exposed to war: practice and policy initiatives. *Journal of Child Psychology and Psychiatry, 45*(1), 41–62.

Bemak, F. (1989). Cross-cultural family therapy with Southeast Asian refugees. *Journal of Strategic and Systemic Therapies, 8*(1), 22–27.

Berkovitz, I. (1972). *Adolescents grow in groups: Clinical experiences in adolescent group psychotherapy.* New York: Brunner/Mazel.

Berman, H. (2001). Children and war: Current understandings and future directions. *Public Health Nursing, 18*(4), 243–52.

Boehnlein J.K., Kinzie, J.D., Ben, R., & Fleck, J. (1985). One-year follow-up study of posttraumatic stress disorder among survivors of Cambodian concentration camps. *American Journal of Psychiatry, 142*(8), 956–9.

Boothby, N. (1994). Trauma and violence among refugee children. In J. Orley (Ed.), *Amidst peril and pain: The mental health and well-being of the world's refugees* (pp. 239–259). Washington, DC: American Psychological Association.

Boothby, N. (1996). Mobilizing communities to meet the psychosocial needs of children in war and refugee crises. In R. Apfel & B. Simon (Eds.), *Minefields in their hearts: The mental health of children in war and communal violence* (pp. 149–164). New Haven: Yale University Press.

Bronfenbrenner, U. (1979). *The ecology of human development: Experiments by nature and design.* Cambridge: Harvard University Press.

Center for Multicultural Human Services. (2002). *Healing traumatized refugee children: Focus on the Sierra Leonean community in the Washington, DC area.* Unpublished presentation.

Cohen, J. (1998). Practice parameters for the assessment and treatment of children and adolescents with posttraumatic stress disorder. *Journal of the American Academy of Child and Adolescent Psychiatry, 37*(10), 4S-26-S.

Cohen, J.A., Berliner, L., & March, J.S. (2000). Treatment of children and adolescents. In E.B. Foa, T.M. Keane, & M.J. Friedman (Eds.), *Effective treatments for PTSD: Practice guidelines from the International Society for Traumatic Stress Studies* (pp. 330–332). New York: Guilford Press.

Deblinger, E., McLeer, S.V., & Henry, D. (1990). Cognitive behavioral treatment for sexually abused children suffering post-traumatic stress: Preliminary findings. *Journal of the American Academy of Child and Adolescent Psychiatry, 29*(5), 747–752.

Donnelly, C.L. (2003). Pharmacologic treatment approaches for children and adolescents with posttraumatic stress disorder. *Child and Adolescent Psychiatric Clinics of North America, 12,* 251–69.

Dybdahl, R. (2001). Children and mothers in war: An outcome study of a psychosocial intervention program. *Child Development, 72*(4), 1214–1230.

Elbedour, S., ten Bensel, R., & Bastien, D.T. (1993). Ecological integrated model of children of war: Individual and social psychology. *Child Abuse & Neglect, 17,* 805–819.

Ellis, B.H. (2004, October). *Trauma systems therapy for refugees.* Paper presented at the International Conference "Anthropology and Health: Cross-Cultural aspects of Mental Health and Psychosocial Well-Being in Immigrant/Refugee Adolescents," Hvar, Croatia.

Felton, C. (2002). Project Liberty: A public health response to New Yorkers' mental health needs arising from the world trade center terrorist attacks. *Journal of Urban Health: Bulletin of the New York Academy of Medicine, 79*(3), 429–433.

Fisher, K., Sanderson, A.Z., & Chew, M.W. (2003). *Community-based programs for youth traumatized by war and other violence.* Paper presented at the Annual Meeting of the International Society for Traumatic Stress Studies, Chicago, IL.

Foy, D.W., Glynn, S.M, & Schnurr, P.P. (2000). Group therapy. In E.B. Foa & T.M. Keane (Eds.), *Effective treatments for PTSD: Practice guidelines from the International Society for Traumatic Stress Studies.* New York: Guilford Press.

Friedman, M.J., Davidson, J.R., & Mellman, T.A. (2000). Pharmacotherapy. In E.B. Foa, T.M. Keane, & M.J. Friedman (Eds.), *Effective treatments for PTSD: Practice guidelines from the International Society for Traumatic Stress Studies* (pp. 84–405). New York: Guilford Press.

Geltman, P.L., Augustyn, M., Barnett, E.D., Klass, P.E., & Groves, B.M. (2000). War trauma experience and behavioral screening of Bosnian refugee children resettled in Massachusetts. *Developmental and Behavioral Pediatrics, 21*(4), 255–261.

Helman, C.G. (1994). *Culture, health and illness: An introduction for health professionals* (3rd ed.). Oxford, England: Butterworth Heinemann.

Ho, M.K. (1992). *Minority children and adolescents in therapy.* Newbury Park: Sage Publications.

Honwana, A. (1998). Discussion guide 4: Non-western concepts of mental health. In *Refugee children: Guidelines on protection and care.* Geneva: United Nations High Commissioner for Refugees.

Howard, M., & Hodes, M. (2000). Psychopathology, adversity, and service utilization of young refugees. *Journal of the American Academy of Child and Adolescent Psychiatry, 39*(3), 368–377.

Jablensky, A., Marsella, A.J., Ekblad, S., Jansson, B., Levi, L., & Bornemann, T. (1994). Refugee mental health and well being: Conclusions and recommendations. In J. Orley (Ed.), *Amidst peril and pain: The mental health and well-being of the world's refugees* (pp. 327–339). Washington, DC: American Psychological Association.

Kataoka, S.J., Stein, B.D., & Jaycox, L.H. (2003). A school-based mental health program for traumatized Latino immigrant children. *Journal of the American Academy of Child & Adolescent Psychiatry, 42*(3), 311–318.

Kaufman, J., & Blumberg, H. (2003). Neurobiology of early-onset mood disorders. In A. Martin, L. Scahill, D. Charney, et al. (Eds.), *Pediatric psychopharmacology* (pp. 124–137). New York: Oxford University Press.

Kinzie, J.D. (2001). Cross-cultural treatment of PTSD. *Treating psychological trauma and PTSD (pp. 255–277).* New York: Guilford Press.

Kinzie, J.D., & Leung, P. (1989). Clonidine in Cambodian patients with posttraumatic stress disorder. *Journal of Nervous & Mental Diseases, 177* (9), 546–50.

Kinzie, J.D., Leung, P., & Boehnlein, J.K. (1987). Antidepressant blood levels in Southeast Asians: clinical and cultural implications. *Journal of Nervous & Mental Disorders, 175,* 480–85.

Kinzie, J.D., Leung, P., & Bui, A. (1988). Group therapy with Southeast Asian refugees. *Community Mental Health Journal, 24*(2), 157–66.

Kleinman, A., Eisenberg, L., & Good, B. (1978). Culture, illness, and care: Clinical lessons from anthropologic and cross-cultural research. *Annals of Internal Medicine, 88,* 251–258.

Koda, V., Charney, D., & Pine, D. (2003), Neurobiology of early-onset anxiety disorders. In A. Martin, L. Scahill, & D. Charney (Eds.), *Pediatric psychopharmacology* (pp. 138–149). New York: Oxford University Press.

Kroll, J., Linde, P., & Habenicht, M. (1990). Medication compliance, antidepressant blood levels, and side effects in Southeast Asian patients. *Journal of Clinical Psychopharmacology, 10*(4), 279–82.

Laor, N., Wolmer, L., Spirman, S., & Wiener, Z. (2003). Facing war, terrorism, and disaster: Toward a child-oriented comprehensive emergency care system. *Child and Adolescent Psychiatric Clinics of North America, 12*(2), 343–61.

Layne, C.M., Pynoos, R.S., & Saltzman, W.R. (2001). Trauma/grief-focused group psychotherapy school-based postwar intervention with traumatized Bosnian adolescents. *Group Dynamics: Theory, Research, and Practice, 5*(4), 277–290.

Lin, K-M., Anderson, D., & Poland, R. (1995). Ethnicity and psychopharmacology: Bridging the gap. *Psychiatric Clinics of North America, 18*(3), 635–647.

Lin, K-M., Poland, R., & Nakasaki, G. (1993). *Psychopharmacology and psychobiology of ethnicity.* Washington, DC: American Psychiatric Press.

Lin, K-M., Smith, M.W., & Ortiz, B.A. (2001) Culture and psychopharmacology. *Psychiatric Clinics of North America, 24*(3), 523–38.

Lustig, S.L., Weine, S.M., Saxe, G.N., & Beardslee, W.R. (2004). Testimonial psychotherapy for adolescent refugees: A case series. *Transcultural Psychiatry, 41*(1), 31–45.

Marmar, C.R., Neylan, T.C., & Schoenfeld, F.B. (2002). New directions in the pharmacotherapy of posttraumatic stress disorder. *Psychiatric Quarterly, 73*(4), 259–70.

Marshall, R.D., & Suh, E.S. (2003). Contextualizing trauma: Using evidence-based treatments in a multicultural community after 9/11. *Psychiatric Quarterly, 74*(4), 401–420.

Martin, A., Scahill, L., & Charney, D. (2003). *Pediatric psychopharmacology.* New York: Oxford University Press.

McClellan, J.M., & Werry, J.S. (2003). Evidence-based treatments in child and adolescent psychiatry: An inventory. *Journal of the American Academy of Child and Adolescent Psychiatry, 42*(12), 1388–1400.

Miller, K.E., & Billings, D.L. (1994). Playing to grow: a primary mental health intervention with Guatemalan refugee children. *American Journal of Orthopsychiatry, 64*(3), 346–356.

Mollica, R.F. (1989). Developing effective mental health policies and services for traumatized refugee patients. In D.R. Koslow & E.P. Salett (Eds.), *Crossing cultures in mental health* (pp. 101–115). Washington, DC: SIETAR International.

Mollica, R.F. (2001). Commentary on "Trauma and extended separation from family among Latin American and African refugees in Montreal:" The trauma story. A phenomenological approach to the traumatic life experiences of refugee survivors. *Psychiatry, 64*(1), 60–63.

Moore, L.J., & Boehnlein, J.K. (1991). Posttraumatic stress disorder, depression, and somatic symptoms in US Mien patients. *Journal of Nervous & Mental Disorders, 179*(12), 728–33.

Muecke, M. (1992). New paradigms for refugee health problems. *Social Science & Medicine, 35*(4), 515–523.

National Advisory Committee on Children and Terrorism. (2003, October). Recommendations to the Secretary. Available on line at http://www.bt.cdc.gov/children/word/working/recommend.doc.

National Child Traumatic Stress Network. (2004). Available on line at http://www.nctsnet.org.

National Institutes of Mental Health. (2002). *Mental health and mass violence: Evidence-based early psychological intervention for victims/survivors of mass violence. A workshop to reach consensus on best practices* (pp. 1–109). Washington, DC: Author.

Neuner, F., Schauer, M., Klaschik, C., Karunakara, U., & Elbert, T. (2004). A comparison of narrative exposure therapy, supportive counseling, and psychoeducation for treating posttraumatic stress disorder in an African refugee settlement. *Journal of Consulting and Clinical Psychology, 72*(4), 579–587.

Nieves-Grafals, S. (2001). Brief therapy of civil war-related trauma: A case study. *Cultural Diversity and Ethnic Minority Psychology, 7*(4), 387–398.

O'Shea, B., Hodes, M., Down, G., & Bramley, J. (2000). A school-based mental health service for refugee children. *Clinical Child Psychology and Psychiatry, 5*(2), 1359–1045.

Pitman, R.K., Sanders, K.M., Zusman, R.M., Healy, A.R, Cheema, F., Lasko, N.B., et al. (2002). Pilot study of secondary prevention of posttraumatic stress disorder with propanolol. *Biological Psychiatry, 51*(2), 189–92.

Resseler, E.M., Tortocini, J.M., & Marcelino, A. (1993). *Children in war: A guide to the provision of services.* New York: United Nations Children's Fund.

Rousseau, C. (1993). The place of the unexpressed: Ethics and methodology for research with refugee children. *Canada's Mental Health, 41*(4), 12–16.

Rousseau, C. (1995). The mental health of refugee children. *Transcultural Psychiatric Research Review, 32*(3), 299–331.

Rousseau, C., Said, T., & Gagné, M. (1998). Resilience in unaccompanied minors from the north of Somalia. *Psychoanalytic Review, 85*(4), 615–637.

Rousseau, C., Singh, A., Lacroix, L., Bagilishya, D., & Meacham, T. (2004). Creative expression workshops for immigrant and refugee children. *Journal of the American Academy of Child and Adolescent Psychiatry, 43*(2), 235–238.

Rubin, A. (1995). *Group work with Cambodian-American adolescent girls: Report of a pilot project.* Paper presented at the annual meeting of the Society for the Study of Psychiatry and Culture, Kohler, WI.

Ruiz, P. (Ed.). (2001). *Ethnicity and psychopharmacology.* Washington, DC: American Psychiatric Press.

Sack, W., Him, C., & Dickason, D. (1999). Twelve-year follow-up study of Khmer youth who suffered massive war trauma as children. *Journal of the American Academy of Child & Adolescent Psychiatry, 38*(9), 1173–1179.

Saigh, P.A., Yasik, A.E., & Oberfield, R.A. (1999). Behavioral treatment of child-adolescent posttraumatic stress disorder. In P.A. Saigh & J.D. Bremner (Eds.), *Posttraumatic stress disorder: A comprehensive text* (pp. 354–375). Needham Heights, MA: Allyn & Bacon.

Saxe, G., Ellis, B.H., & Kaplow, J. (2004). *Treating child traumatic stress: Self regulation and the social environment.* Paper presented at the Boston University Trauma Conference, Boston, MA.

Saxe, G., Stoddard, F., Courtney, D., Cunningham, K., Chawla, N., Sheridan, R., et al. (2001). Relationship between acute morphine and the course of PTSD in children with burns. *Journal of the American Academy of Child and Adolescent Psychiatry, 40*(8), 915–921.

Seeds of Peace. (2004). Available on line at http://www.seedsofpeace.org/site/PageServer?pagename=camphome.

Stein, B.D., Jaycox, L.H., Kataoka, S.H., Wong, M., Tu, W., Elliott, M.N., et al. (2003). A mental health intervention for school children exposed to violence: A randomized controlled trial. *Journal of the American Medical Association, 290*(5), 603–611.

Stein, B.D., Kataoka, S., Jaycox, L.H., Wong, M., Fink, A., Escudero, P., et al. (2002). Theoretical basis and program design of a school-based mental health intervention for traumatized immigrant children: A collaborative research partnership. *The Journal of Behavioral Health Services & Research, 29*(3), 318–326.

Stichick, T. (2001). The psychosocial impact of armed conflict on children: Rethinking traditional paradigms in research and intervention. *Child and Adolescent Psychiatric Clinics of North America, 10*(4), 797–814.

Stichick-Betancourt, T. (2002). The IRC's emergency education and recreation for Chechen displaced youth in Ingushetia. *Forced Migration Review, 15,* 28–30.

Summerfield, D. (1999) A critique of seven assumptions behind psychological trauma programs in war-affected areas. *Social Science Medicine, 48,* 1449–1462.

Sveaass, N., & Reichelt, S. (2001). Refugee families in therapy: From referrals to therapeutic conversations. *Journal of Family Therapy, 23,* 119–135.

Tobin, J.J., & Friedman, J. (1984). Intercultural and developmental stresses confronting southeast Asian refugee adolescents. *Journal of Operational Psychiatry, 15,* 39–45.

Tsui, A.M., & Sammons, M.T. (1988). Group intervention with adolescent Vietnamese refugees. *Journal for Specialists in Group Work, 13,* 90–95.

UNHCR. (2002, October). Refugee children [online]. Website accessed March 2004. http://www.unhcr.ch/cgi-in/texis/vtx/home.

van der Veer, G. (1998). Restoring emotional stability. In *Counselling and therapy with refugees and victims of trauma: Psychological problems of victims of war, torture, and repression* (pp. 125–140). Chichester, England: John Wiley & Sons.

Van Lehman, D., & Eno, O. (2002). *The Somali Bantu: Their history and culture.* Washington, DC: Center for Applied Linguistics.

Wandersman, A., & Florin, P. (2003). Community interventions and effective prevention. *American Psychologist, 58*(6–7), 441–448.

Watters, C. (2001). Emerging paradigms in the mental health care of refugees. *Social Science and Medicine, 52,* 1709–1718.

Weine, S., & Laub, D. (1995). Narrative constructions of historical realities in testimony with Bosnian survivors of 'ethnic cleansing'. *Psychiatry 58,* 246–260.

Weine, S.M., Kulenovic, A.D., Pavkovic, I., & Gibbons, R. (1998). Testimony psychotherapy in Bosnian refugees: A pilot study. *American Journal of Psychiatry, 155*(12), 1720–1725.

Westermeyer, J. (1989). *Mental health for refugees and other migrants: Social and preventive approaches.* Springfield, IL: Charles C Thomas.

Westermeyer, J., & Wahmanholm, K. (1996). Refugee children. In R. Apfel & B. Simon (Eds.), *Minefields in their hearts: The mental health of children in war and communal violence* (pp. 75–103). New Haven, CT: Yale University Press.

Woodcock, J. (1995). Healing rituals with families in exile. *Journal of Family Therapy, 17,* 397–409.

Yamaguchi, T. (1986). Group psychotherapy in Japan today. *International Journal of Group Psychotherapy, 36,* 567–577.

III

LEGAL AND
POLICY ISSUES
RELATED TO CHILDREN
EXPOSED TO VIOLENCE

8

A RESPONSE SYSTEM FOR CHILDREN EXPOSED TO DOMESTIC VIOLENCE

Public Policy in Support of Best Practices

Jeffrey L. Edleson

P ublic concern about the effects of exposure to domestic violence[1] on children's health and well-being has been increasing. A body of research examining children's exposure has emerged (see Appel & Holden, 1998; Edleson, 1999a, 1999b; Fantuzzo & Mohr, 1999; Margolin, 1998; O'Leary, Slep, & O'Leary, 2000; Rossman, 2001), and social interventions to help alleviate the traumatic effects on children are expanding (see Findlater & Kelly, 1999; Groves, Roberts, & Weinreb, 2000; Groves & Zukerman, 1997; National Council of Juvenile and Family Court Judges, 1998, 1999; Whitney & Davis, 1999; see also http://www.thegreenbook.info).

Public policy makers have only recently begun to understand that children may be affected by exposure to domestic violence and are responding with new initiatives in several domains. There is great concern, however, that some public policy enacted or suggested has supported less than best practices for exposed children and their families (see Edleson, 2004; Weithorn, 2001). This chapter fo-

This chapter is dedicated in memory of Susan Schechter, Sheila Wellstone, and B.B. Robbie Rossman, three pioneers in working with children exposed to domestic violence.

I thank the following people for their contributions through telephone interviews and email correspondence: the National Council of Juvenile and Family Court Judges' Greenbook Policy Advisory Council, Jerry Silverman of the U.S. Department of Health and Human Services, Billie Lee Dunford-Jackson of NCJFCJ, Cari Davis from Colorado Springs, Norma Ellington-Twitty from St. Louis, Diana Avery from Lane County, Oregon, Kris Knowlton and Linda Ronson in Utah, and Rosemary Creeden in Cuyahoga County, Ohio.

[1]In this chapter, the term "domestic violence" indicates violence committed by an adult caregiver in the family against another adult caregiver with whom he or she is engaged in an intimate relationship. Sometimes this term is also used to describe other forms of family violence such as elder abuse or child maltreatment. Domestic violence is used here solely in reference to adult-to-adult domestic violence.

cuses on evolving public policies and practices for children exposed to domestic violence. First, the major categories of current public policies in this area are reviewed, including their intended and unintended impacts. Second, the basic values that desirable public policy would promote for children exposed to domestic violence are outlined, and a public policy and research agenda that maximizes safety for children exposed to domestic violence and their families and minimizes negative unintended consequences is suggested.

EMERGING PUBLIC POLICY CONCERNING CHILDREN EXPOSED TO DOMESTIC VIOLENCE

Public policy, most narrowly construed, focuses on legislation intended to benefit and protect children exposed to domestic violence. Since the late 1990s, a great deal of change has occurred in the laws related to child exposure to domestic violence, which focus most often on criminal prosecution of violent assaults, custody and visitation decision-making, and the child welfare system's response (Lemon, 1999; Mathews, 1999; Weithorn, 2001).

Criminal Prosecution of Violent Assaults

Several legislative changes in criminal statutes directly respond to concerns about the presence of children during domestic violence assaults (see Dunford-Jackson, 2004; Weithorn, 2001). In a number of states, laws have been changed to permit misdemeanor-level domestic assaults to be raised to a felony-level charge. In Oregon, a domestic violence assailant can now be charged with a felony assault if a minor was present during the assault. "Presence" is defined in Oregon as in the immediate presence of or witnessed by the child.

In addition, at least 18 states now permit increased sanctions when minors are present during a domestic assault. Assaults committed in the presence of a minor are considered only one factor that may influence the sanctions imposed in most of the states. Some states add sentencing points when minors have been present; one state doubles whatever penalty would have been given without minors present; and still another adds jail time and requires the convicted perpetrator to pay for the child's counseling needs. The definition of when a child is present is left vague by most states, but some define it as "in the presence of" or when the perpetrator knew the minors were present and might be exposed to the violence. At least one state defines presence as within 30 feet of the child's residence, regardless of the child's exposure to the violence (B.L. Dunford-Jackson, personal communication, March 2, 2004).

Utah and at least two other states have taken a more unique approach by defining the presence of a minor during a domestic violence assault as cause for a separate criminal charge. For example, under Utah law (UCA §76-5-109.1) originally passed in 1997, the presence of a minor two or more times during a domestic assault is cause for separately charging an assailant with a Class A misdemeanor. If the assault included a homicide, attempted homicide, or aggravated assault, the law permitted charging a third-degree felony on the first such assault. In 2002, the state amended this statute so that a Class B misdemeanor charge could be brought on a first—rather than a repeated—instance of a minor's exposure.

On the one hand, these new laws are likely to increase the attention of the police, prosecutors, and courts to children's exposure to domestic violence. Greater sanctions are likely to be imposed when it is perceived that there is more than one victim of an adult domestic assault. On the other hand, there is concern about these changes on a number of levels (Dunford-Jackson, 2004). First, given the increasingly scarce resources of police agencies and prosecutors' offices, there is a concern that attention will focus primarily on cases in which children are present because of the likelihood that this will increase convictions or guilty pleas. Another resulting fear is that these children will be brought into court more often to testify in such cases. In addition, some fear that battered women without children will receive less attention because police and prosecutors will see their cases as weaker ones. Many battered women's advocates argue that if *current* criminal statutes were enforced more consistently there would not be a need for these additional laws focused on children. That is, if perpetrators were consistently arrested, prosecuted, and monitored for adult domestic assaults, children in these families would be just as protected without the addition of these new laws and the potential unintended consequences they may create. A final concern about Utah's legislation is that it may be used against battered mothers for "failing to protect" their children from an assailant. The Utah attorney general, at the time of this law's passage, argued that the wording of the law was such that it focused only on perpetrators of assaults. However, the Utah Attorney General's office has not seen this happen. In most cases, it appears that the separate charge is used as a plea bargain and prompts the judge and police to be more sensitive to the presence of children (K. Knowlton, personal communication, March 3, 2004).

There are few data on the impact of these criminal statute changes. In one of the few studies of these laws, Whitcomb (2000) provided interesting data. Whitcomb surveyed by telephone 128 prosecutors in 93 jurisdictions across the United States regarding their work with children exposed to violence and the impact of new laws on them. She also conducted face-to-face interviews in five jurisdictions. She found that 1) none of the jurisdictions had protocols governing

the prosecution of domestic violence and child maltreatment in the same families; 2) prosecutors in jurisdictions in which laws were in place regarding children's exposure to domestic violence were more likely to report domestic violence
cases to child protection agencies, but they were no more likely to prosecute
mothers for "failure to protect;" 3) prosecutors were seeking enhanced penalties
in domestic violence cases when children were also present, even in jurisdictions
where no new laws regarding children exposed to domestic violence were in place;
and 4) 75% of the prosecutors interviewed said they would not report or prosecute a mother for failing to protect her children from exposure to her own victimization, and the remaining prosecutors said they would only do so when there
were additional factors indicating extreme danger to the child. Whitcomb's research is clearly a starting point for additional studies with the multiple factors in
the complex system of social responses to children and their families.

Custody and Visitation Disputes

Most states now include the "presence of domestic violence" as a criterion that
judges may use to determine custody and visitation arrangements when disputed.
In most jurisdictions here and in other western countries, there has been an assumption that both parents have the right and ability to share custody and visitation of their children (Eriksson & Hester, 2001). In approximately 23 states,
however, this presumption has been reversed in what are commonly referred to as
"rebuttable presumption" statutes. Rebuttable presumption statutes generally
state that when domestic violence is present it is against the best interests of the
child for the documented perpetrator to be awarded custody until his or her safety
with the child is assured. California Family Code is an example of a rebuttable
presumption statute. Under Section 3044 "there is a rebuttable presumption that
an award of sole or joint physical or legal custody of a child to a person who has
perpetrated domestic violence is detrimental to the best interest of the child." California's code outlines six factors to consider in assessing whether a perpetrator of
domestic violence has overcome this presumption:

1. Whether the perpetrator of domestic violence has demonstrated that giving
   sole or joint physical or legal custody of a child to the perpetrator is in the
   best interest of the child

2. Whether the perpetrator has satisfactorily completed a batterer's treatment
   program that meets the criteria outlined in subdivision (c) of Section
   1203.097 of the Penal Code

3. Whether the perpetrator has successfully completed a program of alcohol or
   drug abuse counseling if the court determines that counseling is appropriate

4. Whether the perpetrator has successfully completed a parenting class if the court determines the class to be appropriate

5. If the perpetrator is on probation or parole, whether he or she is restrained by a protective order granted after a hearing, and whether he or she has complied with its terms and conditions

6. Whether the perpetrator of domestic violence has committed any further acts of domestic violence (California Family Code, § 3044)

One difficulty in applying rebuttable presumption statutes is defining what evidence of domestic violence will be admitted as part of the custody and visitation decision-making process. Is it a past or present arrest or restraining order? Should it be a prior conviction or guilty plea? These are just some of the ways violence perpetration may be proven. In a rebuttable presumption statute passed by the state of Wisconsin's legislature and signed into law by Governor Doyle in February of 2004, *guardians ad litem* are given the responsibility for investigating all accusations of domestic violence and reporting their conclusions to the judge. The new law instructs judges to make domestic violence their top priority by stating that

> If the courts find . . . that a parent has engaged in a pattern or serious incident of interspousal battery [as described in statutes], or domestic abuse, the safety and well-being of the child and the safety of the parent who was the victim of the battery or abuse shall be the paramount concerns in determining legal custody and periods of physical placement. (Wisconsin Act 130, §25, 767.24(5))

The new law requires training of all *guardians ad litem* and custody mediators in assessing domestic violence and its impact on adult victims and children, and it lays out new procedures for safe mediation.

While legislative developments such as rebuttable presumption laws appear to be positive, there has been little or no evaluation of their impact on children's and non-abusive parents' safety. A number of other critical issues remain mostly unattended in custody and visitation decisions that involve domestic violence. Part of the problem is that many battered mothers are self-represented in disputed custody cases. For example, in a California study, 30% of parents entering required custody mediation were concerned about domestic violence and 55% had records indicating current or former domestic violence restraining orders. In addition, more than half of the families (53%) involved in child custody mediation had at least one parent who was not represented by legal counsel (*pro per*), and in 28% of the families neither parent was represented (see Center for Families, Children and the Courts, 2000). These findings raise concerns about both safety for the adult victims and the degree to which they are well represented in court processes.

Poor representation for adult victims may compound a number of other disadvantages, including 1) the abuser or his legal counsel accusing the mother of purposefully alienating her children from their father using empirically questionable concepts such as parental alienation syndrome (Faller, 1998); 2) using "friendly parent" provisions of custody statutes to accuse a mother concerned about her and her children's safety of being uncooperative; 3) minimizing the impact of adult domestic violence exposure on children's safety and well-being; 4) inappropriately using standardized psychological tests that have not been developed to assess domestic violence to question the veracity of battered women's testimony or her parenting abilities; and 5) appointing custody evaluators or mediators, *guardians ad litem,* and court appointed special advocates (CASAs) who have little or no training on issues of domestic violence to assess and provide advice to the court on custody and visitation arrangements. Each of these issues presents unique policy challenges for the future and policy research opportunities as new policies are implemented.

Child Welfare Response

Some states have approached this issue by expanding the definitions of child maltreatment to include children who have witnessed domestic violence. For example, in 1999, the Minnesota State Legislature expanded the definition of child neglect in the Maltreatment of Minors Reporting Act to include exposure to adult domestic violence as a specific type of neglect (Minnesota State Annals §626.556; see Edleson, Gassman-Pines, & Hill, in press; Minnesota Department of Human Services, 1999).

Exposure to adult domestic violence is commonly used as one component of an operational definition of child neglect in many child protection agencies. The change in Minnesota acknowledged what had long been believed to be the practice in many county child protection agencies across the state—accepting certain reports of children's exposure to adult domestic violence as child neglect.

Minnesota is not alone in including such families in its neglect caseloads. Exposure to domestic violence has been commonly included in published definitions of child neglect (see English, 1998; Kalichman, 1999). The U.S. Office of Child Abuse and Neglect suggests that operational definitions of child emotional neglect include "exposure to extreme or chronic spouse abuse or other domestic violence in the child's presence" (Goldman, Salus, Wolcott, & Kennedy, 2003, p. 18); this definition is found internationally as well. For example, most Canadian provinces already include exposure to domestic violence in their definitions of child maltreatment (Weithorn, 2001). The Australian province of New South Wales passed the Children and Young Persons (Care and Protection) Act of 1998 that defines reportable forms of child risk as a child or young person "living in a household where there have been incidents of domestic violence and, as a consequence, the child or young person is at risk of serious physical or psychological harm" (New South Wales, 1998, Sec. 23d).

The change in Minnesota's Reporting Act definition of child neglect to include children exposed to domestic violence meant that the state mandated a range of professionals to report every child they suspected had witnessed adult domestic violence. A survey of 52 Minnesota counties estimated that the language change would generate 9,101 new domestic violence exposure reports to be screened by child protection agencies each year (Minnesota Association of County Social Service Administrators, 2000). Minnesota responds to a total of approximately 17,000 reports of child maltreatment annually (http://www.dhs.mn.us/). If all of these new reports were accepted, it would represent more than a 50% increase statewide, with some counties experiencing much higher increases.

Though the legislators thought that the language change would merely clarify existing practices, the change in definition did result in rapidly rising child maltreatment reports across Minnesota, creating significant problems for many county agencies. First, current Minnesota law required an immediate response to all child maltreatment reports. Second, there was no specific funding appropriated to implement this change. The Minnesota Association of County Social Service Administrators (2000) estimated it would cost more than $10 million to screen, assess, and provide services to referred children and their families, $19 million for the purchase of adequate community-based services, and another $1.4 million to train law enforcement and county attorneys about the new law. Full implementation would have cost more than $30 million if all of these newly reported children were to be appropriately served.

Social service administrators argued that the change represented an "unfunded mandate" by the legislature. Child protection workers already felt their agencies were inadequately supported, and the large increase of reports threatened to stretch some counties beyond their capacity to respond. County agencies and the field as a whole did not yet have adequate strategies to differentiate those factors in exposure to adult domestic violence that created more or less risk for a child. Administrators and workers alike also began to fear that, due to the large increase in reports being screened and investigated, they would have inadequate resources left to properly serve the families of children experiencing more severe forms of physical and sexual maltreatment. In essence, many more children not requiring the full force of the child protection agency would be screened and investigated, but fewer needing the county's services would receive them. As current and former child protection workers explained, a wide range of children were swept up by the legislation, some of whom were very much in need of child protective services and others who needed services but not these.

The expanded reporting requirements also raised concerns among advocates for battered women who feared that as a result of the new definition child protective services would utilize methods that would blame more mothers for their male partners' violent behavior by substantiating mothers for "failure to protect" (see Magen, 1999). In fact, in the midst of implementing the reporting requirements, one county began to use *per diem* reimbursement requests from local shelters to identify women entering local shelters with children and to refer these mothers to the local child protection agency for fuller screening and investigation. Although only a small percentage of reports to child protective services result in removal of children from their parents' custody (English, Edleson, & Herrick, 2005; Kohl, Edleson, English, & Barth, 2005), many mothers and community members believe otherwise.

Minnesota's legislation has had two outcomes, both of which are frustrating. First, the community responded to the expanded definition of neglect by reporting many thousands of Minnesota children exposed to domestic violence. Many of these children were unlikely to have been identified previously. Unfortunately, the capacity of child protective services to respond was greatly strained, resulting in more identification and screening but probably fewer services to those most in need. Second, almost all Minnesota counties decided to drop the requirement for reporting exposed children to child protective services after the legislature repealed the change. Unfortunately, many thousands of children who were earlier identified were no longer visible and not likely to receive needed services. Clearly, well-meaning policy changes can have far-reaching and unforeseen impacts that require careful advance testing (see Edleson et al., in press, for a more complete discussion of Minnesota's experience).

A FRAMEWORK FOR PUBLIC POLICY

There is a clear need to think more carefully about emerging public policy regarding children exposed to domestic violence, particularly when children come to the attention of public agencies such as child protective services, as well as non-profit community-based social service programs for children and their families. My focus here is a result of two factors: 1) This chapter was written at the request of the U.S. Department of Health and Human Services, which is interested in the understanding and development of human services; and 2) as a result of the Violence Against Women Act and the funding that flows from it, a great deal of attention is being focused on criminal justice issues in the field of domestic violence. Unfortunately, much less attention is being devoted to prevention and the provision of supportive social services for children and their families.

The starting point for a public policy discussion should be specific acknowledgment that not all children exposed to domestic violence have the same experience. Surveys of family violence show a great deal of variation in the frequency, severity, and chronicity of domestic assaults in families. It is also likely that children within the same home will be exposed in differing ways to these assaults, will respond to these events with varying coping styles and behaviors, and will have varying numbers of protective or risk factors present in their lives. Acknowledging these facts most likely precludes defining all children exposed to domestic violence as maltreated children (see Edleson, 2004, for a larger discussion of this issue). Many of these children will enter the child protection system because they are also direct victims of child sexual or physical abuse and other forms of maltreatment.

This great variation among the likely experiences of children exposed to domestic violence calls for varied social responses and policies to support them. In fact, many children exposed to domestic violence do not fit into current child maltreatment categories and may be better served in voluntary, community-based settings.

Recognizing the diversity of children's experiences requires consideration of a continuum of possible responses to them. Developing a continuum of responses requires a consideration of the value base underlying policy formation (see Edleson, Eisikovits, & Peled, 1992). There is a growing consensus regarding the value assumptions underlying such policy. This consensus has been expressed in interviews with professionals in a variety of systems (see Beeman & Edleson, 2000; Weithorn, 2001) and most notably in the National Council of Juvenile and Family Court Judges' (1999), *Effective Intervention in Domestic Violence and Child Maltreatment: A Guide for Policy and Practice* (commonly referred to as the *Greenbook,* see http://www.thegreenbook.info). In short, these interviews and documents suggest that public policy should be formulated so as to

- Ensure to the greatest extent possible the safety, stability and well-being of *all* family members, including child and adult victims in a family

- Hold the perpetrator of violent acts accountable for his or her behavior

- Provide multiple points of service access for the multiple needs of children and families

- Improve multiple service system responses through cross-training, cross-communication, structural changes within systems to better serve safety and accountability, and coordination and/or integration of fragmented services

These values must be considered within a context of "do no harm." In other words, both the intended and unintended consequences of these new policies must

be carefully considered. Although there may be surprise positive consequences
from a new policy, it is often the case—such as in Minnesota's experience—that
there may be unforeseen negative consequences that will overwhelm the service
systems involved and lead to less, not more, support for children and families. Such
policies may also exacerbate other existing problems in these systems, such as the
disproportionate representation of poor children and children of color in the child
welfare system (see Courtney & Skyles, 2003).

Needless to say, there will always be cases in which the safety interests of one
member of the family may not be congruent with those of another member.
These are usually the most difficult cases to address but also the ones in which
safety concerns can be balanced through a better understanding among service
providers across multiple systems. This improved understanding will most likely
be achieved through internal structural changes in how safety is enhanced, greater
cross-agency communication, and closer coordination of social responders.

PUBLIC POLICY AGENDA
IN SUPPORT OF BEST PRACTICES

One of the problems with current public policy is that it is often focused on quick
legislative fixes that are seldom accompanied by the resources necessary to support
children and families. Changes in laws without accompanying support for re-
training of key players in various systems and for supportive social services may
not be of the greatest help for these families.

It is logical to envision a graduated system of care based on the seriousness
of the exposure and its possible impacts on the child. One part of this continuum
of care would certainly be child protection agency responses to children who are
both maltreated and have been exposed to domestic violence. An ideal continuum
would also include early intervention services for children and families in which
direct child abuse has not occurred. This "graduated response" to children exposed to domestic violence has been discussed in some national meetings. As the
co-chair of a subcommittee of the national Greenbook Policy Advisory Committee (GPAC), sponsored by the National Council of Juvenile and Family Court
Judges, I had the opportunity to discuss these ideas with a range of interested par-
ties over several years. In preparing this chapter, I also contacted a number of the
federally funded Greenbook demonstration sites and other programs to elicit the
views of their staff. The result is a proposed care system for children exposed to
domestic violence that is illustrated in Figure 8.1. In this figure, the width of the
arrows indicates both the strength and direction of the relationships between elements in the system.

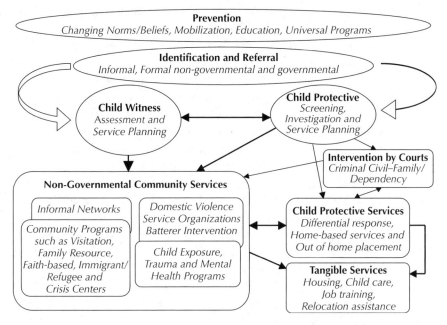

Figure 8.1. Illustration of proposed care system for children exposed to domestic violence.

This system of care is envisioned as a multi-pronged approach to children and families that begins with efforts directed at the *prevention* of child exposure to violence (see Daro, 2000; Daro & Cohn-Donnelly, 2001). In fact, many of the prevention programs mounted in the domain of child abuse or youth violence prevention are highly likely to also address prevention of childhood exposure to adult domestic violence (see Daro, Edleson, & Pinderhughes, 2004). As shown in Figure 8.1, prevention activities that seem particularly promising include mobilizing both informal social support networks (see Budde & Schene, 2004) and communities (see Bowen, Gwiasda, & Brown, 2004; Sabol, Coulton, & Korbin, 2004). Many non-governmental organizations can play an important role in developing public awareness and action as well as changing both norms and beliefs about domestic violence. For example, the Family Violence Prevention Fund has developed a series of highly successful community education efforts aimed at generating appropriate responses within social networks (see Ghez, 2001; Klein, Campbell, Soler, & Ghez, 1997; see also http://www.endabuse.org). Government public health organizations may also play a strategic role in both supporting and carrying out a number of activities, including providing large-scale surveillance of child exposure, studying the epidemiology of the problem, helping to identify protective and risk factors associated with varying outcomes for children and their families, evaluating specific efforts, and encouraging the implementation of empirically proven efforts on a larger scale (Hammond, 2003). All of these prevention activities support other elements in Figure 8.1, including identification, assessment, and intervention.

The *identification* of existing exposed children and *referral* of them to appropriate community or public agencies is facilitated by a variety of sources as shown in Figure 8.1. The direct capacity of any community to respond to children exposed to violence depends in large part on the ability of first responders to correctly identify a child's situation and make referrals. Informal networks that include family members and friends are often the first to respond when battered women seek help. In a study reporting data on battered women using primary care clinic services, the two most frequent sources of help battered women listed were family (65.9%) and friends (61.3%) (Van Hook, 2000). In contrast, only 6.8% of the women said they had used family violence programs, only 11.3% social services, and only 22.5% mental health services. Developing these informal networks to better respond to battered women and their children is a major challenge in developing an effective response system (see Kelly, 1996). Beyond informal networks, there is a wide spectrum of first responders in the formal, nongovernmental sector that can play an important role in identification and referral, including early childhood program staff such as those in child care centers, crisis nurseries, Head Start, and family and parent support programs (Schechter, 2004); teachers and others in school systems (O'Brien, 2001); health care professionals such as emergency medical technicians, nurses, and doctors (Groves, Augustyn, Lee, & Sawires, 2002; Stark, 2001); employee assistance program staff and colleagues; and clergy and congregation members (Fortune, 2001). A variety of governmental agencies may also play a role, including police and other law enforcement officers, public health home visiting nurses, social workers in home visiting programs, and others who have contact with children and families.

Efforts to mobilize the multiple informal and formal networks of first responders in a way that maximizes identification, initial support and safety planning, and appropriate referral are critical components of creating an effective system of response. Referral is likely to be most effective when first responders have a working relationship with the community programs to which they are referring people. This relationship is often a result of prevention education and community mobilization efforts aimed at these providers.

The multiple systems involved in identification of these children and their families must have a clear idea of where to make appropriate referrals. What is an "appropriate" referral will most likely generate some heated discussion. English and colleagues (2005) demonstrated that only about half (56%) of child maltreatment reports in Washington state were accepted for investigation, and a further two thirds of these (68.1%) were then assigned no or low risk after investigation and provided few services.

These data argue that, in the great majority of cases, referral should be made to community-based programs designed for careful *assessment* and *service planning* to address child and family needs. Several examples of community-based assessment settings exist. For example, Cuyahoga County (Cleveland) has funded a nonprofit agency, Mental Health Services, Inc., to operate a centralized assessment program to which primarily police refer families for voluntary and supportive assessment. The county then provides grants to seven community-based agencies to provide support services for these children and their families, based on needs identified in the assessments. Extensive work has been conducted with these seven agencies to enhance their capacity to serve children exposed to domestic violence, and the Ohio Attorney General has supported replications of this project in six children's hospitals in other cities in the state (R. Creeden, personal communication, March 16, 2004).

Other communities have developed the capacity to provide these same services in other ways. Small numbers of programs called "child witness to violence projects" offer both assessment and intervention for children and families affected by all forms of violence (Groves, 1999; Groves & Zuckerman, 1997). Many domestic violence organizations such as battered women's shelters and treatment programs also have the ability or potential to provide assessment and service to these families. Child advocacy centers and family resource centers—originally developed for other purposes—have, in a few locations, also been expanded to provide voluntary and family supportive assessments of exposed children.

A smaller number of identified children will certainly be referred directly to the child protective system and accepted for screening, investigation, and case planning (as shown in Figure 8.1 with a *smaller* circle and arrow from referral sources). Data in state and nationally representative studies clearly show how small this number may be (English et al., 2005; Kohl et al., 2005). Referring *all* exposed children to child protective services might make sense if these services were adequately funded to screen, assess, and intervene with these families. Unfortunately, this is not usually the case.

In a very small number of cases—usually those referred through the child protective system—the courts will also become involved. Even though the numbers are small, the courts have a significant impact on custody, visitation, and out-of-home placement decisions in these families. In some cases, dependency court judges have also used the "reasonable efforts" provisions of federal law (Social Security Act, Title IV-E, Section 471[15]) to require services for battered mothers to permit a child to continue residing with a non-abusive parent. One federally funded Greenbook demonstration site has developed guidelines on using "reasonable efforts" provisions to aid battered mothers and their children (N. Ellington-Twitty, personal communication, March 6, 2004).

The most realistic approach to assessment and service planning for most localities is to clearly differentiate in public policy between children at different levels of risk for harm. Some should be referred to and assessed for abuse by the child protection system, and some should be assessed in a more voluntary and supportive setting because they are exposed to domestic violence but are not themselves at imminent risk for harm. Such an approach would offer multiple pathways to assessment and services and an alternative to flooding the child protective system with large numbers of referrals, perhaps better serving these families' needs. Depending on the size of the community, there may be one or more non-governmental organizations offering voluntary assessment services in any one community.

Some concerns have been raised about the quality of assessments performed on children exposed to domestic violence. First, can child advocacy centers that have long focused on forensic interviewing of sexual abuse victims make the transition to doing family-supportive interviews that do not lead to a case finding or court hearing, but rather lead to a voluntary plan for services for the child and his or her family? Second, commonly used assessors, such as custody evaluators, *guardians ad litem,* and court-appointed special advocates, are sometimes insufficiently trained to understand the dynamics of domestic violence and to accurately assess both the risks and protective factors that both parents may represent in a child's life. Can the capacity of these professional groups be enhanced to the point that they become reliable elements in a community's ability to assess children exposed to domestic violence?

The results of assessment and planning are hopefully referrals to a variety of services. As shown in Figure 8.1, both *governmental and nongovernmental services* as well as *informal supports* are likely to be drawn upon to assist these children and their families. Within child welfare, options include differential or alternative response, intensive home-based services, and out-of-home placements. A variety of community-based programs for children and adults exist and include shelters for battered women, immigrant and refugee services, batterer intervention programs, supervised visitation centers, and programs for children exposed to violence. Informal networks are also increasingly drawn upon to provide safety and support through processes such as community mobilization and family group conferencing (Carter, 2003; Kelly, 1996). Tangible services, such as income and housing assistance, subsidized child care, job training, and relocation assistance are also important basic supports for battered women (see Davies, 1999; Schechter, 1999). In many cases, as the arrows in Figure 8.1 indicate, there will be interaction between the public child welfare system and community-based programs that work with these families.

DEVELOPING A SYSTEM OF CARE

Each community will likely have existing assets that can be leveraged to build this system of graduated care. In each community, the system will evolve differently and with a unique combination of key stakeholders. Ideally, the multiple stakeholders will together systematically develop a communitywide response and then go about the hard work of funding and building the necessary prevention, identification and referral, assessment, and intervention components.

This system will also require funding support. Around the country, a variety of sources are being tapped to support these efforts. Federal funds from the U.S. Department of Health and Human Services and the Department of Justice support six Greenbook demonstration sites. The National Child Traumatic Stress Network (see http://www.nctsnet.org), with funding through the Center for Mental Health Services of the U.S. Substance Abuse and Mental Health Services Administration (SAMHSA), supports a growing number of child witness to violence projects. Interestingly, the Ohio Attorney General has drawn on funds gathered from confiscation of criminal resources (e.g., drug money) to seed replications underway in Ohio. Similarly, in California, Utah, and other locations, Victims of Crime Act (VOCA) funds are being drawn upon to support services to adult and child victims. In addition, in some locations local funds have been allocated by the county board (Olmsted County, Minnesota) and from local court budgets (Johnson County, Kansas). Some sources include Temporary Assistance to Needy Families funds to support battered women and children who have fled to safety (Oregon) and the co-location of multiple providers in local service centers (El Paso County, Colorado). Child welfare and protection funding streams in the U.S. Department of Health and Human Services, and Violence Against Women Act (VAWA) funds from the U.S. Justice Department also support innovative programming and training. Other funding has included state-generated marriage license fees and grants from a number of foundations and private corporations, including the David and Lucile Packard Foundation, Annie E. Casey Foundation, Edna McConnell Clark Foundation, the Doris Duke Foundation, Liz Claiborne, and State Farm Insurance (see Trujillo & Test, 2003).

Federal efforts to expand resources for children exposed to violence have been attempted. The late U.S. Senator Paul Wellstone and his wife, Sheila, drafted the Children Who Witness Domestic Violence Act and co-sponsored it with Senator Patty Murray of Washington State. Work on the Act stalled when the Wellstones died in a plane crash in October of 2002. However, parts of it have been included in the 2003 reauthorization of the Child Abuse Prevention and

Treatment Act (CAPTA) and the No Child Left Behind Act, formally known as the Elementary and Secondary Education Act. Unfortunately, inadequate funding for both of these acts has left the programs for children exposed to violence mostly unfunded.

FUTURE RESEARCH ON POLICY AND ITS IMPACTS

This mapping of a future system of response to children exposed to domestic violence points to a number of roles that research and evaluation can play. There is a great need to work on better definitions of child exposure to violence. Carlson (2000) and Jouriles, MacDonald, Norwood, and Ezell (2001) have suggested that the number of exposed children depends in part on how adult domestic violence is defined. Is it violence between intimate partners of any gender or specifically violence against women? Most would argue for a broad definition that includes violence between any intimate adult partners in the household, but others believe that the definition should be more narrow based on the goals of an assessment. Also in dispute is the inclusion of verbal, emotional, and psychological abuse (e.g., Carlson, 2000). Unfortunately, there is no consistent way in which adult domestic violence is defined, currently making any comparison of different estimates difficult (Crowell & Burgess, 1996).

In addition, few instruments have been developed to measure exposure to violence and its impact. More than a decade ago, Richters argued that "there is a clear and urgent need for intensive, community-based epidemiological research designed initially to identify the children most at risk for exposure to violence in the community as either victims or witnesses, and to assess the consequences of that exposure" (1993, p. 4). His call for the development of measures still rings true today, especially when our ability to assess children exposed to adult domestic violence is in its infancy. There are no existing measures of a child's exposure to domestic violence that have been subjected to rigorous psychometric testing. Mohr and Tulman (2000) have suggested that the measurement of child exposure to violence cannot be univariate and that it must take into account the multiple contextual variables that affect children. There is clearly a need for a comprehensive tool.

There is also almost a total absence of research on the impact of new legislation on children and their families. For example, the impact of Utah's ability to bring charges against an assailant for exposure of minors, Oregon's ability to charge an assault as a felony if minors are present, or the impact of rebuttable presumption laws on custody and visitation decisions are all fertile areas of policy research. Emerging policies are numerous and call out for research that utilizes both in-depth qualitative methods as well as controlled evaluations of their impact on systems and the families for which they are intended.

Even greater is the need to evaluate the impact of various elements of community response and the process whereby such a system of response is created. My colleagues and I (Edleson, Beeman, & Hagemeister, 2000) have suggested that any program evaluation should give significant attention to documenting the unique process of implementation and systems change that develops in a community. A community's response to children exposed to domestic violence should, at least in part, evolve from a *model of change* that is made explicit and used to guide judgments on the degree to which the model is implemented and the value of outcomes achieved. The larger community context will often influence the success of a community effort; therefore, it is critical to document the effects of the local context on the implementation and outcome of the projects through a systematic study of the process of implementation. These system changes are both an outcome of a community collaborative and a means to change for the individuals and families impacted by the system. Therefore, research should identify and measure both indicators of systems change and of the individual and family changes that may result. Finally, the individual intervention elements each require careful evaluation as well. A few such evaluations exist to date (see Graham-Bermann, 2001), but more careful study of the assessment of and intervention programs for children exposed to domestic violence is required.

CONCLUSION

There is a dire need for a comprehensive system of care for the families of children exposed to domestic violence. Public policy and planning in this area must be clearly guided by social values, ensuring safety for victims and accountability for offenders, multiple points of entry to the system of care, and careful collaborative planning among a variety of stakeholders. The care that children and their families require will not result from a simple inclusion of exposed children in the category of maltreated children. There are no quick fixes, and sometimes relatively simple changes bring about unintended negative consequences.

A system of care requires extensive changes in community capacity within informal and formal non-governmental and governmental systems. Adequate caring for these children requires changes in legislation, new prevention efforts, and expanded service delivery systems. Developing such a system certainly requires the allocation and reallocation of financial support from government and private funding sources.

Opportunity abounds for science to make significant contributions to this area of public policy and service delivery. Multiple domains, from definition and measurement to policy and program evaluation, call out for much greater attention and promise to shed light on what can and cannot help children exposed to domestic violence and their families.

REFERENCES

Appel, A.E., & Holden, G.W. (1998). The co-occurrence of spouse and physical child abuse: A review and appraisal. *Journal of Family Psychology, 12*, 578–599.

Beeman, S.K., & Edleson, J.L. (2000). Collaborating for family safety: Challenges for children's and women's advocates. *Journal of Aggression, Maltreatment and Trauma, 3,* 345–358.

Bowen, L.K., Gwiasda, V., & Brown, M.M. (2004). Engaging community residents to prevent violence. *Journal of Interpersonal Violence, 19,* 356–367.

Budde, S., & Schene, P. (2004). Informal social support interventions and their role in violence prevention. *Journal of Interpersonal Violence, 19,* 341–355.

Carlson, B.E. (2000). Children exposed to intimate partner violence: Research findings and implications for intervention. *Trauma, Violence, and Abuse, 1 (4),* 321–342.

Carter, L.S. (2003). *Family team conferences in domestic violence cases: Guidelines for practice* (2nd ed.). San Francisco, CA: Family Violence Prevention Fund (Available on line at http://www.endabuse.org).

Center for Families, Children & the Courts. (2000). *Supervised visitation: A look at the research literature (Research Update).* San Francisco: Author.

Courtney, M., & Skyles, A. (Eds.). (2003). The overrepresentation of children of color in the child welfare system (special issue). *Children and Youth Services Review, 25(5-6),* 355–507.

Crowell, N.A., & Burgess, A.W. (1996). *Understanding violence against women.* Washington, DC: National Academy Press.

Daro, D. (2000). Child abuse prevention: New directions and challenges. In D. Hansen (Ed.), *Motivation and child maltreatment.* (Vol. 46 of the Nebraska Symposium on Motivation, pp. 161–220). Lincoln: University of Nebraska Press.

Daro, D., & Cohn-Donnelly, A. (2001). Child abuse prevention: Accomplishments and challenges. In J. Myers, L. Berliner, J. Briere, T. Hendrix, C. Jenny, & T. Reid (Eds.), *APSAC handbook on child maltreatment* (2nd ed., pp. 431–448). Thousand Oaks, CA: Sage.

Daro, D., Edleson, J.L., & Pinderhughes, H. (2004). Finding common ground in the study of child maltreatment, youth violence, and adult domestic violence. *Journal of Interpersonal Violence, 19,* 282–298.

Davies, J. (1999). *Building opportunities for battered women's safety and self-sufficiency.* Harrisburg, PA: National Resource Center on Domestic Violence.

Dunford-Jackson, B.L. (2004). The role of family courts in domestic violence: The US experience. In P.G. Jaffe, L.L. Baker, & A. Cunningham (Eds.), *Ending domestic violence in the lives of children and parents: Promising practices for safety, healing, and prevention* (pp. 188–199). New York: Guilford Press.

Edleson, J.L. (1999a). Children's witnessing of adult domestic violence. *Journal of Interpersonal Violence, 14(8),* 839–870.

Edleson, J.L. (1999b). The overlap between child maltreatment and woman battering. *Violence Against Women, 5(2),* 134–154.

Edleson, J.L. (2004). Should childhood exposure to adult domestic violence be defined as child maltreatment under the law? In P.G. Jaffe, L.L. Baker, & A. Cunningham (Eds.), *Ending domestic violence in the lives of children and parents: Promising practices for safety, healing, and prevention* (pp. 8–29). New York: Guilford Press.

Edleson, J.L., Beeman, S.K., & Hagemeister, A.K. (2000). *Assessing the implementation of change: Coordinating child protection agencies, domestic violence service providers, and dependency courts.* Washington, DC: The Lewin Group.

Edleson, J.L., Eisikovits, Z.C., & Peled, E. (1992). A model for analyzing societal responses to woman battering: Israel as a case in point. *International Social Work, 35,* 19–33.

Edleson, J.L., Gassman-Pines, J., & Hill, M.B. (in press). Defining child exposure to domestic violence as neglect: Minnesota's difficult experience. St. Paul, MN: Manuscript submitted for publication to *Social Work.*

English, D.J. (1998). The extent and consequences of child maltreatment. *The Future of Children, 8,* 39–53.

English, D.J., Edleson, J.L., & Herrick, M.E. (2005). The presence of domestic violence in a child protective caseload. *Children and Youth Services Review, 27,* 1183–1201.

Eriksson, M., & Hester, M. (2001). Violent men as good enough fathers. *Violence Against Women, 7,* 779–798.

Faller, K. (1998). The Parental Alienation Syndrome: What is it and what data support it? *Child Maltreatment, 3,* 100–115.

Fantuzzo, J.W., & Mohr, W.K. (1999). Prevalence and effects of child exposure to domestic violence. *The Future of Children, 9,* 21–32.

Findlater, J.E., & Kelly, S. (1999). Reframing child safety in Michigan: Building collaboration among domestic violence, family preservation, and child protection services. *Child Maltreatment, 4(2),* 167–174.

Fortune, M.M. (2001). Religious issues and violence against women. In C.M. Renzetti, J.L. Edleson, & R.K. Bergen (Eds.), *Sourcebook on violence against women* (pp. 371–385). Thousand Oaks, CA: Sage.

Ghez, M. (2001). Getting the message out: Using media to change social norms on abuse. In C.M. Renzetti, J.L. Edleson, & R.K. Bergen (Eds.), *Sourcebook on violence against women* (pp. 417–438). Thousand Oaks, CA: Sage.

Goldman, J., Salus, M.K., Wolcott, D., & Kennedy, K.Y. (2003). *A coordinated response to child abuse and neglect: The foundation for practice.* Washington, DC: Office of Child Abuse and Neglect. Retrieved from http://nccanch.acf.hhs.gov/pubs/usermanuals/foundation/foundation.pdf.

Graham-Bermann, S.A. (2001). Designing intervention evaluations for children exposed to domestic violence: Applications of research and theory. In S.A. Graham-Bermann (Ed.), *Domestic violence in the lives of children* (pp. 237–267). Washington, DC: American Psychological Association.

Groves, B.M. (1999). Mental health services for children who witness domestic violence. *Future of Children, 9,* 122–132.

Groves, B.M., Augustyn, M., Lee, D., & Sawires, P. (2002). *Identifying and responding to domestic violence: Consensus recommendations for child and adolescent health.* San Francisco, CA: Family Violence Prevention Fund. Retrieved from http://www.endabuse.org.

Groves, B.M., Roberts, E., & Weinreb, M. (2000). *Shelter from the storm: Clinical intervention with children affected by domestic violence.* Boston: Boston Medical Center.

Groves, B.M., & Zuckerman, B. (1997). Interventions with parents and caregivers of children who are exposed to violence. In J.D. Osofsky (Ed.), *Children in a violent society* (pp. 183–201). New York: Guilford Press.

Hammond, W.R. (2003). Public health and child maltreatment prevention: The role of the Centers for Disease Control and Prevention. *Child Maltreatment, 8,* 81–83.

Jouriles, E.N., MacDonald, R., Norwood, W.D., & Ezell, E. (2001). Issues and controversies in documenting the prevalence of children's exposure to domestic violence. In S.A. Graham-Bermann (Ed.), *Domestic violence in the lives of children* (pp. 13–34). Washington, DC: American Psychological Association.

Kalichman, S.C. (1999). *Mandated reporting of suspected child abuse* (2nd ed.). Washington, DC: American Psychological Association.

Kelly, L. (1996). Tensions and possibilities: Enhancing informal responses to domestic violence. In J.L. Edleson & Z.C. Eisikovits (Eds.), *Future interventions with battered women and their families* (pp. 67–86). Thousand Oaks, CA: Sage.

Klein, E., Campbell, J., Soler, E., & Ghez, M. (1997). *Ending domestic violence: Changing public perceptions/halting the epidemic.* Thousand Oaks, CA: Sage Publications.

Kohl, P.L., Edleson, J.L., English, D.J. & Barth, R.P. (2005). Domestic violence and pathways into child welfare services: Findings from the National Survey of Child and Adolescent Well-Being. *Children and Youth Services Review, 27,* 1167–1182.

Lemon, N.K.D. (1999). The legal system's response to children exposed to domestic violence. *The Future of Children, 9,* 67–83.

Magen, R.H. (1999). In the best interests of battered women: Reconceptualizing allegations of failure to protect. *Child Maltreatment, 4,* 127–135.

Margolin, G. (1998). Effects of witnessing violence on children. In P.K. Trickett and C.J. Schellenbach (Eds.), *Violence against children in the family and the community* (pp. 57–101). Washington, DC: American Psychological Association.

Mathews, M.A. (1999). The impact of federal and state laws on children exposed to domestic violence. *The Future of Children, 9,* 50–66.

Minnesota Association of County Social Service Administrators [Children's Committee]. (2000). *Co-Occurring Spouse Abuse and Child Abuse: Domestic Violence Fiscal Note—January 2000.* St. Paul, MN: Author.

Minnesota Department of Human Services. (1999). *Bulletin #99-68-15: Laws related to domestic violence involving children, including 1999 amendments to neglect definition in Maltreatment of Minors Act.* St. Paul, MN: Author.

Mohr, W.K., & Tulman, L.J. (2000). Children exposed to violence: Measurement considerations within an ecological framework. *Advances in Nursing Science, 23,* 59–68.

National Council of Juvenile and Family Court Judges. (1998). *Family violence: Emerging programs for battered mothers and their children.* Reno, NV: Author.

National Council of Juvenile and Family Court Judges. (1999). *Effective intervention in domestic violence and child maltreatment: Guidelines for policy and practice.* Reno, NV: Author (Available at http://www.thegreenbook.info).

New South Wales. (1998). *Children and Young Persons (Care and Protection) Act of 1998 (Section 23d).* Available on line at Australasian Legal Information Institute web site at http://www.austlii.edu.au/au/legis/nsw/consol_act/caypapa1998442/s23.html.

O'Brien, M.K. (2001). School-based education and prevention programs. In C.M. Renzetti, J.L. Edleson, & R.K.Bergen (Eds.), *Sourcebook on violence against women* (pp. 387–415). Thousand Oaks, CA: Sage.

O'Leary, K.D., Slep, A.M.S., & O'Leary, S.G. (2000). Co-occurrence of partner and parent aggression: Research and treatment implications. *Behavior Therapy, 31,* 631–648.

Richters, J.E. (1993). Community violence and children's development: Toward a research agenda for the 1990s. *Psychiatry, 56,* 3–6.

Rossman, B.B.R. (2001). Longer term effects of children's exposure to domestic violence. In S. Graham-Bermann & J.L. Edleson (Eds.), *Domestic violence in the lives of children* (pp. 35–65). Washington, DC: American Psychological Association.

Sabol, W.J., Coulton, C J., & Korbin, J.E. (2004). Building community capacity for violence prevention. *Journal of Interpersonal Violence, 19,* 322–340.

Schechter, S. (1999). *New challenges for the Battered Women's Movement: Building collaborations and improving public policy for poor women.* Harrisburg, PA: National Resource Center on Domestic Violence.

Schechter, S. (Ed.). (2004). *Early childhood, domestic violence and poverty: Helping young children and their families.* Iowa City: University of Iowa School of Social Work. Available online at http://www.uiowa.edu/~socialwk/publications.html.

Stark, E. (2001). Health interventions with battered women. In C.M. Renzetti, J. L. Edleson, & R.K. Bergen (Eds.), *Sourcebook on violence against women* (pp. 345–369). Thousand Oaks, CA: Sage.

Trujillo, O.R., & Test, G. (2003). *Funding the work: Community efforts to end domestic violence and child abuse.* Washington, DC: American Public Human Services Association (Available on line at http://www.thegreenbook.info).

Van Hook, M.P. (2000). Help seeking for violence: Views of survivors. *Affilia, 15,* 390–408.

Weithorn, L.A. (2001). Protecting children from exposure to domestic violence: The use and abuse of child maltreatment. *Hastings Law Review, 53(1),* 1–156.

Whitcomb, D. (2000). *Children and domestic violence: Challenges for prosecutors.* Newton, MA: Education Development Center, Inc.

Whitney, P., & Davis, L. (1999). Child abuse and domestic violence in Massachusetts: Can practice be integrated in a public child welfare setting? *Child Maltreatment, 4(2),* 158–166.

9

CHILDREN WITH DISABILITIES EXPOSED TO VIOLENCE

Legal and Public Policy Issues

Patricia M. Sullivan

This chapter addresses what is known about the prevalence and consequences of exposure to domestic violence, community violence, and war and terrorism among children with disabilities and the concomitant legal and public policy implications. Its first focus is on defining disabilities in children, including those classifications used in various federal, education, and health care arenas. Current prevalence estimates of childhood disability in the United States of America are presented along with a consideration of varying definitions of childhood disabilities. Second, the current theoretical framework commonly used to conceptualize violence and disability status is discussed. Third, summaries of the existing data on domestic violence, various forms of community violence, and war and terrorism exposure among children with disabilities are presented, including family violence, school violence, and disabilities resulting from exposure to war. Particular emphasis is placed upon co-occurring forms of violence exposure and the systemic violence encountered by children with special needs within institutions and mental health placements. Original data on family stress factors in homes with records of domestic violence among maltreated children with and without disabilities who live in homes characterized by domestic violence and the prevalence and characteristics of school bullying and trauma symptoms among adolescents at a residential school for the deaf are also presented. Finally, the chapter focuses on barriers to obtaining information on domestic, community, and war-related violence exposure among children with disabilities, summarizes pertinent legislation in the field, and makes several recommendations for public policy.

DEFINITIONAL ISSUES

The overwhelming majority of data gathering and research that guides public policy on violence-related issues among people with disabilities has focused on individuals 15 years of age and older (Sullivan, 2003a). As a result, there is a paucity of information about the epidemiology of violence exposure among children ages birth to 14 years. Without surveillance data, we cannot identify the magnitude of their domestic and community violence exposure, the effects of this exposure on their subsequent development and life adjustment, and the components that are within our ability to prevent and address. This lack of data is primarily due to disparate definitions of disabilities among children, variability in age groups targeted in gathering disability data, and the failure to include children with disabilities in existing violence-related surveillance systems.

Disability is a heterogeneous categorization, and various strategies for operationally defining disability status range from medical models of physical impairments to inclusion models of challenges and cultural differences (Sullivan, 2003a). The operational definitions adopted by researchers, medical providers, educators, the federal government, and people with disabilities have determined the data that are available regarding children with disabilities (Sullivan, 2003a). Many groups collect data on disability status among children, which are best described as estimates, with results varying as a function of the agency that is collecting the data. These estimates vary according to how disability status is defined, the severity of the disability, the age range employed in defining disability status, and the need for disability-related services as a function of meeting the defined disability criteria.

It is important to recognize that disability is not simply a health outcome. Rather, it is a demographic descriptor akin to ethnicity, gender, and socioeconomic status. Because disabilities are not commensurable, the heterogeneity of the demographic descriptors must be captured. Among children, this includes information regarding the child's stage of development, age at onset of the disability, as well as the type, severity, complexity, and chronicity of the disability.

It is also important to note that the epidemiology of childhood disability differs markedly from that of adults (Perrin, 2002). Children and adolescents are the fastest growing age cohort with disabilities compared with other age groups in the United States (LaPlante & Kaye, 1998). This is attributed to major new epidemics of obesity, asthma, attention-deficit/hyperactivity disorder (ADHD), type II diabetes, and depression. Children and adolescents also have differential disability trajectories and fewer lasting disabilities than adults. Thus, care must be taken not to simply transpose surveillance methodologies implemented with adults onto children. Different sentinel agencies and target data points apply.

Data on children with disabilities have been tainted by inconsistent operational definitions, poorly defined heterogeneous populations with disabilities, and questionable validation procedures for determining disabilities (Sullivan, 2003b). These problems are compounded by the exclusion of less visible groups of children with disabilities, including those in residential institutions for individuals with mental retardation, those in schools for the deaf, the homeless, and children of illegal aliens. Definition standards of disabilities among children and youth need to be established in order to understand disability statistics. The International Classification of Functioning, Disability, and Health (ICIDH) of the World Health Organization (WHO) encompasses a promising framework by providing uniform language for describing functioning, health, and disability status that includes environmental factors and the social impact of the disability.

PREVALENCE ESTIMATES

Prevalence estimates of children with disabilities in the United States are dependent upon who is counting and why. This stems, in part, from eligibility determinations for receiving health, education, and income services and/or supplements from the federal government. Not surprising, prevalence rates vary with the person counting and the criteria used in determining disability status. Mudrick (2002) provided an in-depth discussion of various paradigms for disability determinations and corresponding prevalence estimates. Health, education, mental health, and federal data sources are briefly considered here, along with correlates of disability status that have been identified.

Health Data

The National Center for Health Statistics (NCHS) within the Centers for Disease Control and Prevention (CDC) conducts telephone interviews within the yearly National Health Interview Survey (NHIS). Some 4.3 million children with disabilities were identified in the 1992–1994 survey (Newacheck & Halfon, 1998). This estimate encompassed noninstitutionalized children younger than the age of 18 with some type of limitation in activities due to chronic conditions reported by their parents. Children with special health care needs (CSHCN) are identified by a need for public assistance to pay for health care services; accordingly, the estimates are limited and do not include children with disabilities from all socioeconomic strata.

The 1996 Survey of Income and Program Participation (SIPP) identified 233,000 children younger than age 3, another 410,000 children between 3 and 5 years of age, and 4 million children between 6 and 14 years of age with some type of developmental delay or physical limitation for which they received therapy or diagnostic services (McNeil, 2001). Available data indicate that 15% of children receiving health-related services in hospitals and outpatient clinics have a record of child abuse and/or neglect, and 64% of these children have some sort of disability (Sullivan & Knutson, 1998a). Prevalence rates for domestic and community violence exposure and victimization among children with disabilities seeking medical services were unavailable in this research.

Education Data

The Office of Special Education Programs (OSEP) within the U.S. Department of Education (DOE) collects the most nationally representative data on children in special education. These data do not include children served in Title I compensatory education programs for disadvantaged children, children without disabilities receiving remedial help, or children with disabilities who do not require special education services. Some 6,726,193 children and youth with disabilities ages 3 to 21 received special education services in the United States during the 2002–2003 school year (IDEA, 2003). Another 272,454 children ages birth to 2 were also served. Data on disability types were available only among children ages 3–21. Children with learning disabilities, speech-language disabilities, mental retardation, and behavior disorders together accounted for 80% of children receiving special education services. Children with other health impairments comprised an additional 7%. The remaining 13% had autism, multiple disabilities, hearing impairments, orthopedic disabilities, visual impairments including deaf-blindness, or traumatic brain injuries resulting from both intentional and nonintentional injuries. Since 1976–1977, the first school year for which data on children served in special education under federal statutes were reported by OSEP, the number of children served has increased by 3 million. This increase is attributed to the growth in the number of children classified with specific learning and speech-language disabilities who account for more than half of all children with disabilities served. Available population-based data indicate that one in three children with a disability receiving special education services is a victim of some form of child abuse and/or neglect, and 17% of these maltreated children with disabilities have co-occurring domestic violence in their homes (Sullivan & Knutson, 2000a).

Mental Health Data

Children and youth with emotional and behavioral problems requiring residential mental health treatment are a burgeoning population in the United States. Available estimates indicate there are some 77,200 children and youth in psychiatric settings and residential group homes in the United States (U.S. Department of Health and Human Services, 1999). Alarmingly, two thirds of juvenile detention facilities hold youth (some as young as 7 years of age) who have not been charged with a crime but are awaiting mental health treatment (U.S. House of Representatives, Committee on Government Reform, 2004). The Surgeon General's national study on mental health found that although some 20% of children and youth have a mental disorder, access to mental health services is limited (U.S. Department of Health and Human Services, 2000). During a 6-month time period, a Congressional study identified some 15,000 youth who were housed in juvenile detention centers while waiting for mental health services to become available. The mental health services required by these children and youth encumber a substantial share of health care dollars. No data are available on the number of children and youth with behavioral and emotional disabilities who are exposed to or victimized by violence while incarcerated and awaiting services. An additional 542,000 children and youth are in out-of-home care, including foster care and kinship care, in the United States (U.S. Department of Health and Human Services, 2003). Violence exposure and victimization data need to be obtained on children in out-of-home care facilities and the prevalence of disabilities among these children.

Federal Income Support Data

For children and youth younger than 18 years of age, the Social Security Administration defines a disability as "a medically determinable impairment or combination of impairments that causes marked or severe functional limitation(s), and can be expected to result in death, or has lasted or can be expected to last for a continuous period of not less than 12 months." There were 959,379 children and youth 18 years of age and younger receiving Supplemental Social Security (SSI) benefits in 2003 (Social Security Administration, 2004). Data are needed on the number of these children and youth with a determined disability resulting from violence victimization and/or exposure. Access to the Social Security database is necessary to identify violence linkages with disability determinations.

Correlates of Disability Status

Irrespective of the prevalence paradigm employed, several demographic correlates of disability status in children have been identified. Disabilities are more prevalent among male children; school-age children; children from low-income families; and children from single-parent homes (Fujiura & Yamaki, 2000; Stein & Silver, 1999). Many disabilities, particularly learning disabilities, are first identified when children attend school. The relationship between ethnicity and disability status is not clearly understood. Although higher rates of disabilities among African American and Hispanic children were reported in U.S. Census data (McNeil, 2001), these findings were not replicated in a smaller study when family structure and income were controlled (Fujiura & Yamaki, 2000). The prevalence study of disabilities and child maltreatment mandated by the Child Abuse Prevention and Treatment Act of 1988 (CAPTA) found Caucasian males to be at the greatest risk to have a disability (Westat, 1993). This finding was replicated when income, parental education, age, gender, and ethnicity were evaluated within logistic regression analyses (Stein & Silver, 1999). Although associations between disability status and gender, poverty, and family structure are fairly robust, the association between disability and ethnicity is unclear. The associations between disability status and domestic and community violence exposure and/or victimization still need to be identified.

ECOLOGICAL–TRANSACTIONAL– DEVELOPMENTAL MODEL OF VIOLENCE

An ecological, transactional, and developmental model of the ontogeny of adverse effects of violence exposure, including domestic violence, community violence, and child maltreatment has been hypothesized (Cicchetti & Lynch, 1993; Cicchetti & Toth, 2000; Lutzker, 1998, 2000; National Research Council, 1993a). Rather than focusing on single causes or short-term effects, violence and maltreatment are viewed in a broader context within a series of developmental and bidirectional transactions between the child and his or her entire environment or social ecology (Lutzker, 1998).

Sobsey (1994) has applied this ecological-transactional-developmental model to children and adults with disabilities. Within this context, the physical and psychological aspects of the potential victim and potential abuser are considered in relation to environmental and cultural factors. Sobsey's integrated ecological model is posited as both an explanatory paradigm for the power inequities between abusers and victim with disabilities, which ultimately lead to violence, and as a set of markers for preventive interventions across the ecological spectrum of the model. Accordingly, child characteristics play an integral role in the occurrence of violence and/or maltreatment. Within this model, the child is viewed as developing within the microsystem of home and family. The microsystem is the context in which family violence and child maltreatment generally occur. The home is embedded within an exosystem comprised of the wider social milieu affecting family life that includes the neighborhood, community, school, and the family's socioeconomic status. This exosystem is embedded in the macrosystem that subsumes cultural values and beliefs that foster violence within families and communities. The model also has an ontogenic level that encompasses factors within the child and parent(s) that influence the child's development, including violence experiences and brain processing (Cicchetti & Toth, 2000). Individual experiences and developmental characteristics are hypothesized to influence the occurrence of violence and maltreatment.

Thus, there is a theoretical basis for hypothesizing an ecological and developmental model of violence exposure among children with and without disabilities. This developmental-transactional-ecological model provides a framework for conceptualizing childhood violence exposure. There is growing research support for paradigms of violence against children that reflect the interaction of parent characteristics, child attributes, and environmental factors in the occurrence of violence (e.g., Azar, Povilaitis, Lauretti, & Pouquette, 1998; Belsky, 1993; Cicchetti & Lynch, 1993; Cicchetti & Toth, 2000; Lutzker, 1998). In such paradigms, there is consideration of child risk factors, and many of those risk factors relate to the possible role of disabilities.

Disabilities can result from both immediate and long-term exposure to violence. Violence victimization and exposure often result in mental health disorders and other disabling conditions. Conversely, children with various disabilities are at increased risk to be victims of violence or exposed to it during childhood. This association between violence and disability is not well understood. The components of the violence to disability and disability to violence equations need to be elucidated (Sobsey, 2004) and mapped with existing theoretical paradigms.

DOMESTIC VIOLENCE

Understanding the effects of violence exposure on children with disabilities requires a consideration of contributing factors that may occur in tandem with the violence and exacerbate or lessen its effects. Unfortunately, there is a paucity of research on the co-occurrence of different forms of violence with disabilities among children. Therefore, what little research exists is discussed briefly here, specifically methodological issues that have plagued researchers studying children without disabilities.

Children's exposure to violence rarely occurs in discrete, unitary forms (Dodge, Pettit, & Bates, 1997; Margolin, 1998; Rossman & Rosenberg, 1998). Often one type of exposure co-occurs with other types of exposure and violent experiences. Risk factors for violence and maltreatment also rarely occur in isolation (Lynch & Cicchetti, 1998), and combinations of risk factors converge at various stages of a child's development in diverse ways to produce a given outcome. Types of co-occurring violence in the lives of children and youth include child maltreatment, domestic violence, and community violence. There are high rates of co-occurrence between exposure to domestic violence in the home and child physical abuse (Appel & Holden, 1998) and between exposure to violence in the community and domestic violence in the home (Bell & Jenkins, 1993; Lynch & Cicchetti, 1998). Emerging data indicate that exposure to multiple forms of violence in the home and in the community is associated with more serious outcomes (Lynch & Cicchetti, 1998; Margolin & Gordis, 2000). This co-occurrence has been called the "double whammy" by researchers (Margolin, 1998). It is important to note, however, that much of this literature is based on studies of the co-occurrence of child maltreatment and domestic violence among those in domestic violence shelters, who often possess a number of other risk factors.

In one of the few population-based studies of violence exposure that have been conducted to date, domestic violence was found to co-occur with child maltreatment in the homes of children with disabilities (Sullivan & Knutson, 2000a). Among the total population of 4,503 maltreated children studied, there were records of domestic violence within the families of 17.2% of the children with disabilities and 16.3% of the children without disabilities. This is almost three times higher than the 6% co-occurrence rate for domestic violence and child physical abuse reported for other community samples (Appel & Holden, 1998). Behavioral disorders, mental health conditions, and speech-language disorders were the primary types of disabilities among children who had records of domestic violence in their families. No data regarding the incidence of domestic violence absent child maltreatment were available in this study.

Maltreated children with and without disabilities are also exposed to a host of additional stressful life events (Sullivan & Knutson, 2000a). The following family stress factors were found significantly more often in the records of maltreated children with disabilities with a domestic violence history in their families than in the families of maltreated children with disabilities without a domestic violence history: voluntary foster care [χ^2 (1, N = 978) = 6.39, p < .05], inadequate parent [χ^2 (1, N = 978) = 67.49, p < .001], inadequate housing [χ^2 (1, N = 978) = 48.74, p < .001], financial problems [χ^2 (1, N = 978) = 27.86, p < .001], marital problems [χ^2 (1, N = 978) = 82.48, p < .001], pregnancy/birth of newborn [χ^2 (1, N = 978) = 10.39, p < .05], parent ill/disabled [χ^2 (1, N = 978) = 16.51, p < .001], mental/emotional problems in parent [χ^2 (1, N = 978) = 41.62, p < .001], parental alcohol/drug problems [χ^2 (1, N = 978) = 97.46, p < .001], social isolation [χ^2 (1, N = 978) = 30.88, p < .001], family involved with the legal system [χ^2 (1, N = 978) = 61.48, p < .001], step-parent/child conflict [χ^2 (1, N = 978) = 14.59, p < .05], fetal alcohol syndrome [χ^2 (1, N = 978) = 13.81, p < .001], and AIDS in family member [χ^2 (1, N = 978) = 10.39, p < .05].

Interestingly, maltreated children without disabilities with records of domestic violence in the home were significantly more likely to be placed in kinship care [χ^2 (1, N = 3,334) = 15.81, p < .001] than foster care when voluntarily removed from the home. However, children with disabilities were more likely to be placed with strangers when removed from the home due to maltreatment with co-occurring domestic violence. In addition, archival documentation of a family member with AIDS was found significantly more often in the records of families with a history of domestic violence and child maltreatment who also had a child with disabilities. These data provide suggestive evidence that there are disability-specific family factors in the domestic violence/child maltreatment equation in need of identification to guide prevention and intervention efforts.

Currently, there is an inadequate database from which to evaluate the extent of co-occurrence of domestic violence and community violence among children with disabilities. Among children without disabilities, research has been limited by the use of domestic violence shelters for samples, which are not representative of the community and do not control for alternative explanations of the adverse outcomes identified. Many studies do not report the type of maltreatment or domestic violence that occurred or the child's proximity to it (Edleson, 2002). Potential relevant variables are often not reported, including demographic information, socioeconomic status, ethnicity, family structure, neighborhood features, substance abuse by parents, and family stress factors (Wolak & Finkelhor, 1998). Population-based prospective and longitudinal research on the co-occurrence of domestic and community violence and child maltreatment must be undertaken (Edleson, 2002; Horn & Trickett, 1998; Margolin, 1998; Wolak & Finkelhor, 1998), and children and youth with disabilities need to be included in this research.

COMMUNITY VIOLENCE

There are three forms of community violence particularly germane to children and youth with disabilities: school bullying, corporal punishment within the school setting, and systemic violence in residential schools and institutions for children with specific types of disabilities.

School Bullying

Bullying in the school setting has been extensively studied in the United Kingdom and Scandinavian countries (Dawkins, 1996; Roland & Munthe, 1989). Defined as physical and/or psychological teasing, name-calling, hitting, pushing, social exclusion, threats, extortion, and theft, bullying is considered to be a form of peer abuse (Dawkins & Hill, 1995). Children with disabilities are the frequent targets of such bullying. Children with visible disabilities (e.g., cerebral palsy, blindness, deafness) who are enrolled in special education programs are twice as likely to be bullied than children with disabilities that are not considered visible (e.g., learning disabilities, behavior disorders). One third of these children are regularly bullied at school, with boys being bullied more often than girls (Dawkins, 1996). These data are consistent with other research that has found children with special education needs twice as likely to be bullied as those in regular class placements (Olweus, 1991, 1993; Whitney, Nabuzoka, & Smith, 1992). School bullying is a contributing factor to feelings of unhappiness, sadness, and depression among children with disabilities, and it affects their ability to benefit from special education services.

School bullying of children with disabilities can escalate to violent physical and sexual assaults outside the school grounds. Although incidence data are lacking on the frequency of occurrence and the dynamics of bullying among children with disabilities, two such incidents during the summer of 2004 in Omaha, Nebraska, are worthy of mention. The first involved a 16-year-old girl with mild mental retardation who was kicked to death by peers at a fast-food restaurant near the public school they attended during lunch time (Omaha World Herald, June 25, 2004). The girl had been a frequent target of verbal taunts and name-calling at school prior to the fatal assault. The second was an incident reminiscent of the notorious Glen Ridge, New Jersey, gang rape of a teenage girl with developmental disabilities (see Lefkowitz, 1997). The Omaha case involved the sexual assault of a 15-year-old girl with mild mental retardation by three members of a parochial high school football team (Omaha World Herald, September 5, 2004). In both cases, the disability of the child victim was prominently featured in the media, noted in police and prosecutorial files on the case, and included in evidence in juvenile court proceedings. However, this information is not consistently recorded in law enforcement and court records. These and similar cases (Sobsey, 1994, 2001) attest to the need to investigate linkages between school bullying and subsequent violence in the community.

Condoned Physical Restraint and Corporal Punishment

Condoned physical interventions dispensed under the guise of therapeutic interventions with children with disabilities can escalate to abusive violence. Examples include physical restraint, holding, and corporal punishment in special education settings. The physical restraint of children and youth by professionals in psychiatric and group home facilities is both controversial and commonplace. Although the Joint Commission on the Accreditation of Healthcare Organizations (JCAHO) has guidelines for the use of holding and restraint, children and youth with disabilities are not mentioned as a special needs group regarding the procedure. Children with cognitive and sensory impairments, in particular, need disability-specific accommodations. Efficacy data are urgently needed to compare physical restraint with other behavioral interventions with children and youth with disabilities in residential mental health settings.

Corporal punishment is permitted in 22 states in the United States and includes the physical striking of children and youth with disabilities within the public schools (American Academy of Pediatrics, 1991; Hyman & Perone, 1998). According to the Center for Effective Discipline (CED), a nonprofit agency that compiles national and international data on corporal punishment of children in the schools, some 342,038 students in the United States received some form of corporal punishment during the 1999–2000 school year. Data released by the CED in February, 2003, on U.S. public schools for the 1999–2000 school year reported four groups of children as the most frequent recipients of corporal punishment in these 22 states: boys, low-income children, minority children, and children with disabilities (National Coalition to Abolish Corporal Punishment in Schools, 2003). The physical striking of children as a means of school discipline remains a controversial issue. However, emerging data link sanctioned corporal punishment in schools to school shooting fatalities (Arcus, 2002) and student aggressive misbehavior (Hyman & Perone, 1998).

There is a need for data on the prevalence, nature, and effects of these noncriminalized violent acts against children and youth with disabilities by peers, siblings, schoolmates, and professionals charged with their care and welfare. Currently, it is unknown if children and youth with disabilities have a higher rate of these types of violence than their peers without disabilities.

Institutional Violence

Approximately 2% of the children and youth with disabilities in the United States live in institutions, including nursing homes; schools for the blind, deaf, and individuals with physical disabilities; institutions for those with mental retardation; and facilities for those with mental illness (Waldrop & Stern, 2003). The problem of violent acts committed against children in institutions is long-standing and has been documented for more than two centuries (Safford & Safford, 1996; Sobsey, 1994). In one study deaf youth attending residential schools, sexual abuse tended to occur in bathrooms, bedrooms, and specialized transportation (Sullivan, Vernon, & Scanlan 1987). Other work suggests that children with sensory impairments may be at increased risk for maltreatment (Brookhouser, 1987; Whitaker, 1987). Numerous states in the United States and provinces in Canada have had major child abuse investigations in residential schools and institutions for children who are deaf and hard of hearing, children with visual impairments, and children with developmental disabilities (Brookhouser, 1987; Sobsey, 1994; Sullivan & Knutson 1998b; Sullivan, Brookhouser, & Scanlan, 2000). Findings from these studies suggest a number of associations between hearing-related disabilities and maltreatment by parents and caregivers in residential schools. First, deaf children with and without cochlear implants are significantly more likely to be victims of harsh physical discipline by their mothers (Knutson, Johnson, & Sullivan, 2004) than hearing children. Second, a residential placement is a major risk factor for experiencing sexual and/or physical abuse; the primary location is the dormitory, and the primary perpetrators are houseparents, older students, and peers (Sullivan et al., 1987; Sullivan & Knutson, 1998b; Sullivan et al., 2000). Finally, for deaf males, a residential school placement coupled with physical and sexual abuse victimization within the school, increases their risk for alcohol abuse, behavior management problems, and the perpetration of sexual and physical abuse against peers (Sullivan & Knutson, 1998b).

These data, and highly publicized episodes of abuse at residential facilities for children with disabilities, suggest that current institutional practices, including condoned physical interventions, which can escalate to abusive violence of residents by their caregivers, should be closely monitored and evaluated. Given the numbers of children and youth with disabilities housed in institutions, the prevalence, nature, and risk factors for violence and abuse need to be determined.

OUTCOMES OF CHILDHOOD DOMESTIC AND COMMUNITY VIOLENCE EXPOSURE

The impact of violence exposure on children, in whatever form, has long-lasting effects (Margolin & Gordis, 2000). Research addressing the long-term outcomes of exposure to childhood violence among adults has identified mental health issues, posttraumatic stress, antisocial, and resilient outcomes (Margolin & Gordis, 2000). However, it is important to note that none of this research has included individuals with identified disabilities in childhood.

Psychopathology Outcomes

Studies of the psychological effects of domestic violence on children without disabilities have identified anxiety, depression, withdrawal, and low-self esteem as common outcomes (Wolak & Finkelhor, 1998). Other research suggests that both witnessing and being a victim of community violence place children at risk for anxiety and depressive symptoms (Fitzpatrick & Boldizar, 1993; Kliewer, Lepore, Oskin, & Johnson, 1998). Being victimized by violence involving family, friends, and acquaintances is associated with greater levels of depression and anxiety than only witnessing the violence (Martinez & Richters, 1993). Other than with deaf and hard of hearing children, however, there is limited research on the effects of violence exposure or maltreatment on children with disabilities. What research exists suggests that children with disabilities exposed to violence experience outcomes similar to children without disabilities. For example, deaf girls who were sexually abused in a residential school were found to manifest anxiety and depression, while boys tended to exhibit aggression and acting out behaviors (Sullivan, Scanlan, Knutson, Brookhouser, & Schulte, 1992). In later work with deaf youth, Sullivan and Knutson (1998b) found that anxiety and depression were prominent symptoms among abused deaf girls and boys with alcohol and drug problems.

The extant research indicates that although some commonalities in psychopathology exist, different children react differently to physical abuse, sexual abuse, domestic violence, and community violence. Such findings underscore the need for the identification of variables that mediate or moderate the impact of these types of violence on children's mental health, in tandem or in isolation. These factors include childhood disability status, along with the frequency, severity, and chronicity of the violence and various neighborhood and family characteristics. Demographic variables such as gender, socioeconomic status, and ethnicity are often not included in existing research and therefore also need to be investigated (Trickett & Putnam, 1998; Wolak & Finkelhor, 1998). Finally, virtually no follow-up studies have been conducted, either longitudinally or prospectively on childhood violence exposure (Trickett & Putnam, 1998); thus, there is a need for such research.

Posttraumatic Stress Outcomes

Trauma and violence exposure are not synonymous. Although childhood violence exposure is a potential source of stress and subsequent trauma, some children are traumatized by exposure to violence and others are not (Glaser, 2000). Thus, it is important for research on the trauma-related factors of violence and maltreatment to attend to the type of violence exposure experienced by the child as well as its duration and severity, the characteristics of the perpetrator, and the victim's response.

Posttraumatic stress disorder (PTSD) symptoms have been associated with domestic and community violence in children and adolescents (Boney-McCoy & Finkelhor, 1995; Osofsky, 1995). An increased incidence of PTSD symptoms has been identified in children who witness physical aggression between their parents (Kilpatrick & Williams, 1997), and PTSD symptoms along with sleeplessness and agitation have been reported in child victims of domestic violence (Osofsky, 1995). There is also growing evidence that children who witness highly traumatic violence, such as the homicide or suicide of a parent, commonly display symptoms of PTSD similar to those exhibited by adults exposed to war (Pynoos, 1993; Pynoos & Nader, 1993). Although linkages have been identified between domestic violence, community violence, and child maltreatment and childhood PTSD, few studies have followed children into adulthood to determine if symptoms persist.

In one study of children with disabilities, pilot data were gathered on adolescent deaf youth attending a residential school to determine their experiences as victims and purveyors of school bullying and their trauma symptomatology, if any. Some 19 deaf youth ranging in age from 13 to 17 were given the Reynolds Bully Victimization Scale (BVS) (Reynolds, 2003) and the Trauma Symptom Checklist for Children (TSCC) (Briere, 1996). These scales were administered in conjunction with an assessment of the extent of bullying within the school and its potential effects on the students. Although the sample size in this study was small and thus limits the conclusions that can be drawn from this work, some interesting data trends emerged. First, the 19 deaf students, comprised of 13 boys and 6 girls, did not report engaging in significantly more bullying behavior toward other students than the hearing students. These students did, however, report being a victim of bullying at significantly higher severity levels than the hearing standardization sample (p = .028). Gender and age of the deaf adolescents were not significantly related to bullying perpetration or victimization.

Second, the findings also suggested that there were some significant associations between the BVS and the TSCC. For both male and female deaf adolescents, there was a significant Spearman correlation (.564) between endorsing bullying behavior on the BVS and the Anger Scale on the TSCC (p = .018). Bullying victimization scores for boys and girls were significantly correlated (.495) with the PTSD Scale on the TSCC (p = .043). Thus, the majority of deaf students self-reported some PTSD symptoms along with being a victim of bullying at school, and being a victim of school bullying was associated with self-reported angry thoughts and feelings, irritability, and aggressive behavior among deaf boys and girls.

In additional analyses, the reported trauma symptoms of the deaf adolescents were compared to the normative data for students with normal hearing in the TSCC manual. On the TSCC critical items, deaf boys endorsed "Wanting to hurt other people" (p = .041) significantly more often than hearing peers. "Feeling scared of men" (p = .027) and "Not trusting people because they might want sex" (p = .000) were endorsed significantly more often by deaf girls than hearing peers. On the Clinical Scales of the TSCC, both deaf boys and girls endorsed significantly more items on the Sexual Concerns (p = .000) and the Sexual Distress (p = .000) Scales than hearing peers in the normative sample. This indicates that the deaf boys and girls endorsed items indicating thoughts and ruminations about sexual matters and that these thoughts were distressing to them.

These preliminary data indicate some clinical utility in the use of the BVS and TSCC with deaf adolescents attending a residential school for the deaf in assessing bullying victimization and resulting trauma. As with any clinical scale, follow-up interviews with the deaf youth are needed to clarify and explore individual bullying victimization, angry thoughts and feelings, PTSD symptoms, fear and trust issues, and sexual thoughts and feelings related to violence exposure and victimization.

WAR AND TERRORISM

The Secretary General of the United Nations is undertaking a study of violence exposure and victimization among children throughout the world. The impetus for the study was multiple reports of violence against children from various countries submitted to the U.N. Committee on the Rights of the Child (United Nation's Secretary General's Study on Violence Against Children, 2005). Children with disabilities are included in the study that focuses on violence against children in five domains: home and family; schools; institutional settings; the community; and, in the workplace. The goal is to compile a global picture of the nature, epidemiology, and causes of violence against children as well as recommendations for violence prevention and reduction. A web site (http://www.violencestudy.org/r25) is maintained and updated periodically as this landmark international undertaking is completed.

To date, however, there is a paucity of data on disability and violence in the United States, and international data are even scarcer. Children are trapped in armed conflicts in as many as 50 countries throughout the globe and serve as bystanders, targets, and conscripted soldiers as well as porters, cooks, and messengers for adults in warfare activities (World Health Organization, 2002). However, record keeping is routinely poor in many parts of the world and is disrupted during warfare (Zwi, Ugalde, & Richards, 1999). Thus, it is difficult to obtain accurate estimates of the disabilities caused by war and terrorist activities. Although the exact figures will never be known, in the decade spanning 1986–1996, it is estimated that warfare killed more than 2 million children, orphaned another 1 million, and permanently disabled more than 6 million children (World Health Organization, 2002).

Sexual violence against women and children is commonplace in war-ravaged nations and often used to terrorize and intimidate the female relatives of opponents (World Health Organization, 2002). Soldiers raped an estimated 60,000 women during the Balkan conflict in Bosnia and Herzegovina, many of them children and adolescents (Ashford & Huet-Vaughn, 1997). Young girls have been raped and subjected to other forms of sexual violence during wartime in countries across the globe (World Health Organization, 2002). In some African countries, children and adults have been maimed and disfigured in order to intimidate and terrorize (Human Rights Watch, 1999).

The remnants of war in the form of unexploded ordnance (UXO), including grenades, cluster bombs, and land mines further threaten the safety and physical integrity of children. The accidental detonation of UXO is a leading cause of disability in war-ravaged nations (Francois et al., 1998). Land mine detonations are a major cause of disabilities and children are frequent victims (Andersson, Pahla da Sousa, & Paredes, 1995). In Cambodia, nearly 10% of the population has disabilities and children account for 20% percent of this, primarily due to land mines (World Health Organization, 2002).

Societal attitudes of shame toward families with children with disabilities are commonplace, particularly in Asia and Africa (Miles, 1995). Women are blamed for having a child with disabilities; as a result, children with disabilities are hidden, often denied critical care, shunned, and neglected by their families (Miles, 1995). The cultural mores of neglect and indifference toward children with disabilities in the developing world are contributing factors to their violence victimization. Individuals with disabilities are at risk to be victims of violence (Sobsey, 1994).

Human behavior is complex, and violent behavior is pervasive throughout the planet and in urgent need of study. The inclusion of disability status of child victims in the ongoing United Nations study will provide needed data and knowledge on the effects of violence exposure and victimization on children with disabilities throughout the world.

LEGAL AND POLICY ISSUES
National Data on Children with Disabilities

A lack of data on the violence exposure and victimization of children and youth with disabilities is universal across many of the criminal justice and child maltreatment databases mandated, compiled, and maintained by the federal government. This greatly impedes our ability to understand the scope and nature of violence exposure in the lives of children and youth with disabilities. A variety of statutory authorities collect public data sets on the disability and victimization status of children. However, the absence of a mandate and resources for a comprehensive demographic study of childhood disability across numerous health, education, social service, and criminal justice agencies makes it difficult to obtain badly needed information on these children. Children and youth with disabilities need to be included and counted in crime victim and child abuse and neglect national databases (Sullivan, 2003b).

The Violent Crime and Law Enforcement Act of 1994 amended the Hate Crime Statistics Act to include crimes motivated by a bias against persons with disabilities. To comply with this federal mandate, the FBI began collecting data on crimes motivated by a disability bias on January 1, 1997. The FBI Uniform Crime Report Handbook defines a disability bias as "a preformed negative opinion of or attitude toward a group of persons based on their physical or mental impairments/challenges, whether such disability is temporary or permanent, congenital, or acquired by heredity, accident, injury, advance age, or illness" (U.S. Department of Justice, 1999). Disability bias crimes are divided into two categories, physical and mental, which are not specifically defined in the Uniform Crime Report Handbook.

In 2003, a total of 7,489 hate bias crimes were reported, 0.4% of which were coded as motivated by a disability (Federal Bureau of Investigation, 2004). No other data are available from the UCR on the types of disabilities of the victims or their ages. These statistics are voluntarily provided by law enforcement agencies across the nation. The labeling of a crime as a hate bias crime and the type of disability is left to the discretion of the individual law enforcement officer completing the crime report. No validity or reliability data are obtained on the disability status of the victim. These are the only national statistics gathered by the FBI that include disability status of the victim. National victim data on disabilities cannot be compiled if disability status is not coded on the original crime reports.

A national effort must be undertaken to train and require police officers to routinely include victim and perpetrator disability status on crime reports. The inclusion of disability status should be the paramount goal rather than requiring the police officer to make a determination that a hate crime occurred. Difficulties in making such a determination may explain the dearth of data on the disability status of victims in the UCR databases.

Inclusion of Children with Disabilities in Research and Public Policy

Children with disabilities have also been neglected in violence research and related public policy. Ideally, research guides public policy. There is a limited research literature on linkages between disabilities and childhood violence exposure and victimization. The Panel on Research on Child Abuse and Neglect of the National Academy of Sciences set forth a national child-oriented research agenda on child abuse and neglect that included a wide range of recommendations for policy, practice, and research. *Understanding Child Abuse and Neglect* (National Research Council, 1993a), which established the National Research Council's agenda for research addressing child maltreatment, failed to include children and youth with disabilities and issues pertaining to their maltreatment. The needs of children and youth with disabilities were also not included in the compendium addressing research, practice and policy in child neglect (Dubowitz, 1999). The violence literature is silent on child and adult victims with disabilities. Two seminal works on violence compiled by the National Research Council (1993b, 1996), *Understanding and Preventing Violence* and *Understanding Violence Against Women*, are also silent on the disability status of both victims and perpetrators. Furthermore, addressing disability status was absent from the research agenda to address domestic violence proposed in both volumes. Currently, there is a critical gap in the research knowledge base on the epidemiology of people with disabilities who are victims of violence as well as those who become disabled by such violence. This gap is a major impediment to the inclusion of objectives in *Healthy People 2010* and future Healthy People volumes that require data driven objectives.

Children with disabilities are particularly at risk to be victims of physical abuse and sexual assault (Levy & Lagos, 1994; Sullivan & Knutson, 1998a, 2000a; Westat, 1993). The seminal study completed on juveniles condemned to death by Lewis, Pincus, Bard, and Richardson (1988) found that the majority of these youth had significant disabilities and child maltreatment histories that antedated their crimes but were not recognized at the time of trial or sentencing. The Commission on Violence and Youth of the American Psychological Association (APA) noted in 1993 that the existing database on abuse and disabilities was incomplete, and comprehensive and reliable prevalence data needed to be obtained to indicate how frequently children with disabilities are victimized and/or engage in violent behavior. A decade later, the American Psychological Association issued a resolution calling for the inclusion of children with disabilities in violence-related research (Clay, 2003).

In response to a mandate in the Crime Victims with Disabilities Awareness Act of 1998 (PL 105-301), the National Research Council's Committee on Law and Justice sponsored a national workshop on Crime Victims with Developmental Disabilities that focused essentially on adults with developmental disabilities. Although the NRC workshop called for research on the nature and extent of the problem, it essentially focused on the needs of victims and the identification of interventions to implement with disabled victims of crime (National Research Council, 2001). Given the limited scope of this workshop, a comprehensive national conference was sponsored in 2002 by eight agencies across the federal government including the Centers for Disease Control and Prevention, Office of Victims of Crime, U.S. Department of Education Office of Special Education Programs, National Institute of Child Health and Human Development, Administration on Developmental Disabilities, Administration on Children and Families, the Children's Bureau, and the Division of Maternal and Child Health. This conference considered all types of disabilities and focused on prevention, public policy, and research needs, culminating in *A Call to Action: Ending Crimes of Violence Against Children and Adults with Disabilities, A Report to the Nation* (Marge, 2003).

Although the Child Abuse Prevention, Adoption, and Family Services Act of 1988 (PL 100-294) mandated the study of maltreatment among children with disabilities, relatively little scholarly and practical attention has focused on the inclusion of children with disabilities as specific fields in child maltreatment archival records. Currently, no data are collected on disability status among children who are victims of child abuse and neglect in congressionally mandated national incidence studies (Sullivan, 2003a). This includes all three national incidence studies (NIS) mandated by the Child Abuse and Prevention Treatment Act (CAPTA) (PL 93-247): the NIS-1, NIS-2, and NIS-3. Ironically, although CAPTA also mandated a national study of the incidence of maltreatment among children with disabilities, which was completed in 1993 (Westat, 1993), data on children with disabilities were not included in NIS-3 and are not being gathered in the NIS-4. The National Child Abuse and Neglect Data System (NCANDS) which collects compiled child maltreatment data from state agencies on reports, investigations, victims, and perpetrators is also silent on the disability status of children who are victims of neglect, physical abuse, sexual abuse and emotional abuse.

Violent crimes committed against children and youth with disabilities can include conventional violent crimes (e.g., homicide, assault, theft, robbery), child abuse and neglect (e.g., neglect, physical abuse, emotional abuse, and sexual abuse), specialized crimes (e.g., abduction by family members, stranger abductions), family violence (e.g., domestic violence, spouse abuse, step-parent abuse), community violence (e.g., murders, drive-by shootings, gang battles, shoot-outs with police, high-speed chases, spousal beatings), and noncriminalized violent acts (e.g., assaults by other children, sibling assault, bullying, physical interventions/restraint). Victimization data are available on children and youth with disabilities for child maltreatment but not for other violent crimes (Sullivan, 2003b; Sullivan & Knutson, 1998a, 2000a). Although the Crime Victims with Disabilities Awareness Act of 1998 proposed to include disability status in the U.S. National Crime Victim Survey, this has yet to be accomplished. This act also mandated research addressing crimes against individuals with developmental disabilities, including children.

CONCLUSIONS AND PUBLIC POLICY RECOMMENDATIONS

The silence of federal and state governments in establishing a national public policy and research agenda addressing children and youth with disabilities is a major barrier to gathering surveillance data and needs to end. A national public policy blueprint addressing children with disabilities needs to be developed. Children and youth with disabilities need to be included in public policy, practice, and research recommendations in the health care, violence, and child maltreatment domains.

A comprehensive demographic study of the disability status of children in the United States needs to be undertaken to obtain accurate prevalence estimates, establish definitional standards, promote research on disabled children, and facilitate linkages between disability data sources. The inability to link data from disability sources to other datasets hampers research efforts. Both public schools and the Social Security Administration have disability databases on children and youth that could assist in research in determining disability prevalence rates of child victims of crime by permitting data mergers of the names of child crime victims with these databases to identify the number of disabled children. Federal law does not permit these mergers (i.e., the Family Education Right to Privacy Act–FERPA and the Social Security Act). Methods congruent with federal statutes need to be identified to permit this research. Collaborative alliances and efforts between federal and state agencies, researchers, program specialists, and practitioners will be imperative to its successful completion. Health, demographic, and violence victimization statistics on children with disabilities should be disseminated in the scientific and lay media.

A descriptive epidemiology of violence-related disabilities in children from birth to 21 years is urgently needed. Disability review teams need to be established at the state level to review the records of victims of violence and abuse and determine if any disabilities have resulted from the violence. It is no longer sufficient to measure only the infant and child mortality outcomes of violence. Disability status as a potential outcome of violence and maltreatment inflicted upon children also needs to be captured in relevant public health surveillance systems.

Finally, funding is needed to support each of these efforts. Unless specific funding sources are made available for research and data collection on children with disabilities exposed to violence, such children will continue to be neglected in national and community databases. This will continue to hamper the conclusions we can draw about these children and limit our ability to properly address the needs of these vulnerable children.

REFERENCES

American Academy of Pediatrics. (1991). Corporal punishment in schools. *American Academy of Pediatrics, 88,* 173.

Andersson, N., Pahla da Sousa, C., & Paredes, S. (1995). Social cost of landmines in four countries: Afghanistan, Bosnia, Cambodia, and Mozambique. *British Medical Journal, 311,* 718–721.

Appel, A.E., & Holden, G.W. (1998). The co-occurrence of spouse and physical child abuse: A review and appraisal. *Journal of Family Psychology, 12(4),* 578–599.

Arcus, D. (2002). School shooting fatalities and school corporal punishment: A look at the states. *Aggressive Behavior, 28,* 173–183.

Ashford, M.W., & Huet-Vaughn, Y. (1997). The impact of war on women. In B.S. Levy, & V.W. Sidel (Eds.), *War and public health* (pp.186–196). Oxford, England: Oxford University Press.

Azar, T.S., Povilaitis, Y.T., Lauretti, F.A., & Pouquette, L.C. (1998). The current status of etiological theories in intrafamilial child maltreatment. In J. Lutzker (Ed.), *The handbook of child abuse research and treatment* (pp. 3–30). New York: Plenum.

Bell, C.C., & Jenkins, E.J. (1993). Community violence and children on Chicago's Southside. *Psychiatry, 56,* 46–54.

Belsky, J. (1993). Etiology of child maltreatment: A developmental-ecological analysis. *Psychological Bulletin, 114*(3), 413–434.

Boney-McCoy, S., & Finkelhor, D. (1995). Psychosocial sequelae of violent victimization in a national youth sample. *Journal of Consulting and Clinical Psychology, 63*(5), 726–736.

Briere, J. (1996). *Trauma Symptom Checklist for Children professional's manual.* Lutz, FL: Psychological Assessment Resources, Inc.

Brookhouser, P.E. (1987). Ensuring the safety of deaf children in residential schools. *Otolaryngology: Head and Neck Surgery, 9*(4), 361–368.

Child Abuse Prevention, Adoption, and Family Services Act of 1988, §§ 100-294 (1998, April).

Cicchetti, D., & Lynch, M. (1993). Toward an ecological/transactional model of community violence and child maltreatment: Consequences for children's development. *Psychiatry, 56,* 96–118.

Cicchetti, D., & Toth, S. (2000). Developmental processes in maltreated children. In D. Hansen (Ed.), *Nebraska Symposium on Motivation 1998: Motivation and Child Maltreatment* (pp. 85–160). Lincoln: University of Nebraska Press.

Clay, R. (2003). APA resolution on maltreatment of children with disabilities. *APA Monitor, 34*(4), 49.

Crime Victims with Disabilities Awareness Act of 1998, §§ 105-301 (1998, October).

Dawkins, J.L. (1996) Bullying, physical disability and the pediatric patient. *Developmental Medicine in Child Neurology, 38,* 603–612.

Dawkins, J.L., & Hill, P. (1995). Bullying: Another form of abuse? *Recent Advances in Pediatrics, 13,* 103–122.

Dodge, K.A., Pettit, G.S., & Bates, J.E. (1997). How the experience of early physical abuse leads children to become chronically aggressive. In D. Cicchetti & S.L. Toth (Eds.), *Developmental perspectives on trauma: Theory, research, and intervention* (pp. 263–288). Rochester, NY: University of Rochester Press.

Dubowitz, H. (Ed.). (1999). *Neglected children: Research, practice, and policy.* Thousand Oaks, CA: Sage Publications.

Edleson, J.L. (2002). Studying the co-occurrence of child maltreatment and domestic violence in families. In S.A. Graham-Bermann & J.L. Edleson (Eds.), *Domestic violence in the lives of children: The future of research intervention & social policy* (pp. 91–110). Washington, DC: American Psychological Association.

Federal Bureau of Investigation. (2004). *Crime in the United States–2003.* Retrieved March 22, 2004 from http://www.fbi.gov/ucr/03cius.htm

Fitzpatrick, K.M., & Boldizar, J.P. (1993). The prevalence and consequences of exposure to violence among African-American youth. *Journal of the American Academy of Child and Adolescent Psychiatry, 32,* 424–430.

Francois, I., Lambert, M.L., Salort, C., Slypen, V., Bertrand, F., & Tonglet, R. (1998). Causes of locomotor disability and need for orthopaedic devices in a heavily mined Taliban-controlled province of Afghanistan: Issues and challenges for public health managers. *Tropical Medicine and International Health, 3,* 391–396.

Fujiura, G.T., & Yamaki, K. (2000). Trends in demography of childhood poverty and disability. *Exceptional Children, 66*(2), 187–199.

Glaser, D. (2000). Child abuse and neglect and the brain: A review. *Journal of Child Psychology and Psychiatry, 41*(1), 97–116.

Horn, J.L., & Trickett, P.K. (1998). Community violence and child development: A review of research. In P.K. Trickett & C.J.Schellenbach (Eds.), *Violence against children in the family and the community* (pp. 103–138). Washington, DC: American Psychological Association.

Human Rights Watch. (1999, July). *Getting away with murder, mutilation, rape: New testimony from Sierra Leone, 11* (3). http://www.hrw.org/reports/1999/sierra/

Hyman, I.A., & Perone, D.C. (1998). The other side of violence: Educator policies and practices that may contribute to student misbehavior. *Journal of School Psychology, 36,* 7–27.

IDEA (2003). *Number of children served IDEA, part B [Data file].* Available from http://www.ideadata.org/tables27th/ar_aa7.htm.

Kilpatrick, K., & Williams, L. (1997). Post-traumatic stress disorder in child witnesses to domestic violence. *American Journal of Orthopsychiatry, 67,* 639–644.

Kliewer, W., Lepore, S.J., Oskin, D., & Johnson, P.D. (1998). The role of social and cognitive processes in children's adjustment to community violence. *Journal of Consulting and Clinical Psychology, 66*(1), 199–209.

Knutson, J.F., Johnson, C.R., & Sullivan, P.M. (2004). Disciplinary choices of mothers of deaf children and normally hearing children. *Child Abuse & Neglect, 28,* 925–937.

LaPlante, M.P., & Kaye, H.S. (Eds.). (1998). *Trends in disability and their causes: Proceedings of the fourth national disability statistics and policy forum.* Washington, DC: U.S. Department of Education.

Lefkowitz, B. (1997). *Our guys: The Glen Ridge Case and the secret life of the perfect suburb.* Berkeley: University of California Press.

Levy, J.C., & Lagos, V.K. (1994). Experience of violence: Children with disabilities. In *Violence and youth: Psychology's response* (Vol. II). Ed. Commission on Violence and Youth. Washington, DC: American Psychological Association.

Lewis, D.O., Pincus, J.H., Bard, B., & Richardson, E. (1988). Neuropsychiatric, psychoeducational, and family characteristics of 14 juveniles condemned to death in the United States. *American Journal of Psychiatry, 145*(5), 584–589.

Lutzker, J.R. (1998). Child abuse and neglect: Weaving theory, research, and treatment in the twenty-first century. *Handbook of child abuse research and treatment* (pp. 561–570). New York: Plenum Press.

Lutzker, J.R. (2000). Balancing research and treatment in child maltreatment: The quest for good data and practical service. In D. Hansen (Ed.), *Nebraska Symposium on Motivation 1998: Motivation and Child Maltreatment* (pp.221–244). Lincoln: University of Nebraska Press.

Lynch, M., & Cicchetti, D. (1998). An ecological-transactional analysis of children and contexts: The longitudinal interplay among child maltreatment, community violence, and children's symptomatology. *Development & Psychopathology, 10*(2), 235–257.

Marge, D.K. (2003). *A call to action: Ending crimes of violence against children and adults with disabilities.* Syracuse: SUNY Upstate Medical University.

Margolin, G. (1998). The effects of domestic violence on children. In P.K. Trickett & C. Schellenbach (Eds.), *Violence against children in the family and community* (pp. 57–102). Washington, DC: American Psychological Association.

Margolin, G., & Gordis, E.B. (2000). The effects of family and community violence on children. *Annual Review of Psychology, 51,* 445–479.

Martinez, P.E., & Richters, J.E. (1993). The NIMH community violence project: II. Children's distress symptoms associated with violence exposure. *Psychiatry, 56,* 22–35.

McNeil, J. (2001). *Americans with disabilities 1997: Current population reports (pp. 70–73).* Washington, DC: U.S. Census Bureau.

Miles, M. (1995). Disability in an eastern religious context: Historical perspectives. *Disability and Society, 10*(1), 49–69.

Mudrick, N.R. (2002). The prevalence of disability among children: Paradigms and estimates. *Physical Medicine and Rehabilitation Clinics of North America, 13,* 775–792.

National Coalition to Abolish Corporal Punishment in Schools. (2003). *Discipline at school.* Retrieved March 22, 2005 from http://www.stophitting.com/disatschool/arguments Against.php

National Research Council. (1993a). *Understanding child abuse and neglect.* Washington, DC: National Academy Press.

National Research Council. (1993b). *Understanding and preventing violence.* Washington, DC: National Academy Press.

National Research Council. (1996). *Understanding violence against women.* Washington, DC: National Academy Press.

National Research Council. (2001). *Crime victims with developmental disabilities: Report of a workshop.* Washington, DC: National Academy Press.

Newacheck, P.W., & Halfon, N. (1998). Prevalence and impact of disabling chronic conditions in childhood. *American Journal of Public Health, 88*(4), 610–617.

Olweus, D. (1991). Bully victim problems among school children: Basic facts and effects of a school based intervention program. In D. Pepler & K. Rubin (Eds.), *Crossnational research in self-reported crime and delinquency* (pp. 187–201). Dodrecht, Netherlands: Kluwer.

Olweus, D. (1993). *Bullying at school: What we know and what we can do.* Cambridge, MA: Blackwell.

Omaha World-Herald. (2004, June 25). *Teen killed in South Omaha.* Available on line at http://www.omaha.com.

Omaha World-Herald. (2004, September 5). *Teens accused of rape held on $1 million bond.* Available on line at http://www.omaha.com.

Osofsky, J.D. (1995). The effects of exposure to violence on young children. *American Psychologist, 50*(9), 782–788.

Perrin, J.M. (2002). Health services research for children with disabilities. *The Milbank Quarterly, 80*(2), 303–325.

Pynoos, R.S. (1993). Traumatic stress and developmental psychopathology in children and adolescents. In J.M. Oldham, M.B. Riba, & A. Tasman (Eds.), *American Psychiatric Press Review of Psychiatry, 12,* 205–238. Washington, DC: American Psychiatric Press.

Pynoos, R., & Nader, K. (1993). Issues in the treatment of posttraumatic stress in children and adolescents. In J.P. Wilson & B. Raphael (Eds.), *International handbook of traumatic stress syndromes* (pp. 535–549). New York: Plenum Press.

Reynolds, W.M. (2003). *Reynolds Bully Victimization Manual.* San Antonio, TX: The Psychological Corporation.

Roland, E., & Munthe, E. (Eds.). (1989). *Bullying: An international perspective.* London: David Fulton.

Rossman, B.B.R., & Rosenberg, M.S. (1998). Maltreated adolescents: Victims caught between childhood and adulthood. *Journal of Aggression, Maltreatment & Trauma, 2*(1), 107–129.

Safford, P.L., & Safford, E.J. (1996). *A history of childhood and disability.* New York: Teachers College Press.

Sobsey, D. (1994). *Violence and abuse in the lives of people with disabilities: The end of silent acceptance?* Baltimore: Paul H. Brookes Publishing Co.

Sobsey, D. (2001). Altruistic filicide: Bioethics or criminology? *Health Ethics Today, 12*(1), 9–11.

Sobsey, D. (2004). *Understanding violence against people with disabilities: Models & mechanisms.* Online presentation from the Conference on Abuse of Children and Adults with Disabilities. Retrieved September 16, 2004, from www.disability-abuse.com

Social Security Administration. (2004). SSI Annual Statistical Report, 2003. Retrieved March 22, 2005 from www.ssa.gov/policy/docs/statcomps/ssi_asr/2003/sect04.html

Stein, R.E.K., & Silver, E.J. (1999). Operationalizing a conceptually based noncategorical definition. *Archives of Pediatric Adolescent Medicine, 153*, 68–74.

Sullivan, P.M. (2003a). Children with Disabilities and Healthy People 2010: A Call to Action. In *Disability and Secondary Conditions: Focus Area 6* (pp. 83–94). Atlanta: Centers for Disease Control and Prevention.

Sullivan, P.M. (2003b). Violence against children with disabilities: Prevention, public policy, and research implications. In D.K. Marge (Ed.), *A call to action: Ending crimes of violence against children and adults with disabilities* (pp. 127–157). Syracuse: SUNY Upstate Medical University Press.

Sullivan, P.M., Brookhouser, P.E., & Scanlan, J.M. (2000). Maltreatment of deaf and hard of hearing children. In P. Hindley & N. Kitson (Eds.), *Mental health and deafness.* London: Whurr Publication.

Sullivan, P.M., & Knutson, J.F. (1998a). The association between child maltreatment and disabilities in a hospital-based epidemiological study. *Child Abuse & Neglect, 22*(4), 271–288.

Sullivan P.M., & Knutson, J.F. (1998b). Maltreatment and behavioral characteristics of deaf and hard-of-hearing youth. *Sexuality and Disability, 16*, 295–319.

Sullivan, P.M., & Knutson, J.F. (2000a). Maltreatment and disabilities: A population-based epidemiological study. *Child Abuse & Neglect, 24*(10), 1257–1274.

Sullivan, P.M., & Knutson, J.F. (2000b). Maltreatment and disabilities among runaways. *Child Abuse & Neglect, 24*(10), 1275–1288.

Sullivan, P.M., Scanlan, J.M., Knutson, J.F., Brookhouser, P.E., & Schulte, L.E. (1992). The effects of psychotherapy on behavior problems of sexually abused deaf children. *Journal of Child Abuse & Neglect, 16*(2), 297–307.

Sullivan, P.M., Vernon, M., & Scanlan, J. (1987). Sexual abuse of deaf youth. *American Annals of the Deaf, 132*(4), 256–262.

Trickett, P.K., & Putnam, F.W. (1998). Developmental consequences of child sexual abuse. In P.K. Trickett & C.J. Schellenbach (Eds.), *Violence against children in the family and the community* (pp. 39–56). Washington, DC: American Psychological Association.

United Nation's Secretary General's Study on Violence Against Children. (2005). Available on line at http://www.violencestudy.org/r25.

U.S. Department of Health and Human Services. (1999). *The AFCARS Report.* Washington, DC: Author. Available on line at http://www.acf.dhhs.gov/programs/cb/stats/afcars/rpt0199/ar0199.htm.

U.S. Department of Health and Human Services. (2003*). The AFCARS Report.* Washington, DC: Author. Available on line at http://www2.acf.hhs.gov/programs/cb/publications/afcars/report8.htm

U.S. Department of Health and Human Services. (2000). *Report of the Surgeon General's Conference on Children's Mental Health: A national action agenda.* Washington, DC: Author.

U.S. Department of Justice. (1999). Federal Bureau of Investigation: Hate Crime Data Collection Guidelines. Washington, DC: Available on line at http://www.fbi.gov/ucr/hatecrime.pdf

U.S. House of Representatives Committee on Government Reform (2004). *Incarceration of youth who are waiting for community mental health services in the U.S.* Washington DC: Author. Available on line at http://www.democrats.reform.house.gov/Documents/20040817121901-25170.pdf

Violent Crime Control and Law Enforcement Act of 1994, §§ H.R. 3355, (1994, October)

Waldrop, J., & Stern, S.M. (2003). *Disability status: 2000* (pp. 1–12). Washington, DC: U.S. Census Bureau.

Westat, Inc. (1993). *A report on the maltreatment of children with disabilities.* Washington, DC: National Center on Child Abuse and Neglect.

Whitaker, J.K. (1987). The role of residential institutions. In J. Garbarino, P.E. Brookhouser, & K.J. Authier (Eds.), *Special children, Special risks: Maltreatment of children with disabilities* (pp. 83–100). New York: Aldine de Gruyter.

Whitney, I., Nabuzoka, D., & Smith, P.K. (1992). Bullying in schools: Mainstream and special needs. *Support for Learning, 7* (1), 3–7.

Wolak, J., & Finkelhor, D. (1998). Children exposed to partner violence. In J.L. Jasiniski & L.M. Williams (Eds.), *Partner violence: A comprehensive review of 20 years of research* (pp. 56–74). Thousand Oaks, CA: Sage Publications.

World Health Organization. (2002). *World report on violence and health: Summary.* Geneva: Author.

Zwi, A., Ugalde, A., & Richards, P. (1999). The effects of war and political violence on health services. In L. Kurta (Ed.), *Encyclopedia of violence, peace and conflict* (pp. 679–690). San Diego: Academic Press.

10

Conclusions
and Future Directions

Margaret M. Feerick & Gerald B. Silverman

A s evidenced by the preceding chapters, understanding children's exposure
to violence and the effects of this exposure on children requires the efforts of researchers and clinicians from a diverse range of disciplines.
Each chapter reflects the specific topics addressed as well as the diversity of individuals and disciplinary paradigms from which they are written. As a result, drawing conclusions that cut across chapters and outlining directions for future work
is a daunting, but necessary, task. In this chapter, we draw from the previous
chapters, as well as research presented at a workshop on children exposed to violence that had as its primary goal the development of a research agenda for the
field (a summary document of that workshop, with its research agenda, is available on the Internet at http://www.nichd.nih.gov/crmc/cdb/cab.htm). Our conclusions and recommendations for future research reflect the summary discussions carried out at the workshop, specific issues raised by particular contributors
to this volume, and our own observations of common issues presented across the
chapters of this book. The themes we identify and the recommendations we make
are not meant to be either exhaustive or exclusive but a first step in systematic research planning for future work in the area of children exposed to violence.

In the research literature, considerable attention has been paid separately to
the consequences of exposure to domestic violence, community violence, and war
or terrorism for children. The chapters in this book provide an opportunity to examine all three forms of violence together and to identify similarities and differences. As the chapters in this book demonstrate, children are affected by violence
in some common ways despite different settings in which the violence takes place.
We know, too, that there could be some differences depending on the circumstances in which the violence takes place. For example, it is critical for children
who have experienced violence to have nurturing caregivers to help them deal

239

with the trauma. In war and terrorism, parents may be victims themselves and may or may not be available to perform that role. In exposure to community violence, the situation in the home may or may not provide stability and care for the children, depending on how functional parents are. Similarly, in domestic violence situations, many factors come into play, bearing on the ability of the non-offending parent to provide support and nurture to the child. We believe that looking across these situations adds nuance and insight.

COMMON THEMES

The chapters in this book, whether they address violence in the home, the community, or society at large, tend to share some common themes and perspectives.

Need for a Developmental Perspective

People who intervene with children must be mindful of the developmental stages of children and how exposure to violence may be experienced at particular stages. Infants, although nonverbal, still are sensitive to what is happening around them and how their parents are feeling and caring for them. Several chapters (e.g., 1, 3, 4, and 5) draw attention to research that shows that children, even at the very youngest ages, can experience traumatic stress symptoms. Responders need to be aware of the cues to their distress. Preschool children may not be able to verbalize what they are feeling in logical ways, but they can express a great deal in their play and interactions. School-age children are more verbal and have a bit more independence than younger siblings and can engage in interventions that utilize these abilities.

Need for an Ecological Perspective

Most chapters in this volume take the perspective that children and families exist in a web of social institutions, programs, and forces that must be accounted for and utilized to help children exposed to violence. It is no longer considered sufficient for helping programs to focus solely on an individual or family. Children are part of extended families; attend schools and religious institutions; use community programs such as recreation and child care; and come in contact with law enforcement personnel, child protective service workers, and other professionals working in a variety of service settings. Families are engaged in multiple economic, ethnic, social, relief, community, and religious groups and institutions that impact on how they interpret what is happening to them and whether they reach out for help and support, and the ways in which they do so. Increasingly, programs are building alliances to aid families and children.

Need to Understand Resiliency and Strengths

Children often bring a number of strengths to dealing with traumatic experiences. Several chapters (e.g., 1, 2, and 3) note that not all children exhibit the same negative responses to serious violence; some children seem to do fairly well in response to what may for many others be very harmful. It is necessary when making assessments of a child's psychological responses to violence to be mindful of the resiliency of children and to look for ways to strengthen this resiliency.

Need for a Relational Approach to Treatment

The treatment of children, especially young children, needs to also help parents strengthen their roles as nurturers and supports of children. Children need the security and support of loving parents or other caregivers. Children who are exposed to violence especially need the stability of such caregivers. Often, however, a child's caregivers are also victims or participants in the violence and are not able to perform a supportive role for their child. The chapters in this book stress the need for treatment programs to help parents to learn how to support the needs of their children and to surmount whatever trauma they themselves may be experiencing.

Need for Safety

Safety is a necessary condition for recovery from violence, both for children and for their caregivers. Treatment without attention to helping children become safe from threats and dangers and assisting caregivers to become safe when they are at risk is likely to be limited and ineffective.

Need for Measured Policy Responses

We need to be wary of policy responses to violence that do not distinguish the seriousness of the exposure. As indicated by several authors, children's responses to violence depend on many factors, including age, violence severity, type of exposure, and caregiver support. We need to avoid responses that, for example, simply equate exposure to domestic violence as child maltreatment. We also need to know more about the consequences of increasing criminal penalties when children are exposed to violence.

A full set of appropriate responses to children exposed to violence should utilize and improve multi-faceted, multi-disciplinary, multi-sector approaches. Many of the chapter authors reference a variety of ways that particular treatment programs engage others in the community to build alliances and create multiple responses for identifying, intervening with, and treating children and their families.

Some programs have developed working agreements with non-traditional mental health treatment sectors of society, such as the police, health care providers, schools, child protective services, and domestic violence providers. Building the capacity of these organizations and providers expands the network of available responders.

In Chapter 8 Jeffrey Edleson lays out a general scheme for describing how a community can organize itself to build the necessary relationships for a multi-disciplinary response to exposure to violence. This model may be useful to some of the emerging programs across the country that are attempting to improve the ways that communities assist such vulnerable children.

KEY RESEARCH NEEDS

Prinz and Feerick (2004) and Feerick and Prinz (2004) outlined an extensive research agenda for children exposed to domestic violence, and community violence and war and terrorism, respectively. Here, we echo and amplify some of these recommendations and add to them recommendations made by the authors of this volume.

Defining and Measuring Violence Exposure

A critical issue in research on children exposed to violence concerns defining and measuring violence and children's exposure to it. Better definitions are needed across all types of violence exposure in order to facilitate communication in this complex research area, as well as to enable scientific progress through better understanding of the independent variables. Clear definitions make it possible to identify the variables of interest, replicate findings reported in the literature, and, ultimately, to specify the components of treatment that have the greatest impact on children.

In defining children's experiences with violence, there is a critical need for more inclusive definitions of violence that include the range of intensity (e.g., verbal aggression through homicide) of violence and the range of behaviors involved (e.g., threats or coercion). Characteristics of violent experiences such as the timing and patterning of exposure (e.g., age of onset, frequency of exposure, single episodes and single victims versus chronic exposure and multiple victims), whether the exposure is direct or indirect (or primary or secondary), the child's relationship to the perpetrator, and the social context of the violence need to be measured and analyzed. In addition, definitions of violence need to take account of contextual factors that may affect children and their responses to witnessing violence such as poverty, cultural and ethnic background, family structure and processes, exposure to other types of violence, disability status, and other forms of victimization (e.g., child abuse).

There is also a need to assess the reliability and validity of reports from a range of reporters and to use multiple sources of information in measuring and characterizing children's experiences. Valid and informative measures of violence, exposure, the child's degree of involvement in and reactions to the violence, parenting, family processes, and developmental outcomes are needed for both identification and assessment purposes. Measures should also be developed that are sensitive to identifying clinical samples, that are sensitive to change over time, and that are capable of demonstrating intervention effectiveness. Finally, measures are needed that can be used with children and parents with special needs and from different cultural and ethnic backgrounds. Finally, in defining and measuring exposure to violence, we must recognize that some children pose special challenges to efforts at surveillance and monitoring of exposure to violence, even once definition and measurement issues are resolved. We are increasingly recognizing the need for culturally and linguistically appropriate approaches to definition and measurement, as well as sensitivity to special populations of children. For example, as Patricia Sullivan in Chapter 9 points out, consideration of the special needs of children (and adults) with disabilities has been largely absent from the discussion about exposure to violence, even though children with disabilities are disproportionately represented among abuse and neglect cases and may lack, by virtue of their specific disabilities, the skills and resources that would otherwise support resilience. Sensitivity to the needs of these children, however, is made more complex due to the fact that current systems that collect data on disabilities and outcomes are often not able to be connected (and indeed, in some cases connections are prohibited under federal laws to protect privacy), and, thus, are not able to provide complete and needed national data. In addition, research on children with disabilities continues to strain resources because, with the exception of broad definitions of disabilities or an exclusive focus on specific and common disabilities, identifying and studying children with disabilities requires substantial samples and screening procedures. However, such studies will ultimately be necessary to determine the effectiveness of different interventions and services on children with specific disabilities.

Designs and Methodologies that Capture the Range of Children's Experiences

There is a significant need for the development of study designs and methodologies that can fully capture the natural variation that occurs among children and their experiences within a developmental framework. In particular, large-scale, longitudinal, and intergenerational studies of children exposed to violence are needed to determine the consequences of exposure to violence at different developmental stages and to identify risk and protective mechanisms that operate over time and across generations. In addition, there is a need for more extensive data on the prevalence of community violence in the general population and children's exposure to it and for longitudinal, developmental studies of children exposed to each type of violence so that the sequelae of exposure at different points in development can be examined. This research should employ a combination of methods and approaches that will produce empirical evidence on how exposure to violence affects children and what factors promote resilience over time and enrich it with qualitative information on contexts and cultural aspects of children's experiences.

Research on children exposed to violence also needs to consider the implications of gender, culture, ethnicity, political context, and child disabilities on every aspect of research planning, development, and execution and to include measures that are appropriate for different ethnic and cultural groups. As suggested in several chapters (e.g., 1, 3, and 7), different ethnic and cultural practices and values may not only affect definitions and reporting of violence but may also act as mediators and moderators of the effects of violence exposure on children. Research in this area needs to examine children who differ in terms of socioeconomic status, cultural background, ethnicity, and immigrant status in order to fully understand the role of socio-cultural factors. Research also needs to examine the meaning of violence from different ethnic and cultural perspectives; theory-driven research on ethnic and cultural questions is essential to identifying effective interventions for different populations of families and children.

In planning studies on children exposed to violence, researchers should employ newly developed and innovative study designs and advanced analytical methods. A number of statistical methods and tools are now available to examine complex, univariate and multivariate effects, while novel approaches to the measurement and analysis of change over time are constantly being developed. Use of these methods and techniques will greatly enhance our ability to examine multiple influences on children, including complex ecological processes and mechanisms.

Theory and Model Development

New theoretical accounts of the effects of exposure to violence must be developed, and current models modified on the basis of new evidence. Such accounts must be comprehensive, taking into consideration that developmental progress may not be linear and that the sensitivity of assessments or measures may vary accordingly. Models must also consider characteristics of the child as key variables in their responses to exposure to violence, including developmental disabilities, gender, culture, and ethnicity.

Specifically, there is a significant need for research that broadens and expands our understanding of the effects of exposure to violence on children. Research has largely focused on outcome in terms of psychiatric symptoms or psychopathology in school-age children. Much more research is needed on short- and long-term outcomes in children of different ages to better understand outcomes or consequences from a comprehensive, developmental perspective. Theory-driven research is also needed on factors and processes that promote resilience in children and that protect them from long-term negative effects. Although there has been a developing body of research on the neurological pathways resulting from violence (see, e.g., Chapters 1, 2, and 3), there is a tremendous need for more research on the neurophysiological and the neuromaturational consequences of exposure to violence, including the short- and long-term consequences on arousal, sympathetic and parasympathetic function, functional brain activity, attention, regulation of emotion, stress reactivity, executive functioning, motor control, and cognitive and linguistic capabilities.

There is also a need for research that examines the medical and health consequences of exposure to violence, including alterations in immune system functioning that may affect vulnerability to infections or increase the risk for autoimmune disorders. Such research should examine whether there are particular medical/health problems that occur with unusual frequency among children exposed to violence and how these may be influenced by poverty, ethnicity, and social class. In addition, much more research is needed on the functional outcomes of violence exposure, including school readiness, school performance, educational achievement, job performance, criminal justice outcomes, and substance abuse and how these outcomes affect long-term adjustment and development.

Finally, there is a need for research on mediators, moderators, and mechanisms of violence exposure, especially parenting, child-caregiver interaction, and family functioning, with particular attention to both competent and compromised parenting, family functioning, and the context in which the child is developing. In particular, research is needed that examines the effects of exposure to violence on family organization and structure, family interaction, parental coping with trauma, and caregiver ability to protect children, as well as how ethnic or cultural differences in parenting relate to how families deal with violence experiences. Research is also needed on community responses to violence and community resilience, and how community reactions and resources affect children, their responses, and their development. More information is needed on the psychological effects of bioterrorism and anticipatory preparedness, as well as how schools and communities can help children who are exposed to the violence of war and terrorism. Such studies will provide an empirical basis for prevention and intervention programs for families and children and for training and dissemination of information to treatment providers and others working with families.

Intervention and Services Research

As we find ways of identifying and defining the factors that place children at risk or that protect them from harmful consequences, we must be able to provide these children with targeted interventions and services that have demonstrated effectiveness. Children exposed to violence often come into contact with many formal and informal systems, such as the health care system, mental health system, educational system, and justice system. They also interact with a variety of informal systems that include relatives, extended families, neighbors, friends, and religious and community groups. There is a need for research that explores how such system contacts affect children over time and under different circumstances and that evaluates the effectiveness of specific programs and interventions. Specifically, there is a tremendous need for large-scale, multi-site intervention research to determine the earliest time for effective intervention, the optimal intensity of the intervention, the appropriate length of the intervention, the necessary skill levels of interveners, the best candidates for that role, and the best delivery methods (e.g., small groups or one-to-one) and settings (e.g., clinic, shelter, in-home). There is also a need for longitudinal studies of both short- and long-term interventions with multiple outcome measures across developmental domains, as well as prospective longitudinal studies of early interventions that document developmental trajectories. Such research should address which interventions are most effective, for whom, and under what circumstances.

There is also significant need for research that can help inform current efforts to prepare providers to respond to violent events (including school violence and large-scale terrorist attacks) and to respond to the needs of individual children, families, and communities. Thus, there is a tremendous need for studies that examine the effectiveness of different programs and interventions at the individual, family, and community levels. Such research should address a number of significant issues such as how do we help schools protect and treat children, what are the most effective crisis intervention models, what are the most effective treatments for children exposed to war or terrorism violence either directly or indirectly, what are the effects of quarantine and anticipatory preparedness programs, which interventions are most effective for families experiencing grief and loss as a result of violence, and which are the most effective training models for non-mental health providers and other first responders. Such research also needs to document treatment protocols and models, involve providers and community participants in the development of treatment programs, include methods to minimize attrition, include multiple data sources, and evaluate the cost-effectiveness of different approaches. In addition, intervention studies should focus on functional outcomes for children and families, and should be ethnically, culturally, and developmentally appropriate for the populations they serve.

Finally, as multi-disciplinary and multi-sector interventions are proposed, we need research models in which the unit of analysis is the community. Since such a focus does not lend itself to more traditional experimental designs, we need creative thinking about how to measure community change in a systematic and rigorous way, while doing justice to the complexity of the interventions.

Research on Effective Policies and Practices

There is a need for research that rapidly identifies the consequences of new legislation and policies designed to better protect or help victims of violence and their children. Specifically, such research needs to examine the impact of the legislation and whether there are any unintended consequences. For example, studies are needed on how public policy, as reflected in changes in criminal justice and child maltreatment statutes, affects families. Many states are increasing penalties for violence committed when a child is present. We know little about whether this increases safety for children and non-offending parents or whether there are unintended negative consequences that in fact harm children over the long term. With concern for the harm often experienced by children in homes with domestic violence, some states are moving to equate exposure with child abuse. If done in an inflexible and unexamined manner, child protective services may inappropriately intervene with children who would be better served in less coercive settings. In addition, such public policy has the potential to overburden child protective services; should protective services determine that removing children from the home is necessitated by new policies, foster care and other non-parental care systems would potentially be overburdened, even amid ongoing concern about the viability and safety of such systems.

Studies are also needed on the impact and success of media campaigns and educational efforts designed to increase understanding of the effects of violence exposure, how to prevent exposure and/or its effects, where to find appropriate services and interventions, and how best to prepare for large-scale violent events. Although a number of such campaigns and programs have been developed, little is known about their effectiveness and whether they may have unintended adverse effects on children, families, or communities. Research can potentially inform distinctions between media broadcast of important news and information (as in the immediate coverage following the attacks of September 11th), which serves an important public good, and media broadcasts that result in ongoing secondary exposure to violence through the media.

SUMMARY AND NEXT STEPS

Together, the chapters in this volume represent the current state of the science across numerous disciplines in addressing children's exposure to violence. While specific chapters address particular aspects of this larger problem, together they converge around a common set of themes, which lead directly to an indication of research needs. Although there is much known about preventing or responding to children's exposure to violence, there is still much to be learned. Exposure to violence can occur in a broad array of environments, on a number of different scales. Much of what is done currently to respond to these experiences has been developed specifically in response to each new type of exposure; children in homes with domestic violence may be treated in one way, children from violent neighborhoods in perhaps another way, and children who witness, as a group, a large-scale violence event, may be treated in still yet a different manner. The results of such a progression in the development of the field is that although there may be specific strategies that can be mobilized, there remain large gaps in our knowledge that require a wide-range view of the problem as a whole. This becomes the challenge, then, to the community of researchers, policy makers, and practitioners who concern themselves with the needs of children who are exposed to violence.

REFERENCES

Feerick, M.M., & Prinz, R.J. (2003). Next steps in research on children exposed to community violence or war/terrorism. *Clinical Child and Family Psychology Review,* 6(4), 303–305.

Prinz, R.J., & Feerick, M.M. (2003). Next steps in research on children exposed to domestic violence. *Clinical Child and Family Psychology Review,* 6(3), 215–219.

INDEX

Entries followed by *f* denote figures; those followed by *t* denote tables.

Economic status
  and risk of exposure to community
      violence, 30–31
  of war-affected families, 164
  see also Poverty; Socioeconomic status
Education
  of children displaced by war and
      terrorism, 62
  on effects of violence exposure, research
      needs on, 247–248
  emergency, 176–177
  peace, 177–178
Education systems, and mental health
      interventions for war-affected
      children, 176
Educational outcomes, exposure to
      community violence and, 41–43
Emergency education, 176–177
Emerging Programs for Battered Women and
      Their Children, 110
Emotional development
  in children of abused women, mothers'
      perceptions of their children and,
      16
  of infants and young children, intimate
      partner violence and, 8–9
  of school-age and older children,
      intimate partner violence and,
      10–11
Environment
  characteristics of, and occurrence of
      violence, 219
  and medication effects, 169
Ethnicity, see Race/ethnicity
Ethnopharmacology, 168–169
Exosystem
  background violence in, effects of, 38
  in child's environment, 32, 34
  and violence and abuse, 218

Families First, Michigan, 127
  contact information for, 134
Familism, protective effect of, against
      intimate partner violence, 16
Family(ies)
  affected by war and terrorism
      changes in, 59–63
      mental health interventions for,
          162–164
      short-term trauma-focused therapy
          for, 163
      socioecological needs of, 164, 181

changes in, war and terrorism and, 60
characteristics of
  and effects of community violence,
      45–46
  and risk of exposure to community
      violence, 31
exposure to community violence and,
      44
functioning of, research needs on, 245
interventions for, research needs on,
      246
legal difficulties, and co-occurrence of
      domestic violence and
      maltreatment of child with
      disabilities, 220
as protective factor, 163
single-parent, and childhood disability,
      217
stresses on, war and terrorism and, 60
structure of, and childhood disability,
      217–218
Family conflict, and exposure to
      community violence, moderating
      effects of, 45–46
Family context, and effects of intimate
      partner violence, 17
Family members
  adult, affected by war and terrorism,
      effects on children, 61
  loss of, in war and terrorism, 59–60,
      160
Family stress factors, and maltreatment of
      children with disabilities, 220–221
Family therapy
  culture and, 166
  with war-affected children, 165–166
Family Violence Prevention Fund, 123,
      201
Fear
  in children exposed to violence, 63
  posttraumatic, 69
Feelings, child's symbolic expression of, 93
Fetal alcohol syndrome, and co-occurrence
      of domestic violence and
      maltreatment of child with
      disabilities, 220
Financial problems, and co-occurrence of
      domestic violence and
      maltreatment of child with
      disabilities, 220
First responders, and children exposed to
      domestic violence, 201–202